Julia Baird is a bestselling author and award-winning journalist. She hosts *The Drum* on ABC TV and writes columns for the *New York Times* and the *Sydney Morning Herald*. Her first book, *Media Tarts*, was based on her history PhD about the portrayal of female politicians. After moving to the United States to take up a fellowship at the Harvard Kennedy School, she became a columnist and senior editor at *Newsweek* in New York. Julia's biography of Queen Victoria was published in several countries to critical acclaim and was one of the *New York Times's* top ten books of 2016. Her most recent book, the number-one bestseller, *Phosphorescence: On awe, wonder, and the things that sustain you when the world goes dark*, won the 2021 Australian Book Industry Awards Book of the Year. She lives near the sea with two children and an abnormally large dog.

MEDIA TARTS

JULIA BAIRD

ABC
BOOKS

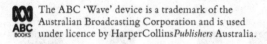 The ABC 'Wave' device is a trademark of the Australian Broadcasting Corporation and is used under licence by HarperCollins*Publishers* Australia.

HarperCollins*Publishers*
Australia • Brazil • Canada • France • Germany • Holland • Hungary
India • Italy • Japan • Mexico • New Zealand • Poland • Spain • Sweden
Switzerland • United Kingdom • United States of America

First published in Australia in 2004 by Scribe Publications
This edition published in 2021
by HarperCollins*Publishers* Australia Pty Limited
Level 13, 201 Elizabeth Street, Sydney NSW 2000
ABN 36 009 913 517
harpercollins.com.au

A catalogue record for this book is available from the National Library of Australia.

ISBN 978 0 7333 4192 2 (paperback)
ISBN 978 1 4607 1400 3 (ebook)

Cover design by Andy Warren, HarperCollins Design Studio
Cover images: Plaster Busts Of Young Woman by Yaroslav Danylchenko / stocksy.com / 2670101; egg by shutterstock.com
Author photograph by Alex Ellinghausen
Typeset in Sabon LT Std by Kelli Lonergan
Printed and bound in Australia by McPherson's Printing Group
The papers used by HarperCollins in the manufacture of this book are a natural, recyclable product made from wood grown in sustainable plantation forests. The fibre source and manufacturing processes meet recognised international environmental standards, and carry certification.

To my parents, Judy and Bruce
and my friend Martha

Contents

A Deployment of Fashion

In Australia, a lone woman
is being crucified by the Press
at any given moment.

With no unedited right
of reply, she is cast out ...

... she goes down, overwhelmed
in the feasting grins of pressmen, and Press women ...
It is done for the millions.

Sometimes the millions join in
with jokes: how to get a baby
in the Northern Territory? Just stick

your finger down a dingo's throat.
Most times, though, the millions
stay money, and the jokes

are snobbish media jokes:
Chemidenko. The Oxleymoron.
Spittle, like the flies on Black Mary.

After the feeding frenzy
sometimes a ruefully balanced last lick
precedes the next selection.

Les Murray, 1997

Foreword

Rereading Julia Baird's seminal book *Media Tarts* gives me two distinct feelings. One is admiration — nearly two decades after it was first published, this book still stands up well. The other is depression, because the reason it still stands up well is that the issues *Media Tarts* documents for women in parliament haven't gone away.

Since its publication, of course, women have made astounding inroads. There's been a female prime minister, a female governor-general, two female foreign ministers, two female defence ministers, and a mounting horde of female MPs who have managed the juggle of young children with parliamentary careers in a way that still seemed exotic in 2004. Baird, who charted the shocking experience of Ros Kelly in 1983 when she became the first federal MP to give birth while in office, cannot but be heartened, one assumes, by the baby boom of recent years, including the talented young Labor MP Anika Wells who in the plague year of 2020 welcomed twins.

There's been a fleet of female premiers — so many that they have ceased to be particularly unusual — though new inductees into this league still run the risk of vapid media coverage like the sort afforded to Lara Giddings by the *Australian* in 2011. Under the front-page headline 'Leftist Lara Still Looking For Mr Right', the first paragraph of the news story announcing Ms Giddings's elevation to the premiership read: 'Lara Giddings says she still hopes to meet the "right man" but for now she's happy to give all her time to being Tasmania's first female Premier.'

The occasional facepalm moment notwithstanding, progress has unquestionably been made.

And yet, in early 2021, we witnessed a spectacular eruption of what has lain beneath, all these years. The volcanic emergence of Brittany Higgins's story of alleged rape in the ministerial wing of Parliament House has redrawn the political landscape. Female politicians and staffers have begun to talk about episodes and experiences they had erstwhile kept secret.

For a building in which the *Sex Discrimination Act* was created — drafted and propelled through the Hawke cabinet and then the parliament by the late Susan Ryan, who was at the time the only woman at the cabinet table — it appears that the parliament harbours an extraordinary subculture of sexist behaviour and harassment.

It's been shocking, particularly for those who have addressed themselves to the numbers task of getting women elected to parliament, trusting that equal representation would bring its own reward of a fairer and more balanced culture in parliament.

What has become clear is that for women, getting into parliament is one step. Being heard and respected once you're there is another. And the first does not presuppose the second.

*

The year 2021 marks the centenary of Edith Cowan's election. In March 1921, she became the first woman elected to any

Australian parliament when she won the seat of West Perth in the WA parliament.

She was treated differently from day one, as you can imagine. There was no toilet for her in the building (she had to duck home when nature called). The long-held tradition of listening to the maiden speech of a new MP in courteous silence was — in Edith's case — not observed. She was interrupted and jeered more than a dozen times.

To honour Edith's anniversary, I set about interviewing some of Australia's surviving female political 'firsts' for an ABC documentary series reflecting on the experience of parliament for women over the century. These interviewees came from a variety of party backgrounds and eras. But the one thing almost all of them had in common was this observation: when they found themselves in a meeting with lots of men, they noticed that their ideas would sometimes be ignored, only to be picked up with enthusiasm once a man repeated them. We found archival footage of Nancy Buttfield (the first female senator from South Australia, elected in 1955) remarking upon this phenomenon, and a chorus of current and former female parliamentarians echoed her observations in arrestingly similar terms. Everyone from Julia Gillard to Sarah Hanson-Young to Bronwyn Bishop said the same thing.

How extraordinary that the experience of finding oneself somehow inaudible in a room was so common that women joked about it regularly between themselves.

This question of audibility is a central one. The woman who is ignored in a committee meeting and the woman who chooses not to speak about being sexually assaulted for fear of losing her career are deeply connected. They're responding to the same culture. It's a culture that prizes men's experience over women's, that listens out for men's voices and erases women's.

But it's changing. The courage of a new cohort of young women who refuse to shoulder a burden of guilt and shame that does not belong to them, plus the influence of senior female journalists who do not minimise the significance of sexual harassment and assault, have created a new age of audibility for women in politics.

It's a perfect time to revisit *Media Tarts*, which is almost an oral history of women in the parliaments of Australia; a conversation between women across party lines and across the generations that is only now becoming audible to a wider audience.

Julia Baird – herself a young journalist when she conducted these interviews and compiled the book – has matured since its publication into one of Australia's most thoughtful and erudite writers on gender. Her warmly perceptive style is evident throughout the work, coaxing recollections from female MPs about details of their professional lives from the relatively trivial to the profound.

How often are women in politics asked in depth about gender? Most are familiar with the handful of questions at the end of an interview; pretty much every woman I spoke to for the ABC series harbours, I know, a deep caution about discussing gender 'too much', lest her gender become all that people see when they look at her.

It's only when you hear all their accounts together, in a book like this, that the near-unanimity of experience is laid bare. I found *Media Tarts* striking and instructive when first I read it. In a new era of attentiveness to women's experience, let its new iteration fire the pistons of change.

Annabel Crabb
May 2021

Introduction to 2021 edition

Lava flows slowly. Following an eruption, a burning mass of melted rock can snake down slopes, hills and streets for months, steadily glowing red, quietly devouring anything in its path. It cannot be controlled, hurried or hushed. It can only be respected, as molten earth should be, and allowed to run its course.

This is what I saw when I stood on the fringe of the crowds at the Women's March 4 Justice in Sydney in March 2021, taking notes with my teenage daughter by my side.

It was an unstoppable lava flow of dissent, which saw thousand-strong crowds throng the streets of Australia — Adelaide, Brisbane, Canberra, Darwin, Hobart, Perth, Melbourne, Sydney, and a host of regional towns, including Alice Springs, Armidale, Bathurst, Bundaberg, Byron, Cairns, Gosford, Kangaroo Island and Warrnambool.

I had never seen so many women so angry as in the few weeks prior. Deeply, implacably, unmovingly angry, as though pent-up fury was steadily spilling from their collective core.

The marching slogan was clear: 'Enough is Enough'.

This wasn't a spontaneous outburst, but the eruption of long-held, boiling frustration at the absence of accountability and consequences for perpetrators of sexual assault, the failings of the criminal justice system, the lack of interest and action by our most powerful politicians — and the fact that most of them are still male.

On 15 February 2021, former Liberal staffer Brittany Higgins told journalists she had allegedly been raped on a ministerial couch in a ministerial office two years earlier, which her superiors had failed to respond to, and which she had not reported to police because she feared losing her job. A stunning series of stories exposing misogyny and treatment of women swiftly followed, ranging from the unethical to the criminal.

The next — and even more politically explosive story — was an allegation that the attorney-general Christian Porter had sexually assaulted a woman thirty years earlier. The story sickened thousands, not just with horror but with familiarity. Porter robustly and repeatedly denied the allegations, and began legal proceedings against the ABC for defamation.

The police were unable to investigate this case because the alleged victim was now dead, having taken her own life. Her friends asked to testify on her behalf, proposing an independent inquiry.

And Prime Minister Scott Morrison's insistence that to establish any kind of inquiry into the matter, given that the charges were being made against the nation's most senior legal figure, would flout the 'rule of law' — even though leading lawyers had suggested it would uphold the same — and his lack of interest in familiarising himself with the facts of the case had inflamed women across all sectors of the community. Higgins left politics; Porter changed portfolios but remained in cabinet. After mediation, he dropped his case against the ABC. In turn, the public broadcaster affixed a note to an online article about the allegations saying they 'did not intend to suggest that Mr Porter had committed the criminal offences alleged'. They added: 'However, both parties accept that some readers misinterpreted the article as an accusation of guilt against Mr Porter. That reading, which was not intended by the ABC, is regretted.' The calls for an independent inquiry have continued.

At the rally, the placards repeatedly expressed utter weariness.

'I'm twelve and already sick of this shit.'

'I can't believe I still have to protest this shit!'

One woman dressed as a suffragette held in her gloved hand a sign reading: 'Still protesting this shit ... FFS, it's ~~1911~~ 2021!!'

It was obvious that what was being protested was not new, just another iteration of an ancient story of women being assaulted, belittled, ignored, slut-shamed, punished and shoved aside as powerful institutions somehow, just naturally, as though requiring no effort whatsoever, continued to protect the men involved, even from allegedly criminal acts.

A story of women ousted and blamed, bearing the consequences for men's bad behaviour, while the men marched on mostly unscathed in official positions.

The Prime Minister, who floundered when trying to respond to the claims of rape in an office metres from his own, as well as allegations of rape by one of his most senior cabinet members, at one point, grabbing at any potential solution, said he would now be open to the idea of quotas in his party to get more women into parliament.

The Liberal Party has long held the position that quotas would undermine the idea that purely 'merit' determines a path to parliament, even though it has become apparent that 'merit' has historically just meant 'being male'. The party had introduced soft targets in 2016 (of 50 per cent representation of women in parliament by 2025), but since then the number of women in parliament had gone slightly backwards at less than a quarter of the House of Representatives. On the other side of the house, a long fight for equal representation and quotas had resulted in a near fifty-fifty split of women and men in the ALP.

It appeared the PM now believed two things. First, soft targets hadn't worked (and aren't quotas just targets that need to be met?). And second, that having more women in the parliament might clean things up a bit, make it nicer and less ... what's the word? Rape-y. Former Sydney alderman Kathryn Greiner, a member of the Liberal Party for fifty years, told me she resented the idea of women needing to be 'God's police' and said the blokes should tidy the place up themselves; after all, it's their mess.

This idea is nothing new. Women have long been expected to bring buckets and mops to public spaces, ministries and troubled or failing governments. This has been part of the problem.

And in response, men have masturbated over female MP's desks and sent each other videos of it. What a lark! *Who's got a mop?* In the aftermath of the Higgins revelations, we also learned some members of cabinet considered themselves part of a group they called the 'big swinging dicks club' (and acted in concert to try to prevent former foreign minister Julie Bishop from replacing Malcolm Turnbull as leader of the Liberal Party). Of course, they protest too much.

It has long been assumed that once women have seats in parliament it's all going to be tickety-boo: nicer, calmer, cleaner. But we know from history that until there is a critical mass, the fact that women are cast as outsiders, as interlopers in a male space, or as gentler operatives, more morally virtuous and altruistic politicians, will work not to cement their positions in a house of power designed for and by men, but make them more precarious.

*

History is crucial. We already know that treating women as decorations, subordinates and playthings, even and sometimes especially in our houses of power, is not new. We don't need more reports, rumination or research. We know that from the moment women walked into parliament and took up space alongside men, they have been treated as objects: openly salivated over, described lasciviously in print, pursued and placed on pedestals simply by virtue of their gender — only to find the simple fact of their being on a pedestal, of having a high profile or powerful position, was used to argue they were ill-equipped for political office. They have been asked to pose with vacuum cleaners and in bikinis, to have makeovers, to endure being fawned over or ignored. And they have been asked to exist in an environment where sexual harassment has been tolerated and normalised and gone unreported, and where women who speak about sexism are derided as playing a 'gender card'.

When men were featured often in the press, they were rising stars.

When women were featured often in the press, they were media tarts.

For decades, it has been the female MPs who have been sexualised — their bodies scrutinised, private lives gossiped about. They have been the first to be exposed when having affairs. They have been called sluts and 'alley-cats on heat', with one even effectively pushed out of parliament after being falsely accused of exposing her private parts to a male colleague. And all the while, the sexual indiscretions or 'bad behaviour' of their male counterparts have been hidden behind a press gallery code, created by men, that a politician's private life should not be written about unless it directly impacts their political work (or they're a woman). Even former National Party leader Barnaby Joyce's affair with a staffer was not exposed until she was obviously pregnant.

When writing this book almost 20 years ago, I thought that upholding this code would protect women from prurient questions and gossip. But I now see it's not women it was protecting, but primarily men. What is now clear is that what has also been hidden is not just the odd sexual tryst or clumsy come-on but decades of harassment, sexual assault and misbehaviour by the men running our country. And all while this has been happening, they have been calling women in their ranks whores and simpletons.

We must know the history of women entering parliament if we are to fully understand how this has happened, and how long we have tolerated the public, sustained abuse of prominent women, particularly those who make mistakes. And we must know it if we are to understand the grotesque nature of the abuse endured by our first female prime minister. It has all happened in plain sight, in front of our eyes, sometimes at our incitement.

It's not just the last few months or even years. It's the last few decades.

*

When I wrote this book, in the early 2000s, the political landscape was littered with the smoking effigies of women who had been touted as leaders then vilified as losers. It was astonishing, picking my way through this graveyard of characters whom had become cautionary tales for the next generation of young female MPs like Julia Gillard, Tanya Plibersek and Marise Payne — women who hoped that through dint of sheer hard work they could avoid the 'flamed out meteor' syndrome, avoid being cast as imposters. I was trying to understand what had happened, and I had years of research for my history PhD at my disposal to help.

For that thesis, I had examined the media files of every single female Australian MP from the 1940s onwards, eventually focusing on the decades after 1970. This involved spending years researching in state and territory parliamentary libraries — including Adelaide, Brisbane, Melbourne, Perth and Sydney — burrowing into yellowing clippings files and whirring through dizzying microfilm spools. I spent most of my time, though, in the federal parliamentary library in Canberra, wrestling with mammoth files devoted to the major players, the likes of Carmen Lawrence, Ros Kelly and Amanda Vanstone.

When not in a library, I was interviewing more than one hundred current, former and aspiring female politicians who generously gave me hours of their time to reflect on their experiences, even though, as one said to me, a political career can feel much like you're 'thrown in the washing machine on the day you're elected, and you only stop spinning on the day you leave'.

What I wanted to know was how the press refracted the experiences of female MPs back to the public, how reporters and photographers depicted women entering a world made up almost entirely of men, and if there were any repetitive patterns or stereotypes that impacted the careers of those women.

What I found was decades of evidence showing how odd, and unnatural, we considered the pairing of women with power and authority to be. There were several dominant frames, or tropes. Women were diminished as 'Grandma MPs'. They were asked who would do the dishes or mind the kids if they won a seat (the Housewife Superstars). They were drooled over if young and considered conventionally attractive, then quickly dismissed as shallow and ungrateful if they complained (the Cover Girls). They were described as peculiarities, a combination of metal and velvet, who were considered very surprising if successful and cast as unbending 'iron lady' autocrats if decisive (the Steel Sheilas). They were asked constantly about being women, were declared to be acceptable feminists if they appeared to also groom, and yet often asked about little else (the Feminine Feminists). Then, by the 1990s, they were canonised then crucified (the Sinning

Saints). While their male colleagues were seen as individuals, women were viewed as part of a group.

These frames showed the persistence of the idea that politics is a man's game that women could only dabble in, often at their peril. It matters because it means women are then promoted less frequently, ousted more readily and ignored much more easily. It also means they are depicted as interlopers and imposters, and urged not to change a culture but conform to it.

It's important to remember, too, that there was a significant emotional toll in many of these stories. Some women were destroyed by this cycle of adulation then hate, overwhelming even before the onset of social media; some had breakdowns and hospitalisations, ongoing struggles with mental health, and were forced to leave politics and never return — all as a nation watched and women still remaining in political parties took note. In the 1990s and 2000s, the lessons were: keep your head down, don't attract too much attention, shave the edges off your personality, fit in a box and stay there. Don't, in other words, upset the status quo. Don't disrupt. Women were punished for any overt signs of flair or glamour, while their male colleagues were just considered rakish and charismatic.

Let's not forget, for example: former Democrat leader Cheryl Kernot was slut-shamed nationally for months for wearing a pretty red dress and a feather boa on the cover of the *Australian Women's Weekly*. Jeff Kennett, who posed with models draped around his legs and shoulders when he was the premier of Victoria, with his hand patting the head of one woman on the floor much as one might a toddler or a dog, was simply called a 'Model Premier'. (The portrait is currently part of the National Portrait Gallery).

As I outline in this book, Cheryl Kernot was also slut-shamed for years after being exposed by a gallery veteran for having had an affair with a Labor colleague, Gareth Evans. She left the country for several years. Evans meanwhile carried on unscathed, serving on influential international commissions and being appointed chancellor of the Australian National University.

By 'slut-shamed', for those who wince or puzzle at the term, I mean having one's character or morals impugned by the suggestion of being sexually active. Which, of course, does not happen to men. The Cambridge Dictionary defines it as: 'to talk about a woman's sexual behaviour in order to embarrass her and make people disapprove of her'. Interestingly, the first example they give is: 'Her political career was brought to an end by gutter journalism that slut-shamed her.' It's now a well-established pattern — the examples are legion.

*

I called this book *Media Tarts* because the media was so obviously conscious of their role in the rise and demise of female politicians, well aware that they could create then deflate public reputations with ease. All politicians are media tarts — dependent on good coverage for visibility and electability — but only the women were derided for having sustained favourable coverage. And there was a creepy kind of subtext in much reportage that implied that the sexual appeal of women in the public eye was inexorably linked with their political fortunes, as it was assumed to be for women in so many arenas. That, in an instant, they could be praised then shamed for being female, or feminine, or flawed. Tarts, even.

*

After the book's initial publication, it seemed like things were getting better, that inching progress was being made. Then overnight, suddenly and shockingly, a woman became prime minister. Julia Gillard successfully toppled Kevin Rudd in 2010, saying the government had lost its way, and it seemed, briefly, as if this could be the tipping point for women, the moment at which it could become normal to see a woman wielding real power.

But despite the fact that Gillard was widely popular as a deputy leader and respected as a sharp and pragmatic operator, the moment she placed her hands on the nation's helm, the souring began. By the end of her tenure, we had witnessed a kind of mass misogynistic hysteria that was unprecedented in its volume and vitriol. For the three years and three days that Julia Gillard was prime minister of Australia, we debated the fit of her jackets, the size of her bottom, the exposure of her cleavage, the cut of her hair, the tone of her voice, the legitimacy of her rule and whether she had chosen, as Liberal senator Bill Heffernan put it, to be 'deliberately barren'. (Anyone who would do that deliberately, he said, has 'got no idea what life's about'.)

When was the last time you heard a man called barren?

The fact that Julia Gillard had no children and had not married her partner somehow opened her up to abuse. The CEO of Australian Agricultural Company, David Farley, called her a 'non-productive old cow' and Liberal opposition leader Tony Abbott suggested she should 'make an honest woman of herself'.

The sexism was visceral and often grotesque.

There were placards crying 'Ditch the Witch', toys designed for dogs that encouraged them to chew on the fleshier parts of her anatomy, and a menu offering 'Julia Gillard Kentucky Fried Quail — small breasts, huge thighs and a big red box.' By the end of her term, on 27 June 2013, the disrespect was so pervasive that the prime minister struggled to be heard above the sexist ridicule. Violent threats became commonplace. In Brisbane, she drove past a man who pointed at her, making a sign of a noose.[1]

When Gillard spoke about some of these slurs, she was accused of igniting 'gender wars.' When female colleagues came to her defence, they were tagged the 'handbag hit squad' by their Liberal opponents. Any discussion of the misogyny that was marbling public debate was dismissed as 'the gender card'.

Gillard was not flawless — that was not the issue. Much of her problem arose from the way she acquired power. When she deposed Rudd, it was the first time that a sitting prime minister in Australia had been overthrown by his own party during his first term. Three years later, of course, Rudd returned the favour, after polls suggested that the party would be annihilated at the coming election.

Uneasiness over the way Gillard came to power fed deep currents of sexism throughout her time as prime minister. Yet in political scientist Blair Williams's analysis of the prime ministerial ascension of both Malcolm Turnbull — who successfully challenged sitting prime minister Tony Abbott in September 2015 — and Julia Gillard, she found that while Gillard was depicted as a 'backstabbing murderer', Turnbull was seen to be 'taking back the reins'.[2] Positive terms spotted the coverage of Turnbull: 'rejuvenate', 'innovation', 'exciting', 'welcomed', 'triumph'. His win over Abbott was a 'spectacular reprise' and he was described as 'seizing the PM's job ... in a sudden and extraordinary ballot'. Whereas of the 380 articles Williams analysed about Gillard's successful challenge, almost half portrayed Gillard as a Lady Macbeth: she was depicted in the coverage as 'a murderer thirsty for Rudd's blood, employing words such as "knifing", "decapitation", "ruthless assassination" and "execute".' Gillard was disloyal; Turnbull was successful and ambitious.[3]

The polls were favourable, though — in her first week as PM her party's two-party preferred vote rose by 14 per cent, and leader satisfaction by 38 per cent — and Gillard quickly called an election for August 2010. The results were close and she was only able to form a minority government by negotiating deals with the Greens and three independents. The Greens wanted a price on carbon and Gillard agreed, even though she had said during the campaign that there would be 'no carbon tax under a government that I lead'. (Incidentally, the price on carbon saw a drop in emissions in those companies subject to it: it worked.)

Tony Abbott, who was prime minister from 2013 to 2015, spent years branding Gillard as a liar because of her move on the carbon price, with some effect. He promised repeatedly during the 2013 election campaign to lead a government that 'says what it means, and does what it says'. But analysis by the *Australian Financial Review* found that in his first year of office, Abbott had broken his word on 14 pre-election promises, including 'no cuts to education, no cuts to health, no change to pensions, and no cuts to the ABC or SBS'. The headline read: 'Abbott government breaks more promises than it keeps'.[4]

It's not hypocrisy that is the most problematic finding here, but the idea that men are expected to do politics this way — to lie, backflip, play dirty, abuse opponents, topple leaders. But when a woman was forced to break a promise because she did a deal that would allow her to form minority government, she became 'JULIAR' and was unable to shake the tag. A common descriptor was 'the lying bitch'.

As leader, Gillard struggled to project her natural warmth, humour and empathy or convince the public of her sincerity. She was slow to condemn corruption in her party, opposed marriage equality, passed welfare reforms that disproportionately disadvantaged single mothers, and negotiated a limp tax that failed to reap significant revenue from Australia's mining boom. But she was pragmatic and effective, presided over solid economic growth, called a royal commission into institutional child abuse, and enacted historic reforms in the areas of education, paid parental leave and disability.

Women across Australia had clinked glasses at her ascension:

at last, the mould was smashed. She was an unmarried red-haired atheist with no children, living with a hairdresser boyfriend who often rose early to tend to her tresses. Gillard had fought the 2010 election hard, ignoring the sneers, the contempt and the catcalls.

Then, in 2012, her father died. While she was still grieving, a radio shock jock named Alan Jones — who had previously said Gillard should be put in a chaff bag and dumped out at sea — declared that Gillard's father died of shame. Shortly afterward, in Parliament, Tony Abbott, the leader of the Liberal opposition, said that Gillard's government should 'die of shame'.

And Gillard, spectacularly, stood up and delivered a blistering response, a speech of such force and conviction that it ricocheted around the globe. She said:

> The Leader of the Opposition says that people who hold
> sexist views and who are misogynists are not appropriate for
> high office. Well, I hope the Leader of the Opposition has
> got a piece of paper and he is writing out his resignation.
> Because if he wants to know what misogyny looks like in
> modern Australia, he doesn't need a motion in the House of
> Representatives, he needs a mirror.

She would not be lectured to, she said, by a man who had stood next to placards calling her 'bitch' and who had suggested that men had a better temperament for leadership (asking an interviewer: 'what if men are by physiology or temperament, more adapted to exercise authority or to issue command?').

'My father did not die of shame,' she said coolly. 'What the leader of the opposition should be ashamed of is his performance in this Parliament and the sexism he brings with it.'

Many still remember where they were when they heard this speech; I was at home, writing, and was suddenly charged with electricity. I hopped from foot to foot, calling my newspaper editor to see if she wanted me to file a piece on it, and when she asked me to wait until Saturday, I laced up my sneakers and dashed out the door for a run, trying to find a way to burn up the energy. When I saw the papers the next day, I was staggered — I flipped pages, looking for someone who got it, who saw how momentous that speech had been and would remain. But, with one rare exception of a small piece by Jacqueline Maley, the press gallery, distracted by the daily politicking, missed it, astonishingly.

While this speech was globally lauded, the irony was, as Gillard's popularity dropped — especially among men — her failings were pegged to the fact that she had dared to talk about the perils of female leadership. With gender dominating front pages for months, the media described her daily as a failed experiment. Even her fiercest critics conceded in the final weeks of her leadership, that no other prime minister was ever treated with such vitriol. Radio host Ray Hadley, who had called her an 'imbecile' and a 'vitriolic, bitter, condescending, arrogant facade of a prime minister' said, apparently without irony: 'I don't think there's been any prime minister who has been subject to the sort of attacks Julia Gillard has received.'

At her last news conference as PM, Gillard said being the first woman to hold the office 'does not explain everything about my time in the prime ministership, nor does it explain nothing'. Her voice quavered when she said, 'What I am absolutely confident of is that it will be easier for the next woman and for the woman after that and the woman after that, and I'm proud of that.'

Gillard had suffered the most extraordinary foul attacks on a woman we have seen in this country. Both her success and her failure acted like pipe songs, luring the snakes of contempt and woman-hating from their baskets. Disrespect was rife. School students threw sandwiches at her. And all of the ancient tropes had roared back into life — the focus on her lack of children and an empty fruit bowl in her kitchen (Housewife Superstars), on her appearance (Cover Girls), the horror that she compromised on a promise, which is pretty standard political behaviour (Steel Sheilas), the view of her successful leadership challenge as sinister (Steel Sheilas) and murderous (Sinning Saints), and the punishment for talking about bias against women (Feminine Feminists). All of them dormant, then revived.

It would be difficult to underestimate the impact this public vivisection of a powerful woman had on women in Australia, especially young women. A 2017 Plan International survey of more than 2000 Australian girls and young women aged between ten and 25 found that precisely zero per cent of women aged 18 to 25 wanted to go into politics. Not one. They had been paying attention. As had other women, who as they went about their daily lives, working and caring and parenting and striving, remembered the contempt, the scorn and the ugliness ladled out upon the head of our first female prime minister and wondered what had happened and why things became so frenzied and so irrational once a woman was finally in charge.

*

In her recent book, *Sex, Lies and Question Time*, former federal Labor minister Kate Ellis describes the guilt she and some of her female colleagues felt — and still feel — about the treatment of our first female prime minister. Could they have better protected Julia Gillard when she was being disrespected and savaged daily? Ellis writes: 'if we had been more forthright in calling the culture out earlier, would the appalling misogynistic attacks on Julia Gillard still have occurred? Could we have stopped things before they exploded so dramatically?'[5]

Deputy opposition leader Tanya Plibersek believes they let Gillard down, telling Ellis: 'You and I, in particular, because we both went in quite young, we were toughened to it because we had gone through it ourselves. It was our view, and it was Julia's view as well, that you just get on with doing a good job. I didn't call it out in the way I should have.'6

Senator Penny Wong, a cabinet member in Gillard's government, wonders the same: 'By not raising things earlier, did we actually not confront norms which then enabled it to go so far in the national abuse of the prime minister?'7

But Gillard hopes her experience will provide women with blueprints for future political careers. She told Ellis: 'Women starting in the parliament now have got the fantastic benefit that they've seen this movie before. And when you think you've seen the movie before, your ability to think in advance about how you will react and what you will do if these moments come in your political career is far better than it's ever been. That is such a huge advantage.'

The problem is, that is almost exactly what she told me, almost two decades ago.

And here we are.

*

The story of women in parliament in Australia is the story, in vast part, of white women trying to enter places created for, controlled by and policed by white men. The vast majority were heterosexual, able bodied, cis and middle class. They were told to look and act in the ways white men would approve. They were told to make themselves physically pleasing to white men.

People of colour were largely excluded. In 1901, Aboriginal Australians were not even included in the constitution Australia adopted when it became a federation. It was not until 1967 that a national referendum gave citizenship and the power to vote to Aboriginal and Torres Strait Islander people.

The first Indigenous member of federal parliament was Neville

Bonner, who became a senator in 1971; it was 42 years before Australia had its first female Indigenous senator, decorated athlete Nova Peris, in 2013. And it was not until 2016 that Linda Burney, a proud member of the Wiradjuri nation, became the first Indigenous woman to be elected to the House of Representatives (in 2003, Burney had been the first — and only — Indigenous member of NSW parliament). This means it had taken 73 years after the first white woman entered the lower House towards the end of World War II for an Indigenous woman to follow — a stunning, shameful gap.

In her first speech Burney said she had been told when she was 13 years old that her ancestors were like stone-age men. 'The Aboriginal part of my story is important, it is the core of who I am,' she said. 'But I will not be stereotyped and I will not be pigeon-holed.'

In hers, Nova Peris, a descendant of Yawuru, Kiga and Murran/Iwatja tribal nations, had urged her colleagues to become champions for the inclusion of first nations people in the Australian Constitution, adding that: 'Aboriginal Australians are symbolic of triumph over adversity. We represent knowledge and wisdom held in land and country, because in our hearts we know that we do not own Mother Earth; the Earth owns us.'

Peris's entry to parliament had been marked with controversy as she had been a 'captain's pick' by Julia Gillard, replacing an incumbent. But Peris resigned at the end of her term, after a considerable period of horrific racial abuse, including death threats.

She told the told the audience of the ABC's 'Q&A' program in 2020, that because she started to speak out about Indigenous rights she was 'attacked by racist trolls' almost daily. She continued:

Mail was sent, phone calls [saying], 'Get back in your box, you black bitch.' I had death threats. The AFP were tracking down mail that was sent to me. This is what I had to endure...

People fear when an Aboriginal person speaks out. When you're an Aboriginal person in this country and speak out and start calling racism out, you get attacked, because for so long this country has had this thought process. Racism is about inferior races. White is up here. Black is down there. That's how this country has been built. Nineteen ninety-three was when the Eddie Mabo High Court decision was made. It knocked out the notion of terra nullius. They had inherited mentally that the country belonged to 'no man'. So it meant our lives as Aboriginal people, we were nothing.

And so when people often talk about the history of this country, the history of this country is violent. There's been the attempted genocide. There's been the massacres. There's been the poisoning. There's been the rapes. There's been so much, and it's horrible. The truth just gets to people and they don't want to have a bar of it. But us as Aboriginal people, we inherit that every day. If I don't acknowledge that then I am denying everything that makes me who I am.

The abuse was exhausting, and Peris left parliament. She said her family needed her, and she felt as if she was being asked to compromise who she was as an Aboriginal person, which is what she is 'first and foremost'. What a disgrace, that our first female Indigenous senator, elected well more than a century after federation, who brought so much knowledge and life experience, endured such savage, nasty abuse.

The whiteness and lack of diversity in politics has long been obvious, yet remains. In 2018, fewer than twenty of the 226 federal parliamentarians had a non-English speaking background, even though 2016 Census data showed more than half of Australians had parents born overseas, or were born in other countries themselves. Almost one in four speak a non-English language at home.

A 2019 Per Capita report found that since 1988, the proportion of Australians born in other countries had shot up from 22 per cent to 33 per cent, but their representation in parliament had stagnated at 11 per cent.[8] As the *Sydney Morning Herald* put it: 'culturally and ethnically, Parliament is in a time warp'.[9]

It's also in a time warp on gender. Former PM Malcolm Turnbull has often stated that when it comes to attitudes to women, federal politics is like corporate Australia was back in the 1970s and 1980s. Several women MPs who entered from the private sector have told me they were shocked to discover this for themselves.

As is clear in this book, no political party has been or is free of sexism. But currently, the Liberal party is steadily losing women voters — a two-decade trend — and failing to increase the number of women in its parliamentary ranks. In March 2021, I obtained a copy of a confidential internal report on why there were so few female leaders and MPs in the party, carried out for the Liberal Party Federal Executive in 2015 by the Women's Working Group (WWG).[10] This document revealed that many of the issues women preselected in the 1960s and 1970s wrestled with — and the frames and tropes identified in *Media Tarts* — are still current. For example, 'a preselector bias against women of childbearing age' (still! Still asked who will mind their children, and who will cook the meals!), and the attitude of some older party members that: 'If you are a woman and have children you should be staying at home and looking after them.' Some women reported being viewed as 'tea makers' by male LNP members. Revealingly, they found 'some men in the party see women in an old-fashioned way where they were present to support the men and not be a force of their own' — and that these kinds of male MPs groomed male staffers as their replacements.

There were also findings of a 'boys' club culture', 'chauvinistic behaviour from men', and the bullying and intimidation of women.

Women said they were silenced at meetings, and the report tellingly recommended they be able to speak out 'without fear of being cut down and removed from any position they held'. Women would change the culture of the party if more of them were in there, just as happened in the Army, argued the WWG, although presciently concluding: 'sadly, a significant number of Liberal men in Parliament are still either uncomfortable with the idea of women as political equals, or they simply ignore the whole issue'.

This report, which was finalised in December 2015, was effectively buried. It was not released publicly and was generally ignored. Just a couple of years later, Brittany Higgins was allegedly sexually assaulted by a Liberal staffer on a Liberal minister's couch. Two years after that, she spoke out. She was quickly called a 'lying cow' by the minister she used to work for (who hastened to stress had not been referring to the rape allegations, but to Higgins saying she had not been supported subsequently) and a 'silly little girl who got drunk' by a veteran radio host. A Liberal senator was alleged to have insulted Higgins by telling another MP she had been 'disgustingly drunk' on the night of the attack and 'would sleep with anybody, [and] could have slept with one of our spies and put the security of our nation at risk'.

And so the lava began to flow.

If we understand our history, we will know there is no more time for patience. And we will see the tropes a mile away, along with the pitfalls and the traps and the rubbish. We will see them coming, name them, call them out and move on. We have all the evidence we need — much of it contained within these pages.

Julia Baird
Cabbage Tree Bay
2021

Introduction to 2004 edition

tart: 1. (derogatory) a promiscuous woman. 2. a prostitute.
3. any woman. 4. (obsolete) a female sweetheart.

frame: an enclosing border or case, as for a picture ... the
body, esp. the human body, with reference to its make or build;
a structure for admitting or enclosing something ... (Snooker)
a. the triangular form used to set the balls up for a game.
b. the balls as so set up. c. the period of play required to pocket
them; ... (framed, framing) ... to conceive or imagine as ideas,
etc ... to shape or to prearrange fraudulently or falsely as a
plot, a race, etc; (colloquial) to incriminate unjustly by a plot,
as a person ... (obsolete) to direct, as one's steps.

                                           — *The Macquarie Dictionary*

Joan Kirner was a 'fat whinger'. Cheryl Kernot a self-obsessed
'whore'. Meg Lees was an ageing headmistress with the
personality of a laxative. Natasha Stott Despoja was a vapid
yuppie princess. Amanda Vanstone was the charge nurse from
hell. Bronwyn Bishop was a rottweiler with lipstick. If you

believed the insults flung by their detractors, aired in the press, you'd think female politicians were a pitiful bunch. How did they become such caricatures? Each of the women who blazed most brightly through the political firmament over the 1990s had been pursued with an unprecedented enthusiasm. They were courted and feted by the phalanx of reporters who hanker for a touch of colour and difference in the blokey world of politics they daily scour for stories. Then, with few exceptions, they were dumped or discredited with an intensity that surprised even the most experienced observers.

For a century after women started seriously agitating for the vote, it was often suggested women would scrub Parliament House clean once they were elected to political office. They would make it more open, honest, and accessible. Just as Christians are told to be *in* the world but not *of* the world, so it was thought that women would be in, but not of, politics. They would float above it, gazing with pity and scorn at the muck beneath. They would be promoted when they deserved it, or a man stepped aside, not because their ambition propelled them forward. They would not be pragmatic premiers, driven leaders, or vicious backbenchers who sought publicity, undermined enemies, and relished playing the game of politics. Their chastity and virtue depended on their removal from the heat of the political fray. Parliament was not their natural home; they were intruders in whom signs of difference were alarming, and signs of sameness — or political acumen — even more so. In this atmosphere, their flaws became monstrous.

The difference between what it has been suggested women should bring to politics and what they actually do has played havoc with the careers of our most successful female politicians. An assumption — often fostered by women to their own advantage — that women are cleaner, more ethical than men, and that their presence will bleach politics of grime, has been their greatest burden. Trumpeted as sincere, honest, and accessible, when they turn out to be human and flawed the pundits marvel and sneer. Women and power; water and oil. Or at least that's what you might think if you relied only on the headlines for information.

*

The letters pages of metropolitan broadsheets are among the bestread parts of their papers. They have a loyal, witty, and committed readership. When I first began as a cadet at the *Sydney Morning Herald*, the letters editor, Sam North, sat several feet away from me and I could hear him chuckling all day as he waded through the rivers of correspondence from our readers, plucked out the best and placed them on his page. They were a good way to gauge the thoughts of readers, and community reactions to daily events, then. For many female politicians, the letters pages have provided a welcome contrast to the exacting judgement of political commentators. When Carmen Lawrence resigned from the ALP opposition front bench over its refugee policy, readers responded far more fervently and positively than did many commentators, who slammed her as pious and a poor team player. When Natasha Stott Despoja was compared to glamorous tennis player Anna Kournikova by political guru Alan Ramsey, readers wrote to complain, as they did when the front-page headline to a story about the distinguished psychiatrist Professor Marie Bashir becoming the first female governor of NSW was 'Phillip, Bligh, Macquarie, Grandma'. (Yes, that really was the headline in 2001.)

But by the early 2000s, some people were also writing in to ask if it was actually worth having women in politics. Don't they just stuff things up? Don't they cause more problems than they solve? Were women, as one prominent commentator said to me, the political experiment that had failed? There was a cluster of failures: former Democrat leader and Labor minister Cheryl Kernot lost her seat in 2001; Natasha Stott Despoja challenged Meg Lees for the leadership of the Democrats and won, before being forced to resign less than 18 months later; and Lees resigned from the party she had previously led. Some letter writers snorted into their cornflakes as they read the newspapers — women were just as dirty as the men! They backstabbed, pursued personal ambitions and openly criticised each other. On 30 July 2002, after Meg Lees quit the Australian Democrats, these appeared on the *Herald*'s letters page:

> First Cheryl Kernot, now Meg Lees. Not long ago the electorate was being told by the women's lobby about the positive, transforming influence women would have on Australian political culture if only they were given the chance. Get away from the aggressive, confrontational boys' culture, we were told.
>
> Oh well. Back to the drawing board.
>
> David James, Epping, July 29

> I love seeing women in politics. They really are so much fun to have around. They are so tolerant and exhibit all those nice qualities of collaboration and interpersonal skills so lacking in men.
>
> What great entertainment, and perhaps a thrilling constitutional crisis brewing ... Hopefully we will now be spared the sanctimonious twaddle about the superiority of women over men.
>
> Paul Murphy, Illawong, July 29

This belief — of women's superior morality — is why parties pushed more women into marginal seats, and handed them portfolios muddied by the corruption or incompetence of the men before them, in the belief that they would have — or at least appear to have — some kind of purifying effect. It is also partly why women have failed to reach the top.

It took almost a century to see women reach their mid-2000s quota of more than a quarter of all MPs in this country. In the mid-1990s, with women finally in key leadership positions, excitement about women 'storming the citadel' was palpable. In February 1994, *Herald* journalist Mike Seccombe argued that there was an arms race going on between the major parties, where women were the missiles: Bronwyn Bishop for the Liberals, Carmen Lawrence for the ALP, Cheryl Kernot for the Democrats. It was widely believed that the feminisation of politics was about to occur. In 1990, when Carmen Lawrence became premier of Western Australia, ALP pollster Rod Cameron declared it was a watershed for Australian politics. In the same year, Joan Kirner was made premier of Victoria; Rosemary Follett had been chief minister of the ACT in 1989 (and was again from 1991 to 1995); and Kate Carnell was elected first woman leader of the ACT Liberal Party in 1993. This was, apparently, the Era of the Woman, finally coming as a counter to the Millennia of the Man.

Then, over a decade, Australia watched prominent female politicians topple like ten pins under a barrage of media criticism. One after the other, with careers destroyed, credibility damaged, prospects of leadership slim or non-existent: hyped as heroines, then cast as villains or fools, or just made invisible. Bronwyn Bishop, feted then hated. Cheryl Kernot, desired then destroyed. Natasha Stott Despoja, pinup then media tart. Carmen Lawrence, canonised then castigated (although cleared by the courts) for her role in the Penny Easton affair. Others failed through their own lack of ability or bad timing. In many cases, the women were partly to blame or complicit in their demise, yet the bias that frequently emerged in the media made their transgressions grotesque, their mistakes almost sinister — a hall of mirrors that exaggerated their flaws and made them lethal.

By 2004, the political horizon was almost devoid of charismatic, powerful female MPs who were potential leaders. There were a handful of ministers, a deputy leader of the federal ALP, Jenny Macklin, but only one female leader nationally: Clare Martin in the Northern Territory. All female cabinet ministers were in their 50s, and most were senators, meaning they are not likely to be contending the leadership of their parties. (On the opposition front bench, shadow health minister Julia Gillard was the one most widely — and correctly — regarded as having a chance of future leadership.) With the exception of talented young MPs like Tanya Plibersek (now deputy opposition leader), Marise Payne (now minister for foreign affairs and women) and Nicola Roxon (who became the first female attorney general, in 2011), a generation of younger women were discouraged from going into politics because of what the country witnessed in the late 1990s: who wanted to be the alley cat on heat, the plastic piranha with balls under her skirts, or the blonde bimbo party girl? Political pundits declared parties didn't want another emotional Cheryl, a discredited Carmen, a lightweight Natasha, a despised Bronwyn. Their grisly heads were displayed on spikes in political memory, serving as warnings to those who wish to follow them. In the noughties, women MPs were told to keep their heads down: fly too high, too close to the throbbing heart of power, and you will be shot down. And look like a fool while you fall. So what went wrong and what needs to change?

The current commentary provides few answers. A century after women first exercised the vote at federal level, and several decades after winning the right to sit as members of state parliaments, there is something tired and deflated about the debate regarding women MPs. Clichés are resorted to, tired assumptions are reproduced, and the rhetoric about their relationship to the media has been marooned between two strands of thought. The first claims there has been no bias, and the second exaggerates that bias, assuming it is unassailable and overwhelming.

Academics and activists have frequently assumed the press is a monolithic block of anti-woman propaganda, which is clearly untrue. Many argue that there has either been no change in the press since the 1970s or it has become worse, while showing little awareness of what has changed over the past three decades, and what impact women, and the women's movement, have had. Few recognise that part of the problem for women MPs is not necessarily disdain from journalists, but excessive enthusiasm, as women such as Carmen Lawrence have found.

Some political journalists argue that to talk of gender means introducing an intellectually weak, lame excuse for bad behaviour: the 'gender card'. The ghosts of a thousand thwarted ambitions roam the corridors and offices of parliament houses — those men and women who would be/should have been/almost were ministers, leaders or prime ministers (or those who were-but-then-were-robbed-of-victory-or success-or-acknowledgement). Politics is timing, luck, talent, and resilience. It is also about withstanding the attacks of your enemies — and of course the more powerful you are the more you'll have. It is easy to dissect and dismiss the individual experiences of women MPs, but when viewed collectively it is clear that a specific way of viewing women has frequently interfered with the way they are seen and the progress of their careers. The fact remains that the position of women is more tenuous and their grasp on power more slippery by virtue of their gender and the intense scrutiny — both sympathetic and hostile — of the media.

It is true, also, that female politicians are not simply victims of vicious politics, or sexism. The fact that some women, like many male politicians, can use the media for their own political success adds to the cynicism of journalists and commentators, who no longer view them as victims of a sexist press but agents of their own profiles. That journalists both resist and expose any attempts at manipulation makes controlling the media a difficult task. But not impossible. In this book, I will look at how many women politicians — like Flo Bjelke-Petersen and Natasha Stott Despoja — have exploited the stereotypes and superficiality of press coverage for their own gain.

It is difficult to generalise about the media. It is a large, sprawling beast with thousands of heads, all talking at once. Journalists are trained to be suspicious and cynical, and dissent is part of the trade, seen in daily disagreements with colleagues, editors, publishers and subeditors within their own papers, let alone other newspapers. Each day is a mad scramble to break stories, get the facts right, edit and correct copy, and spin the plates of newspaper rounds like health, education, rural affairs; the work can be systematic, deliberate, and chaotic all at the same time. This is why it is important not to buckle to conspiracy theories. Timing and personality, along with the daily news flow and the views of key commentators, are often more influential in determining news coverage than any predetermined agenda.

Nor are newspapers the simple hierarchical, entirely male structures many people assume them to be. Editors can of course place their stamp on stories, but the rapid pace of news means often the people who have the most influence on the nature and placement of news coverage are the individual reporters and key figures including the chief of staff, news editor, night editor and chief subeditor. There are multiple, competing voices within media organisations, and often just one edition of a newspaper contains several different approaches to reporting on prominent women. Throughout the 1970s and 1980s, for example, despite a frequently dismissive attitude to the women's movement from reporters, editorials were often devoted to the lack of women in parliament, and they usually supported the right of women to be there on equal terms with men.

However, a large, differentiated organism like a newspaper still suffers from wheel alignment problems in the way major events are reported: a veering towards a blokey sensibility; to the way it has always been done; to what political scientists call predetermined 'frames' — or today, tropes — which decide the way stories are written and presented. Often a failure on behalf of a reporter or chief of staff to produce correctly framed stories means those pieces will not get a run. The majority of newspaper editors and bureau chiefs are still men, reflected in the language which differentiates between 'hard' and 'soft' stories, and refers to the running of a story as 'getting it up'. Recently I heard one editor tell another he didn't want the 'soft cock' stories to be dumped on his section at the end of the day — he only wanted 'hard news'.

While researching this book, I went from analysing the press gallery from afar to sitting in it myself. I started as a reporter and editor at the *Sydney Morning Herald* in 1998, when I was a cadet. I spent only six months in the state and federal press galleries, but as a reporter and opinion editor I have interviewed and worked with dozens of politicians. I also worked briefly on the closest thing the *Herald* has to a gossip column, then titled 'Stay in Touch', and witnessed the ready reversion to diminishing clichés when poking fun at female MPs: reference was made to Jackie Kelly's cleavage at a ball, and Amanda Vanstone's physique at a sausage and beer party she hosted for the press gallery. Broadsheets have a long tradition of trying to disguise sexism as satire. But personal comments are not always necessarily sexist. As a trainee asked to write a colour story about an unremarkable first day of federal parliament, it was oddly difficult to refrain from referring to the fact that, in a mob of dark suits, Cheryl Kernot and Bronwyn Bishop wore matching white skirts and jackets. Opposite sides of parliment, diametrically opposed views, but exactly the same clothes. Trivial, yes. But these kinds of human details are what gives life to a story, what reporters crave, and why they flock to unusual politicians who dress or speak differently. (In the end I didn't mention it, although journalists from other newspapers did.) We should be able to describe people's appearance — journalists are often told they are the eyes of their readers — but it should not be done gratuitously, repetitively or selectively. It is appropriate in personal profiles, and men should be treated the same way.

*

Former *Sydney Morning Herald* journalist Margo Kingston wrote that, three years before she finally stood for leader, Natasha Stott Despoja asked for her advice, as she had asked many journalists, about whether she should run, saying the media wanted her to. Kingston warned her: 'You're the touch of excitement and attractive product the media drools over. But if you rely on the media to bring you up, it will just as quickly drag you down. The shift from media darling to media tart can come in an instant. The media is a fickle, dangerous support base.' These words proved to be prescient. In the 1990s, many female politicians were accused of being media tarts, as journalists wooed them then ridiculed them. By the journalists' rationale, news stories that trivialised or stereotyped women were not the sign of a superficial or image-obsessed press, but the outcome of vain, ambitious women who craved the spotlight and pretended to be better than the men.

The story of female MPs and the media is a story of shouting matches in newsrooms, of senior journalists who cross swords in print and stop talking to each other for years, of too-cosy relationships and betrayal. It involves gossip, innuendo, dirty tricks, voyeurism, nervous breakdowns, tears, and odd alliances.

It is also a tale of women fighting back, using stereotypes to their advantage, verballing journalists, refusing photographers' requests, and learning to laugh at themselves. It is a story of women who, like Pauline Hanson, have been determined that there was 'no way in the bloody wide world' they were going to allow the media to make them lose their seats or their sanity.

'A rare kind of woman politician': Margaret Thatcher's visit to Australia in 1976

Mrs Thatcher made it plain she would prefer less publicity about her hair and more about the content and impact of her speeches. But all the same, her new hair-do is an enormous success, as Australians will soon see. Margaret Thatcher, who is 50, is slim, has a peaches and cream complexion that has been left unlined by the English climate, and Australians who don't hate her politics are going to 'Ooh' and 'Aah' over her, without any doubt.[1]

She had been described as a steely blonde bombshell, the Marilyn Monroe of British politics, the Iron Lady, the Ice Maiden, and a politicised Edna Everage. And now she was coming to Australia. On 13 September 1976, Margaret Thatcher, the first female leader of the British Conservative Party, stepped off a plane in Sydney, prepared for what a local reporter described as a great test: facing the Australian media. Until then, journalists had read only second-hand accounts of the former barrister and chemist who, two months into International Women's Year, had defied all the pundits and become the leader of the Tories. Words of praise and astonishment tumbled over each other in articles that questioned how she could be both attractive and strong, and how she could remain immaculately groomed while working hard. She was described as an exceptional kind of woman who men desired and women admired. A woman who was unlike other women, who scared her male colleagues and outshone them. On the tabula rasa that was the powerful woman in the popular imagination, Thatcher came to embody everything a woman could be — and everything most women were not.

The *Sydney Morning Herald*'s London correspondent, T.S. Monks, wrote that Thatcher's visit would provide Australians with 'a chance to study a rare kind of woman politician'. While there were dozens of conservative women who looked like her, few had her ambition, he wrote, or her background of academic success and rapid political promotion. What was most astonishing, however, was how good she looked: 'Only tough women can have done all this, and the few in the world who have reached political pinnacles have tended to look tough. But Mrs. Thatcher does not. Nor do her fine-boned features ever look ruffled or agitated.' Despite the long political hours, Thatcher reportedly bloomed in parliament due to an ability to get by on four hours sleep a night, and came through these long ordeals 'with not one of her blonde hairs out of place'.[2] (Which is, after all, the aim.)

Glowing descriptions of her looks were ubiquitous in the coverage of the woman who had once modelled tweed suits for London's *Daily Telegraph*, although when mentioning this, most reporters hastened to add that she was also capable and intelligent. Many journalists, male and female, exclaimed over her beauty, detailing the perfection of her skin, legs and dresses.

Jilly Cooper, writing in London for the *National Times*, said she had not been prepared for her prettiness: 'Old-fashioned parasol-cherished looks, an apple-blossom complexion, pearly white arms emphasised by the black dress, long beautiful legs set off by expensive black shoes.' Ros Dunn claimed Thatcher was 'supremely aware of being a woman. She has only to look in a mirror for confirmation: at 49, she looks at least 10 years younger, pretty and feminine, with soft gold hair, blue eyes, cream complexion and a nice pair of ankles. But behind the soft facade is a whip-lash mind and a tongue more biting than hydrochloric acid.'[3] Perhaps the London *Sun*, on the day she was made leader of the Tory Party, summed it up most succinctly in the headline: 'She's no powder puff! She's charming — and tough.'

These articles appear risible now, knowing the immense power Thatcher went on to wield both in her own country and in global politics. On the day she arrived in Australia, *Woman's Day* ran an article declaring that Thatcher was 'tough, but still feminine', quoting her saying, 'Clothes are immensely important to a woman. It's always first impressions that count ... Luckily I don't have too much of a problem with my figure; I can wear an off-the-peg size 14 all the time.'

The fact that journalists frequently referred to her appearance led Thatcher to protest that she was not vain and not always tidy: 'People complain I'm too immaculate to get any work done, but look, look, there's ink on my hands and my hair's a terrible mess.' She told one journalist, who had asked if it was a hindrance being so good-looking, that she was barely conscious of it, adding, 'By the time I've been writing a speech at three o'clock in the morning my hair is looking dishevelled. I haven't even got a mirror in this room.' Despite her protestations, Thatcher continued to be described again and again as an impeccably styled, good-looking woman, and changes in her hairstyle were noted by the Australian and British press.

When Thatcher campaigned for the leadership, from late 1974 to early 1975, she employed a strategy of portraying herself as an ordinary wife and mother, to counter a public image of a cold, snobbish Tory with twin-sets, pearls, and a fondness for expensive hats and Derby porcelain. In December 1970, she had earned the title of 'Thatcher Milk Snatcher' when, as secretary of state for education, she stopped free milk for eight- to 12-year-olds, and by 1971 the *Sun* had declared her to be 'the most unpopular woman in Britain'. In order to prove she did not lack 'the common touch', Thatcher took the advice of former television producer Gordon Reece and deliberately cultivated the image of a dedicated housewife: allowing herself to be photographed dusting, cooking, washing up, baking cakes, putting out empty milk bottles, peeling potatoes, and sweeping paths wearing a lacy cap. She told the *Daily Mirror* in February 1975: 'What people don't realise about me is that I am a very ordinary person who leads a very normal life. I enjoy it — seeing that the family has a good breakfast. And shopping keeps me in touch.' In Australia, photographs of Thatcher were labelled simply 'suburban housewife'.

After Thatcher was elected leader of the Tories, headlines in articles written by London correspondents for the Australian media proclaimed: 'The Leader is a Wife too!' Photographs of 'the smile of victory' were compared to 'the smile of content' as she stood at the kitchen sink washing the dishes. Readers were assured that 'the twins, Mark and Carol ... had their good-night kiss and tuck in without fail over the years'. She was reported to put 'all her academic brilliance into cooking', and to be a kind and sensitive hostess who, even in the midst of intense discussions with colleagues at her home, was 'forever checking on people's glasses and replenishing their cups with fresh tea and coffee'. Just as all leaders do.

The news of Thatcher's election as leader of her party came in the middle of the decade in which second-wave feminism, encapsulated in books such as *The Female Eunuch*, *The Feminine Mystique*, and *Damned Whores and God's Police*, had clambered onto the front pages of newspapers, shaken a fist in the face of the establishment, and was slowly gaining a voice in mainstream politics. However, her triumph was represented in the press not as a breakthrough for women's liberation but, paradoxically, as an affirmation of the ideal of the 'wife and mother' role for women. Following Thatcher's leadership coup, Dr Claire Ibister of St Leonards wrote a letter to the editor of the *Sydney Morning Herald*, expressing relief: 'Whatever our political attachments, we family women must say thank you Mrs Thatcher, and perhaps there is yet hope that our contribution to society as mothers and home-makers will be recognised in International Women's Year.'[4] Thatcher told journalists she owed nothing to women's liberation and did little to promote other women in the Tory Party, or the interests of women generally.

Yet her achievement and carefully cultivated image created a legacy that set the standard for female politicians from all parties in Australia. Newspaper editorials constantly asked where our own Thatcher was, while reporters did their best to find a local replica. There were few to choose from, however. Until the 1980 election, there had been only four women in the House of Representatives, only one of whom lasted more than a term, and 12 in the Senate. Between 1950 and 1965 there were no women in the House of Representatives. In 1976, the time of Thatcher's visit, there were again no women in the House of Representatives and only six in the Senate: Margaret Guilfoyle, Ruth Coleman, Kathy Sullivan, Jean Melzer, Shirley Walters and Susan Ryan. The Fraser government had only one woman in cabinet, Margaret Guilfoyle, who had been minister for social security since 1975, and there were no women in the shadow cabinet. There had been no women ministers in Labor prime minister Gough Whitlam's cabinet. While Fraser had said he wanted more women in parliament to 'brighten up the place a bit', the *Daily Telegraph* wrote that he 'might find himself squirming a little if Mrs Thatcher asks him a few pointed questions on female representation in parliament'.

Thatcher had already inspired a dozen different nicknames by the time she landed on Australian shores for the first time as party leader. She was called the Iron Lady by the Russian press in January 1976, following her first foreign policy speech as leader of the opposition in which she criticised Russian expansionism and armaments. Even before this, she had been referred to as a ruthlessly ambitious 'iron butterfly' in the British media. The 'iron lady' label appeared in many guises, including the Iron Maiden, the Ice Lady and the Cold War Warrior. She had also been described by the *Daily Telegraph*'s London correspondent as a 'peaches-and-cream sedate Marilyn Monroe of British politics', a 'sort of politicised Edna Everage of England', a Boadicea, the 'blonde, steel bombshell of British politics', and a 'stern, starched, impeccably tailored but coldly-grey angel of political doom'. The female allegories — as yet unmined for female political leaders — were seemingly endless as the press probed what was considered a peculiar hybrid of power and femininity. She was the Iron Lady with a feminine side, the most powerful woman in Britain who cried when things got too much, and relaxed by doing the ironing.

The articles on Thatcher are extraordinary because reporters are so continually astonished at what women are capable of: thinking, working, *and* looking good! Imagine if, instead of a woman called Margaret Thatcher entering a world of men, the press were reporting on a man called Merv Hatcher entering a world ruled by women, giving hope to all Aussie blokes with an eye to power.

If we were to follow closely the formulae and descriptions used for Thatcher in what I read in several hundred articles about her, this is how stories of Merv would read. The (usually female) journalists would cluster around him, gasping at the thickness of his hair and the tautness of his physique, noting that he also had opinions on Russia *and* economic policy. After describing his physical attributes in detail, the copy would continue:

And to think: he manages to lead the party and still fetch the paper in the morning, bright as a button after only four hours sleep. Proving his devotion to his family, he also manages to mow the lawn on the weekend.

His wife does not mind him working at all, and is happy to stay in the background while he speaks, even though she is often spotted napping in her seat at functions. She is the butt of jokes from other women, who tease her about having a working husband, but she is proud of him. Miraculous Merv's stamina has also been the subject of much surprise. Sometimes, after long parliamentary sessions lasting until 4.00 a.m., while his female colleagues stumble about having consumed far too much wine over dinner, their hair unkempt and clothes crumpled, Merv emerges without a trace of stubble, hair neatly combed and shoes shining like mirrors.

His hair is raven-coloured, thick, and styled according to the latest trends, thanks to his barber, Stan, at Hedge Hairdressing. His legs are shapely, his waist trim, and his buttocks strain ever so slightly against his tailored pants from Harrods, leading some of his colleagues to, *ahem*, admire his charms. 'I believe it's important to look one's best at all times,' he says. 'Clothes are very important for a man.'

For all his good looks, charm and sex appeal, it would be a fatal error to mistake Merv for a himbo. His female opponents have tagged him 'Metallic Merv' for his ability to make a decision without changing his mind or breaking down in tears. Merv is known to be not just intelligent, but tough — although remarkably, with his pressed off-white shirts and navy ties, he looks more of a gentleman than a tough, surly, unattractive kind of fellow.

Women lust after him and fear him. Men don't trust him, and while some may admire his courage, will they vote for him?

A psychiatrist who studied Merv has concluded he is smart and has the stamina to work more than an eight-hour day. 'He's a freak,' says Dr Diddle, 'a highly unusual man, but I think he could have what it takes.' A leading party official said he was 20–30 per cent stronger than any woman, and had to work twice as hard to prove himself their equal. He is tough, but still masculine, which may be the key to his success, says advertising executive Don Knowal.

Metallic Merv has also been called the 'Wonderboy', Batman, 007, Muscleman, the Brunette Bomber, Napoleon, 'Margaret Thatcher in pants', Saint Merv, the Freak and That Bloody Bloke.

The Iron Lady in Australia

Thatcher's visit to Australia was structured to maximise positive publicity. She told British journalists the three-week tour, which also included Pakistan, Singapore and New Zealand, was part of her preparation for the prime ministership.[5] Patricia Morgan, in London for the *Advertiser*, wrote that Thatcher knew she was 'going to a country where, on the whole, women are almost unrepresented by women in Parliament'. Her challenge, then, was to garner good coverage in a country almost entirely unused to a woman in her position. To that end, she was accompanied by her parliamentary private secretary, Adam Butler; her constituency secretary, Alison Ward; and her public affairs adviser, Gordon Reece. Reece, Morgan said, had been 'widely credited with advising Mrs Thatcher to adopt a softer hairstyle, more feminine dresses, as part of the task of selling the politician as an attractive and feminine woman'. Morgan wrote that although Thatcher had made it clear she would like less publicity about her hair and more about the content of her speeches, 'all the same, her new hairdo is an enormous success, as Australians will soon see'.

On her first day in Sydney, Thatcher held a press conference in the Boulevarde Hotel. While this was reported on the front page of major Sydney newspapers the next day, there was very little discussion of her policies or views. The *Sydney Morning Herald* began by describing Thatcher as splendidly British: 'all peaches and cream and red, white and blue'. Reminding us that 'she has been described as Dresden china and stainless steel', Lenore Nicklin described how she answered questions efficiently, while leaning forward like an 'encouraging schoolmarm'. Thatcher was clearly loath to discuss discrimination: 'To all those questions about how she felt being described as an Iron Lady ... she simply said, "If I'm never called anything else I'll be very pleased."' Asked if her political achievements would have been easier if she were a man, she said, 'I don't know, I've never tried it.' The *Daily Telegraph* declared she had lived up to her iron lady image by fielding a variety of questions skilfully: 'like a schoolmistress telling pupils how the game should be played'.

It was the female reporters, the *Daily Telegraph* claimed, who were most interested in how a woman came to lead the Tory Party, and how her husband would cope with being the spouse of a British prime minister. In the *Australian*'s front-page story, her husband, Denis, was made the centre of attention, photographed sitting alone in a chair as reporters crowded around his wife with microphone and camera lights aloft. The headline read: 'Behind every successful woman there's a man'. He was quoted saying, 'I just keep my mouth shut and let Margaret get on with it ... Margaret answers the questions far better than I ever could.' A more serious article on Thatcher's views on the Soviet presence in the Indian and Pacific oceans ran on page three. A couple of days later, the *Mirror* also featured Denis in a series on 'men behind the throne'.

The full implications of the conservative Thatcher's interaction with a stronghold of Australian unionism at Broken Hill were largely glossed over by the media here, who portrayed her as being charmed by the rugged 'outback' miners. On 14 September she flew out to western NSW to inspect the North Broken Hill Ltd mine and the Royal Flying Doctor Service, as well as attend a barbecue. The next day newspapers featured photographs of the British leader in the mine — drilling in white overalls, a red tin hat, and blue and white socks and boots — and pointed to the irony of her warm reception in the heavily unionised Broken Hill: 'capital city of all she dislikes and distrusts'. The *Sydney Morning Herald* cried, 'Ice lady of conservatism breaks through the Barrier'. What the Iron Lady needed, it seemed, was a sausage sandwich and a beer with the men at Broken Hill. James Cunningham wrote that Thatcher, 'who has been known as the Ice Lady of the British Conservative Party, thawed out yesterday in eight hours of winning hearts and minds in this rugged citadel of trade-unionism'. The *Advertiser* quoted Thatcher saying, 'There was a companionship among underground workers that was unequalled in almost any sphere.' In her memoirs, however, Thatcher described how horrified she was by what she saw as the 'blatant infraction of liberty' which she understood to mean that no one could live or work in Broken Hill unless they were members of the union.[6]

According to the reports, in just a few days Thatcher had charmed Australia's politicians, journalists and public. The *Sun-Herald* opined it was still uncertain if male prejudice would keep her out of office, but that she had been impressing Australians as 'a very remarkable woman, fully equipped to seize the chance offered by a dearth of male leadership talent in the Tory party'.[7]

Martin Beesley, who accompanied Thatcher on her tour, praised her preparation and application, as well as her ability to remain 'ever charming and in control'. She had impressed all who heard her with 'an extraordinary ability to retain and quote facts on any subject'. The tour, he surmised, had been 'more successful than her advisers dreamed possible. Conservatives in Australia and New Zealand would welcome her as Prime Minister of the country many of them still refer to as home'.[8] It is interesting to note that Thatcher's brief recollections — of a country unused to her 'unapologetic conservatism' because of a culture of protectionist economics and an advanced welfare state — were entirely different, perhaps because her focus was on policy, not sandwiches and legs.[9]

Despite all the editorial predictions that Thatcher's election would ease the path for ambitious women in all democracies, and that her visit would 'make [electors] realise that there is no limit to what a woman can achieve in politics', Thatcher's visit in 1976, and the accompanying publicity, seems only to have emphasised that there was no limit to what the woman who was Margaret Thatcher could achieve.[10] Other women simply had to try harder. In the 1970s, many commentators had argued that it was women's own fault that they were not represented in parliament, firstly for not voting for other women, and secondly for not trying hard enough. John O'Hara of the *Sydney Morning Herald* wrote that 'women are sadly underrepresented by their sex in the Australian parliament for one predominant reason — they don't try to be represented ... that they do not choose to is largely because politics does not interest them ... [because of] a woman's temperamental dislike for public wrangling'. Thatcher herself said in 1974 that 'the shortage of women politicians in Australia, the US and Britain is the fault of the women themselves', adding that in Australia it was also the pressure of travelling long distances to Canberra, because 'Australian women, like all women, do not like to be separated from their families and politics frequently separates a woman from those she loves'. There was some truth to this view, even if the future British PM skipped over any discussion of whether men might like to be separated from their families. Throughout the 1970s and 1980s Thatcher continued to be portrayed as the exception to the rule.[11]

*

Thatcher was, from the mid-1970s onwards, renowned for her stamina, ability and intellectual prowess. Because of her longevity and international prominence, she represented a new realm of possibilities for Australian women. But her media coverage also emphasised the unattainability of what she had achieved, as a former chemist and barrister, mother of two, who became prime minister and was praised for her beauty while allegedly surviving on four hours sleep a night. After becoming PM, she stopped promoting herself as a housewife. According to the *Guardian*, in 1983 'the Prime Minister no longer wheels out her femininity to win hearts and minds. She relies instead on an image of steely resolution'. In the 1980s she was increasingly seen as a warrior queen and Iron Lady, as the 'ordinary woman' disappeared behind a suit of armour, or gun-lined tank. As Beatrix Campbell wrote, she wanted to be seen as a woman, but more than a woman, and more than a man.[12]

Fifteen years after she first visited Australia as the new Tory leader, local female MPs were still gnashing their teeth about the impossibility of the ideal Thatcher represented. Queensland Liberal Kathy Sullivan complained in a radio interview that, while Thatcher had demonstrated what women were capable of, 'what is unfortunate is that you'd have to be thought as good as Margaret Thatcher to be any good at all. You know, do you have to be Bob Hawke to be able to succeed in the Labor Party?

No, of course you don't. You need all the mixtures and you've got to have people at all levels'.[13]

When Thatcher was elected prime minister in 1979, the *Sun* exclaimed: 'She knew, and we knew, and the whole world knew, that the Housewife had become a superstar.'[14] Thatcher was no housewife, of course, but she was a woman who had reassured the electorate that her power would not compromise her domestic skills. She was able to manipulate, then transgress, stereotypes because of her intellect and ability — and because she became prime minister of Britain. In Australia, the tendency of journalists to refer to her as the iconic — or only — politician for women to emulate was a source of frustration for many MPs, who insisted they had their own views, their own style, and their own way of managing their household affairs — out of the public eye.

CHAPTER ONE

Steel Sheilas: female MPs, ambition and power

Q: Why do so many people take an instant dislike to
   Bronwyn Bishop?
A: It saves time.

Q: What's the difference between Bronwyn Bishop and
   a Centurion tank?
A: Eyeshadow.

— Jokes circulated around federal parliament
in the early 1990s

In 1994, Bronwyn Bishop's face was just about anywhere you cared to look. Even the biannual photograph of the Canberra press gallery featured, instead of the diverse mob who report on politics from the hindquarters of Parliament House, a mass of Bishop faces. Journalists had been given a fierce-looking mask of the famous Liberal frontbencher to wear for the shoot on the steps of Parliament House, and only one wore a mask of John Hewson. It was a light-hearted shoot, playing on the fact that *Sydney Morning Herald* cartoonist Alan Moir had been drawing

Bishop as a crowd of clones, a woman with a grin like a grimace who was everywhere all at once. Fairfax photographer Mike Bowers, who took the photograph, said, 'It was Bronnymania and we were just swept up in the whole thing.' The mask is ghoulish: eyes cut out, black and white features beaming, hair puffed up in a chignon.

The right-wing Bronwyn Bishop was the politician journalists loved to hate, and laugh at. She was widely parodied, and called a piranha, the Barracuda, a hot pink steamroller, Superwoman, Battling Bron, Boadicea, Ice Queen, Battleaxe, Bovver Boy Bron, Edna Everage, Dolly, Australia's Margaret Thatcher (or Iron Lady), Marge Simpson, Senator Doubtfire, Mosman's answer to Evita, Senator Bobbitt, a pit-bull, and Attila the Hen. Legendary for her ubiquity, she was loathed by her colleagues, despised by her opponents, and loved by the grassroots of the Liberal Party. The amount of coverage she received was virtually unprecedented for someone who was not a leader, and the fascination journalists held for her was both intense and fickle. Members of the press drew the curtain as quickly as they had shone the spotlight on Bishop, blaming each other for her popularity and profile, and chafing at opinion polls that supported her. In November 1993, the front page of the *Bulletin* magazine posed the question: 'Will Bronwyn be our first female prime minister?' Political commentator Malcolm Mackerras predicted that she would be. A year later, in October 1994, another front page asked, 'Whatever happened to Bronwyn Bishop?' She was, briefly, a star in a dull male firmament, but her fire quickly faded, if her ambition did not.

*

The first time I interviewed Bishop I was a university student, and she'd had several months of extraordinary publicity. I was shocked by how rude she was. I was ushered into her office in Parliament House, introduced, and then stood clutching my notepad for several minutes while I waited for her to acknowledge me. She lifted her head when her mobile phone rang and asked me to pick it up off the couch and hand it to her. I then took a seat as she checked her diary entry and rolled her eyes when she said, 'What are we talking about today? *Oh*, women in politics.' She then bent her head and kept working. I started to explain myself, and, after an exchange about the subject of my thesis which completely baffled me — I told her I was planning to write a PhD about women in post-colonial governments, which she perhaps interpreted as a republican rant — she stared at me coldly and told me to leave. 'Get out. *Immediately.*' I was longing to turn on my heels and go, but curiosity and a 300-kilometre trip from Sydney drilled me to my seat. I explained again and we had a difficult, strained interview as she batted away questions about women dismissively. Not a problem. Nothing to do with her.

When I went to see her in 2003, when she was a backbencher and I was a journalist, she was smooth as silk, chatty and accommodating. Her honey-coloured hair was tied at the back of her head, not dragged skywards in a stiff sweep of blonde, and her trademark pearls bulged from her neck (yes, I know, even I repeatedly fell into the trap of describing her attire, as it was so eccentric, eye-catching and consistent). I admired her leopard-print coat, draped over a chair in her electoral office, located on the bustling Pittwater Road that winds along Sydney's northern beaches. She smiled often, and gave me meaningful looks. At one stage she even said to me, 'I have to say, Julia, I enjoy talking to you, and I have been quite frank with you in a way I wouldn't be with others. Because in a way I see you facing a number of the challenges I faced earlier on, wanting to do it on your merits.'

In the span of a decade, I had witnessed both the charm and the venom of the woman renowned for ruthlessness and tenacity.

I was more intrigued by her thoughts as a backbencher than the terse comments she had made when she was a shadow minister. She seemed more reflective, and willing to discuss the question of gender — she seemed to have come to the conclusion that she had been done in by her party because she was a woman, or at least a particular type of woman. She had told me in 1994 that the Liberal Party was accommodating of ambitious women: 'To be ambitious was strange for a woman but ... [now] it is just fine to be ambitious.' Nine years later, she clearly implied that tough, aggressive and ambitious women often get short shrift from men who prefer their women to be at home, compliant and supportive:

> There's always this concept that if women come into something it's all going to go soft and soggy. Well, that's just rubbish. The women who are coming through are strong, determined women. Well, I was addressing a sports conference this morning ... and Pru Goward was there and we were having a chat and talking about whether people liked it if women were strong or whatever, and Pru just made a throwaway line and said, 'Well blokes don't like it much — look at what happened to you!' But that's not going to change the way I am going to feel in politics because I think the world needs strong women just as much as it needs strong men. But there are still men out there who want women to stay at home and look after the household and look after them. And I suppose there are some women who like to do it. I am not making a judgment about the women; maybe I am making a judgment about the men.

Bishop's support was always higher among women. But when I discussed Bishop's new-found feminism with one of her female colleagues, the woman laughed, 'but I thought she had never even admitted she *was* a woman!'

Surprisingly, Bishop also told me in 2003 that she believed the way the press reported on the Mackellar by-election destroyed her hopes of leading her party — and possibly the country.

While often likened to the long-lasting populist Joh Bjelke-Petersen, Bishop was in fact the first female political celebrity — to be followed by One Nation's Pauline Hanson and Democrat leaders Cheryl Kernot and Natasha Stott Despoja.[1] She says she became like a brand: 'Kleenex tissue or CocaCola; it's like a breakthrough point where your identity is something that makes you public property.' Celebrity took a long time to come to Bishop, and she worked hard for it. She tried to get elected to parliament seven times before she finally entered the Senate in 1987. A critical moment came in 1992, when her relentless interrogation in the joint committee of public accounts, particularly of the commissioner of taxation, Trevor Boucher, earned her a reputation for toughness. After this, a series of polls cemented her reputation as a growing political force, and a potential leader. These polls, conducted throughout 1993 and 1994, showed she had a clear lead — of as much as two to one — as preferred leader over John Hewson. She was no longer a stereotype, a tough Liberal woman with a blonde beehive; she was a future leader of her party at a time when the current leader, Hewson, was under threat after losing what had been considered the unlosable 1993 election.

Much of the coverage surrounding Bishop was marked with astonishment: where had this woman come from? Could she actually become prime minister? What was her motivation? Some explanation for her success in creating and sustaining a profile can be found in the relentless search by the Australian press for our own 'Steel Sheilas' over the two decades before Bishop entered parliament. In the 1970s and 1980s, patterns of reporting had been established which saw an earnest search for Australia's first female prime minister accompanied by genuine surprise: first that a woman could be capable of such ambition, and second that she could still appear well groomed. The search for our own 'iron lady' had occupied many reporters and editorial writers, but usually the subject of their hopes was either unwilling or unlikely to be voted into a position of leadership. Few had the support of their colleagues, and found journalists — or even the public, if we are to believe the polls — far more eager than the men they worked with to see a woman in a powerful position. The interest of the media can be likened to that of an overexcited labrador bowling over a stranger at the gate: for all their enthusiasm and good intentions, the object of their affection usually just ends up muddied, dribbled on, or looking silly.

*

The decades-long search for Australia's Steel Sheilas was clear in the *Bulletin* article published in 1981 which predicted the appearance of a female PM:

> Britain has its Iron lady; the Philippines its Iron Butterfly, Imelda Marcos; and America the Steel Magnolia, Roslyn Carter. For its part, Australia is finally on the way to tempering its own formidable first lady. Women are flocking into politics in numbers that mean it is only a matter of time before one of them outwits, outmanoeuvres and overwhelms the male contenders for the role of top dog — or bitch. The first female prime minister may well be dubbed, as convention demands of women in power, the Steel Sheila.[2]

Iron Butterfly. Steel Sheila. Iron Maiden. Ice Maiden. The 'iron hand in the velvet glove'. Mrs Ironpants. Once the epithet 'iron lady', with its simple juxtaposition of strength and femininity, was established as a title not just for Britain's Margaret Thatcher but for any woman in a position of power, the number of antipodean adaptations flourished. In the 1970s, most women running for parliament, irrespective of their political beliefs, were asked the same question: are you like Margaret Thatcher?

From the mid-1970s, journalists were keen to see an Australian Thatcher — or, at least, were interested in the idea of one. Women who were elected to either upper-house positions or lower-house seats were asked if they aspired to be leader of the party, the state or the country at first gasp (even if not possible). When a woman was appointed to cabinet, commentators made predictions as though calling a horserace: would *this* be the first female premier or prime minister? The hunt has usually been counterproductive and unrealistic.

For many women, the comparison to the 'iron lady' was welcome, as it implied success, efficiency, and competence. Thatcher herself appeared to be far from displeased with the label. She told reporters in 1975: 'I get very wild with people who don't realise that under all this … [*tapping a gold suit button*] there's a bit of tough steel that is me.'[3] In the 1970s, female politicians were battling stereotypes that portrayed women as uninterested in politics and incapable of withstanding its physical and mental demands. Donald Horne wrote in *A Time of Hope* that for most of the 20th century the prevailing culture in Australia included sexist strains which considered it 'obvious that men were stronger, more practical minded, less emotional, more able to run things than women'.[4] In 1978, former prime minister Sir William McMahon said women were too soft for 'the tough and ruthless job of prime minister' and Australian women were unlikely to occupy the position he had filled. 'I think women are more kind-hearted to the underdog than men and I think this is an enormous disadvantage in political life,' he said. 'I don't think you would find a woman with the toughness and relentlessness.'[5]

Women who were effective or competent were cooed over as marvels, women not of flesh but steel. The 'iron lady' label, used most frequently for conservative female politicians who became ministers, emerged when they were simply exercising authority or making decisions. In the 1970s and 1980s, the tag was applied particularly to an elite and powerful group of state and federal Liberal MPs who rose to ministry positions: Senator Margaret Guilfoyle, NSW MLC Virginia Chadwick, West Australian MLA June Craig, and NSW MLA Rosemary Foot. All were considered possible future leaders, and all were described at some stage as the most powerful female politician in the country. The 'iron lady' label meant their competence or assertiveness was exaggerated, so they seemed crueller, tougher and harder: not just than other women but their male colleagues as well.

The first 'woman of steel' was Victorian Liberal MP Margaret Guilfoyle. Initially headlined as 'a mother with political ambitions', by the mid-1970s Guilfoyle was known nationally as the 'Iron Butterfly'. She also quickly, predictably, drew comparisons to Thatcher because of her first name, conservative political views, professional training, neat appearance, and — apparently — the fact that she too was 'quietly proving that she's not just an attractive face'.[6] One reporter claimed Guilfoyle was being compared with Thatcher simply because 'like Mrs Thatcher, Sen. Guilfoyle has a husband and a family'.[7] She was widely respected as an excellent minister though. Press gallery veteran Michelle Grattan believes she was a 'stand-out' politician, canny and clever.

Guilfoyle, an accountant, was elected to the Senate in 1971 after working her way up through the influential women's branch of the Victorian Liberal Party. She aimed to keep press coverage limited to her work, and, from the moment she was elected, refused to divulge details about her private life. Speculation about her leadership potential emerged in 1975 and continued for several years. The *Sun-Herald* political correspondent Chris Anderson wrote: 'Her party supporters claim that she could be promoted as a non-Labor leader like Britain's Mrs Margaret Thatcher.'[8] According to press gallery journalists, however, these rumours were never taken seriously. Guilfoyle, called 'Australia's most successful woman politician' in 1979, continually denied having any aspirations beyond cabinet, telling journalists neither politicians nor the public were ready for a woman political leader, and that she and her female peers lacked the necessary experience, unlike Thatcher.[9]

Rosemary Foot had a similar experience. After winning the blue-ribbon NSW seat of Vaucluse for the Liberal Party in the 1978 election, and being appointed opposition spokeswoman on youth and community services in 1980, she was frequently asked about Thatcher. Even the *South China Morning Post* called her the 'Iron Lady of Down Under'.[10] Foot told journalists she considered Thatcher a role model, and allowed herself to be photographed with a renowned Thatcher impersonator, British actress Janet Brown, drinking tea at the Boulevard Hotel. However, like Guilfoyle, she was careful to point out the comparisons were superficial:

> Margaret Thatcher did not become Prime Minister until she had been in politics 20 years; certain people expected me to be ready for a leadership role after I had been in politics two years. There are several things that must not be forgotten about Margaret Thatcher. She has been a career woman all her life, except for the four months she took off to have twins. With 35 years of professional experience, degrees in law and science, and the capacity to live on four hours sleep a night, she's a hard act to emulate ... Would I want to be prime minister? I do believe I've got leadership qualities, but I would never nominate myself for a top job if I didn't feel

entirely equal to it ... If the cards fall in the right way, if my physical stamina is what I hope it will be in 10 years, and if my learning curve keeps at its present rate — then yes, those top jobs would interest me.[11]

Top jobs interest most politicians. It's just not always a realistic prospect.

Journalists regularly felt the need to point out that successful competent female politicians were also feminine and attractive. Journalist Catherine Menagh wrote that Liberal West Australian minister June Craig gave 'an impression of calm elegance rather than the hard-headedness one might expect to see in a woman who has risen to a cabinet position'.[12]

When under pressure as a minister, NSW Liberal MP Virginia Chadwick was frequently physically scrutinised for signs of stress and strain. The neatness of her appearance was often referred to by journalists in times of crisis, as though she was expected to emerge from her office with wild hair and torn clothes. *Sydney Morning Herald* journalist Matthew Moore compared the disasters springing up in her portfolio to an apparent 'effortless manner and poise': 'This week, everything fell to bits except the unflappable hairdo.'[13]

Australia's Steel Sheilas were called tough when simply doing their job — particularly if cutting resources, making unpopular decisions and displaying resolve. As the minister for social security, just about any decision Guilfoyle made was depicted as severe. This happened frequently when she was forced to face the 'razor gang' which oversaw the finances of federal government departments, and, in the late 1970s, was annually under pressure to reduce budgets.[14] Virginia Chadwick was similarly dubbed an iron maiden after she was made minister for family and community services (FACS) in 1988, and had signalled her intention to shake up and streamline the department.[15]

As Chadwick told me in 1996, comparisons with Thatcher were:

> ... a natural corollary if you're having to do tough things, like closing things, sacking people or restructuring things ... I did get that a bit, and funnily enough I don't think it was to do so much with Thatcherite politics ... as a very simple way of people [thinking] a person capable of making tough decisions therefore must be like Maggie Thatcher ... What I always found somewhat amusing, quite apart from the fact that it's physically impossible, is that it is just the language that always goes back to the male — that if you're strong and resolute, it's not because you've got backbone, it's because you've got balls, so there's always a reference back to male vernacular in terms of a woman who is strong or resolute, and often that can be as negative as it can be positive ... it's like she's not a real woman, so it is a double-edged thing.

'Iron Lady' was a cliché both trivial and lazy. Did it matter at all? In the 1970s, Guilfoyle shrugged it off as generic and unoriginal, saying she had never thought of it as a personal nickname: 'Most women in politics are dubbed with that title, or a variation of it, at some time ...'[16] But Anne Summers, then a *National Times* reporter, wrote at the time that Guilfoyle was visibly perturbed about her tough image.[17] What she objected to was the implication that the minister or department responsible for welfare payments to the nation's unemployed, ill, elderly, and disabled was cold and uncaring. As she told journalist Alex Kennedy, the 'hard woman' stereotype did bother her, 'especially if that image of myself is in any way transferred to my department. We try at all times to be fair and reasonable'.[18]

After the 1983 election, which saw Labor's Bob Hawke voted in as prime minister, Guilfoyle did not seek reappointment to the shadow ministry, announcing she would retire at the next election. After this, she disappeared from newsprint. But even the article about her retirement contained a reference to an apparent contradiction between her femininity and her job, as well as to a rapidly fading memory of her reputation and competence: 'It's difficult to imagine that this immaculately attired woman with the delightfully genial manner could have carried out the tough and uncompromising roles of both social security and finance minister. But carry them out she did and, during the Fraser years, was responsible for many hard decisions on government spending. Those heady days are gone.'[19]

Heady days!

But by the late 1980s, a growing cynicism about politicians meant that those who were seen to deviate from the norm were increasingly welcome. It was no longer considered to be an automatic liability to be female and in 1990 two women became state premiers. The critical shift occurred in the late 1970s and early 1980s, as political scientists began to point to election results with two critical findings: female candidates were not voted against on the grounds of their gender, and women voted differently to men. Women became increasingly aware of, and able to exploit, the fact that many voters believed them to be different from men, to be more honest, idealistic and untainted by a corrupt political system. As education minister, for example, Virginia Chadwick continued the policies of her male predecessor, but because of what was perceived to be a more feminine, consultative, compassionate approach, she was considered more acceptable.[20] Women historically have been disproportionately allocated more nurturing, 'soft' social portfolios, such as education, health, family and consumer affairs, as an extension of a caring, motherly role.[21] However, the expectation of virtuosity in women often proves to be a burden for those who are percieved to fall short of these standards.

*

It was not Bronwyn Bishop's virtue that was the problem, though. It was her supposed vices: ambition, and determination to go further than any woman ever had — the Lodge. It took many attempts, and at times bloody and botched preselections, before she was successful in gaining a seat in parliament. Bishop was prepared to be the woman journalists had been hunting for. Asked, like so many women before her, if she wanted to be Australia's first female prime minister, the answer was an unambivalent *yes*. At last, here was the woman willing to dispense with the velvet glove and unsheath the iron fist.

Bishop consciously modelled herself on Margaret Thatcher, and displayed on her desk a framed photograph of herself shaking Thatcher's hand. This photograph was reproduced and referred to countless times. Journalists made the comparison so much it turned what was already a tired cliché into a convention. True to historical form, the comparison was usually made in a superficial way: it was about being a conservative female politician with blonde hair and an apparent ambition. The most striking similarity, apart from some physical attributes (a fondness for pearls and unmoving hair), was that they both claimed they could survive on four hours sleep a night. Bishop usually brushed off the comparisons without discouraging them. In 1989, she protested to *New Idea*: 'People have been kind enough to make comparisons, but the truth of the matter is she is the leader of Great Britain, she is Margaret Thatcher and I am Bronwyn Bishop, here in Australia.'[22] In 1992, she told a Canberra reporter: 'The Iron Lady might be just a term of strength, I don't know, but I am me, I am my own person, I decide my own priorities. I find it interesting that people find it necessary to say a woman politician has to have a model.'[23] Many commentators dismissed the comparisons to Thatcher as lacking in substance. But after political journalist Paul Lyneham described her as a mix of Edna Everage, Margaret Thatcher and a Sherman tank, Bishop placed gladioli on her desk alongside her photograph of Thatcher, and ordered a staff member to find her a toy tank for a party she was holding that night.

Just as Thatcher inspired fear in men, Bishop inspired a kind of hatred. The loathing expressed was quite extraordinary and excessive. A recurring theme in articles about her is the vitriol of Liberal MPs who freely spoke to journalists off the record. David Leser, Bishop's unofficial biographer, records Liberal MP John Hannaford saying that, in his 25 years in the party, he never knew anyone who was so prepared to use people then dump them. NSW Liberal John Dowd said she was 'foul', 'ugly' and 'very unpleasant' at times. Members of the Labor Party were also vehemently critical, particularly Gareth Evans, Labor foreign minister from 1988 to 1996, and the government leader in the Senate when Bishop was there. He once threatened to garrotte her in parliament. Liberal Ted Pickering, a member of the NSW upper house from 1976 to 1995 and NSW police minister from 1988 to 1992, said she represented 'the unacceptable face of the Liberal Party', and that she had taught her daughters to urinate standing up because she was so angry about the treatment of women.[24] Bishop was indignant when told this: 'That is such a lie. I'll tell you a story. [A prominent woman lawyer] when she got pregnant said that "the only way my daughter will get to be chief judge on the High Court is if I teach her to urinate standing up." So he can't even get his story right.'

Was it her naked ambition that upset her colleagues? Bishop had been telling friends since she was a teenager that she wanted to be prime minister of Australia, as blokes sometimes do. Her standard response to journalists' questions of whether she wanted to be PM was: 'I came into politics to serve my country and my party, and I'll do it whichever way I'm asked.'[25] The headline to a profile by Peter Ward in the *Australian Magazine* in March 1989 was 'Bronwyn Bishop: The Woman who would be Prime Minister'. The photograph featured Bishop in football shorts. Sports commentator and columnist Mike Gibson said she had attracted more publicity then any other politician because she was:

> The most voraciously ambitious woman Australian politics has ever seen ... Name any other female politician who has courted so much media attention, been so avidly analysed by so many commentators, attracted so many words on everything from the bricklayer who does her hair, to the shade of her lipstick and the height of her stiletto heels ... Bronwyn Bishop is so tough, she blow dries her hair in the exhaust of her limo.[26]

Some sympathetic commentators insisted she was being treated unfairly because of her gender, and that her ambition was regarded as grotesque simply because she was a woman. Alan Ramsey warned against misreading her: 'While she can look like an insufferable, mannered, middle-class matron who is thicker than two planks, she behaves like a political gorilla. Her appetite for politics is enormous. So are her ambition and her capacity for work. The worst mistake to make with Bronwyn Bishop is to underestimate her.'[27] Frank Devine, columnist with the *Australian*, wrote that her colleagues called her an 'airhead. Pushy. Uncontrollable. Not a team player. Unarmed in policy matters.' Pushy was the most substantial accusation, he wrote, but was it also 'the sort of word applied almost reflexively by male reactionaries — of which the Liberal Party is not devoid — to women who don't know their place'?[28] Many journalists argued that it was not ambition in itself but the expression of it that bothered people, and insisted men exhibiting the same ruthlessness would also be disliked.

Bishop now believes the hostility towards ambitious women springs from a more selfish source:

> Let's face it, if women are able to compete equally, what you do for men is, you double your competition. So the more people you can keep out of the game, the lesser your competition and the better your odds are ... I think it's a bit of a worry. In the general population now, women have a huge participation rate: 66 per cent; it's huge. Kids growing up ... are looking at two-income relationships; you are looking at sharing workloads; I mean, that's the way life is. But for — how do I say this? — if you look at our front bench, most of the blokes have stay-at-home wives. Now I am not criticising that situation but it doesn't reflect what the rest of the country's like. And it does have an impact on policy.

Bishop often provoked people to joke about her being a man in drag, or having 'balls under her skirts'. After the *Australian Magazine* featured her kicking a football in 1989, the photograph was displayed in a 'very senior' Liberal's office, after someone had drawn male genitalia hanging out of her football shorts.[29] In October 1993, Australian reporter Kate Legge asked: 'How much of the attraction [to Bishop] is voyeuristic of the sideshow freak variety? "Roll up. Step inside. See a real tough woman with balls."' Bishop clones marched along Oxford Street in the 1994 Sydney Gay and Lesbian Mardi Gras, and Bishop drag acts sprouted in Sydney and Melbourne. Long-standing enemy and preselection rival Chris Puplick called her '[Liberal Party head-kicker] Wilson Tuckey in drag'. She was also called Menzies in a frock.[30]

More important than Bishop's ambition, in media reports, was the way she looked. Her appearance was widely commented on, frequently parodied and occasionally praised, in particular her 'beehive' hairstyle — comedian broadcaster Andrew Denton once joked it was 'not hair but twelve pounds of plastic explosive' — her tailored clothes, and tooth-flashing smile. She was famous among photographers for sweeping into a room for photo shoots and barking, 'Teeth, or no teeth?' Some photographers claim she was overtly sexual. For years they joked about huddling together in corners for safety at parties she held. The rumours about her alleged sexual aggression were legion but unproven — as prevalent as the gossip about any woman taking a seat in parliament. For decades, single women working in Parliament House have found themselves fending off fake rumours about seeking, giving or demanding sexual favours, even if completely chaste.

Another trope often used for female politicians in this era was suggesting they have a 'makeover' to make them more palatable: in Bishop's case, in order to win leadership. On 3 July 1993, the front page of the *Telegraph Mirror* provided a spectacular example of this. In a paean to her strength in challenging Prime Minister Paul Keating to debate her on television rather than criticise her publicly, the headline screamed: 'BE A MAN'. Next to it was a large photograph with a doctored image of Bishop. Her face had been pasted onto the head of a woman with thick, wavy hair and long, dangly earrings, whom readers were told was American actor Candice Bergen. It was an injection of Hollywood into Canberra in an image that represented Bishop as a sexual creature who challenged blokes to be real men — just at the moment she was revealed to be a real woman. The caption read: 'She already outranks Dr. John Hewson as the most popular choice for leader of the Liberal Party — but Bronwyn Bishop is being urged to undergo a complete image overhaul to snatch his crown away ... We use a computer-enhanced graphic to show just what a winner she could look. Her party will never see her in the same light again.' Inside, journalist Sue Williams urged:

'Let down your hair, Bronny B ... Clip on some sparklers and soften those suits. How much *more* popular could you be if you loosened up a little and mellowed that stiff, starchy image that sends shivers of fear and loathing up the spines of the incumbent Liberal leadership?' Williams praised the computer image: 'A North Shore matron becomes a potential parliamentary pin-up.'

What is odd is that, in 1991, the same reporter had chastised NSW National Party MP Wendy Machin for posing in a leopard-print gym outfit: 'The day an ambitious, high-profile woman politician tries to win a few more votes by flashing a little flesh and flaunting her fashion sense is a sad one indeed.'[31] Two years later, Williams was quoting hairdressers, make-up artists and designers with tips for Bishop.

*

The key question about the wax and wane of the Bronwyn Bishop phenomenon, posed by many journalists at the time, is whether her influence was exaggerated by the press. Many journalists and commentators blamed other members of the media for being indulgent and fuelling a silly story. But the polls revealed growing public support for Bishop, particularly among women and young people. According to Newspoll figures, in March 1993 she was considered the best candidate to lead the Liberal Party by 17 per cent of voters, while 36 per cent supported Hewson. Four months later, the Morgan poll figures showed 18 per cent supported Bishop as leader, while only 15 per cent supported John Hewson. The media interest grew even more intense. Her colleagues told journalists this 'publicity orgy' exaggerated her influence, and repeated that she had no party room support. However, public support for her continued to grow. By 2 November 1993, she was the preferred party leader by a two–one majority in a Herald Saulwick poll. The next day the *Herald*'s editorial argued this could be partly due to former ALP pollster Rod Cameron's theory of the feminisation of Australian politics: 'Voters and particularly women voters ... are being turned off by politicians who are confrontational and who engage in vicious name-calling. Despite the tough rhetoric ... and the barbs about sharks and piranhas, Senator Bishop, on television and in person, presents herself in a reasonable and soft-spoken manner.'

The crucial year for Bishop came in 1994, and she flamed then fell in a matter of months when she moved from the Senate to the lower house. She went from being the preferred leader to the fourth choice. What went wrong? First, the hype was just that: exaggerated excitement based on unrealistic expectations. Second, she failed to translate her alleged electoral appeal into votes during a by-election. And third, the press had had enough of her anyway. While the cameras had continued to click throughout 1993, and her face still rolled off the presses, Bishop failed to impress the Canberra gallery or significant portions of the business community on policy matters. The most common complaint was that she lacked intellectual rigour, or policy depth. She did, however, have the support of some powerful men. She lunched with Kerry Packer and Liberal Party powerbroker Michael Kroger — and, she said, talked ideas.[32]

As the momentum grew, and senior Liberals puzzled over how to contain her, in January 1994 Bishop was moved from the back bench to the shadow cabinet as spokeswoman for urban and regional strategy. The following Newspoll figures showed 39 per cent of voters preferred Bishop as leader, 21 per cent wanted Hewson, and 13 per cent John Howard.[33] The head of the Saulwick polling group, Irving Saulwick, said her profile was 'extraordinary ... You could describe it as a "Superwoman" image and I am not sure where it comes from.'[34]

A move to the House of Representatives — from where leaders are chosen — seemed inevitable for Bishop as each poll was interpreted as nudging her closer to the Lodge. Her chance came when Jim Carlton indicated he was going to resign from his seat, in the electorate of Mackellar in Sydney's northern beaches. The by-election was to prove her undoing. Although the ALP did not field a candidate, she had one unexpected opponent. Author Bob Ellis stood against her as an independent with the intention of destroying her chances of leadership. He told broadcaster John Laws he had decided to stand 'in response to arguably the worst woman in the world coming into my turf, threatening with her hair-spray to pollute the water and kill fish for miles around'. He dogged her steps on the campaign trail and insulted her at every opportunity. But *Sydney Morning Herald* journalist Sally Loane wrote that when Bishop was asked to comment on Ellis's description of her as 'fanatical, overdressed, perfume-drenched and ideologically insufferable', she replied, 'Is that a policy?'

Ellis believed Bishop was a threat to Australian politics: 'She was a fascist.' He claimed his campaign cost $125,000, including his own loss of earnings. Ellis also believed Bishop was talented enough to exploit the Liberal leadership vacuum: 'She was a good interviewee, she had a good radio voice, she was an inspiring right-wing speaker to vacuous old people in old people's homes.' Bishop believes she was considered such a threat by the men on both sides of politics that they conspired to delay her entry to the lower house. She told me:

The date for my by-election was arranged between Keating and Hewson. I was preselected in November; I did not have an election until March. Which meant because of Easter and Anzac Day we didn't sit in April. I didn't actually go into the parliament until May, and Jim Carlton flagged his resignation in November. There has never been such a long time for a by-election.[35]

Hewson bluntly denies any involvement, telling me: 'This is incorrect. I had nothing to do with her by-election. I always considered Bronwyn a bit of a joke — I never thought of her as a "threat" and indeed publicly welcomed her "competition".'

But Ellis claims Labor helped him: 'one of the wiliest things' he'd done was to call Labor powerbroker Graham Richardson and ask him to delay the election by six months: 'And he said "done". I said "no Labor candidate", and he said "done". And I wanted six months so I could run a presidential-type campaign and he said "done". And in those days when Graham Richardson said "done", it would be.' Richardson did not believe he could win, but Ellis said he wanted to deliver him a prize: 'a wounded tigress on the floor of the House of Representatives'.

Bishop won the seat, but lost kudos when there was a swing against her — especially since there had been a swing towards Labor's Carmen Lawrence in a by-election in Western Australia. Newspapers reported the swing was 4.36 per cent, which cast doubt on the wisdom that Bishop had tremendous, untapped, and enduring vote-pulling power. Analysis of by-elections held since 1949 showed it was the only time an opposition had received a swing against a candidate in an opposition-held federal city seat. The front page of the *Sunday Telegraph* screamed: 'SHOCK RESULT FOR BRONWYN'.

Bishop insisted that the media simply swallowed the spin coming from her political opponents. The primary vote had dropped by about 5 per cent, but there were seven candidates running against her. According to the Australian Electoral Commission, the two-party preferred vote went from 61.16 per cent in the 1993 election for Jim Carlton to 60.27 per cent in the 1994 by-election. But on the same day in Warringah, Liberal Tony Abbott had won his by-election with a swing of 5.1 per cent on the two-party preferred vote, and a 1.2 per cent swing against him in the primary. The nameless 'senior Liberals' who continued to speak off the record to reporters did not hide their glee: the damage to Bishop's status was 'the biggest burst since the South Sea bubble'.[36]

The front page of the *Sydney Morning Herald* on the Monday after the election was the subject of debate for several days afterwards. While the headline — 'BISHOP IN, BUT LIB VOTE FALLS' — and article were sober, the photograph, by Peter Rae, depicted Bishop standing at the bottom of a penis-shaped arch. Rae said he was not conscious of the way it could be interpreted at the time of shooting it at Sydney's InterContinental Hotel, and that he was just aiming to have a nicely framed photograph. He was, however, 'astounded' by the number of calls he received congratulating him for depicting her as a 'dickhead'. A letter was published the next day thanking the *Herald* for the 'wonderful' and 'very apt' image, with the question: 'Did yesterday's front-page photo have anything to do with the Bishopric or Bobbitt affair?'

This result marked the beginning of a downward spiral for Bishop. When Hewson, forced by the polls, finally called a leadership spill in May 1994, Bishop told journalists she would support Downer, who successfully challenged Hewson and became the next leader. In 2004, she clearly had some regrets. When I asked why she did not run, the exchange went like this:

> *BB*: The timing at that point in time was — I decided it
> would be better to back Downer.
> *JB*: You didn't have the numbers?
> *BB*: No, I didn't. But it would have been interesting if I had
> [run] in hindsight.
> *JB*: Do you wish you had run now?
> *BB*: I would just say it would have been interesting ... I had
> a conversation with [then Liberal Party president] Tony
> Staley down at a dinner in Melbourne not long after that
> and he said to me, if you'd had a 5 per cent swing to you

instead of against you, you would be leader today. The truth of the matter was I didn't have a 5 per cent swing against me, but that's what certain people put forward.[37]

Once Bishop was in the lower house, and appointed to ministry positions, she made a series of gaffes that compounded the view that she had been hyped, and promoted, beyond her ability. In May 1994, for example, after she became opposition spokeswoman for health, in a very short time she was rebuked by then leader Downer when she questioned the amount spent on AIDS research and argued tobacco advertising should not be banned. She then attacked Carmen Lawrence, the health minister at the time, asking her if she supported the decriminalisation of marijuana seeing as she had admitted to smoking it. Lawrence shot back that Downer had made a similar admission.

At the end of June 1994, Bishop was forced to sack a staff member after it was revealed that Rodney Adler's FAI Insurance had paid his wages before and after Bishop's appointment to the shadow health portfolio. She later rehired him. In mid-July, further trouble followed a story about bad behaviour on an Ansett flight, where it was alleged Bishop had demanded to use her mobile phone, and entered the cockpit so she could tell the pilot to land instead of circling while waiting for bad weather to clear. She dismissed the allegations as 'rubbish' and 'complete nonsense', saying, 'I've never tried to get into a cockpit in my life.'

By November, in a Liberal leadership poll, Bishop had only 13 per cent support, compared with 20 for Howard, 18 for Downer and 14 for former NSW premier Nick Greiner. Hewson was at 9 per cent.

Bishop went on to be minister for defence industry, science and personnel from March 1996 to October 1998, then minister for aged care until October 2001. The aged care portfolio effectively destroyed her chances of promotion, as a series of scandals about nursing homes unravelled daily. The most damaging and memorable story was the discovery that 57 residents in a Melbourne nursing home had been given baths with kerosene to prevent a scabies outbreak. Images of systemic abuse and neglect flashed in the media for months: maggots in wounds, infected bedsores, residents locked in cupboards, dismal standards of care. Referred to as the 'minister for caged hair', Bishop spent almost $350,000 monitoring the media coverage of the debacle. The *Courier-Mail* slammed her performance as 'abysmal', the *Age* argued 'serious questions' remained about her refusal to take responsibility, and the *Australian* insisted we deserved better.

After the 2001 election, Bishop was dumped from the ministry. There was a notable silence from women's groups. Michelle Grattan wrote in 2001 that, despite the media hype, her chances of leading the Liberal Party had been, 'realistically, zilch. When the "Bishop bubble" burst,' she wrote, 'it was hard to understand how anyone had taken it seriously.'

*

Bronwyn Bishop resigned in 2015 following revelations she had chartered helicopter flights from Melbourne to Geelong in order to attend a Liberal Party fundraiser and claimed them as travel expenses. Her parliamentary career had lasted three decades, encompassed a range of ministry positions — with varying degrees of success — as well as a stint as Speaker. But at the time I was writing this book, in 2004, she had won some respect for her sheer tenacity. The *Daily Telegraph*'s political editor, Malcolm Farr, told me:

> I always thought it was a scream that people used to
> think Bronwyn could be the first [woman] prime minister,
> because she's quite thick. But I have got to tell you, her

determination and her hard work and her ability to get up there and make things happen are absolutely impressive; she's quite a remarkable woman. A lot of people hate her — not just dislike her, hate her — and this doesn't bother her a bit, and when she lost her portfolio, she didn't sit home and whimper and weep, she got up and did things and I admire her; I think she's terrific in that area. I'd never vote for her but I think she sets an example for MPs, male and female ... There's nothing like her. She's this tiny creature who enjoys life to the full. You go to a party and there she is drinking, joking, dancing, carrying on. She's a very extroverted woman. She was a combination of all these things — she was a woman who thought she could have a good time and do the hard work and she did.

Alan Ramsey said he liked her because she was tough: 'Bronwyn has a shell like you wouldn't believe. Her attitude is "fuck you all", essentially, and she really was very, very tough mentally ... She was not liked, but she had this determination, or stronger; she was resolute, stoic ... you could knock her over ... [*smacks his hands*] and she'd be straight up again. And she'd do some of the silliest things, but she always learnt from them ... Bronwyn was a real politician.' Like Farr, he believes the suggestion that she could be PM was nonsense, even though she liked to encourage it:

And, of course, there was this strange bloody woman getting around looking like Marge out of 'The Simpsons', and it just washed over her. You couldn't humiliate or embarrass Bronwyn; she couldn't humiliate or embarrass herself. And I just thought, you get top marks from me ... this is terrible, but she had three times the balls of most of the men. Now that's a very sexist remark, but in this place, that's what she had. Really. She knew if she was going to get anywhere she had to do it on her own bloody merits and she had to force people to take notice of her.

Early in her career, Bishop rarely acknowledged there could be a bias against women. In 1993, she would only agree to speak to Kate Legge off the record about chauvinism, 'woman to woman'. Legge concluded: 'She would rather die before complaining publicly of sexism. "You just get on with it," she snaps. Square jaw. Stiff upper lip. Squibbing prohibited.'[38] In 1994, she was nominated for an Ernie award, organised by women from the NSW Labor Party, for 'unbelievable harm to the cause of increasing women's representation in office'.

Bishop told me, in 1994, that being parodied in the media was 'just part of politics': 'Now of course ... everybody has got biases one way or another ... but at the end of the day, if the heats gets on, either you can stand it or you can't.'

Having long believed Australia was 'ready' for a female PM, Bishop did not relinquish her dreams of leadership. As she said to me a decade before she left in disgrace:

> BB: I am not one to pack up my bags and go. By the way,
>   I am here for the next encounter.
> JB: What encounter?
> BB: You never know what is around the corner, what issues
>   there are. The one thing I can say about politics is you
>   never know when it is going to turn.
> JB: Well, look at Howard.
> BB: Precisely.

CHAPTER TWO

Housewife Superstars

Some there are who say, 'If we permit women to go beyond her sphere, domestic duties will be neglected.' In plainer language, 'If we acknowledge woman is human, we shall not get so much work out of her.'[1]

    — Henrietta Dugdale, president of the Victorian Women's Suffrage Society, 1883

Were political office to become the latest craze of fashion, there would be many dreary and neglected homes throughout the country sacrificed on the altar of political ambition.

    — Editorial, the *Age*, 15 March 1921, following the election of Australia's first woman MP, Edith Cowan, to the West Australian parliament

In 2003, the federal opposition spokeswoman for health, Julia Gillard, was asked without warning to come to the on-set kitchen and whip up a pasta dish at the end of an interview with Kerrie-Anne Kennerly. It was for a television show aimed at housewives and daytime viewers. In a modern twist, however, it was sprung upon her because she does not cook: the gnocchi she attempted was a flop. Her press secretary said, 'It was all rather bizarre', but her predecessors would have laughed to see her struggle with the flour and dough. Ever since they began to be elected to parliament, women have been asked by photographers to hop back over their garden fences and pose in contrived displays of domestic competence. It has been a long-running cliché. It is as though, at the moment women were elected to positions of prominence in the public sphere, the press firmly pushed them back into the private, to both explain their deviance and assure readers of their normality. Some women have played along, some have suggested they pose doing something else, while others have laughed and blown raspberries.

In 1981, when a daily newspaper sent a photographer early one morning to the home of former Fairfield mayor Janice Crosio, newly elected to the NSW Legislative Assembly for the ALP, to catch her washing the dishes, her firm refusal was reported several times. She told him:

> No, you cannot. Get out of my house. You can come in
> and do an interview with me, more than welcome to it.
> But no, you are not going to catch me under the hair dryer;
> no, you are not going to catch me with curlers in my hair;
> no, you are not going to catch me cooking bacon and eggs
> for my husband for breakfast, nor are you going to catch me
> cooking his dinner at night ... You want to talk to me, [you
> can] whether it is down the sewerage pipeline or whether it's
> at the forest or whether it's at any other program.

The 1970s was the decade when women began to fight back, taking control of the way they were portrayed and refusing to cooperate with clichéd or demeaning photographs. Labor politician Joan Child, for example, was famous for telling women never to allow themselves to be snapped in the kitchen. In 1974, she was the first woman from the Labor Party to be elected to the House of Representatives — and the fourth from any party.[2] As she celebrated her victory with friends, a Fairfax photographer came to her house and asked if she would pose doing the dishes or hanging out the washing. She resisted, and was photographed instead with a champagne glass in her hand, standing next to the washing line, over which was draped a sheet with 'Great Going Gough' written on it.[3] The photographer was drawing on a decades-old tradition, but with five children and a lifetime of both paid and unpaid housework behind her, and a parliamentary career ahead of her, Child understandably believed it was inappropriate. When her husband died of a heart attack at age 42, she had been left to bring up the children on her own. She worked in a factory and cleaned other people's homes. When she ran for federal parliament for the first time in 1972, she was still scrubbing other people's floors to finance her campaign. Despite her efforts, the headline in the *Australian* on the day after her victory assured readers that even though she had been elected to parliament, she 'always got home to cook the tea'.

Refusals to be photographed doing housework became the symbol of female politicians' defiance of a sexist press and discriminatory political system, and a popular hook for stories in the 1970s. By the 1980s, these requests were regarded by journalists themselves as anachronistic and discriminatory, even though some women still agreed to them.

Domestic work has always played a central role in debates about female citizenship, and the participation of women in politics. One of the intellectual hallmarks of first-wave feminism was an argument that women deserved the vote, and a voice in parliament, because their work as wives, mothers and house-workers gave them a vital perspective that men lacked. In the early 1900s suffragist Rose Scott extended the metaphor to the nation state, arguing the vote would enable women to 'have a voice in the national housekeeping'. Marilyn Lake has written

THE LADY OF THE HOUSE

Mrs. Joan Child, member for the Victorian seat of Henty, makes history as Labor's first woman MHR. She will be the only woman in the House of Representatives and hopes that her success will be only one of many more for women in politics.

ABOVE: The new member for Henty, in her campaign rooms at Carnegie, Melbourne.

Seventeen-year-old Roger Child, of Carnegie, Melbourne, was a little disgruntled during the recent elections.

Almost 18, he just missed out on being able to vote.

"After all, it's not often a boy is able to vote for his mother," he said.

His mother is Joan Child, who has just become Australia's first women Labor Member of the House of Representatives in the Commonwealth Parliament.

Although other women have been elected to the House, she is currently the only one.

By
SELENA SUMMERS

Mrs. Child, a widow, with five sons, stood for the Victorian seat of Henty against Liberal candidate Max Fox.

In the 1972 elections Max Fox defeated her by just over 300 votes — but this time she won.

"The phone's been going like mad ever since," said Mrs. Child, "and there's been an avalanche of flowers and telegrams from friends and party members. I even received a short cable from England which said. 'Knew you'd make it'.

"My sons didn't even doubt my win, but I was apprehensive.

"My family were just great. At home the housework turned into team work. Whoever came home first, put the dinner on. My sons all dived in and helped. They can all cook.

"They also helped my campaign and handed out leaflets."

Mrs. Child said she didn't feel exhausted after the campaign. "I loved the hustle and bustle of it all. What do I think of making history? Well, I'm only sorry it took

so long, I hope this'll be the start of many more women in politics.

"I also feel people are now thinking about issues in a better, more nationally-minded spirit — not so much through their hip pockets, I think this is good.

"Education, child care, and improvements in the welfare of migrants and handicapped people are a few of my particular interests.

"But while I'm very involved with women, I'm not a spearhead to concentrate solely on women's issues. I was elected on a Labor party platform and will be working for the welfare of all people — not just women."

Quietly spoken, intelligent, and sincere, Joan Child gives intense and flattering concentration to every question asked.

"I quite surprised myself one day when I went to a meeting and hecklers wouldn't let me talk they were making so much noise.

"I just had to shout above them and I was startled to discover the volume of voice I was capable of.

"I remember a little bloke coming up to me after and saying in a surprised way, 'You do have a loud voice, don't you?' But I certainly needed it."

Mrs. Child entered politics actively about six years ago, after the death of her husband. "But I've been an ALP supporter for 30 years at least."

She has been secretary of the Glenhuntly branch of the ALP and, in the past year, research assistant to the Trade Minister, Dr. Cairns.

"My working day now won't be that different. In my job as research assistant I spent maybe two days a week at Parliament. Now I'll spend about three days there a week.

"Still, I've got a lot to learn about parliamentary procedure.

ABOVE: Mrs. Joan Child in the kitchen of her Carnegie, Melbourne, house. During her campaign, her sons helped with the housework, including cooking.
RIGHT: Mrs. Child with two of her sons, Roger (standing), 17, and Gary, 20, both apprentices. Other sons are Geoff, 22, in England. Peter, 28, married, pharmacist, and Andrew, 24, married, a student at Latrobe University.

Pictures by Les Gorrie

"In the past year I've been getting a little temporary help with housework, but I'll have to make more permanent arrangements.

"Also, I'm not wearing a hat to the opening of Parliament," she said with a smile. "I haven't owned one since I was 24. Although come to think of it, I did buy one of those

jockey caps. One of my sons took it though. He said it looked better on him."

Asked about any special ambitions for the future, Joan Child just smiled.

"I don't want to be a nine-day wonder. I hope to win the Henty seat again, next time round."

In a rare moment, done only for a women's magazine, Joan Child was photographed for the *Australian Women's Weekly* in a flowered apron, stirring a pot on her stove, 5 June 1974. *Australian Women's Weekly* about a long tradition of feminists who have appropriated a nationalist discourse — also propelled by racism and imperialism — on the importance of motherhood to promote the rights and interests of (mostly white) women. This brand of feminism was attacked by second-wave feminists, who argued that by elevating the domestic work of women, the private rather than public sphere was assumed to be their natural abode.[4]

The domestic imagery was also extended to the parliament itself, where the first women members were portrayed as housewives coming in to sweep up crumbs of corruption, bad language and rowdy behaviour; as moral guardians; or, quite literally, to decorate the place. Suffragists hastened to assure opponents their political work would not be carried out in place of their domestic labour; instead, it would be enriched by it.

By the 1960s, growing numbers of women were starting to assert that housework was, in fact, drudgery. The second-wave feminists seriously interrogated domestic work, arguing it was key to their oppression. As one wrote, 'We women have been brainwashed more than even we can imagine. Probably too many years of seeing media-women coming over their shiny waxed floors or breaking down over their dirty shirt collars. Men have no such conditioning. They recognise the essential fact of housework right from the very beginning. Which is that it stinks.'[5] The restlessness and boredom of full-time housewives — many of whom in Australia were bombed out on Valium — was what Betty Friedan had famously called 'the problem that has no name', or '[a] strange stirring, a sense of dissatisfaction, a yearning ... That voice within women that says: "I want something more than my husband and my children and my home."'[6] Feminists wrote personal accounts of the tyranny of labour in the home as well as histories of the housewife. Many of these histories were informed by Marxist critiques of the sexual division of labour in an industrial capitalist society, where the function of women was to provide male workers with physical, emotional and sexual support for their work outside the home. The ideology of domesticity was argued to be not an immutable truth, then, but a cultural creation.[7]

Another reason domestic work was hotly debated in the 1960s and 1970s was that large numbers of women were flocking to the workforce. By 1975, almost a third of women with children under 12 years were in the workforce.[8] The proportion of married women who were in the labour force rose from 13 per cent in 1954 to 29 per cent in 1966. By 1979, it was 41 per cent.[9] By the end of the 1970s, only 964,000 of Australia's 3.8 million families conformed to the traditional image of a working husband, a dependent wife and dependent children. The traditional 'nuclear family' was no longer the family unit of most Australians.

The Australian press often portrayed women who joined political parties as wide-eyed innocents awakening from a long sleep or drug-induced stupor: 'Thousands of Australian housewives have discovered an alternative to suburban isolation and boredom by taking an interest in the world around them.'[10] Headlines such as 'Housewife takes to politics!' abounded, and housewives were stereotyped as naive, bored, and ill-informed. Journalists often exclaimed upon meeting intelligent or articulate women that you could have mistaken them for a 'quiet housewife next door'.[11] Peter Blazey, in an article headed 'Battler Joan Child still takes it all in her stride: Grandmother MP is as popular as ever', wrote that 'it is easy to misread Joan Child by thinking her naive and housewifely'.[12]

Articles on women in politics in the 1970s often followed a formula of the 'battle' between contesting ideologies about women: should they work or stay at home? This was usually played out with women from different political parties, although sometimes men who believed women should be at home emerged to provide a foil for feminists. In June 1975 David Taylor, a

Waverley Council alderman, told the *Daily Telegraph* that Australian women should be 'back in the kitchen where they belong', and argued that the money allocated for International Women's Year should be channelled into relief for unemployed men. The headline 'Angry alderman hits back at home role for women' was accompanied by a photograph of 'Bronte housewife, mother of five and fellow alderman' Ann Symonds ironing a shirt. Symonds, who was later elected to the NSW upper house, retorted: 'A woman's place is everywhere — not only in the kitchen, but in decision-making areas which affect the life of everyone. Unlike Mr Taylor, who is single and lives with his mother, I am married and look after my husband and five children ... I don't think my baby or any other of our children are neglected.'[13] Symonds later saw that article as an 'awful experience' of being manipulated by the media:

> I was young and silly, of course, and didn't say 'no', which I would now, but they are an intimidating force, the press ... 'Stand here, do that, do this. Have you got a washing basket full of nappies? Can you just lean on the ironing board here?' And they had this great huge photograph of me, leaning on the ironing board with my nappies, just having been elected as deputy mayor.

The truth was, Symonds's husband did all the ironing in their household.

The kitchen photograph was, of course, an old trick. In 1943, the election of the first woman to the Senate was followed by an article in *Pix* magazine that featured a neatly aproned Dorothy Tangney taking a roast out of an oven. The caption read: 'The Senator is perfectly at Home in the kitchen, whether cooking the family's dinner or doing [the] large wash-up which follows.'[14] In 1955, Mabel Miller, who was both a barrister and the deputy lord mayor of Hobart, was the first woman to be elected to the Tasmanian lower house. The day after her election, the front page of the *Mercury* pictured the Liberal MP mixing a salad and assuring readers that she had carried out her chores 'like any other housewife' the day before. 'Naturally it's a great thrill to be a member of parliament,' she said, as she bustled around in her Sandy Bay home preparing the family meal, 'but I've still got to do this.'[15] When Mabel Furley was preselected as the first female Liberal Senate candidate in NSW in 1961, the *Mirror* declared that she had conceded — while mixing a soufflé in her 'modest Mosman flat' — that she would have to give up sewing if elected.[16]

From Federation to 1972, only 42 women were elected to state or federal parliament. In 1960, there were 12 women in the country's parliaments, and in 1972, when a record number of women ran for parliament, the number was 16 women out of 728 seats, forming 2.2 per cent of the total. Joan Child won the seat of Henty in 1974 but lost it in 1975, making the House of Representatives once again an all-male house, which it was to remain until 1980. By 1981, when Flo Bjelke-Petersen entered parliament, there were three women in the House of Representatives and nine in the Senate. Bjelke-Petersen brought the total to ten. The early 1980s saw an increase in representation across the country, not just in the federal parliament. By December 1982, there were 58 women MPs in Australia.

In the 1970s, many women became increasingly defiant. These women, many of whom had been attempting to persuade their own political parties not to restrict them to 'political housework', such as door-knocking, fundraising, and cleaning up at functions, were mostly from the ALP. In 1979, Jeanette McHugh, who had been a full-time housewife before entering politics, and told journalists she was proud to be a 'mother of three', refused to be snapped by the *Sydney Morning Herald* in her kitchen, saying,

'I'm a housewife, but not a housewife superstar.'[17] She was photographed sitting at a desk instead, talking on the phone. In 1980 the *Sun-Herald* reported that Labor MP McHugh was tired of newspaper stories about women which were headlined 'She Always Got Home to Make the Tea'. She said, 'Male politicians are never asked questions about their kids, or whether they mow the lawn. The fact is that politics is just as draining on families whether you're male or female.'[18]

Some women, like the influential Margaret Guilfoyle, refused to participate in contrived housework shots on the grounds of privacy, as well as the belief that it diminished women and set them apart from their male colleagues: 'I don't think that's got anything to do with your private life at all ... If you don't photograph the local judge doing something like that, I don't see why you should photograph anyone else.'[19] The fact that she had a housekeeper was her own business.

Other politicians refused these requests because they saw it not just as sexist, but contrived. When Democrat leader Janine Haines was asked if she deliberately projected her femaleness in an election campaign, she was emphatic that she would not do something she would not normally do, as she believed Margaret Thatcher did: 'Everybody knows that the Prime Minister of Great Britain is not your average mum, that she has people to do these things for her. I don't.' However, she was happy to be photographed doing chores that were part of her weekly routine, like shopping with her husband.[20]

Feminist politician Susan Ryan, who was elected in 1975, also refused all requests to pose doing housework, on similar grounds to Haines:

I was always deliberately against what Margaret Thatcher
did so dishonestly, which was to run around the supermarket
with a trolley and get pictured in the kitchen, as if a woman

working as hard as that has got time to do all that domestic
stuff ... It is very discouraging to women who can't afford to
pay to have their housework done or who feel somehow it's
a failure to do it and who then feel 'Oh my God I'm trying to
hold down my job and do the shopping and the cooking and
the housework and I'm a wreck', and yet there's Margaret
Thatcher sailing around doing it all.[21]

She says that on the one occasion when she agreed to be
photographed with her family — because her son wanted to
promote his rock band — the photographer said, 'Would you just
get out the vacuum cleaner and do a bit of vacuuming for me,
Senator Ryan?' And the children just laughed their heads off and
said, 'We've never seen Mum with a vacuum. She wouldn't even
know where it was.'

At the same time, women MPs were actively countering bias.
In Australia in the late 1970s, parties were still reluctant to
endorse female candidates because of the belief that they lost votes
simply because they were women. In 1977, Malcolm Mackerras
compiled evidence proving this was untrue, arguing it was a
mere prejudice on the part of party preselectors 'who use it as a
justification for their own refusal to select women for winnable
or safe seats'.[22] Between 1960 and 1969, women accounted for
less than 5 per cent of total candidates. This jumped to almost
10 per cent between 1970 and 1979, and more than 18 per cent
between 1980 and 1989.[23]

How women wished to be portrayed was influenced by more
than their personal views of the role of women. Women who were
standing for a lower house seat were under more pressure to draw
votes from local constituents than candidates for the upper house.
Another concern was whether their electorate was marginal or
safe, conservative or more mixed, as well as whether their parties
were campaigning on progressive, proto-feminist policies or a

more conservative, 'family first' platform. The problem facing all women, though, was a broad cultural anxiety about the impact on families of women's movement into the workforce. In 1977, the *National Times*, claiming the housewife was still the 'dominant image' of women in Australia in the 1970s, cited a poll which had found 46 per cent of respondents believed women could not both run a home and work, and 60 per cent thought children suffered when their mothers worked.[24] The professional work of male politicians was not seen to be threatened or destabilised by private responsibilities: it was only women who were seen to have two worlds, or roles, in constant conflict.

Nervousness — or prejudice — about female candidates was reflected in the questions from preselectors about what would happen to their children, or even who would get their husbands' dinners if they were elected to parliament. Myriad female politicians have complained of this during the 1970s and 1980s. Virginia Chadwick advised women candidates in the NSW Liberal Party to be prepared for a deluge of questions about their families from all quarters over this period, and to be polite while privately laughing them off:

And the one that used to frustrate me so much is people, particularly other women, who [say] — as if they're bringing something to your attention that you couldn't possibly have thought of before — 'Have you thought about what you're going to do about your children?' What are you meant to say? 'Oh no, look, thank you for raising it, of course not.' So I've often said to women, just play along, say what you have to say but in your mind you think, 'Oh yes, I've got it all worked out, I'm going to tie them to the Hills Hoist and leave a bowl of water.'[25]

Some women played along with the housewife stereotype, believing it would boost their chances of election, or re-election, and appeal to those who held traditional views about women. Some wished to reassure their electorates that they were not neglecting their families. NSW Labor politician Deirdre Grusovin, elected to the upper house in 1978, said she was only asked once if she would pose doing housework. She agreed to a shot of her making sandwiches for school lunch, with one of her children up on the kitchen bench because it would mean 'people knew her children were being looked after and not ignored'.[26] She said she suffered from a 'constant guilt complex', like many working women.

Victorian Liberal Gracia Baylor, who was captured grinning while pulling a tray out of her oven by her local paper, insisted there was 'nothing wrong with being a housewife' and that her background running a house gave her useful practical and organisational skills. Housewives could run the country better than the men in Treasury, she said often, and it irked her that housewives were undervalued by society.[27] In the lead-up to the 1980 election, Labor candidate Ros Kelly, then a 32-year-old former teacher, published *Mrs Kelly's Cookbook* as part of her successful election campaign in a previously Liberal-held electorate, telling journalists she did not care if feminists did not like it: 'I've had terrific support from women at home. I've been meeting a lot of housewives and I believe it's an important part of my campaign.'[28] The launch was held at her home, and Kelly was pictured behind rows of clean tea cups and saucers, reading her book. The photographs of her running or playing tennis would have prevented her being typecast as a housewife, she told me later: 'I was never a big sort of house person type, so I was never going to be stereotyped like that anyway so it didn't really worry me ... It definitely wasn't an image I developed over time.'[29]

Many women who closed their doors in the faces of newspaper photographers opened them up to reporters from women's magazines or local newspapers. Even Joan Child was photographed in a flowered apron stirring a pot on her stove for *Australian Women's Weekly* in 1975.[30] Queensland Liberal senator Kathy Sullivan was also snapped in the kitchen, standing next to her oven and leaning over two saucepans, for an article in *Woman's Day* just after she was elected. Sullivan (nee Martin), called 'the new blonde Senator' with 'plenty of fight', was quoted on a range of subjects including women's liberation, which she said had 'thoroughly buried the old "back to the kitchen, woman" syndrome'. The reporter, Lorraine Palmer, continued: 'Just the same, the kitchen is a favoured place with Kathy, who entertains gourmet-style at her flat in Brisbane with meals such as fondue, steak bermuda (steak stuffed with ham and bananas and cooked in wine), or beef stroganoff.'[31] Sullivan felt this was a positive article, because women she would not have otherwise reached now knew she existed, and many would have related to the fact that cooking was one of her hobbies.[32] West Australian Labor politician Lyla Elliott said she was photographed gardening for a woman's magazine, but argued the woman who was doing the article 'was a feminist, so it was okay'.[33]

Part of the appeal of women's magazines had long been their high circulation figures, which meant that at one time a magazine like the *Australian Women's Weekly* was estimated to reach half of Australian women each week. In 1971, it had a circulation of 820,000, and, according to one survey, was read by 47.5 per cent of Australian women, compared with 35.2 per cent who read *Woman's Day*, and 27.8 per cent who read *New Idea*.[34] In the 1970s, dozens of new titles were launched, providing more opportunities for women politicians to reach voters who did not read daily metropolitan newspapers.[35]

Some women continued to promote themselves as housewives in the mainstream media well into the late 1980s. Liberal

Senate candidate Bronwyn Bishop snapped up the opportunity in July 1987 when she ushered a journalist and photographer from the *Sun* newspaper into her North Shore home. After an interview, in which she spoke of her admiration for Thatcher, the photographer asked Bishop if she would pose with a carpet sweeper, as though she were doing her daily chores in her high heels. She readily agreed.[36]

The National Party's Yvonne Chapman was photographed elbow-deep in suds a couple of months after being appointed Queensland's minister for welfare services in 1986, saying that she wanted to be 'a mum to all the kids out there'.[37] After her next appearance in the *Courier-Mail*, dressed in an apron, holding a kettle, standing under frilly white curtains in her kitchen, and grinning broadly, a debate began in the letters page. One reader

Liberal Senate candidate Bronwyn Bishop poses with a carpet sweeper in her North Shore home, July 1987. *John O'Gready/Sydney Morning Herald*

complained the picture was a 'worn-out stereotype' which was 'quite offensive and an insult to her intelligence', while another insisted it revealed Chapman 'conveying the lighter side of life and a caring nature in both busy roles as a housewife and State parliamentarian'.[38] Clearly not all readers viewed women as victims of the press.

*

Tropes, or 'frames', of reporting are remarkably resilient. When Carmen Lawrence was elected premier of Western Australia in 1990, the front cover of the *Australian* featured a file photograph of Lawrence standing in a kitchen, next to a stove, with the caption 'Dr Lawrence can stand the heat.'[39] The photograph had been taken some time before, when she was minister for Aboriginal affairs, opening a housing estate. The reference to heat came in part from the fact that Lawrence inherited a government suffering from the stigma of corruption, following allegations that the two previous Labor premiers had acted improperly in dealings with business, which became known as WA Inc. But the headline also neatly summarised the question that ran through much of the housewifely reportage: 'Can women handle power?'

CHAPTER THREE

Florence Bjelke-Petersen: pumpkin politics

'I'm far from a dumb blonde,' she quipped, patting her greying hair. 'I'll make it in Canberra and I'll emerge, I hope, more of a woman.' Senator Flo agreed that she knows exactly where she is going. 'Home to cook some pumpkin scones.'[1]

— *Daily Telegraph*

Florence Bjelke-Petersen told journalists one of the highlights of her life, both as a senator and as wife of the longest serving premier in Queensland's history, was a state reception in Brisbane for the Prince and Princess of Wales. Prince Charles stood up in front of the crowd and said that he had been visiting Queensland since he was a little boy, and now he was a grown man and Joh Bjelke-Petersen was still the premier. He was starting to wonder, he said, if Sir Joh's stamina came from eating Lady Bjelke-Petersen's famous pumpkin scones. When asked how he'd heard about the scones, he replied that his mother, the Queen, had told him. Being a fierce royalist, Flo was 'absolutely tickled pink' to hear the head of the British Empire knew of the scones she had concocted in the kitchen of her northern Queensland home.[2]

It was not necessary for most Australians, however, to have a chat with the Queen in order to hear about Flo's pumpkin scones. She was rarely alluded to in print without a reference to her baking skills, and her husband's favourite snack. 'Mention pumpkin scones and lamingtons,' said broadcaster Clive Hale, 'and the name Flo Bjelke-Petersen inevitably springs to mind.'[3]

Flo Bjelke-Petersen, who with her scones was a regular presence in national newspaper headlines from 1979 to the mid-1980s, glorified what other women had resisted. Just as many journalists began to recognise and record the sexism implicit in photographing women doing the housework, she proffered them a plate of scones and beamed as they devoured them. It was a colourful and evocative image which was replicated hundreds of times. While it was based on a dish Bjelke-Petersen appeared to genuinely enjoy baking, not on a Thatcherite public relations campaign dreamt up by advertisers, Bjelke-Petersen clearly used it to her benefit. By nominating for the Senate in 1979, after more than a decade of heated debate about the place of women, the responsibilities of working mothers (and fathers), and the nature of housework, this aproned housewife from Kingaroy walked onto the national stage declaring that although a woman's most important role was looking after her family, a good scone maker could be a good politician. The proud, hardworking wife and mother, who boasted at luncheons, dinners and morning teas across the country about her favourite recipe, entered an environment of uncertainty about the place of women and constant questioning of female politicians' domestic skills. She placated anxieties, filled empty stomachs, and marched around the country delivering homespun wisdom from the 1950s, seemingly untouched by the turmoil of the intervening decades.

Florence Bjelke-Petersen was a member of the Senate for the National Party from 1980 to 1993. Before she was elected, her fame was built on two factors: her marriage to Joh Bjelke-Petersen, who had been the Queensland premier since 1968 (and would be until 1987 after a royal commission into police corruption revealed an extensive political culture of wrongdoing), and her reputation as a good baker. Joh Bjelke-Petersen's particular brand of conservative politics meant he was renowned mostly for who he did not like: Aboriginal people, homosexuals, feminists, unions, the Labor Party, former Labor prime minister Bob Hawke, many elements of the Liberal Party, environmentalists ('Greenies'), protesters ('rent-a-crowd'), journalists ('scum'), and anyone with left-wing beliefs ('Commies').[4] He reserved a particular brand of scorn for the media, whom he referred to as chooks that required regular feeding. His wife, while sharing his views, presented a friendlier face, and was a popular speaker who travelled throughout the state entertaining audiences with cheerful homilies, as well as tales of living with the premier and satisfying his seemingly insatiable appetite for pumpkin. Before she became a senator, Bjelke-Petersen spent so much time attending functions in her husband's electorate that she became known as the member for Barambah, while Joh was known as the premier. Her popularity was not limited to Queensland, however, and she was asked to campaign for the National Party in the 1980 Victorian election.

Many commentators argued Bjelke-Petersen's political work was vital as an adjunct to her husband's, as she added warmth to his hard-line authoritarian approach.[5] Ron Boswell, who entered the Senate in 1983 as number three on a ticket headed by Flo Bjelke-Petersen, surmised recently: 'Joh had magic, but he was too right-wing for the people of Brisbane. But when you threw motherly Flo in, she softened his image ... Flo and Joh were magnets for voters.'[6] Their rhyming names were regularly linked as 'the Flo and Joh show'. Several wives of other high-profile politicians had become celebrities by bringing glamour into the political scene, with former model Jill Hickson marrying the

NSW premier Neville Wran, Sonia McMahon wearing dresses split to her thigh on a trip to the White House with her prime minister husband, and Susan Peacock's modelling of sheets in a controversial advertising campaign which prompted her Liberal MP husband, Andrew Peacock, to offer to resign.[7] Flo Bjelke-Petersen injected domesticity, a brand of femininity that was familiar, comforting, and unthreatening. She was the standard bearer for middle-aged mothers, 'the epitome of Queensland motherhood', a woman who did her own washing, ironing, and cooking, and milked the cow with her own hands.[8] She represented women who were happy with looking after the needs of men, and excelled at it. A woman who had a homely kitchen with a large poster of Queen Elizabeth II and Prince Philip taped to the wall. She stood for, wrote Queensland journalist Hugh Lunn in 1979, 'everything the *Australian Women's Weekly* stands for: Prince Charles, the Queen, lamington recipes and babies'.[9]

In 1979, when Bjelke-Petersen nominated as a candidate for the Senate, she told reporters she was now ready to stand if the party wanted her, because her daughters would soon be married. Her husband baldly informed reporters it was a way of extending his influence into the federal political arena: 'We work together very closely, 100 per cent, and I would be there indirectly ... She's pretty good when it comes to politics.'[10] Her detractors said her candidature was only possible because her husband had done her dirty work: she would be there merely as his puppet, and to keep an eye on the Liberal Party, with whom he often clashed.[11] Bjelke-Petersen's plan to enter the Senate was a big story. Two days after the *Weekend Australian* revealed her plans, the story was still the page one lead in metropolitan papers. When Brisbane television reporters flew to Kingaroy to interview her, they were, naturally, invited in for tea and homemade scones.

Newspapers in Victoria and NSW poked fun at the idea of the housewife from Kingaroy going to the Senate, while

Queensland journalists who had witnessed the hard work and growing popularity of Bjelke-Petersen cautioned their southern counterparts not to underestimate her.[12] The *Australian*'s Hugh Lunn, who had broken the story about her candidacy, led an article with: 'Florence Bjelke-Petersen may be a figure of fun to many but since announcing her hope to run for the Senate there are few Liberals and Australian Democrats who want to laugh any more.'[13] Since Gough Whitlam, whom the Bjelke-Petersens loathed, won the 1972 election, breaking a 23-year period of Liberal Party rule in Canberra, she had toured the state from top to bottom on her own. Although some regarded her as naive, a *Courier-Mail* journalist argued she possessed 'a toughness and shrewdness below the motherly exterior. No longer is she the Little Woman, if she ever was. One can see her becoming more and more independent.'[14] Janet Hawley warned that after 30 years of being a politician's wife, 'Flo is beginning to enjoy the smell of real power and wants to become the real thing herself at last.'[15]

But Bjelke-Petersen's entrance to parliament was marked with controversy. She had been elected to a six-year term as a senator in October 1980, and was due to enter parliament in June 1981, but was nominated to fill a casual vacancy in March. It soon became clear that by entering the Senate three months early, she would be eligible for an additional $80,000 in superannuation. A journalist from the *Age* wrote: 'Mrs Flo Bjelke-Petersen may soon put aside her beloved pumpkin scones and dream up a new recipe: what to do with a big, juicy windfall of $150,000.'[16] The *Australian* editorialised: 'The pumpkin scones that Senator-elect Flo Bjelke-Petersen bakes in her new kitchen in Canberra had better be scrumptious — for they will be downright expensive.'[17] It was not just the newspapers who brought up the scones, however. In a letter to the *Australian* in which she defended herself about the superannuation allegations, Bjelke-Petersen ended with, 'My pumpkin scones are always made of the best ingredients and always rise to the occasion.'[18]

Bjelke-Petersen's cooking ability had clearly turned into a joke. Cartoonist Alan Moir, together with Mac Vines, wrote a book titled *Flo Goes to Canberra: The Intimate Diary of a Kingaroy Housewife*, which depicted her bumbling about the nation's capital, clueless yet enthusiastic. Moir told me it was great stuff for comedy: 'Ma and Pa Kettle going to Washington'. Don Dunlop wrote an indignant review for the Melbourne *Herald*: 'Mrs Bjelke-Petersen isn't really a funny person, either peculiar or ha-ha. But there are some who find this important lady hilarious ... It's all good clean fun — unless you think it is maybe time we took the senator seriously.'[19]

Flo Bjelke-Petersen also wanted people to stop laughing. It was at the point of campaigning for the Senate, in mid-1980, that she began to tell journalists she was more than a dab hand in the kitchen, adding that she was in Canberra to represent Queensland, not her husband. After her first fortnight as senator-elect she professed reluctance to judge a pumpkin scones competition at a town outside Brisbane, saying to the journalist present, 'It is becoming a bit of a gimmick. Some say I have to stop this image now I am to be a Senator and I don't want to be known purely as someone who can make a good morning-tea.' To demonstrate her diversity, she baked pikelets for a reporter.[20]

When she was about to leave for Canberra, Flo Bjelke-Petersen told journalists that she was hoping interviewers would ask her about politics rather than pumpkin scones, adding: 'Of course I, like very many women, like baking, not only scones but pikelets, tea cakes, little cakes. We had the family up last week and a batch of little cakes I made disappeared overnight.'[21] *The Daily Telegraph* cried: The day of the scone is over for Flo!'

Once a politician, Bjelke-Petersen had an ambivalent attitude to the symbol of the scones, protesting then promoting them, and at other times defending it. There was nothing wrong with being able to cook, she said, arguing, 'If you can make good pumpkin scones then you can be a good politician.' She complained about the media, while in the next breath dictating her famous recipe. She said that although she had made a statement about MX missiles, she bet they would only print what her husband said, adding, 'But they seem to love it when I talk about pumpkin scones.'[22] She was indignant that 'people have equated the fact that she can cook with innate stupidity'.[23]

Although she continued to insist women's most important role was that of wife and homemaker, she told a journalist, while munching on a pumpkin scone, that she had 'shown many people that a woman's place is no longer only in the home'.[24] She intended to bring attention to family issues, such as family allowances and support for full-time mothers. She stressed that family issues were different to women's issues, and that women were treated fairly in Australian society — they just were not as 'pushy' as men.[25] She argued her work in Canberra would only make her more of a woman, not less.

Flo Bjelke-Petersen drew the line, however, at comparisons to Edna Everage, the character created by cross-dressing comedian Barry Humphries and based on a parochial, garrulous housewife from suburban Victoria. The anomaly of a housewife on a stage, talking about the colour of her carpet and toilet seat covers, was at the core of the humour of Humphries's act, as evident in the title of the 1976 show 'Housewife/Superstar!'. The parody was based on an obsession with domestic detail, 'seeing the whole world through the Venetian blind of the kitchen window: seeing everything in terms of household arrangement, cleanliness ... ' Edna was someone who had 'merely strayed from the kitchen to the stage', Humphries said. In the mid-1970s she declared herself the 'housewife superstar', while she became a 'megastar' in the 1980s.[26] In some ways Edna, who claimed to be an intimate friend of Margaret Thatcher, paralleled the entry of women into the public sphere and participation in political life. The housewives of the 1960s became the 'housewife superstars' of the 1970s, whose presence on the public stage was thought to be inextricably linked to their gender. Female MPs were not seen as politicians, but 'women politicians', whose celebrity sprang from the apparent contradiction in terms.[27]

Bjelke-Petersen was probably compared to Edna Everage in the Australian press more than any other female politician, including Thatcher. It was usually ridicule. Bjelke-Petersen claimed she did not see the similarity with Edna, and said, 'I think that's a very silly sort of comparison — I should say, "Who's she?"'[28]

When Bjelke-Petersen took up her place in federal parliament, it became apparent that expectations of the Queensland housewife were so low, she was praised even when she did absolutely nothing. This can be the only explanation for the rash of compliments from journalists who watched her first week in parliament closely and concluded that, as she had made no grave errors and kept quiet, she must be able. After surviving a week in the Senate without making any gaffes, Laura Veltman declared Bjelke-Petersen could no longer 'be regarded as a joke' and 'the laughing stock of Australian politics', despite the remarks of those who said 'she's politically naive, generally silly, and male chauvinism's strongest argument for keeping women in the kitchen where they belong'.[29]

'She's smart,' Barry Everingham decided, 'and tough as nails' despite being an archetypal grandmother who had come to Canberra with her policies tucked away with her 'twin sets, pearls and sensible shoes'.[30] Alan Reid from the *Bulletin* also warned at the end of March that there was a 'lot more to her than culinary expertise on how to produce pumpkin scones or a toothsome pavlova'.[31] Still, Bjelke-Petersen's views on policy drew only fleeting attention, although there were some references to her support for a flat rate of personal income tax, which she shared with her husband. Her policies, which mostly represented the Queensland National Party platform, included splitting the family income to reduce the level of taxation, increased welfare spending for families, cutbacks in overall government spending, more money for Queensland roads, and lower petrol prices.

While Bjelke-Petersen was acknowledged to have gained her position owing to her husband's clout, she was clearly popular in her own right, winning a huge vote in the 1983 election (and drawing two other senators in with her). Her diary overflowed with appointments to speak across the country. Audiences loved her. She was described as politically shrewd, and 'one of the hardest working and most popular politicians in Australia'.[32]

In 1981, Bjelke-Petersen persuaded her husband to accept a one-off federal grant for Queensland under new health care arrangements, despite his publicly expressed anger that it was not enough money.[33] This peace-making role between the federal and Queensland governments earned her respect in the Canberra press gallery. Anne Summers wrote she had surprised her critics, who had mistaken a pumpkin-scones image for an entire persona. During a Telecom strike, people had said she would not be able to function without daily advice from her husband on the telephone, but Summers noted she had asked a number of questions during that period. She was accessible, attracting an exceptionally high volume of mail; was popular with her colleagues on both sides of the house; and regarded as sharp and intelligent. A lonely Joh had lost his wife for a good part of every week, Summers wrote, while Flo Bjelke-Petersen was 'blossoming with her independence, working hard and having a thoroughly good time'.[34]

What earned Bjelke-Petersen her loudest accolades in Canberra was the stand she took on sales tax. The federal government was introducing legislation that would impose a 2.5 per cent tax on various items, including books, food and newspapers.

Flo believed the proposal should have excluded basic family needs such as footwear, clothing and building materials. She crossed the floor to vote against the government. She promised to support the Democrats in the committee stages but vote with the government on the more far-reaching amendments proposed by Labor. She told the *Courier-Mail*, 'The sales tax will seriously affect those in our community who are least able to afford it.' Overnight, she had gone from being a naive housewife to 'the champion of lower income earners'.[35] Former prime minister Gough Whitlam called for 'three cheers for Flo' at an anti–sales tax rally. Michelle Grattan described her as a 'smart-broker' in Canberra–Queensland relations, arguing that while the image was homely and trite, 'the reality is rather different.'[36]

Jane Cadzow declared in the *Australian* that Bjelke-Petersen was a 'housewife superstar in her own right'. She was nominated for Queenslander of the Year. She campaigned for the National Party before the 1982 South Australian elections, and, even though she was not up for re-election in 1984, was the major focus of the campaign, featuring in all advertisements. After the large vote she attracted in the 1980 election, she was also used in a by-election campaign in Victoria in 1984. She was reported to be the favourite to take over the Senate leadership in 1984, although her husband did not want her to as she would be away from home too much. She told reporters she would not take the job, if offered it, because her first priority was carrying out the duties of the premier's wife.

Frequently, signs of Bjelke-Petersen's political acumen were contrasted with her femininity. To be a housewife was assumed to be benign, but to be political while appearing feminine was dangerous, even sinister. She was described by one Queensland MP as a 'thug dressed as a granny'.[37]

Other journalists recognised Bjelke-Petersen's brand of campaigning as clever because it appeared to be 'good sense' or motherly advice, while she was in fact pedalling policies. Michael Gawenda, watching as she stood talking to a greengrocer while campaigning in Melbourne, observed that:

> [This] was a mind which could concentrate on watermelons and cantaloupes and the perfect bananas while all the while, on another level altogether, wait for the chance to slip in an absolutely outrageous comment which, because of the timing, and because it came from a woman who seemed so totally unselfconscious, so artless, would sound like a piece of grandmotherly common sense. This, we thought, was a politician to be reckoned with. The key to this very shrewd politician is that she doesn't sound like a politician at all. If anything, she sounds very much like Dame Edna Everage.[38]

While Bjelke-Petersen's career demonstrated women could make effective and popular politicians, she used her success and platform to espouse her belief that the home was the preferable location for women. She was fervently opposed to the sex discrimination and equal opportunity legislation of 1984 and 1986, due to her view that it undermined the family unit and diminished the role of home-makers.[39] She would never have allowed her name to be put forward, she told audiences, if her children were not grown up. In fact, going to the Senate was not even her idea in the first place. Now, she travelled so much, she was rarely at home.[40]

*

Bjelke-Petersen's reservations about scones lasted only six months. By November 1981, she was confident she had 'overcome her early pumpkin scone image', and cheerfully gave out the recipe on radio and for auctions: 'it's done me no harm. It has helped me relate to people.'[41] Bjelke-Petersen's mantra was that the scones helped her relate to the women who made them and the men who ate them. She used her scones in a dispute Joh was having with striking coalminers in 1983, bringing a batch of freshly baked scones and promising to make her husband negotiate. The headline on the front page article was 'pumpkin scone diplomacy'.

In June 1985 the *Bulletin* declared, 'At last Lady Joh — i.e. Flo — Bjelke-Petersen has admitted what her frustrated opponents have sworn for years — that her political success is due largely to pumpkin scones.' Fellow Queensland senator Kathy Sullivan argues: 'When they voted for her, women used to go to voting booths and vote for themselves. She played them at their own game magnificently — the pumpkin scones thing was brilliant — and she was listened to when she spoke on other issues. But she wouldn't have got a break if she hadn't been the wife of the premier.'

Bjelke-Petersen baked pumpkin scones for visiting journalists for years, as well as tourists who came in busloads to meet the former premier and senator, struggling financially in their retirement. Her profile subsided in the mid-1980s, probably due to her absorption in her husband's problems as the damning 1987 Fitzgerald royal commission uncovered widespread corruption in the Queensland police force, and Joh later faced court.[42] In 2005 Joh Bjelke-Petersen died; and Flo in 2017.

*

Flo Bjelke-Petersen was a smart, capable woman. When her political instincts proved to be more than a mere mirror of her husband's, the element of surprise expressed in political commentary revealed how a focus on women's domestic skills often masked their suitability for political life. She cleverly capitalised on this focus, however, and her popularity provided evidence of an able political tactician who was patronised and petted yet earned respect in her own right. What many other women resisted and attempted to redefine, Bjelke-Petersen embodied and glorified, manipulating media interest in politically active women's domestic competency until it defined her completely. If she had been made a cabinet minister, it would have been a difficult tag to shake. But as a tactic for a rising political star, both her pumpkins and her populism were brilliant.

CHAPTER FOUR

Political Superwomen and MP Mums

In 2004, Treasurer Peter Costello had a message for the women of Australia: 'You should have one for the father, one for the mother and one for the country.' Concern about the ageing population and declining fertility rate led to a rash of policies — including a $3000 'baby bonus' — trying to encourage Australians to procreate, three times. After all, Costello had three children, as did the prime minister, John Howard.

The suggestion was widely mocked. But the cultural anxiety was real. In the late 1990s, and then the noughties, the public debate about fertility and whether mothers should work had become almost hysterical in tone, remonstrative and shrill. Much of this debate centred on the fact that a growing proportion of women in their 20s and 30s were single and childless. It was usually assumed that they were 'selfishly' or 'foolishly' delaying, or refusing, to have children simply because they did not want to sacrifice their careers. The truth was a lot more complex — and certainly one of the most significant reasons for the delay is the search for the right partner. But as the finger was pointed again and again at feminism for daring to suggest women should have more choices than their mothers (inaccurately, distractingly, called 'having it all'), many young women had become worried and fearful. A distinct lack of successful role models in many professions, and particularly in politics, feeds the belief that women still must choose either work or family.

Over these years, conservative columnists lined up to lecture young, single women, to blame feminists for encouraging women to work, and to wage an ideological battle about the impact of childcare on young children. Single female MPs continued to be grilled about whether — and when — they wished to have children, just as 'MP mums' were asked about how they coped. An extraordinary kerfuffle resulted from a photograph taken during the 2001 federal election campaign, when then Democrat leader Natasha Stott Despoja was photographed holding a baby, grimacing towards the camera. It was reprinted widely during the course of the campaign. Her facial contortions were interpreted as a sign that she was uncomfortable with children — calling in the tired assumptions that young professional women are opposed to families, or children, and that women can be divided neatly along ideological lines: worker or mother. In fact, as Stott Despoja later explained in a letter to the *Herald*: 'It was a split-second shot that captured me in the middle of exclaiming, "She's so tiny. I can't believe she's only four days old; I hope I don't drop her."'[1] Stott Despoja fell pregnant only a couple of years later.

*

Kirstie Marshall was an Olympic aerial skiing champion; a young, fit, cheerful and dedicated sportswoman. In 2002, she successfully slid from snow-slopes to back bench when she was elected to the Victorian parliament. When it was revealed, during the campaign, that she was pregnant, some observers grumbled.

Bettina Arndt wrote, in a column for the *Sydney Morning Herald* and the *Age*, that having a baby was not a 'charming diversion' but 'a potentially hazardous, extremely demanding undertaking which brings many unstuck':

> The life-changing experience of giving birth will not always slot neatly into the background of a demanding political career. International research highlighting the importance of parental care for infants brings into question the usual glib assumptions that the new political mother can easily minimise her parental involvement ... Does this mean pregnant women should never stand for political office? Obviously not, but surely the electorate has a right to consider these issues when deciding how to vote.

Arndt went on to question the argument that having 'more politician mothers would lead to more enlightened political decisions about issues affecting women and children'. Rather than supporting the real needs of women and children, she concluded, 'mothers who are forced to compromise their own instincts may end up promoting policies, like more infant childcare, that justify their own hard choices.'[2]

After Marshall was elected, the speaker of the Victorian parliament evicted her for breastfeeding her baby in the chamber on the grounds that there was a 'stranger' in the house: her baby. The story landed on the front page of the *Age* and the *Australian*, and was debated vigorously on talkback radio. Most of the sympathy went to Marshall. (A notable exception was Senator Amanda Vanstone, then the minister assisting the prime minister for the status of women, who said, 'I feel sorry for the baby being fed in a noisy and testosterone-filled televised parliamentary debate ... Female parliamentarians can generally look after themselves and I can see no reason why they should get a better deal than anyone

This photo, showing a grimace on Natasha Stott Despoja's face as she held her colleague Andrew Bartlett's tiny baby, was replicated several times throughout the 2001 election campaign. *Patrick Hamilton/Newspix*

else.') Shortly afterwards, the speaker of the Victorian Legislative Assembly, Judy Maddigan, said she had decided to make an exception to the 146-year-old 'strangers' rule for babies who were being breastfed. She told reporters: 'I have decided ... that if it is her view that it is in the best interests of her child, she is welcome to bring it into the chamber at times when she is required to be there.' Marshall welcomed the news, but said she did not expect to find herself in an emergency breastfeeding situation again.

This incident neatly exemplified the juggling act female MPs need to perform if they have families, the insistence of some that their two roles — mother and politician — need not necessarily clash, and the fact that there will always be a vocal rump of sexism in the community. Broadcaster Ron Casey was awarded an Ernie for his comment that Marshall was 'a second-rate politician with a first-rate publicity stunt. I mean, how else could a member of the lower house of Victorian state government get her name and boobies splashed all over the national press?'[3]

A century earlier, a cartoon in the Melbourne *Punch* featured a cartoon of a woman addressing parliament, as a bewigged speaker sat in the background nursing a child. The caption read: 'Some foolish people imagine our ladies will neglect their family duties. Quite a mistake. 3 a.m. That dear good old creature, Mr Speaker, is kind enough to take the blessed infant while the Hon. Member addresses the house.'[4] Maybe it's not such a crazy idea.

*

In many ways, the female politician is an iconic working woman, and her incremental progress provides a potent symbol of the struggle of all women to take up powerful positions in Australia. As Bronwyn Bishop indicated, at the heart of many of the attacks on the female politicians dubbed the 'women most likely to' has been a challenge to the right of women to occupy space in a parliament run by men. This has been in part driven by a supposed fear of what women's entry into the workforce may do to the children they leave behind.

In the 1980s, pregnant politicians insisted they could combine children and career effortlessly, wary of preselectors and constituents ready to level accusations of child neglect at them. Over the decade, a significant number of women who had young children — and had worked — were elected to parliament, unlike those elected in the 1960s and 1970s, who were either single or had grown-up children, and had promoted the joys of a traditional family life. The number of women who were appointed ministers also tripled in the 1980s, particularly due to the Hawke and Keating Labor governments between 1983 and 1996.[5]

In the 1990s, people who criticised mothers for working were scoffed at. Over this time, a seismic shift in the way working women were regarded had occurred, largely because so many women had moved into the workforce. When NSW Liberal candidate Wendy Jones was critical of her Labor opponent, Gabrielle Harrison, in 1994 for campaigning when she had a young child, she was howled down. Harrison's politician husband had just died of cancer and she had decided, at the age of 30, to run for his seat of Parramatta. Jones's comments on radio were laced with judgement: 'I have some concerns as a mother that perhaps now is not the best time for Gabrielle to be standing ... from a mother's point of view I'd be focused on my child, or children in my case.' Harrison received a large amount of sympathy: she was supported by the vast bulk of talkback callers, and after she appeared on Channel Nine's 'Midday Show', elderly women shouted out, 'Good on you.' There was a 10 per cent swing to Labor in the by-election; she said it was a 'victory for working mothers everywhere'. At the time, Harrison dismissed Jones's remarks as 'contemptible', but in 2001 she told a journalist: '[it] still stings after all these years. Nobody asks a male politician who's minding their child, but I was being judged as a mother.'[6]

A year before Marshall put her hand up for parliament, Anna Burke, the Labor member for the Victorian federal seat of Chisholm, concealed the fact that she was pregnant with her second child when she stood for re-election. She eventually wrote to the *Age* to announce her pregnancy, saying she 'chose not to tell anyone our great news so I could get on with the job of holding the seat without public distraction. Nor had I informed the ALP of the future birth of our second child, because I did not want to be excluded from consideration for advancement.'

Burke had given birth to her first child during her first term and taken six weeks off before returning to work. She insisted that being a mother had not stopped her from performing her duties as a politician, and that 'no male in parliament has ever been questioned about his ability to be a father and an MP at the same time.'[7] Burke later told me she regretted writing the letter to the *Age* because by then she believed she did not have an obligation to tell anyone: she was in her late 30s and her pregnancy was in an early stage. She said she was prompted to do it by constant references to the pregnancy of Jackie Kelly, a federal Liberal MP from Sydney, in the press: 'It's no one's business; I was in an early stage in the middle of my campaign. But every time I looked at the paper, it was pregnant Jackie. It was the annoyance of it, that somehow we are these altered beings, that I would have been a different being because I was pregnant.'

It has long been assumed that the families of male politicians make sacrifices; the families of female politicians suffer. That, after having children, the careers of male politicians coast along while those of women are under threat. Because of this, the first female MPs to have babies in office were defiant about their ability to combine motherhood and politics. Queensland Liberal MP Rosemary Kyburz told a journalist during her first pregnancy in 1982 that she and her husband shared the housework and intended to share childcare: 'I am certainly going to make sure I'll be back in Parliament within a month of the birth. I couldn't stand being a fulltime mother and wife.' She was determined to transform expectations of working mothers, and was credited with bringing 'romance and baby-feeding routines to the Queensland Parliament'.[8]

When federal Labor MP Ros Kelly returned to work, air cushion in hand, a week after giving birth, she sniffed at suggestions she should be at home with her baby. It was 1983, she worked close to her home in the ACT, her mother helped with childcare, and it was, frankly, nobody's business. As Australia's first federal MP to give birth while in office, she was emphatic about her responsibilities as a working politician. Initially, the newspapers expressed only a mild interest, reporting that she'd had a 15-hour labour, forceps delivery and stitches, and had no time to do antenatal exercises. The *Sydney Morning Herald* reported that becoming a mother was not expected to disrupt her career.

After one of Kelly's parliamentary colleagues, Liberal MP Bruce Goodluck, attacked her for neglecting her child, however, scrutiny intensified. 'Why doesn't she stay at home a little longer?' he asked. 'Her husband's got a good job and I'm sure Parliament would be only too happy to give her maternity leave. If children are put straight into child minding centres after birth, God help us. Who wants the socialisation of babies?' Several female journalists leapt to Kelly's defence. Kate Legge wrote: 'The old saying "Mother knows best" was turned on its head last night when a male parliamentarian claimed he knew better.'[9] Kelly insisted it was a private family matter and 'a personal decision, not the launch of a campaign for working mothers'. She told one reporter that being a mother made her a better politician because it made her more relaxed.[10] If she protested too much, it was because she felt she had to. As another journalist argued, the 'MP mum' was keen to minimise any concerns about her heavy workload because she was under 'great, if subtle pressure, to appear as if absolutely nothing has changed'. She went through her daily routine in painstaking detail for several reporters.[11] She told one that she wore rouge on her cheeks over a light foundation because 'it helps when you are tired. People are always looking for signs that you're not coping.'[12]

＊

Unlike housework, mothering cannot be easily delegated. While in the 1980s the vacuum cleaner requests largely subsided, journalists continued to ask what became known as the 'casserole question': how do working mothers cope? Victorian Labor MP Kay Setches, who was elected to parliament in 1982 and went on to be a minister in the Cain and Kirner governments, found that: 'The press always wanted to know first about the nurturing side of you, and the responsibilities that you have as a woman, and how you are handling them, and whether they are clashing with the other responsibilities you have as a public person.'[13] Like others, she was torn between the desire to prove women could do it all and the need to explain how difficult it could be, and argue for policy and attitude change. It was a difficult position to be in: while 'MP mums' shared the guilt and exhaustion of many working women, they were constantly forced to prove their ability to combine both effortlessly.

Carmen Lawrence, dubbed 'Lawrence of Suburbia' when first elected to state parliament, tried to be candid about the complexity of being a working parent. She was elected as the Labor member for Subiaco in Western Australia in 1986, held a series of portfolios, and went on to become Australia's first female premier in February 1990. Her government was the first in Australia to have five women in the cabinet at the same time. Although she was then the nation's most powerful woman, she was happy to be photographed in the kitchen, because she said she wanted to provide a positive portrayal of motherhood without diminishing the difficulties many people experienced in parenting. She told me in 1997:

Because you also don't want to deny that [you are] a mother ... to deny that I had that additional responsibility would be to sell a lot of women out too ... I like the things that women do. I like to cook. Having my son and bringing him up was one of the most potent experiences of my life, and I know that is true for many women. On the other hand, being the only one to do that — being required to do it — is onerous ... At one level you want to say, 'Look, I'm a politician making decisions that affect you and the sort of person I am doesn't matter.' But on the other, there's this sense of being a woman in a political system. A novelty. And [it is] important to represent the breadth and complexities of women's lives. Because they can't just walk out the front door in most cases, and close it behind them.

Many women were uncomfortable with the glossy image of the 'superwoman', glorified in the 1980s and 1990s in the way the housewife had been in the 1950s, which implied women could manage everything just by their immense organisational ability, effortlessly combining careers with having families. This was fed by photographs of women cheerfully stirring pots on the stove after 14-hour working days, and articles where women said they easily coped with the workload by sheer efficiency, or some other mechanism such as paid help, lack of sleep, or otherwise unemployed grandparents.

Journalists, however, were often more sympathetic than political parties. When June Craig's husband fell ill in 1981, and colleagues spread rumours that she would resign to look after him, a female journalist, Leslie Anderson, wrote an opinion piece arguing that when men worked hard for the community, they were praised for good citizenship, while women were accused of neglect.[14] Similarly, Prue Leggoe, a Victorian lawyer, faced a preselection contest for a state seat in 1981 — when she was Prue Sibree — which she survived without controversy. Her second preselection, in 1984, was bitterly disputed on the grounds that she had separated from her husband, was in another relationship, and was facing a fight for custody of her children. While some branch members threatened to resign if she was selected, and circulated rumours about the illegitimate child she had borne at the age of 19, Leggoe said she found journalists 'very supportive':

> All of them to a 't' said, you know, 'Anything we can do, you
> know we're with you. Everyone's saying these blokes who are
> trying to run against you are a pack of shits.' ... They didn't
> want to pry too much into the private life and they sort of
> said, 'Well that's your business.' ... I think perhaps the press
> saying publicly that they thought the thing was not the right
> way to go, it was an unfair sort of thing to happen [which]
> probably swayed some people to think twice about it all.

Leggoe won the preselection and remained in parliament until 1988, when she resigned.[15]

*

The prospect of role reversal was something that made our forefathers shudder, and argue vehemently against the vote. Tasmanian MP Sir Edward Braddon sketched the dreaded scenario in the debate over the Commonwealth Franchise Bill 1902:

> Does the honourable gentleman think of the case when the
> woman will not take her husband along with her [to vote
> at polling booths], but will go alone and leave him at home
> to look after the baby and cook the dinner? That is what
> the honourable gentleman has to think of as a possibility in
> many of the homesteads throughout the Commonwealth.[16]

The spectre of the 'househusband' was frequently used as a derogatory term in the 1970s and 1980s. Possibly the most famous of them was Democrat senator Janine Haines's husband, Ian Haines, who looked after their two daughters in Adelaide when parliament was sitting. Janine Haines's domestic arrangements were often described as ideal for women who wanted to succeed in politics, but she was irritated by the fact that she was asked throughout her career how her family would cope when she went to Canberra. She told journalists her husband was supportive and they had 'always split the task of looking after home, hearth and children, with him taking the larger share for the most part'. She admitted that, yes, she felt awful when her girls cried as the Commonwealth car came to pick her up and take her away for the week, but said she refused to let the guilt tear her up. In November 1984 she told the *Bulletin*, '[Working in Canberra] stuffs up your family life.'[17]

After being appointed deputy leader in 1985, she was asked again how she managed to be both a senator and a mother. She retorted, 'Probably the same way men manage to be both senators and fathers ... Ian is how I manage it. Every politician needs a supportive spouse ... He is placid, easygoing with a very secure sense of his own worth. He runs the whole thing. I don't interfere even when I am at home.'[18] It was an 'obviously touchy subject', wrote the *Canberra Times* in 1986. Haines said, 'When people say to me, "How do you feel about leaving your husband and children at home while you go to work?" I tell them that I'll answer that question when it is asked of a man first.'[19] Their arrangement was almost marvelled at. The *Sydney Morning Herald* reported she had 'an extraordinary amount of help and encouragement from her husband, despite his personal lack of political ambition'.[20] Haines was photographed at home with her husband several times; he was shown cooking, or bringing her cups of tea.

By 1987, some journalists were writing about the fact that *other* journalists were asking Haines questions about her domestic arrangements. Her frustrations became a new hook for stories, in the same way women's refusal to pose doing their housework had been. Her complaints were printed at length:

> The day I was appointed [in 1977] to fill Steele Hall's casual vacancy, the second question asked of me was 'how will the family cope?' Baden Teague was elected the same month. No one asked him how his family would cope. My children were at school and my husband was at work, unlike Cathy [Teague] who had two pre-school children and no one over 18 inches to talk to. It was much harder for her. My husband once had to explain to a journalist that it actually didn't take a giant IQ to push the buttons on an automatic washing machine. Well, we're still married and our children are not wards of the state.[21]

It was at this point that the Denis Thatcher jibes began to emerge. In 1986, when Ian Haines chose to take four years unpaid leave instead of a forced transfer that would have sent him to a small town in the south-east of South Australia, he was tagged 'Mr Mom' in two newspaper articles for not wanting to disrupt his family life.[22] Haines later said her husband 'got pretty stroppy' with a male journalist who asked him how he was going to cope, because 'to argue that only by having a woman in the house do you have a well-run establishment, I think is a bit bizarre in this day and age.'[23]

Denis Thatcher was a name associated with complete emasculation. He was not a target for ridicule because of anything he did or said. It was simply that he was married to a woman substantially more powerful than he was. This fact alone made him a laughing stock — as though to be a real man it was necessary to dominate your wife.

Janine Haines's partner, Ian, was frequently referred to as the model househusband. In this photo, he brings his wife, who was recovering from pneumonia, a cup of coffee.
Craig Golding/Sydney Morning Herald

Like Ian Haines, Tony Vanstone, the husband of South Australian Liberal politician Amanda Vanstone, was also often called 'Denis', much to his annoyance. Even Ros Kelly's second husband, David Morgan, an influential economist who went on to be CEO of Westpac, was dubbed 'Denis' occasionally, which, he said, 'hit a little sharper' than being called Mr Kelly.[24] NSW Liberal minister Virginia Chadwick resented the jokes her husband Bruce was subjected to:

> Perhaps some people are quite kind, and they think you haven't heard a Denis Thatcher joke before, but it does get very wearing, and it is debilitating, and it's just another little chipping away at the capacity of couples to actually make it work in this sort of environment ... It's really hard for a bloke who has been brought up in a traditional environment

who's trying to make all of those adjustments and be very
modern and supportive who then amongst their own peers
is belittled, even though they mightn't see it as belittling.

The questions fired at Ian Haines revealed a belief that his
position was unenviable and unfortunate. Did he regret anything?
Did he feel he had missed opportunities? Peter Coster from the
Melbourne *Herald* described his discomfort: 'Ian Haines was
clearly used to deflecting loaded questions: he denied being
Haines' husband brought "demands", that life was difficult with
two teenage daughters, or that they were resentful.' But then
Coster went on to ask: 'Would he agree that some husbands
might feel resentful of what is a role reversal more public than
perhaps any other in Australia?'[25] In a similar vein, Ivo Crosio,
the husband of NSW Labor politician Janice Crosio (who became
the first female cabinet minister in NSW, in 1984), had to reassure
the *Sun-Herald* that he'd 'never really had any sort of problem
about being married to a "famous" woman — people expect
you to, but honestly, it's never really crossed my mind.'[26] It seems
many journalists expected them to.

It is not unusual for female politicians to say they wish they had
a 'wife' to support their political careers; however, few women
MPs have actually had househusbands who looked after young
children full-time. (They were more likely to be the partners of
Green, Democrat or Labor women.) In fact, many marriages
dissolved under the pressure of being a political spouse. Meg Lees
told the *Sydney Morning Herald* that when she left her 25-year
marriage her husband was seeing someone else, but that she was
'quite happy to put on the record that one of the reasons he gave
for going was that I left him with too much responsibility for the
kids and too much responsibility for the housework'.[27]

There were others. Victorian Labor politician Valerie Callister
partly blames the break-up of her marriage on the media attention

and discomfort of her husband with an at-home, non-traditional role. He was reported frequently in the media as a househusband, she said, and 'in the long haul it didn't rest easily with him, and I think it's a tall order to ask anyone to turn the whole sociology of their upbringing on its head ... It didn't really last because I think that males are still defined in society largely by what they do ... and he wasn't used to any sort of media attention; it used to make him nervous. He just wanted to be an anonymous person, which is understandable, and it just did not work out.' Victorian senator Jean Melzer also says her marriage broke up because her husband disliked being an ancillary to a senator.[28]

Wives of male politicians can be similarly resentful of the workload and publicity, but they do not have the added burden of aspersions being cast on their femininity, nor suffer sympathy for their bad luck at being married to a successful man.

Most articles on househusbands centred not just on the abnormality of the role, but its undesirability. The actual chores the men carried out were described at length, as though it were miraculous and extraordinary that a man could choose to do menial work or look after his family to such an extent: 'He drove them to and from school and he cooked them dinner when he brought them home. When one of the girls developed appendicitis, he held her hand and took her to the hospital.'[29] The home was still assumed to be the domain of women. Any divergences were prodded curiously and held up to question.

*

Anxieties about working women are still lived out in public disputes about life decisions of female politicians: whether to run for office, stay at home, accept promotions, and how to cope with young children. Female MPs remain symbols of a cultural ambivalence about women working. The 'feminist' position has long been wrongly assumed to be a singular, unchanging, and relentless push to get women to work no matter what the cost. Just as each female MP grapples with her own decisions and responsibilities, so do all of her female constituents.

When it was discovered that Labor MP Michelle O'Byrne was pregnant, her Tasmanian electorate — and talkback radio — was abuzz. Would she still be an effective MP if she had a child? She won the next election, with an increased margin, and got pregnant again. O'Byrne was one of a group of federal MPs with young children in the 2000s, which included Tanya Plibersek, Kirsten Livermore, Kate Lundy, Anna Burke, Jacinta Collins and Jackie Kelly. Some women have trumpeted their pregnancy or motherhood in their campaigns. In NSW in 2001, the 13-month-old daughter of an ALP candidate, Carolyn Neilson, featured on campaign posters in the safe federal Liberal seat of Wentworth in Sydney's eastern suburbs, grinning and saying, 'Vote for my mum!'

The most telling part of the debate is that it was still about women. Men still worked, were assumed to work, and male politicians were not grilled about their responsibilities, even when they had babies or toddlers. Liberal MP for the federal seat of Parramatta Ross Cameron was not challenged about the fact that he had four young children under six — including twins — as a young MP. Similarly, Christopher Pyne, another young Liberal senator from South Australia, was elected when he was 25, and his wife gave birth to four children during his political career. He took a month off work when his twins were born prematurely and kept in intensive care. He took a week off when his third child was born. Fatherhood and politics are assumed not just to be an easy mix, but an effective one. Being a father is an asset, not a liability, and it is considered career-enhancing to have children and a wife. Family portraits are used with some effect in campaign material.

While today the number of women politicians who are mothers is greater, the task is no easier. By the mid-2000s most cabinet ministers were childless or had grown-up children, and there had been few examples at a federal level of women ministers with young children. Lynne Kosky, who was made Victorian education minister in 2002, told one reporter she had to abandon her son Jack when he was halfway through surgery at the hospital to carry out some duties. She said she felt compelled not to miss Question Time: 'You're seen to be weak if you use that [children] as an excuse not be there.'[30] Stories like these are why federal sports minister Jackie Kelly, then pregnant with her second child, resigned from the front bench after the 2001 election. Kelly, who has often railed against the pretence and pressure of the 'supermum' image, was criticised in the press but told me she was cheered by her constituents:

> I got a lot of responses from working women and women
> who'd been trying to juggle both. And there was a lot of
> sympathy like 'Yeah, good on you. We find it hard too, and
> we're only doing a nine to five job.' It is hard, it's very hard.
> We have set women up for falls in terms of you can be the
> housewife, the mother, and a working woman as well. It's
> an awesome amount to take on because the blokes in our
> society are still not doing their fair share of the housework
> … It is hard and the women in my electorate at least
> basically said, 'Well yeah, it was another reinforcement that
> she is human. It's an awful lot to take on.' I didn't realise
> how tired I was. Just shattered.

Feminist commentator Eva Cox was disappointed, arguing Kelly's decision signified that 'clearly in the higher echelons of government having a baby is still regarded as a liability'. She argued Prime Minister John Howard should have overruled her and made appropriate arrangements to help her, like providing a temporary minister to fill in when she was on leave. Bettina

Arndt slammed Cox as an 'ideological troglodyte' who had lost sight of the fact that feminism was about choice. Kelly told me that women still face the fact that 'kids under five wake in the middle of the night and they want Mum; that's it. You can have all your feminist ideals as much as you want but at the end of the day they want Mum and you have to learn to cope with that, and that's challenging.' While she gave up her ministerial position, she continued to work, however, and Howard appointed her his parliamentary secretary. Kelly, like others, pointed out how many male politicians have supportive wives, some of whom attend functions in their place: 'I am lucky if my husband will go to the State of Origin with me [*laughs*].'

In one of the most ancient of tropes, some women still like to claim they are mothers to their constituents, or indeed — in Pauline Hanson's case — to the country. Danna Vale, Liberal MP for the federal seat of Hughes, declared in 2001: 'My four boys have grown up, but I've now got 88,000 people to mother.'[31] Old stereotypes die hard, and the maternal imagery is powerful, but the problem for women in the noughties is still often posed in public commentary as an either/or scenario: babies or promotions, families or careers, lonely success or loving sacrifice. The truth, of course, is that most women do both.

Postscript, 2021

The fact that it is more difficult for mothers than fathers to be federal politicians has remained true. In 1983 Ros Kelly was the first member of the House of Representatives to give birth but it took sixteen years before another woman did — Anna Burke in 1999. And it was another eighteen years after that before the first cabinet minister had a baby while in office — Kelly O'Dwyer in 2017 (also noting that when she resigned in 2019, she said she needed to be around her kids more often). O'Dwyer was reportedly annoyed when the government whip, Scott Buchholz, asked her to express more breastmilk so as to not miss parliamentary duties — even though under parliamentary rules, breastfeeding mothers are able to get a proxy vote.

Annabel Crabb has called it the 'wife drought', saying women in demanding jobs need the same kind of domestic and personal support their male colleagues have in their partners. (As she has pointed out, the fact that the current prime minister, Scott Morrison, and his treasurer, Josh Frydenberg, have run the country while raising small children has gone almost entirely without comment and certainly without interrogation.) Economist and Labor MP Andrew Leigh calls it 'The Motherhood Tax', and conducted research that found in the federal parliament of 2013–16, the average male politician had 2.09 kids, while the average female politician had 1.22. Only one in five male politicians had no kids, while the number was more than one in three for women.[32]

On the upside, there is now childcare in Parliament House, and plenty more women MPs are mothers. Deputy Opposition Leader Tanya Plibersek now has grown-up kids. In 2016 the House joined the Senate in allowing breastfeeding in parliament. In June 2017, Greens MP Larissa Waters stood up while breastfeeding and proposed a motion about a condition affecting coal miners. The Tasmanian election was called this year when the opposition leader Rebecca White was due to give birth, but she declared the timing was of no consequence.

CHAPTER FIVE

Feminist Politicians: 'waving the flag of feminine feminism'

Late one afternoon in Canberra, 1975, almost 200 women marched through the streets of Australia's capital city to the offices of the *Canberra Times*, holding placards they had painted with 'Media Oppress Women' and 'Watch out Media'. Women in their 20s, wearing jeans and sporting jaunty afros, walked alongside grandmothers in their 60s, wearing plaid skirts and cat-eye glasses. All had come to Canberra to take part in a Women and Politics conference, which had been thoroughly derided by the press. Finally, they had decided to make their fury heard. They forced their way into the newsroom, and, standing on desks, chairs and filing cabinets, shouted angrily at the acting editor, John Farquharson, demanding space to respond to an offending editorial. Max Prisk, then *Canberra Times* news editor, remembers the women cutting phone lines with nail clippers and refusing to leave. The photograph published in the *Sydney Morning Herald* the next day, of women crowded into the newsroom, clutching folders, handbags and banners, is a powerful image of women of all ages tackling a male-dominated press.

Journalists had taken great delight in poking fun at the conference held to coincide with International Women's Year. Editorials across the country had attacked it as an extravagant waste of taxpayers' money, and those who attended it as badly behaved extremists. The money that had been allocated for International Women's Year activities the year before was headlined in the *Age*: '$2 million for the Sheilas: Surprisingly It's Not a Joke'. Coming at a time when the Whitlam Labor government was facing accusations from the opposition and a growing number of political journalists about economic incompetence and wastage, the fact that money was being allocated to a group of women wishing to discuss the women's movement was grist to the mill.[1] Sydney's *Daily Telegraph*, before the conference began, said the money was being poured 'down the great Labor drain', and dismissed it as a talkfest for talentless women: 'Obviously there should be more women involved at higher levels of decision making. But we can't help feeling that those who need a conference like this to tell them how to do it wouldn't be very good at it anyway.'[2] Attacks intensified when the conference began.

The opening reception was held in the dignified surrounds of Kings Hall in Old Parliament House. According to newspaper reports, 'not-nice' women spray-painted 'Lesbians are lovely' in the ladies toilet, food was trampled into floorboards, and drinks were spilt. The *Sydney Morning Herald* wrote that Prime Minister Whitlam, who had struggled to be heard over interjections such as 'sexist' and 'Margaret still takes second place', 'stood silent and grim faced' as a group of 50 Aboriginal women demonstrated about racism in the women's movement. A group of Labor women also stood behind Whitlam holding placards, protesting his stand on East Timor. The *Daily Telegraph* said it was a 'drunken display of exhibitionism which under normal circumstances would have required police intervention'. One disgruntled delegate told the Melbourne *Herald* that many of the women at the conference were 'lady mafia members who would not hesitate to punch or kick ... The language has been disgusting, drink has been frequent and behaviour in general has been very bad. The congress is a socialist forum for a lot of women yahoos who run around in men's clothing.' After this reception, the *Canberra Times* ran an editorial that argued feminists were trying to prove against nature that there were no differences between men and women. Their error was evident, the editorial argued, in the fact that, while women may have taken literally the 'lounge suit' dress code on their invitation to the opening, they still carried handbags. Firebrand African-American feminist Flo Kennedy responded: 'If I wore pearls they'd think I was an oyster.'

John Farquharson talks to women from the Women in Politics conference who had invaded his *Canberra Times* newsroom, September 1975. *Sydney Morning Herald*

The women of the conference, who were by now thoroughly annoyed with the way they were being trivialised, held a meeting, chaired by journalist Liz Fell, to discuss how to respond. They decided to head to the *Canberra Times* and extract a promise from Farquharson that he would run a critique of the editorial. In their long day of negotiations, the women were enraged when they asked Farquharson what feminism was and he responded: 'femininity'. When he refused to publish the statement they submitted, and asked for a rewrite, about 80 women returned to the newspaper offices and stayed there until 3.00 a.m. Their statement was eventually published, with some cuts. According to Fell, a group of women went to the printing presses at Fyshwick to sabotage the delivery of the papers. Twenty police were waiting.

An editorial in the conference newspaper, *New Dawn*, concluded that the coverage showed the male-dominated Australian press had felt 'immensely threatened' by the fact that a large group of women had met to discuss politics: 'In the long run, whatever course we take, the ultimate aim should be a re-definition of what is news. Right now let's do what Flo Kennedy says and "get down to kicking arse".' While the march on the *Canberra Times* was a spontaneous eruption, reacting to coverage of a specific event, it followed years of resentment and frustration with the media about how women, and feminists, were portrayed. The 'action ideas' the women drew up included a total embargo of sexist media; the setting up of a government newspaper, like the ABC, with 51 per cent representation of women at all levels; sit-ins at radio and television stations; forming a woman's radio station; and law suits. One of the suggestions was to issue 'requests that "successful" women stop dissociating themselves from feminism'.

*

In the noughties, feminism was considered by many to be passé. Younger women frequently dismissed their female elders as too '70s feminist' — outdated, earnest and hard-line. Conservative commentators still liked to pore over the supposed excesses of the chaotic and theoretically diverse so-called second wave of feminist thought (there have been many more than two). What is curious is the 'evidence' given for the claim that the time of feminism was finished. The prime minister, John Howard — not generally renowned for his insights into feminist thought — claimed that in the noughties we were in a post-feminist phase because women under 30 thought the battle had been won. Telstra businesswoman of the year in 2003, 33-year-old Gabrielle Molnar, said she was not a feminist because, 'I don't think it serves or supports my cause. And when you're managing a corporate career, you also manage the perception around that, and you don't want to get pigeonholed.'[3] A cursory study of history shows that this was nothing new, and hardly surprising. There has always been a swathe of women who have been hostile to the central tenets of the women's movement, and resisted every incremental victory in the emancipation of women. From the vote to equal pay, from women priests to female politicians, there have been women urging men not to support change. And feminism was long a dirty word. Even second-wave feminists were equivocal about using it, preferring the term 'liberationists' to something associated with their foremothers, whom they saw as dry, censorious and sexless. But the use of the word by women in the public sphere has long been a battle of conscience and identity for the women involved. As Molnar's words revealed, when women were interested in getting ahead in blokey realms such as politics or corporations, it often did not augur well to associate yourself with something vilified as — in the 1970s — hairy-legged, unaccommodating, or extremist; or, in the noughties, something associated with whingeing or demanding special treatment. Her words could have been uttered by hundreds of women MPs since the 1960s.

Since the 1970s, there has been a Herculean shift in our understanding of feminism, partly due to the activist shock troops of dissenting women. The term 'feminist' has been bandied about, claimed and disclaimed, owned and disowned, attacked and trumpeted as change has inched forward — and occasionally backward. Women who entered parliament were grilled relentlessly by journalists about whether they considered themselves feminist. And, generally speaking, mostly the younger, progressive women owned the term, while older, conservative women disowned it. Most qualified it, proffering their own definition. The battle over this word reflected more generally on fears about what women MPs were supposed to be doing — and how a pleasing appearance could make just about anything palatable for many (usually male) journalists.

But there are other reasons why women might have been loath to identify themselves as feminists keen to fight for 'women's issues'. Female MPs often worried they would be stereotyped if they said they were feminists. Former actor Elisabeth Kirkby, who was a candidate for federal parliament in 1977 and 1980, and entered the NSW upper house in 1981, felt she had to 'temper my women's liberation enthusiasms so that the label of being a "radical" feminist would not jeopardise my future or that of my party'.[4] Many female MPs were keen to avoid being thought of as separatists who wished to work apart from and against men at a time when they were working hard, and often alone, to win the respect of their male peers. As NSW Labor MLC Edna Roper told a *Sydney Morning Herald* journalist in 1973, 'I am not a women's libber — I don't believe in dividing the sexes.' Victorian Liberal Margaret Guilfoyle said in 1997 that she probably would not have described herself as a feminist when she was elected to the Senate in 1971, despite thinking women had the right to reach their full potential in their chosen profession, because: 'At that time feminism was rather regarded as displacing men rather than working together.' She also wished to emphasise she was not a spokesperson for women, as it was assumed feminists were.[5] Many spokespeople for women found they were rarely asked about anything else.

Some women politicians described feminism as a sign of weakness. Janice Crosio, who was a member of the NSW lower house from 1981 until 1990, when she moved to federal parliament, insisted that she was not a feminist because she had never personally experienced discrimination.[6] She said she was concerned with women's rights, but was no 'women's libber' because she had not had any problems: 'Primarily I'm an individual, but being a woman has never gone against me.'[7] She told reporters she was tough, and dismissed their questions about bias as though they underestimated who she was: 'My height has a certain advantage. I'm 175 cm in bare feet, 182 cm in high heels, and I invariably wear high heels. The men certainly can't patronise me or pat me on the head and say go home little girl. It's not the point whether you're a man or a woman but whether you can get the point across.'[8] This was a feminism predicated on personal body space: as Crosio had a commanding physical presence, and no parliamentarians had pawed her, she told journalists she did not need it.

By the 1990s, however, Crosio told me her views had changed:

I thought I was free even the first day I took my own breath ... but to be called a feminist, I probably said no in those days, what do you mean by feminism, do you mean that you are not free to do, to think, to speak? Since then, of course, I have seen a lot of problems with females not getting the same wages, not getting the same representations in what they are able to do ... I'm fighting the fight for the people I represent

129

and half those people — in fact now it's more — happen to be women … Maybe I was doing it and maybe I was acting it, maybe I was living it, without all of those platitudes and rhetoric going on behind — I don't know.

Crosio's insistence that she personally had no need of it, and was tall or talented enough to fend for herself, was representative of a more widespread view that feminism was a cop-out or soft option for those who wanted to leapfrog to the top by claiming they represented the absent voice of women. This was a nascent version of what came to be known as 'the gender card'.

Other women politicians were simply ideologically opposed to feminism. They argued, in a decade where public debates about the role and status of women centred on sex discrimination and affirmative action legislation, that women were not disadvantaged by their sex. National Party politician Flo Bjelke-Petersen said she thought that feminists sought to eradicate the differences between the sexes; were opposed to motherhood; and were generally angry, 'hard-hitting' women dressed in overalls. Some, like Bronwyn Bishop, sought to portray feminists as whingers who lacked sufficient talent to achieve on their own merits.[9] Many politically conservative women shied from being linked to the women's liberation movement because it was strongly associated with a critical Marxist or socialist class analysis in the 1970s, and increasingly with the Labor Party in the 1970s and 1980s.[10] However, some women from the ALP Right objected to the women's movement for the opposite reasons, and resented what they believed was a request to place gender before class. Joan Child thought feminists irrelevant, and was irritated that, as the member for a marginal Labor seat, she was portrayed as a representative of women before she had opened her mouth.[11] She argued feminist policies were too sectarian for a staunch Labor MP, who represented both men and women. Child believes the greatest problem she had politically was not the press but women's groups who criticised her for not representing their interests and a lack of sympathy to problems faced by women.[12]

And women of colour were rarely asked for their views or included in any discussion of feminism. Definitions of feminism varied widely. Ros Kelly, for example, told me: 'Of course I'm a feminist if you believe in women developing to the fullest and doing everything you can to support them.' Victorian Liberal MLC Gracia Baylor called herself a 'right-wing feminist', and claimed feminism was about gaining power, not lobbying those who had it.[13] This was partly because the term feminist was associated with a broad set of demands, few of which formed part of their own political platform. But from the mid-1980s a growing number of female MPs, especially those from the ALP, owned the word without qualification.

In newspaper coverage of the women's movement in the 1970s, feminism was as closely associated with the 'burning bra' symbolism in Australia as it was in America.[14] By focusing on a trivial aspect of feminist activism — which was in fact most likely a fictional event — women MPs could laugh off any suggestions that they were 'women's libbers' who refused to pander to conventional codes of feminine dress and behaviour in order to make themselves attractive to men.[15] 'Burn my bra?' asked Janice Crosio, a couple of years after her cleavage was displayed on the front page of the *Sydney Morning Herald*: 'I need all the help I can get.' Jean Melzer said she believed in women's equality, but not women's lib: 'I'm much more comfortable in a bra.'[16] Liberal MP Kathy Sullivan, who was sympathetic to the goals of the women's movement, told me in 1997 that she had always avoided the 'misleading' term feminist. In 1974, being a feminist meant 'to burn the bra', she said, and she 'wanted to be listened to on other topics'. She found 'some of the feminist rhetoric at the time very offensive'. She wanted to be taken seriously by a 'very heavily male chauvinist' press and believed calling herself a feminist would have put her 'at the mercy of these male journos' who tended to stereotype feminism.

Behind the jokes were fears that the label feminist could marginalise women in parliament. Identifying as a feminist was interpreted not just as having a particular view about the place of women in society, but as *only* having views on women.

*

The term 'feminist', which had originated in Europe more than a hundred years earlier, was not used unquestioningly by those active in the Australian women's movement in the 1960s and 1970s.[17] According to Anne Summers, author of *Damned Whores and God's Police*, an activist and later a journalist, second-wave feminists did not wish to be called feminists because it was considered an old-fashioned word: 'Feminists, we thought, were quaint relics with their fixations on peace, abstinence from alcohol and an obscure concept called rights. We weren't for women's rights ... we were women's liberationists!'[18] According to Ann Curthoys the term 'women's liberation' was gradually dropped around 1973–74 and replaced by 'feminism' and for some time the 'women's movement'.[19] A rough correlation can be seen in the words used by journalists, and by the mid-1970s feminist was the term most frequently used.

Australian feminism has always been multiple and diverse: consisting of intersectional *feminisms*, and not just one single view, perspective or theoretical framework, though those of white middle-class straight women usually dominated. The women's movement which burst onto the political scene with such exuberance into the late 1960s was influenced by several strands of thought, and riven with debates about how to prioritise class, race, gender and sexuality, as well as the most appropriate strategy to employ to effect change. Few of these ever appeared in newsprint. It was strongly influenced by the critiques of British and American writers, such as Juliet Mitchell, on the sexual and material subordination of women, Pat Mainardi's deconstruction of the politics of housework, Kate Millett's analysis of patriarchy, and Shulamith Firestone's utopian vision of a world where women would be freed from the burden of reproduction.[20]

Woven through much of the more radical literature were the voices and experiences of First Nations women, and women of colour, but in the public eye, in press reports, they were often absent. Notable exceptions were civil rights activist and South Sea Islander Faith Bandler, who was a high-profile member of the NSW Women's Electoral Lobby in the 1970s, Kuku Yalanji woman and lawyer Pat O'Shane, who became Australia's first Aboriginal magistrate and often confronted white feminists about racism in the women's movement, and Yaegl elder Joyce Clague, who campaigned for the rights of Indigenous Australians, ran for parliament and worked on councils advising the NSW premier about women.

Radical feminists (women's liberationists), who sought revolution and employed consciousness raising as a means of personal transformation, were frequently at odds with liberal feminists (from the Women's Electoral Lobby), who sought to reform existing institutions, usually by lobbying the government or through bureaucratic channels.[21] Unlike activists in the United States and Britain, many Australian women flooded into the state and federal bureaucracies after the election of the sympathetic Whitlam government in 1972, which enacted a range of pro-women policies, such as equal pay in the Commonwealth Public Service, paid maternity leave for public servants, funding for women's refuges, the abolition of the luxury tax on the contraceptive pill, as well as the appointment of an adviser on women's issues. But many women MPs also faced accusations from others in the women's movement that they had sold out, allowing themselves to be co-opted by a masculinist, capitalist political system in a pursuit of personal power.

The Women's Electoral Lobby (WEL) was formed in Melbourne in 1972 specifically for the purpose of political lobbying. It was most prominent during the 1972 federal election, when members canvassed candidates for their views on a range of policies affecting women. Female journalists were recruited (often by other women journalists) to help with media strategy, with great success.[22] Nancy Dexter wrote in the *Age* that 'the 1972 federal election must go down as the first in which the average woman is really interested. Much of this interest is due to WEL.' Another *Age* journalist, Sally White, argued WEL's success meant 'that Women's Lib is not a dirty word to the media if they are approached in the correct way'.[23] There were 164 press articles on WEL in 1972, many written by women journalists, and only three were unfavourable.[24] A significant number of members went on to become politicians.[25]

For many journalists, WEL was the acceptable face of feminism.[26] Members were described by the press as different from other 'women's libbers' because they wore nice frocks, brushed their hair, were mostly married with children, and aimed to improve, not overthrow, institutions. WEL's public relations officer, Wendy McCarthy, told interviewers she was not a women's liberationist, because 'WEL defined its role as reformist, not revolutionary.'[27] It was the rowdy elements of women's liberation — particularly anything to do with breasts — that had captured the imagination of the press, however, and became the standard by which journalists compared women politicians. By 1975, the undefined and open-ended question 'Are you a feminist?' had become critical in a self-conscious formation of identity.

*

Susan Ryan was elected as senator for the ACT in 1975 under the slogan: 'A Woman's Place is in the Senate'. Unlike the 14 women who had entered federal parliament before her, her political career was spawned by the women's movement. She was elected as a feminist, supported by her own feminist faction in the ALP, and voted for on the understanding that she would promote the views of, and policies for, women. She was different from her female colleagues, wrote Phillip McCarthy in the *National Times*, because she had 'used feminism as a political weapon and never seen it as a liability'. When she first appeared in the press, as a candidate, headlines read 'Women's libber aims for the Senate' and 'A Woman on the move'.

Ryan was of particular interest to the media because she was articulate, young and a divorced mother of two — someone to be welcomed as a source of entertainment in the dull and conservative 'old men's House' of the Senate. It was often implied that Ryan's appearance was the spoonful of sugar that made the feminism go down: 'It helps ... that she is feminine as well as feminist, a woman who never forgets she is one. She is petite and attractive, dresses well and always aims at looking good.'[28] She still managed to look attractive to men despite her views, wrote Dorian Wild.[29] 'It has to be said that despite once belonging to a fairly militant women's lib group, Susan Ryan is a very feminine feminist,' he wrote. Another reporter declared:

> Senator Susan Ryan is a together lady, although she'd
> probably consider such a description demeaning. It is indeed
> a sexist comment about a woman whose success in Canberra
> has come as much from her personable ability to wave the
> flag of feminine feminism in a manner which has the male
> dominated corridors of power willing to listen as from her
> undoubted political prowess.[30]

Largely because the word was considered pejorative, many journalists were careful that the labelling of Ryan as a feminist — and socialist — was her responsibility, not theirs. They usually said it was 'self-described', or put the word feminist in inverted commas. But most of her coverage in the late 1970s was positive. She was touted as a 'brilliant Labor Senator' who, predictably, was considered to be 'a Prime Minister in the making'.[31] Ryan was appointed shadow minister for communications, arts and letters after Labor lost the 1977 election, and was described in a spate of articles as a credible, passionate 'optimist in the Senate'.[32]

Over the next few years, however, Ryan's feminist views gradually came to be seen as a liability. Ryan had been hugely successful in making her party take the views of women seriously, particularly when she utilised research that found that if women had voted for the ALP in the same numbers as men, Labor would have won all elections since World War II, including the 1977 election.[33] She convinced the ALP leadership to change their policies for women, embarked on a national publicity campaign, and put the gender gap on the political agenda. Labor won the 1983 election, and the gender gap closed for the first time when more than 50 per cent of women voted for the ALP.

At the same time, complaining she was being typecast by print journalists who were only interested in her views on women, Ryan began to downplay her image as a feminist mouthpiece. She argued that women's issues had moved to the centre of Australian politics. Some of her fellow feminists accused her of selling out.[34]

But Ryan's rhetorical shift away from feminism as a defining identity was viewed by many journalists as a sign of maturity, revealing again how feminism was seen as being marginal to the political process, and how women were portrayed as peering over the edge of 'real politics'. The *Sydney Morning Herald*'s Jenni Hewett wrote that, for Ryan, feminism had become 'the fall back position rather than the battering ram'. Ryan told her:

I don't see myself so much as a feminist representing women. I see politics as broader and with more complex interactions than when I started. I've gone from concentrating on specifics like child care much more into the mainstream. What we call women's issues are really marginal. Though I support campaigns like women's refuges — and people still identify me with them — I see them as peripheral to issues which affect women's position such as access to employment, tax policies, distribution of income.[35]

Both male and female journalists interpreted the shift as signalling Ryan had become tougher, more ambitious and more adept at the political game. She had toughened as a politician and no longer 'let her heart bleed in public', wrote one.[36]

After Labor's victory in 1983, Ryan became the first woman in a federal Labor cabinet when she was made minister for education and youth affairs and minister assisting the PM on the status of women. As Ryan grew in status, her feminist views were no longer considered cute, or quirky. They began instead to be described in the press as liabilities, as her opponents used her views to attack her. This was triggered by the active role she played in driving the ground-breaking sex discrimination and equal opportunity legislation through the federal parliament. There was a protracted, powerful and hugely personal campaign orchestrated against her in 1984 as she introduced and fought for the Bill which outlawed discrimination on the grounds of sex, marital status and pregnancy in employment, housing, goods, services, education, accommodation, and finance, and made sexual harassment unlawful in employment and education. Andrew Symon wrote in the *Advertiser*, 'A year in Government has left Susan Ryan in no doubt about the price she must pay for her feminism ... she says she has been a target of extreme conservative groups opposing Labor policies because she personifies the changes in society they oppose.'[37] But the passage of the *Sex Discrimination Act*, a critical pieces of feminist legislation, was a momumental feat. 'Suffragette Susan' considered it her greatest political achievement.

*

In 1977 a 31-year-old Janine Haines entered the Senate to fill a casual vacancy for the then fledgling Australian Democrats. The party had been formed by former Liberal cabinet minister Don Chipp in 1977, and was intended to be a third political force in Australia, located somewhere between the two major parties.[38] Coinciding with a period during which a greater number of women were becoming involved in political parties, the Democrats 'seemed to present an ideal opportunity to create a party free of patriarchal legacies', with more transparent decision-making processes, and a structure that sought the involvement of party members at a grassroots level.[39] The party prided itself on avoiding male-dominated machine politics, and consistently fielded a high number of women candidates. Although Haines — who only stayed in parliament until 1978 but was re-elected in 1981 — had identified herself as an advocate for women from the start, in the early stages of her political career she was ambivalent about the word feminist. In 1981 she said that although she supported equal rights for women, calling her a feminist because she opposed injustice to women was like calling her an Aboriginal person because she opposed injustice to Aboriginal people. However, by 1984, journalists reported that Haines described herself as a feminist. In 1989 she insisted she still did not like the use of labels, but accepted they were often used: 'They are meaningless statements by and large but, given we are stuck with labels, now when I'm asked I will say, "Yes, I am a feminist. The fact that I look like a reject from the Liberal Women's Council of Victoria is totally irrelevant.'"[40] Haines consistently aimed to voice the concerns of women, saying when she first entered the Senate chamber, she was 'struck by the maleness of the place' and felt it to be 'awash with testosterone'. Women's groups hailed her as a heroine.

Journalists highlighted Haines's rapid-fire delivery and frank approach to interviews, and often represented her feminist views as the emotional, savage and shocking outbursts of a political firebrand.[41] This may be why photographs of her with her mouth open, looking intense and angry, were used so often with articles. Her attacks on sexism in the parliament and the press were considered good copy, but were used as examples of someone who was unguarded and liable to offend. For example, when she was annoyed by reporting that focused on her looks, the '32-year-old mother of two' told a reporter: 'People say how nice it is to have a young, and other adjectives, woman in the Senate, and say that I'll be a decoration to the place and so on ... But they wouldn't dream of going up to one of the nice-looking younger male senators or members of the House and saying the same thing. They'd get a punch in the nose.'[42] These comments were often referred to over the following decade, not as an incisive observation about sexism in politics, but as an example of an alleged tendency of Haines to upset people.[43]

Haines attempted to broaden the definition of women's issues from what particularly affected women — families, childcare, reproductive rights, discrimination and violence — to what women were interested in, thereby covering the entire political spectrum. She argued for specific legislation to protect or elevate women's interests, and insisted women were interested in all legislation, as Ryan did, over the years she was in parliament.[44] But these two positions were often seen as contradictory: the affairs of women were assumed to be outside, or tangential to, 'real' politics. Comments like 'Although she has strict feminist ideas, she has the widespread respect of the party' were typical.[45]

By 1986, the Democrats had a fully developed policy on women; however, Haines quickly became frustrated that the press 'only quote us when we speak on rape, abortion, pornography'.[46] Like Ryan, her desire to move away from being seen as solely interested in 'women's issues' was heralded as a mark of maturity. But the competency she displayed in other areas was still recognised by the press. By 1984, the compromises she had extracted over Medicare and her work in the Senate committee that investigated the conduct of Justice Lionel Murphy had earned her the reputation of a shrewd parliamentary watchdog. By the end of 1984, she was tipped to be the leader who would follow Democrat founder Don Chipp. The headlines read: 'Fiery senator not afraid to tilt at windmills' and 'Janine Haines: now taken seriously'.

In 1985, Haines was elected deputy leader of the Democrats, becoming the first woman to hold a leadership position in a federal parliamentary party. The leadership contest was well-reported: internal brawls in the party were good copy, and the tales of disgruntled men who disliked Haines were aired regularly. Even before she went on to be elected leader, one of the Senate candidates resigned due to concerns over an increasingly 'strong feminist element' in the Democrats.[47] Commentators speculated on what impact her 'outbursts' on sexism or views on women's issues would have on her chances, as well as the way she looked. Many journalists clearly believed that engaging in 'women's issues' was not a good recommendation for leading a parliamentary party, but, at the same time, recognised her gender could be an advantage in leading a young and progressive political party. One wrote that Haines had shouldered all of the political 'women's areas', like community service and welfare, 'yet, ironically, being a woman is not going to hurt her chances of being elected as leader, and could even help them.'[48]

Haines won easily, to the surprise of many commentators, who had underestimated her appeal. A poll at the beginning of September 1986 showed support for the Democrats had shot up from 5.4 per cent in 1984 to a substantial 11 per cent.[49]

As leader, Haines continued to critique sexism in parliament, and she worked hard to link women's issues to broader economic debates. Unlike Ryan, Haines's views on women became part of her package, not her defining characteristic, partly because as leader of a party her views were sought on a wide range of subjects. But she was increasingly conscious of the liability of being represented as an 'archfeminist', a tag which she argued was applied to any outspoken woman. She told the *Age*:

> I'm damned if I do and damned if I don't. If I raise questions
> of pornography, child abuse, incest, domestic violence, they
> say I'm obsessed with sex. If I raise equality of opportunity,
> difficulties women face, they say I'm a man-hating feminist.
> If I'm flippant about myself it's lack of confidence; if I'm
> flippant about them, I'm a sarcastic bitch. If I make strong
> statements I'm aggressive; if not, I'm weak. If I'm angry,
> I'm emotional.[50]

Haines brought women into the public arena in a very real way. She spoke about rape, postnatal depression, how politicians were often 'up themselves', and were 'troglodytes' engaged in 'stag fighting'. While she, like many other women, equivocated about the word feminist, she did not waver from her belief that women's issues formed a central plank in the Democrats platform. She supported Ryan during the passage of the sex discrimination legislation. She was scathing about the way women were treated by the media, arguing in 1981:

If [women politicians] make statements of state or national
importance but on topics outside the realm of so-called
'women's issues', we are ignored; if we make a passing
reference to a topic such as rape, sexism or pornography, we
are labelled hysterical, reactionary, fun spoiling wowsers —
or just plain whimsical ... I and a lot of other women are
becoming fed up with the treatment we receive at the hands
of the media. We are constantly being trivialised, patronised,
decried and stereotyped. We are depicted as mothers,
grandmothers, wives and daughters. We are described in
terms of size, age, and hair-colouring. Our comments are
edited into idiocy. We are considered mindless twits with
nothing of value to offer the community outside the kitchen
and the bedroom.[51]

Haines's popularity defied the pundits who thought a woman
with feminist views and no business experience would struggle
to keep the Democrats afloat after Chipp left. When the
Democrats won seven Senate seats in the 1987 election, she was
called 'Australia's most powerful woman'.[52] Her ability to attract
publicity on a wide range of topics was regarded with awe by the
major parties. Dozens of journalists described her as the most
popular politician in the country. The *Bulletin* named her one
of Australia's top ten politicians in April 1989. *Sydney Morning
Herald* columnist Alan Ramsey said Haines was 'developing a
public profile as somebody who means business'.[53]

Then, in 1990, at the peak of her success, Haines decided
to run for a seat in the House of Representatives because she
wanted to improve the Democrats' profile. She believed it was
impossible to attract media interest on a day-to-day basis while
in the Senate. Her popularity provided the impetus, as well as
her ability to handle the media, and the future of the party was
seen as hinging on her success.[54] For months, the polls predicted

she would win. In the long series of articles that followed her announcement, journalists began to treat the Democrats more seriously, and once it became apparent the Democrats could begin to exercise considerable political clout, articles critically examining their platform began to appear.[55]

It should be remembered that Haines's popularity coincided with a distinct change, over the decade she was in power, in the way female candidates were viewed. By 1990, women began to be seen as a more honest, credible alternative to male politicians.[56] Some reporters, and especially paternalistic editorial writers, had been promoting this view since the 1960s. Haines capitalised on this, and added to it with her straight-shooting exposés of how parliamentary business was conducted to suit the interests of an elite group of middle-aged men. Haines, like many who followed her, was canonised as 'Saint Janine'.[57] Polls showed she was seen as honest and trustworthy.[58] Her rival for the seat of Kingston, sitting Labor member Gordon Bilney, clearly resented the perceived advantage her gender gave her. He told Peter Smark: 'It's more than just an attempt to sell her as a saint. She's being sold as someone not just sanctified but attended by a band of angels ... I just say she's a cold, calculating polly.'[59]

Haines lost her bid for the seat of Kingston. She came third, capturing 26 per cent of the vote, behind 38.4 per cent for Bilney and 32 per cent for the Liberal candidate, Judy Fuller.[60] Nationally, however, the Democrats peaked in popularity, with 12.6 per cent of the Senate vote. Her mistake was to think she could win a seat in the lower house given our system of preferential voting, but her personal vote was remarkable.

*

In the 1970s and early 1980s, the Australian press took a great interest in female politicians who were feminists. The problem was, the women who sought to be heard on matters to do with women were rarely given the chance to speak about anything else. By the middle of the 1980s, feminist views were increasingly recognised as just one facet of a political personality, and were no longer considered sufficiently novel to lead articles with. In the 1990s, Natasha Stott Despoja not only did not shy from the word feminism, but claimed it was a personal religion. Others insisted women were now embedded in the political process and should not be considered separately. Many journalists just lost interest. In 1994, Doug Aiton of the *Sunday Age* wrote a feature piece about Cheryl Kernot: her strengths, her background and her views. He wrote: "'I was going to ask you,' I said, 'your thoughts on feminism. But I've decided I can't be bothered.' She nodded, 'We should have gone past that by now.'"

We hadn't, though.

CHAPTER SIX

The Cover Girls: 'Forget policy, I've got great legs!'

You can control a story by the way you look or get a story up by the way you frame it. You can manipulate it by superficial things such as appearance.
— Former MP Wendy Machin, 1997

I think it would be a lot easier for me if I was ugly, because what you've got to do if you're a blonde, you've always got to prove yourself, you've always got to prove that you're not stupid and that is a very big problem.
— Ros Kelly, 1997

For many female politicians, entering federal parliament was an experience akin to walking into a male-only university residential college, pub or building site: catcalls all around. The absence of women in the blokey world of politics meant that many fairly normal looking women, walking in to take their places alongside men, have been leered at and lusted after as though they were 18-year-old barmaids. NSW National Wendy Machin was called the 'spunkette MP', South Australian MP Barbara Wiese a 'page three girl', and, later, Cheryl Kernot was dubbed 'Ballot Box Barbie' and Natasha Stott Despoja a 'blonde enchantress'. When Pauline Hanson stepped off a plane during the 1998 election campaign, with the wind blowing her skirt up around her knees, the front-page headline on the *Daily Telegraph* cried, 'Forget policy: I've got great legs!' Which pretty much sums it up — even if the next day a reader, R. McCormick from Bridgewater in South Australia, wrote in to challenge the point: 'Pauline Hanson has not got great legs. They are skinny and shapeless. The super high heels she wears would make any woman's legs look better.'

Women MPs have consistently complained of a gratuitous and discomfiting focus on their appearance. In the 1990s, some were even accused of exploiting it, and mocked for trying to play the 'beauty card'. In 1990, for example, Ros Kelly, then a federal Labor minister, agreed to pose draped in a red sheet for an exhibition about the sensual side of powerful women. Photographer Heide Smith's aim was to skewer the assumption 'that if a woman is beautiful she must be dumb and if she's brainy she can't be good-looking or sexual'. After the exhibition, called Because Beauty Is Timeless, opened at the Canberra Press Club in July, journalists discovered Kelly, then minister for the arts, sports, environment, tourism and territories, had asked Smith to take out a particular photograph of her with a swathe of red material draped across her head. The headline in the *Daily Mirror* read: 'BANNED: Hawke Minister bars this photo'. It was accompanied by a cropped photograph of the portrait, which made it look as though Kelly was naked. *Canberra Times* reporter Marion Frith, while arguing the press had over-reacted, wrote that 'Mrs Kelly looks, well ... she looks sensual, sexual even, a look until now unassociated with figures of such political status.'[1] The *Sydney Morning Herald* joked, 'Popular wisdom in Canberra has it that the high profile Minister for the Arts, Sports,

Environment, Tourism and Territories, Mrs Ros Kelly, will do anything to get her picture in the papers. For a while yesterday, it looked like the joke had been proved true by pictures of Mrs Kelly clad only in a bed sheet.'[2]

Sex, power, a bare-shouldered cabinet minister draped in red: the story was irresistible. When Cheryl Kernot posed in a deep red bordello dress for the *Australian Women's Weekly* in 1998, with a now famous feather boa, it was frequently claimed that her action, and the ensuing hullabaloo, was unprecedented. This is incorrect. Partly due to the timing of the shoot, the reaction to her frock-up was more prolonged, fervent and damaging than the others. But several women had posed in similar, if perhaps less flamboyant, attire for newspapers and magazines. Former Democrat leader Janine Haines agreed to be photographed fully made-up for the *Australian* in 1989, in a sequined evening dress, and, unusually, without her glasses. The headline read: 'the real Janine Haines'.[3] In 1993, Ros Kelly dressed in a long, one-shouldered evening gown, split to mid-thigh for *Woman's Day* shortly after the prime minister's wife, Annita Keating, had modelled clothes for *Vogue*. The female reporter wrote Kelly, 'in her favourite little black dress, blonde hair glamorously coiffured and handsome features highlighted to great advantage ... faced up to the camera like a cover girl'. Readers were told it had taken a 'great deal of persuasion', before Kelly agreed, due to her belief that 'it takes a very confident woman in politics to be seen as a woman'. The headline cried, 'Yes Minister!' The reporter exclaimed she 'proves without doubt that you can be a pollie and a super-attractive woman too!'[4] Just what we were all worried about.

All of these 'glamour shot' articles claimed to be peeling back the political layers to the 'real woman' underneath, even though the images were highly stylised. There were no corresponding images of male colleagues draped in doonas or tight-fitting pants, with headlines revealing this was the 'real' or 'true' man. It was the professional garb of working women that was seen as artifice, not the make-up and borrowed dresses.

*

In the 1970s and 1980s, there was a handful of young women dubbed MPs with 'model looks' by the press, including NSW National Party MP Wendy Machin (27, 'blonde, slim and single'), Liberal senator Kathy Sullivan (33, 'blonde, slim and recently divorced'), South Australian Labor politician Barbara Wiese (30, 'brunette, slim and single'), and federal Labor MP Ros Kelly (32, 'blonde and married'). Each endured a series of debates in the press about whether they were 'just a pretty face'. The stereotype of most women the press dubbed 'blonde bombshells' was eventually used against them by political opponents who accused them of being vain and shallow. The flipside of this, of course, was that there were many women considered not to be model girls, and therefore less worthy of media attention. Women judged to be frumpy or — the worst of sins — 'housewifely' were frequently the subject of articles where experts commented on how they could be 'made over' in order to win votes or party support.

Kathy Sullivan: 'the Kissable Senator'

Queensland political science graduate Kathy Sullivan (then known by her birth name, Kathy Martin) was elected to federal parliament in 1974, when there was almost a complete dearth of women politicians in Canberra. A total of five new federal female MPs were elected, which the media hyped as a landslide. 'Every television station, every current affairs program just zeroed in on me — fabulous publicity for a politician,' Sullivan later told ABC radio. Within a short period of time, she became known as the 'Kissable Senator' — a tag that originated from a comment she made to a journalist that 'everyone kisses me. They don't want to shake hands — they all want to kiss.'[5] On her first day in parliament, a *Daily Telegraph* headline declared: 'One girl among the new boys: Kissing Senator arrives'. Digby McLean from the *Canberra News* said he had found out why everybody had wanted to kiss her: 'Senator Martin has a charming personality, and a warm smile she always manages at the right psychological moment,' he wrote. 'Her soft, husky voice is one of the sexiest I have heard.'[6]

Sullivan said she deliberately attempted to project an image of 'somebody who is businesslike, but still female'. She stopped smoking cigars in public, stopped wearing her favourite knee-high boots and quickly complied with instructions to grow her hair to a 'neat, businesslike sort of style'.[7]

After Sullivan was elected, stories about her first husband, who was convicted of murder after their marriage broke up, soon appeared, with headlines proclaiming: 'New Glamour Senator Was Wed to a Killer'. When she married again, at age 33, in 'floral chiffon' on 20 December 1975, her wedding was reported in the *Australian* ('Senator marries'), the *Courier-Mail* ('Senator Kathy becomes Mrs Gray'), and the *Canberra Times* ('Big week for the Senator').[8] Martin's separation from her second husband two years later, in seemingly acrimonious circumstances, was also widely reported.[9] Her third marriage, to Robert Sullivan, in December 1983 received little attention. 'It never was my intention to announce it to the press,' she told the *Courier-Mail*. 'I'm fairly sensitive to intrusions into my private life.' However, she agreed to speak to the *Courier-Mail* on their one-year anniversary in an article containing a progress report on the relationship and the couple's search for a five-bedroom home on the Gold Coast.

While Sullivan complained to journalists that the interest in her personal life was prompted by an interest in the way she looked, her discomfort provided hooks for another round of stories, which verged from mocking to sympathetic. Journalists, while recording her frustration, simultaneously implied she was a loose cannon.[10] For example, Queensland journalist Hugh Lunn, from the *Australian,* wrote a story after Sullivan had accused the press of a sexist bias in the coverage of her personal life 'simply because I am a woman and blonde'.[11] Although the *Australian* ran a supportive editorial about how difficult it was for politicians to maintain their marriages, Lunn later referred to her 'funny lady' comments as evidence that she was a wild card, had 'stormy relations with the media' and was a potential liability for the government.[12]

By the mid-1970s, sexism in political reporting had become a fashionable story — usually written by female journalists. In 1982, Queensland journalist Sally Loane wrote an article about Sullivan and the 'peeping Tom' press. The article began: 'Like some beastly King Kong pawing over the blonde Fay Wray, the Queensland press has for years held Senator Kathy Martin in its hairy palm.' Sullivan told Loane the print media were far worse than the electronic, and singled out the Queensland press as particularly chauvinistic. When she crossed the floor and resigned from her position as deputy whip because she opposed Prime Minister Malcolm Fraser's simultaneous election referendum proposals, the headline in the *Courier-Mail* screamed, 'Canberra's Blonde Bombshell': 'The blue-eyed blonde from Brisbane, one of the standard-bearers of new-look Liberal politics, has become a bombshell.'[13] The article clearly trivialised a serious — and damaging — political move. Over a decade later, Sullivan attributed the years she spent on the back benches to her decision to cross the floor. It led to a 'very cold' relationship with Fraser, which affected nine years of her political career, she said, and made her 'a lot of enemies'.[14]

Sullivan believes the greatest problem of her 25-year political career was not being trivialised but receiving coverage only for her views on women.[15] The bulk of newspaper articles about her centred on her looks and the discrimination she experienced.

Barbara Wiese: the 'page three girl'

South Australian Labor politician Barbara Wiese was considered a conventionally beautiful woman. This fact made her a constant presence in the major South Australian newspapers, the *Advertiser* and the *News*, in the 1980s. Few articles about her were printed without a photograph or reference to her looks. She was 30 years old when she was elected to the state parliament in 1979, having worked as a short-hand secretary and stenographer, and risen rapidly in the ranks of the ALP executive. The small cluster of male journalists who covered politics in Adelaide sat up. In 1980, when this 'very female feminist' was elected the first woman president of the South Australian Labor Party, the *News* declared it 'the day the ALP went chic'. Tony Baker, who took a particular shine to Wiese, self-consciously gushed that he did not object to her views about women: 'In the case of Barbara Wiese feminism comes in a very fetching package. That observation may be sexist but it is irresistible and apposite because Miss Wiese is as attractive as she is intelligent — and she is highly intelligent.'[16] However, he attributed her success to luck and accident, and alleged her appointment was tokenistic. She was qualified, he wrote, but basically she was 'the right woman in the right place at the right time. Being a good looker in a still male-dominated party also does no harm at all.'[17]

It was difficult to be taken seriously by members of the press who were dumbfounded by the combination of brains and femininity. Wiese told me Baker 'seemed to be surprised that a person could be attractive and intelligent as well if they were a woman, so for that reason he seemed to find me even more attractive.' Male journalists were baffled by her objections, she said, because they saw a focus on her looks as a drawcard: 'Why should I whinge about such a thing when one of the reasons they wanted to come and talk to me was that they found me attractive and interesting?' The Wiese profiles quickly became formulaic: her beauty was both a drawcard and a liability, she was single, and she was beautiful. She was repeatedly asked to explain her achievement, and told journalists she worked hard and had no distractions like a family.[18]

Wiese's profile grew substantially when, aged 35, she became the first female Labor minister in a South Australian cabinet. The *Advertiser* published a feature which began with a reference to her appearance, and expressed surprise that she stayed calm and performed well at her first press conference: 'Barbara Wiese is every inch a politician, albeit an unusually decorative one. She veils her excitement at being South Australia's first woman Labor minister with decorous calm. She sits at press conference, hands in lap, head held high, fielding questions as if she were born to do so.'[19] Gosh! A 35-year-old woman able to answer questions.

Predictably, the question of tokenism emerged instantly. Many female politicians appointed to ministry positions in the 1980s faced criticisms that they were only showpieces, particularly if their elevation came when their parties were publicly acknowledging the need for more women in parliament. If they were ever under intense pressure, made mistakes, or became embroiled in a controversy, allegations that they lacked the necessary skill, grit or competence quickly surfaced. Wiese's appearance was again described as an impediment, and a distraction from being taken seriously. She told reporters:

I found when I first joined the party it took quite a long time for me to make people realise I was a serious person who had something to say and wasn't just a pretty face. But in many ways it's probably also helped me. People are attracted to people they find attractive and in that sense it has probably provided entrees I might not otherwise have had. But having reached that point I really find sometimes it's more difficult to get to the next step — which is to be taken seriously and to have people listen to you — because they are distracted by the first part.[20]

These comments could easily have applied to journalists as well as politicians, as the tenor of the 'beautiful Barbara' articles remained the same. Comparisons were drawn between her appearance: 'attractive, an elegant dresser, and softly spoken in manner', and her competence, as though the two were naturally at odds.

Wiese was conscious early in her political career that photographers were often seeking sexualised shots of her. She told me that when she became junior vice president of Australian Young Labor, 'the photographer was particularly keen for me to turn side-on so that he would be able to get a good silhouette of my bust.' She refused. On a trip to Hawaii, a photographer asked her to pose in a bikini by the pool. She refused. She says photographers 'would want me to recline somewhere or just pose in a position that I didn't think was fitting or becoming for a politician. I wasn't a model or a movie star, I was a politician.' The requests continued when she was a minister, and her profile grew. When minister for tourism, she often appeared on page three. She was photographed bearing a spade and wearing a helmet, drinking a beer at the close of the Adelaide Grand Prix, riding a camel, inspecting a new wing of the Mortlock Library, with hat and torch in a copper mine, in an earth-moving machine at a marina, patting a wombat, feeding a wallaby, and throwing a pamphlet in a bin. Her many appearances prompted cynics to call her a 'Barbie doll' and 'page three girl'.

It was Wiese's female political opponent, Jennifer Cashmore, the opposition's spokesperson on women, who first publicly aired the 'page three girl' tag after a large photo of Wiese with a python curled around her body appeared on page three of the *News* with the headline 'Oh, Minister — you're a charmer'.[21] Politicians and journalists alike sprang to Wiese's defence when Cashmore said she needed to be more than 'a page three girl, charming snakes and spinning dice' while her department was in 'critical condition'. Premier John Bannon, asked if he would be moving Wiese from the ministry, replied, 'Why should I when someone is performing so well? The sour grapes attitude of Ms Cashmore is just extraordinary.'[22]

After Cashmore's attack, Wiese released a seven-page defence to the media. Cashmore was slammed by commentators. Wiese said, 'They just absolutely went for the jugular ... The other side of the coin was that she was a pinched old woman who was being nasty and was suffering from sour grapes because there was this younger, more attractive woman who was having a go. I think it was a double-edged media response which was just as horrible.'

Although many of Wiese's colleagues and talkback hosts had defended her, in an often chivalrous fashion, the debate revived suggestions that Wiese was in cabinet only for cosmetic reasons. Articles suddenly began to appear posing the question: 'Is Barbara Wiese's rising star waning?', accompanied by photographs of Wiese as she opened Port Lincoln Marina, released a dove and inspected a mine. The *Advertiser* alleged Cashmore's comments had 'struck a raw nerve', and that the opposition had targeted Wiese as a 'weak link' in the Bannon cabinet. Critics condemned her parliamentary performance, a perceived aloof bearing at social events, reliance on political advisers, lack of sensitivity to issues, lack of knowledge of local government, and a 'tentative' media performance. The

Advertiser quoted detractors who said Bannon had appointed her as a 'PR asset' in the 1985 election, and that the 'Barbie doll' tag had been earned because of the 'number of occasions she gets attention from press photographers and TV cameramen'. 'It might be sexist to say it,' wrote Kym Tilbrook, 'but photos of Ms Wiese add a certain charm to newspaper columns and television news items. And Ms Wiese is politically wise enough to know that to be photographed holding snakes or climbing down mines will not do her any real harm.'

There was a growing insistence by journalists in the late 1980s and 1990s that women — especially those considered good copy — played a role in shaping their coverage, and benefited from the exposure. The question of whether she was 'more than a pretty face', it seems, was never satisfactorily resolved.

In retrospect, Wiese said she felt 'schizophrenic' about the media during her career because the gushing descriptions embarrassed her. She believes the focus on her looks damaged her relationships with female colleagues. She claims the press only ever conducted 'soft' interviews which probed how and why a woman could enter a male environment, and she found it hard to have people listen to her views on policy. Because of this, the tourism portfolio was considered appropriate for her, she believes, because 'it was always light-hearted; it was froth and bubble in terms of the media focus, and so because I was being viewed that way I could get that part of the message across.' The difficult part was getting across news about policy decisions.[23] She was asked questions about how she managed to be both attractive and intelligent throughout her career: 'You might expect it when you first burst on the scene and that that might be the focus initially — "she's good-looking and gee she's got a brain as well" — but you don't expect to be still reading that article in that vein ten years later.'[24]

Wendy Machin: the 'spunkette' MP from Gloucester

After 'young spunkette MP' Wendy Machin walked into the NSW parliament in the mid-1980s, her physical appearance was frequently described in print. In 1985 Machin, a 27-year-old public relations consultant, was the first woman preselected by the National Party for a winnable NSW seat. Although she differed from older National Party colleagues because she was in favour of a republic, supported the decriminalisation of homosexuality, and was prochoice, this was not discussed in the many 'first woman' stories published when she was elected. 'She wears homemade clothes,' cooed the *Daily Mirror*, 'but manages to look as if she has stepped from the pages of *Vogue*.' Journalists hinted at a wild side of the woman who 'showed a penchant for leather clothes and outdoor rock concerts during her time on the [North Sydney] council'.[25]

A large part of Machin's appeal was assumed to be cosmetic. Reference to her looks and youth were closely followed by expressions of surprise that she was also intelligent. The *Daily Telegraph* defended her from charges of tokenism, raising them and dismissing them in the one breath.[26] When she was later appointed deputy speaker, a profile in the *Daily Telegraph* said she exuded 'cool confidence' about the formidable task ahead, and, although it was not clear why she would have been expected to, Machin was showing 'no signs of apprehension or self-doubt': 'And with her easy demeanour, neatly bobbed platinum blonde hair and short black skirt revealing aerobically exercised legs, Wendy is no pushover.'[27]

Dorian Wild, a gossip columnist with the *Daily Telegraph*, constantly described Machin in sexual, lascivious terms. He instantly dubbed her 'the spunkette MP for Gloucester' who, just ten days after entering parliament, had 'started setting various hearts a-flutter'. Marking her as both sexually desirable and available, he wrote that the 'unwed mother of none' had been wearing some daring dresses: 'On Tuesday it was a tan number with a faint leopard spot ... yesterday it was a white cotton skirt, slit nicely to the knee, and set off by a pair of sporty red and white shoes.' The next day, he wrote the 'unattached' Machin had dressed down for work after the publication of his article on how 'she had been knocking people out with her stunning frocks and whatever'. 'She might be the prettiest thing in the NSW Parliament,' he wrote, 'but ... [Machin] sure knows how to disappoint a chap ... Instead of the white skirt, slit to the knee, that set political pulses racing on Wednesday, she wore a dreary white blouse, stripy blue and grey jacket and a fawn skirt that could have done with an iron.'

Wild clearly liked portraying himself as a provocateur. Following an exchange with Machin, he wrote that she told him, while 'marvelling at the ways of modern journalism', that 'I haven't been making any particular effort. They're dresses I've had in the wardrobe for some time.' Wild soon became the self-appointed monitor of media mentions of Machin, and champion of her sexual attributes. Three years after she was elected, he was still referring to her as a 'spunkette', and wrote that her time in parliament had not 'flattened the womanly shape' of the 'political spunkette'. He wrote that as she walked to her seat in parliament wearing a floral frock, 'Wendy was easily the best thing to look at in Parliament on Wednesday — she strode to her seat flashing an acre of thigh — and a very good thigh indeed'.[28]

Open, unabashed sexism.

Machin said Wild's columns made her feel spied on and were 'just stupid — a bit embarrassing'. She tried to avoid him: 'I just had to cop it ... I wasn't going to sue him or anything like that and that wouldn't have stopped him anyway. So I think you've just got to roll with the punches, take it with good grace, get on with the job and be a bit mature about it, and that in itself eventually sends a message.'[29] Wild told me Machin was a 'good sport' about his columns, because she sensibly 'knew very well that as soon as you start bleating about what the media does to you, the media will do more of it'.[30] Complain, and you will be punished.

Machin's looks were not just the preoccupation of gossip writers. A curious cross-party debate ensued when a National Party MP, Roger Wotton, told parliament that Machin was 'not just a pretty face'. Labor frontbencher Janice Crosio accused him of sexism and was ejected from the house for repeated interjections. Crosio said she was insulted by Wotton's remark that Machin was the only lady in the house.[31] The 'single' Machin responded she would fight her own battles. The *Daily Mirror* splashed it on the front page with the headline 'MP's Good Looks Spark Row: "I'm not just a pretty face"'. Machin was photographed sitting in a chair, smiling, the lens angled to emphasise the long bare legs crossed in front of her.[32] The tabloid newspapers followed the story for several days.[33]

Since the 1970s, it has been the tabloid newspapers that have championed women MPs considered conventionally attractive, caricatured those who have fallen short of the ideal, and given the most prominence to debates about their bodies. This was particularly the case in 1991, after Machin modelled a series of outfits, including gym wear, for her local newspaper, the *Port City Pictorial*. The photographs were first picked up by the *Sydney Morning Herald*'s satirical gossip column, Stay in Touch, which printed a selection of photographs from the 'steamy double-page spread' of Machin — in sleeveless sundress, leopard skin bike shorts and crop top, and strapless evening gown. She was ridiculed for agreeing to be photographed this way: 'National Party MP Lady Wendy Machin shows that being the Deputy Speaker and the Chairman of Committees in State Parliament doesn't stop her burning desire to be a top catwalk siren rivalling even Elle Macpherson.'[34]

Days later, the *Telegraph Mirror* splashed the photograph of the leopard print outfit on its front page, with the headline 'Dressing down for a model MP'. The article concentrated on criticisms from upper house Labor MP Ken Reed, who called the shots 'irresponsible and demeaning to her position'. Machin said they were 'lighthearted', but added, 'Some people could not handle it. They are too immature and for that reason I wouldn't do it again.'[35] The editorial, headed 'Machin whoopee', defended her for bringing humanity to politics and argued Reed's comments were 'nasty, politically inspired rubbish': 'Ms Machin is an attractive as well as an intelligent woman and she is obviously and quite correctly not prepared to disguise any of these facts. There is nothing wrong with that, as indeed her picture shows. Vive la political difference!'[36]

Sue Williams, a columnist for the *Telegraph Mirror*, disagreed. She criticised the 'prim pin-up' for failing to recognise the photographs would be controversial, and argued she was letting women down. 'The day an ambitious, high-profile woman politician tries to win a few more votes by flashing a little flesh and flaunting her fashion sense is a sad one indeed,' she wrote. 'Does she want to be admired for the cut of her curves and the flounce of her frills or for her tough-talking, no-nonsense political acumen? Why can't winsome/lose some Wendy realise the two are mutually exclusive?'[37]

Were they though? Regardless, on the day of her retirement from politics, Machin said her only regret was posing in the leopard print gym gear.[38]

In the early 1990s three events changed the way the press viewed Machin: she got married, had a baby, and became a minister. After the birth of her son, James, in 1992, the references to her hair and sexuality died down almost completely.[39] When in 1993 she was touted as most likely to replace the vacancy in cabinet left by Wal Murray's resignation, she was dubbed 'young mum Wendy Machin'.[40] She was praised for having 'handled the demands of motherhood and an increasingly onerous career'.[41] But the continual questioning about how she coped, she said, implied 'every time something happened I was going to retire'.

In 1993, Machin was appointed minister for consumer affairs: the first female member of the National Party to be a minister in New South Wales. As a minister who was also a mother, there was another distinct change in the way she was portrayed, and the reporting of her views on policy issues such as credit laws, toy safety, junk mail, warranties, door-to-door selling, and HomeFund.[42] The profiles shifted from glamour to her ability to juggle babies with politics, as she, of course, was quickly made a spokeswoman for working mothers. She was quoted refuting a study's findings that daycare is harmful to children, and defending Labor MP Gabrielle Harrison when criticised for not staying home with her son.[43] She formed part of a 'nappy power' push for childcare facilities in Parliament House and portrayed as heralding a new era in NSW politics.[44]

The problem was, as Wiese found, the attributes that helped to create a profile would resurface in times of strife. A 'party girl' tag was also used by members of Machin's party to undermine her and, she believes, affected her political advancement. She claims the added exposure led some of her colleagues to think she was a 'flibbertigibbet' or media junkie who chased publicity. Some still say, off the record, that they consider her to be a lightweight. She now thinks this may explain why she was so rarely asked to chair committees.

However, Machin used her profile to her advantage and insisted women could control stories by the way they looked, and '"manipulate" the media by superficial things such as appearance':

I occasionally would wear something outrageous just for
the hell of it, or I would do something just for fun, and

from time to time I used it. And it would be dishonest of me or any woman to say that they weren't conscious of the benefits of exposure. But women politicians are able still to exploit the difference because we are still a little unusual so from time to time you can get an issue up perhaps by dint of the fact that you are a woman ... The exposure could be a benefit. The problem is, it is hard to control.[45]

And there, as the cliché goes, lies the rub.

*

In 1984, the NSW minister for natural resources, Janice Crosio, was splashed on the front page of the *Sydney Morning Herald* in her swimming costume, sweeping her hair off her face, her breasts spilling out, knee-deep in the Bondi surf. It was a spectacularly revealing photograph, for a politician. Crosio, who was facing allegations that Bondi Beach was polluted by sewage, decided to go for a swim to prove that the water was safe. She alerted journalists, drove to the beach with her press secretary, and stripped down to her swimming costume. 'With a look of steel and a determined stride,' the *Daily Telegraph* wrote, Crosio, surrounded by press photographers and news cameras, 'marched defiantly to the water's edge and dived in'.[46]

Crosio was horrified by what she saw the next day. The photo selected by the *Sydney Morning Herald* for its front page emphasised her deep cleavage, and almost made her look as though she were posing for the cameras, with one arm sweeping her hair off her face, her other hand on her knee. The photographer, Rick Stevens, said he filed several photographs that day, most of them more flattering than the one selected. The *Daily Telegraph* pictured her reclining in the shallows, leaning back as her legs pointed upward, with the heading 'She's up to her neck in it'. The *Sun* printed shots of her backside and breasts with the headline: 'Surfer Jan cops a towelling'. The *Mirror* sniggered, 'She's thrown her weight behind arguments that our beaches are clean and the water crystal clear.'[47]

Crosio now blames her decision to enter the water on a female reporter who egged her on to prove the water was safe, but the media reports implied that she had invited journalists for that specific purpose. Stevens said she had prepared for the shot by coming to the beach in a swimming costume and robe, and repeated the stunt for the *Daily Telegraph*, who arrived late.

What was significant about the front-page photograph of Crosio coming out of the water was the number of times it was used again, in both the *Daily Telegraph* and the *Sydney Morning Herald*, to accompany profiles or simply as a 'head shot' with a political story. When it was used once with a serious article about the delay in relocating stormwater drains, the photograph was cropped to include her breasts.[48] When Crosio leapt to her feet to attack Roger Wotton for calling Wendy Machin 'not just a pretty face', Premier Nick Greiner waved the photograph in the air, reminding her of her embarrassment, again pitting women against each other. This was five years after the photograph was first published.[49]

*

Crosio was not the only one to be featured on the front page in her bathing suit. When Joan Kirner, who later became the first female premier of Victoria in 1992, was appointed deputy premier in 1989, the front page of the *Australian* displayed an old photograph of her sitting in a spa in a swimming costume. The headline was 'Kirner shapes up as first woman Deputy Premier'. Joan Kirner, who as premier was nicknamed 'Miss Piggy' and 'Mother Russia', was frequently criticised about her body shape. But the caricature

Many Sydneysiders still remember the day Labor minister Janice Crosio stripped down to her bathing suit at a press conference and landed on the front page of the *Sydney Morning Herald*, 21 December 1984. *Rick Stevens/Sydney Morning Herald*

used in cartoons was not just of a well-proportioned woman but a harassed housewife, drawn with drops of sweat or frustration springing from her brow. The subliminal message, she suggested later, was 'How could an ordinary housewife cope?': 'And I'm sure that's why they constantly want to photograph you in the kitchen, because they can cope if you maintain your links with being an ordinary housewife. But once you don't, it's not you who can't cope, it's them.'

Her friend and cabinet colleague, Caroline Hogg, was appalled by the press Kirner received:

I used to ring her first thing in the morning at 6.30 and say, 'Listen, there is a bloody awful cartoon in the *Sun* ...' It was very painful for some time. It was very painful for me as her closest friend in the cabinet at the time ... It was the way she was portrayed physically in cartoons. For middle-aged women that's hard stuff. I think however much one is in control of all those things to do with appearance, nonetheless, to see oneself day-in, day-out blown up into some terrible overweight bullying polka-dotted figure which couldn't be further from the truth was just disgusting.[50]

Then Kirner confronted the cartoonist Geoff Hook, drew the media's attention to the phenomenon, and elicited public sympathy in a kind of media masterstroke. At first, she said, she took it personally, which encouraged both Hook and the newspaper. But one day she cornered Hook and asked, 'Why do you do it? I don't even own a polka-dot dress, and I'm certainly not harassed all the time.' He responded, 'Well, Mrs Kirner, I know how to draw Henry Bolte and I know how to draw Bob Hawke, or John Cain or Paul Keating, but I've never had to draw a woman in power before and I don't know how to draw you.'

After this conversation, she viewed the cartoons not as a personal but political attack: 'The editor and his cartoonist were showing their own prejudices — their view of how a housewife could cope — to get at me politically.' As she told a conference in 1994, 'I could then ask the questions, "Who is this attack serving?"; "What is the intent behind focusing on my appearance?"; "Who profits if I respond in kind?"; "How can I turn the attacks around?" Having asked and answered those questions, I could then shape my response. And that was to maintain an image, my own, which treated myself and other women with respect and integrity.'[51] Kirner fought back, by showing herself in the media in positions of control, visiting factories and making speeches, and displaying a sense of humour with events like the fundraising 'Spot-on Joan' concert. While she did eventually agree to change her hairstyle and changed the cut and colour of her clothes, she firmly controlled her image and refused to do anything she was uncomfortable with. She placed the issue of sexism in the media on the public agenda in Melbourne, provoking dozens of articles dissecting gender bias. She won public sympathy for what commentators called a 'dignified' way of reacting to sexist comment and criticism, while gaining the respect of many journalists for not 'forever whingeing about the media'. As John Hurst wrote, 'She resisted pressure to do anything against her will, however beneficial it might seem in public relations terms.'[52] Kirner, as premier, was in a privileged position, with greater access to the media and more power to dictate the political agenda than a backbencher or even a minister, but her story is an important one.

In the federal sphere, South Australian senator Amanda Vanstone had suffered constant jibes about her weight since being elected in 1985, particularly when she was the high-profile minister for education. She was nicknamed 'Fatty' and 'Roseanne', told she 'couldn't get a job as a road hump', featured as a gargoyle in the Sydney Gay and Lesbian Mardi Gras parade, and had plump effigies burnt by angry students.[53] The taunts entered cyberspace and, at one point, on an American website called Johnny Howard's Comedy Store, images of her face were pasted on pornographic photographs of obese women. For a long time she was called 'The Incredible Bulk'. But the quick-witted Vanstone fought it off — famously telling one of her political opponents: 'Better big in the backside than bulldust for brains.'

What kind of impact does this coverage have? Well, firstly, it is a serious disincentive for other women to join politics. Heather Southcott, formerly a Democrat in the South Australian parliament, said the caricatures of her figure led her to abandon any political ambitions. 'I decided that unless I could lose weight, have a streamlined image, wear smart executive clothes, I would not be any good to the party because I would be a sitting duck for cartoonists.'[54] Secondly, it is an added pressure for women already in the public eye. Ros Kelly told columnist Miranda Devine that she had only begun to worry about her weight after she became a politician. 'After a while in politics,' she said, 'I perfectly understand why women get bulimic and get eating disorders.'[55] She told another female journalist she never wore pants because she thought her bottom was too big.[56]

*

Early in 2001, federal sport and tourism minister Jackie Kelly received a letter instructing her to get a makeover. The anonymous complainant wrote: 'Where do you [and Bronwyn Bishop] buy your clothes — St Vinnies' op shop? Ever heard of a makeover? You and Bronwyn (lost the plot) Bishop are badly in need of one. Two of the most pathetic frumps in Federal Parliament. You might look all right in McDonald's Parramatta like that, but not in Parliament in front of cameras, representing the country.'

The *Sunday Telegraph* came to her defence, splashing the story indignantly on page three with a headline: 'Kelly was a victim of sexist hatemail'. The woman often called 'Trakkie Dakkie Jackie' told reporter Nathan Vass that women should just be themselves and not worry about 'the whole image thing': 'Women in public life are under enormous pressure to live up to impossible expectations, [like] we should all look like Elle Macpherson. I have news for you — it ain't going to happen. My advice to women is this: just be true to yourself, don't try to cater to other people's image of you and, even under enormous criticism, just stick to it.' She earned some respect for that approach. When Vass referred to a Melbourne newspaper that had quoted a 'style guru', saying

Kelly needed to get a haircut and 'her whole appearance needs work', Kelly's response was, 'I am not paid to be a cover girl. I am paid to achieve things for my community.'[57]

She told me the story was a boon for her:

> [It] resonated with my electorate because the women in my electorate said, hey if it's an occasion, we can get dolled up — what woman doesn't look gorgeous when you pluck a few eyebrows, shave a few legs, put on a frock, makeup ... But at the end of the day, we've got to get the kids in the car, packed up — you can't look like that all the time and that's what's made me so electable in my electorate; I don't have that classic Liberal do, that rigid, you always looks the same, twin-set and pearls ... I think it's been pretty important for me to bust out of that pigeonhole.

The fact that the *Sunday Telegraph* wrote a sympathetic story is an interesting shift. In the 1980s, tabloid papers were fond of asking image consultants to 'make over' female MPs, and turn them into what they considered to be sexy, modern women. This often happened when the MPs were under threat, as though it were kindly advice offered from an older sister about how to pick up boys at the local pub. The consultants tended to advise the women either to look more masculine by exuding authority, arrogance and power, or to look more youthful and beautiful: like models, not mothers. In 1984, in an article about the alleged lack of style of Australia's women politicians, Janine Cohen from the *Melbourne Herald* quoted a 'national wardrobe consultant' who claimed 'poor image and dress sense hold women politicians back'. Alongside the article ran two photos, comparing the Victorian minister for community services, Pauline Toner, and the wife of the NSW premier, Jill Hickson, a former model. Toner was dressed for work in a jacket, skirt, court shoes and pearls, while a younger, leaner Hickson oozed glamour in a shimmery evening gown, with a cape, and a corsage pinned on her shoulder. The fact that Toner was dressed for work and Hickson for a party went unrecognised.[58]

Some women MPs actually agreed to be 'made over' due to pressure from their parties as well as journalists. When faced with threats to her leadership, Janet Powell, who had succeeded Janine Haines as leader of the Democrats, agreed to have a makeover filmed by '60 Minutes'. Powell, a former teacher, had a strong intellect and debating style, according to colleagues, but a low profile. She had been called matronly, 'the forgotten woman of politics', and nicknamed 'Senator Sensible'. She had performed 'stolidly in a hard role', but, just like future leader Meg Lees, she was said to lack the 'razzamatazz' necessary for a 'marketable image and flair'.[59]

In August 1991, newspapers revealed the white-haired and bespectacled former Adelaide academic John Coulter, 60, and Senator Paul McLean, who also wore glasses and was aged 54, would be running against Powell in a leadership spill.[60] Although neither of her opponents were catwalk models, or appeared to be lusted over by female journalists, the following day Powell agreed she would consult professional image-makers.[61] The *Herald-Sun* contacted a range of experts who said they were 'itching to go to work' on Powell, 48. In a telling comment, one image consultant said, 'She looks like a suburban mum. There's nothing wrong with suburban mums — I love them dearly — but I don't want one telling me what to do.' Another said she should lose weight, since 'trim and taut people look ready for action', as well as change her clothes: 'They say "let's go shopping", not "let's get cracking and get down to business".' A third consultant said again that she looked too 'mumsy' and should seek out tailored clothing. This wasn't a criticism, she said, but Senator Powell's public and peers were looking for a leader, not a mother.'[62] It's a

YES, MINISTER!

Ros Kelly casts off her no-nonsense political gear to show her sexy side

WE ALWAYS knew it, now here's the proof – Ros Kelly is political dynamite! In her favourite little black dress, blonde hair glamorously coiffed and handsome features highlighted to great advantage, the Minister for Arts, Sport, the Environment and Territories faces up to the camera like a cover girl. Rather like a certain Prime Minister's wife we know.

Paul Keating must be rubbing his hands with glee at having discovered two secret weapons so far into the election campaign – his wife Annita, who dazzled the electorate with a glossy fashion spread (complete with straightened hair), and now Ros, who proves without doubt that you can be a pollie and a super-attractive woman too!

However, it took a great deal of persuasion to get the Minister to agree to a few hours of pampering and a photographic shoot for *Woman's Day* at Sydney's Park Lane hotel.

"It takes a very confident woman in politics to be seen as a woman," she explains. But it *was* just days before her 45th birthday, so why not!

Ros arrived at Scissors Haircutters in the Town Hall Connection, Sydney, with eight-year-old son Ben in tow.

After washing the Minister's hair, stylist Joseph Bitar gave her a soothing scalp massage to ease away the stresses of the campaign trail. He then blow-dried her hair and curled the ends for a fuller, more romantic look.

Then it was time for glamour make-up. Natural colours lightly applied emphasised Ros's wonderful bone structure, and bold red lips completed her stunning new look.

She chose to wear her own slinky one-shouldered, side-split Carla Zampatti gown for our photographs, offset by elegant earrings from David Jones.

Ben preferred his Mum as she was before our pampering, but Ros was thrilled with the makeover. "It would make an interesting campaign photograph!" she says. ∎

Story: Angela Donaldson

Ros Kelly posed in an evening gown for *Woman's Day* on 8 March 1993 after a great deal of persuasion — five years before Cheryl Kernot frocked up for the *Australian Women's Weekly*. *Woman's Day* revealing dichotomy. It was decided Powell had failed to project confidence, egotism, power and assurance, and she was advised to dress in navy blue.

Despite her efforts, Powell was dumped by her party — for reasons discussed in chapter nine — after little more than a year in the position, and John Coulter was voted in as leader. Powell resigned from the party less than a year later, after 15 years as a member of the Democrats. She stood as an independent in the next election, but failed to gain a seat.[63]

Most of the makeover articles are just silly and trivial. When Carmen Lawrence became premier of Western Australia, a Sunday newspaper asked local fashion consultants to make over her hairstyle, glasses and clothing. Pauline Hanson, who has defied many of the conventions of political behaviour to her advantage, was filmed being 'made over' for her senatorial race in March 2001. Yet frequently, if women do not measure up to an ideal of young, slim, stylish femininity, they are advised to lose weight, cut their hair and buy new clothes. If they do measure up, and newspapers feature articles that portray them as attractive or desirable, they were often victim to charges of superficiality and tokenism.

*

The scrutiny of public figures intensified in a culture of celebrity where politicians were encouraged to groom themselves as visual performers, cultivate a profile, and measure the amount, not the substance, of the ensuing publicity as the standard of their success. Many male politicians tinker with their appearance to satisfy the demands of a fickle electorate and image-driven media. Prime Minister John Howard capped his teeth and trimmed his eyebrows, former Labor leader Kim Beazley was on several diets, and John Hewson changed his banker-style shirts. Bob Carr and

Peter Cook dumped spectacles for contact lenses, and Bob Collins went on a salad diet. Andrew Peacock was famous for his vanity, his hair (allegedly dyed), perennial tan, and smooth demeanour. While there have been some male politicians who have been the subject of interest or speculation due to their dress — such as South Australian premier Don Dunstan for wearing pink shorts to parliament; federal MP Al Grassby, who was likened to a 'spiv' or used car salesman because of his flamboyant fashion sense; former NSW Labor premier Barry Unsworth for his cardigans; and Prime Minister Paul Keating for wearing Italian suits — no male politician's body has been the subject of the kind of debate Machin or Wiese has experienced. When former prime minister Harold Holt was photographed in his swimsuit in the 1960s, it was the bodies of his daughters-in-law who surrounded him, and not his own, that were most commented on. Labor PM Bob Hawke also appeared occasionally in his Speedos without exciting comment.

In the noughties, things were changing for men. One notable example was the week-long debate in the national media about Mark Latham's 'manboobs', snapped when he was playing a game of cricket in a t-shirt. The *Daily Telegraph* also ran a page two story about Latham's hair being unkempt, accusing him of having too frequent bad-hair days: 'Other politicians have battled an image issue and the Opposition leader's thatch appears to be his bugbear. His staff freely admit he sometimes sports a "rooster" — the technical term for that annoying clump of hair that springs up on the back of the head.' A Sydney hairdresser advised him to use 'some serious product' to keep it down. Latham's adviser told the journalist he did not believe it was a serious issue in an election year, but the reporter retorted: 'Prime Minister John Howard's eyebrows made headlines when they became unruly. One colleague remarked at one stage the PM appeared to have two koalas asleep on his forehead.'[64] And here

I must confess — *mea culpa* — that I once wrote a story about David Kemp, then minister for education, shaving off the facial hair which had earned him the moniker 'weird beard'.[65] I cringe!

Often it is fellow politicians, not journalists, who are the worst culprits. An unnamed Victorian Liberal backbencher caused some excitement when he was widely quoted saying the then deputy opposition leader Louise Asher had not performed well but was 'the one with good legs who wears short skirts'.[66] Victorian National Party MP Ron Best won a political Ernie in 2001 for saying to Minister Monica Gould that her 'breasts were so small that her front was indistinguishable from her back'. Erstwhile NSW opposition leader Kerry Chikarovski was accused of having hormones to make her voice deeper, and of wearing long skirts to hide her legs. Still, when Labor MP Peter Black shouted across the chamber at her in 2000, telling her she should 'get a facelift', he was chastised by both journalists and colleagues. The *Sunday Telegraph* ran a story, headed 'Giving this MP a taste of his own medicine', where a plastic surgeon claimed that with $20,000 of plastic surgery, he could make Black look 20 years younger.

Many of the first young female MPs to come into parliament cleverly capitalised on all kinds of media attention. But while some women have been ogled and petted by journalists, others have been ignored, or lampooned for not being thin or pretty enough. It all adds up to a scrutiny that can make it very uncomfortable for women in the public eye. And, as Natasha Stott Despoja was to discover, it can make their position far less secure.

CHAPTER SEVEN

Natasha Stott Despoja: the 'impossible princess'

The chief glory of a woman is not to be talked of, said
Pericles, himself a much-talked-of man.
> — Virginia Woolf, *A Room of One's Own*

I have to be pretty if I am going to get over and I have to get
over if I am going to f … the system up. And I'm gonna f …
it up.
> — Courtney Love, quoted by Natasha Stott Despoja
> in 'Stott in the name of Love', *Sydney Morning Herald*,
> 22 January 1999

The first time I saw Natasha Stott Despoja was at the ARIA
Awards in the year 2000, when she was photographed with a
fake tattoo and accused of posing as a pseudo celebrity. I was
with a star-struck journalist friend who could not keep his eyes
off her, and claimed she was the most desirable woman in the
country. The second was in the wee hours of Mardi Gras 2002,
upstairs in the VIP room, where board members, party organisers
and their friends unwind with cold beer or cups of tea and watch

the crowds grind and soar on the dance floor in the Royal Hall of Industries below. I was standing in the bathroom, squashed between a couple of enormous drag queens and a purple-clad photographer. Stott Despoja emerged from a cubicle, pale and tiny, and stood in front of the mirror, adjusting her hair. She was immaculate, untouched by the sweat and steam of the dance floor. A drag queen, towering over her in painful-looking heels, cooed, and tried to crush her to her heavily padded chest: 'Oh, *Natasha*!' Stott Despoja smiled, then washed her hands. Looking apologetic, the photographer leaned forward and asked if she could take a shot. The drag queen beamed and looked hopefully at Stott Despoja, who politely shook her head and walked out.

Everywhere she went, the photogenic Stott Despoja was a target. At 26, she was the youngest woman to be elected to the federal parliament, and she capitalised on this fact in order to be able to air her views about young people and their alienation from politics. When she was elected leader of the Democrats, there was a palpable excitement among many women, particularly those disaffected with mainstream politics and the suited men who controlled it. Friends from a range of parties said they would consider voting for or even joining the Democrats once she was leader, and there was much interest in the fact that a woman of her age was wielding serious political power. Many journalists were unrelenting fans who praised her with fawning prose; likened her to the vulnerable, blonde Princess Diana; and wrote flatteringly about her physical appearance. They defended her from attacks, and gave her ample space to air her views on a range of subjects, including the opinion pages.

The fact that many in the media liked her was, predictably, used as evidence that she was shallow. When I worked in the federal press gallery I was struck by the cynicism of the reporters towards Stott Despoja's appearances in forums which had endeared her to my peers — she outwitted blokes on the ABC TV show 'Good News Week', made politics accessible and somehow possible when talking on Triple J, and showed herself to be human. But according to a growing sentiment in the gallery, she had a high profile and, ergo, was vain. She was a show pony, a celebrity, a ballot box Barbie, a woman who was young, good-looking and therefore insubstantial. *Sure*, many of them argued over time, she looks good in a frock, but what about *policy*? The 'more sizzle than sausage' cliché was repeated to a mind-numbing extent. She was forced on countless occasions to defend herself from the charge, and stubbornly refused to change her strategy of appearing in as many different forums — and in many different guises — as she could, including *Cosmopolitan*, *Cleo*, *Rolling Stone* and *Juice*.

Reading through the reports again while working on this book, I felt frustrated with the press, who did not recognise how complicit they were in this. Given the prevalence of these charges, why not sit her down and grill her about a raft of policies, instead of just speculating about her intellectual depth? It was odd. Why not count the number of times she had spoken, and what she had fought for? Only a sprinkling of senior journalists took this approach.

Stott Despoja, introduced as a 'part-time politician and full-time enchantress' on 'Good News Week', and voted the 70th sexiest woman in the world by men's magazine *FHM* in 1998, was the ultimate 'media tart' journalists eagerly pursued then mocked. She once wrote that women should 'manipulate the media' in order to get their voices heard. The problem was, the press who adored and replicated her image eventually despised her for allowing them to do so.

Since it was the media who first touted and endorsed Stott Despoja as leader, then dismissed her as naive and lightweight, the key question is this: was her media strategy wrong? Should she have pruned back the personality cult in order to impress the heavyweights of the gallery? Or was she just battling a series of dodgy assumptions about young women? Was there, as a good Democrat might ask, a middle way, between media darling and media tart?

*

Stott Despoja's name was synonymous with Doc Marten shoes from the moment she walked into the Senate. They became the defining symbol of her youth. Sensible, chunky, and solid, Docs were popular among middle-class youth of university campuses, and feminists who refused to wear high heels. They became a cliché in her press coverage, starting from the day of her swearing-in ceremony in 1995, when she decided to wear a pair of Doc Martens — they were comfortable, practical and emblematic of a younger generation — and the press hungrily lapped it up, with headlines like: 'These boots will walk right into the Senate'; 'Senator goes in — boots and all'.[1] In a piece she wrote the next day for the *Canberra Times*, Stott Despoja referred to her shoes several times. 'My decision to wear Doc Martens into the chamber was a sign of the times — and a need for sensible shoes and, in some respects, it is the dress code of a generation.'[2]

The Doc Martens references lived on for years — to complain about it revived it. But Stott Despoja continued to refer to them in interviews and speeches. Her frustrations with the 'Doc Martens' image were reported throughout her bid to be leader of the party five years later.[3] She was forced to defend herself from the charge that she was a 'Doc-wearing pretender' in at least two newspapers. When she wore heels, instead of Docs, this was reported on.

When I asked her if she regretted the Doc Martens image, she responded:

> I'm proud of a symbolism that says I represent my generation
> and heaven help the woman with a punk hairdo when she
> gets in ... It makes conformity very appealing, it really does
> ... I walked into an environment where there were not a lot
> of women and there was no one my age or younger — did I
> really want to emphasise that difference any more? I didn't
> need to, I didn't want to, but inevitably that was part of the
> role of me working with the media and part of the media's
> excitement or role to play as well because that sold stories
> and that got my party publicity. Pretty simple exchange.

Along with the Docs, the other symbols of Stott Despoja's youth were her predilection for Diet Coke and chocolate, along with her use of the phrase 'cool bananas'. She admitted she had smoked marijuana, watched the cult American soap 'Melrose Place', and went to clubs and raves. As Democrats spokeswoman for youth affairs, she put out press releases headed 'Gen X has Senator on Side'. She was the champion of 'Gen HECS' in the university debate. She was not the only person under 30 to have been elected to parliament (Paul Keating, Gary Punch, and Christopher Pyne were all elected at 25, and Bill O'Chee at 24), but her gender, position, and approach cemented her status as The Voice of Youth.

In part, Stott Despoja's 'cool' image was a poor reflection on the conservative and stifling atmosphere of federal parliament, and the fact that there were few other young people there. To an outside observer, she appeared to be an earnest, serious young woman committed to accessing power for herself and her party. It amazed me when I heard people call her a bimbo — as though a woman who spent her precious university years at Democrats meetings, lobbying, electioneering, and politicking could really be classified as someone with a head full of bubbles. Many young people spend their 20s clubbing, travelling, making mistakes and having tragic relationships. Yet because the neatly dressed, and apparently well-behaved, Stott Despoja wore a backpack and Doc Martens, and listened to bands like Powderfinger, she was constantly described as 'hip', 'groovy', 'chic' and 'cutting edge'. For those not sedated by the valium of federal politics, 'Australia's coolest MP' was not radical but fairly normal. This was in fact her appeal. Buckets of young women drank Diet Coke; lecture halls and rave parties were studded with Doc Martens; and millions listened to Triple J. The fact that she spoke politics so forcefully and effectively at the same time is what made her so popular.

In the mid-1990s, the young, photogenic senator had a protracted honeymoon with the press. Many journalists were lyrical about her attributes. They were sympathetic to her claims that she was patronised because of her youth. She was frequently profiled. A close examination of her clippings files reveals Stott Despoja was active across a range of her portfolios in the 1990s, particularly tertiary education.[4]

Stott Despoja's success was such that when her party leader Cheryl Kernot defected to the Labor Party in October 1997 she was immediately touted as a potential leader. She declared the party should be bold, and asked reporters 'whether the media or the public is bold enough to back a woman under 30 in a leadership [position] in Australian parties. I'm not so sure they would.' A Taverner poll found she was the most popular candidate. She later said she thought the media was pushing her to run: 'I would have to say that 98 per cent of the publications were saying either "You have no choice" or "Whether she likes it or not, this is her responsibility" ... It was almost this anointment by the media.'[5]

After much agonising, she decided not to stand, and was elected deputy leader. She told Virginia Trioli that she was conscious of the fact that her high profile was important to the Democrats, and that she was in the best position to promote her party. She wondered out loud: 'Where am I best spent? Unlimited travel running around the country, campaigning for everybody, doing high-profile media stuff, or is it controlling a parliamentary team and being responsible for mammoth legislation, some of which I don't have a handle on?'[6]

From this point on, the possibility of leadership for the bright young spark who pounded the popularity polls like an Easter Show strongman preoccupied many journalists. And she continued her policy work.[7]

*

Allegations that Stott Despoja was light on policy and heavy on publicity emerged less than a year after she entered parliament. The genesis of this criticism came earlier. Her opponents frequently told journalists that she was preselected after an ABC-TV report showed her being 'photographed like a *Vogue* model'. By late 1997, journalists were writing that she was 'wearied and worried by constant accusations of being a media manipulator, a headline hound'. She became preoccupied with her image. Virginia Trioli wrote that her 'cognisance of the media, its influence and its appetite is complete'.[8]

The accusations grew louder the following year, when she appeared in a slinky Armani dress in *Cleo*, as 'dewily doe-eyed as any starlet'. It was a glamorous but not overtly sexual shot, as she reclined with her hair waved and face made up. She later defended her decision: 'Many women voters want alternatives to boring old men in government. The National Party boys call me the *Cleo* Senator, they go — how embarrassing! — but why shouldn't we do this? These men are stunned when you tell them the magazine circulations.'[9] She repeatedly insisted she did not drop IQ points when she put on a dress, and that: 'You can be a

179

politician and look however you want.' She added that she had refused to wear fake breasts with the dress as requested.

Many men in the gallery and political parties told me they desired Stott Despoja. Editors were observed blushing in her presence. Websites were devoted to her, and bedecked with glamour shots. A former gallery stalwart told me that after one reporter had a relationship with Stott Despoja, all the other men in the gallery were fascinated, and plied him for details. Another gallery reporter asked me why, if she wanted to avoid scrutiny of her personal life, she dated journalists: 'How could she keep her private life private if she was having serial affairs with the media? There was no separation; it was a convergence.' Even in sympathetic articles, she was frequently asked about her boyfriend, and if she planned to get married. Once, Greg Callaghan from the *Weekend Australian* wrote: 'I quickly scrub my next question — what kind of men do you fancy? — and leap straight to my Serious Issues list.'[10]

The interesting thing about Stott Despoja was that although she was aware of the criticisms, she did not moderate her behaviour. Over time, she cut her hair shorter, replaced the Docs with heels, started to wear glasses, and adopted neatly tailored suits, but she continued to appear on a variety of television shows and in women's magazines. Her rationale was fairly consistent: she was being human, making politics accessible, the public loved her, and the requests continued to flow in — so why change for the dictates of the gallery? She also justified it on a feminist basis, insisting women were multi-dimensional and complex beings.

In a feature-length piece she wrote for the *Sydney Morning Herald*, Stott Despoja interviewed singer and actor Courtney Love, champion of bad-girl 'femme-inism', and paralleled her own experience at the hands of the press with Love's. It is this article that provides the best insight into Stott Despoja's thinking.[11] 'Why is it,' Stott Despoja asks, 'that the minute you put on a glamorous frock or wear flattering tennis shorts, your IQ is presumed to plummet?' She quotes Love saying, 'I have to be pretty if I am going to get over and I have to get over if I am going to f ... the system up. And I'm gonna f ... it up.' It was, then, a means to an end. Love's target was music, Stott Despoja's politics.

But the cumulative effect of Stott Despoja's appearances in the mainstream media seemed to confirm the suspicions in the press gallery that the 'new kid on the block' lacked serious political intent. Querying the length of time Stott Despoja spent in Albania visiting refugee camps while missing a tax debate in the Senate, the chief political reporter of the *Daily Telegraph*, Malcolm Farr, wrote in 1999:

> Senator Stott Despoja will still be in demand as a guaranteed crowd puller for TV shows, quiz nights and speaking engagements requiring celebrity reinforcement. But her commitment and depth as a politician and Democrat deputy leader are being questioned by her peers, of all parties, as never before. The general and strengthening view is that Senator Stott Despoja's good at being seen and heard but not so good at the hard yakka and teamwork of politics ...[12]

Asked what he thought of Stott Despoja in 2003, Farr answered:

> I think there are few people more lightweight in this building. She has a view of herself which is compounded by huge self-absorption which she uses to ignore or treat with contempt any criticism. She lives in a fantasy world, in my view ... There's a definite view that there's not much substance there, which is unfortunate because ... Stott Despoja does get up and join in debates with a certain amount of information and fluency which is not something

181

you can say of a lot of people, the Greens' leader included.
I guess I am being a bit harsh. Because she is an attractive
young woman, gnarled and ancient creatures such as myself
take that view, but I don't know, it's hard to get rid of ...
[*Why?*] Because she doesn't have any substance [*laughs*].

He was not alone. But he was being harsh. She was clearly hardworking and intelligent. Surely one of the surest signs that Stott Despoja had 'substance' — or a clearly enunciated and thought-out philosophical position and agenda for the party — was her stance on the goods and services tax in 1999. She indicated at an early stage that she would not support a GST on books, and stuck to it as her party leader, Meg Lees, negotiated with the government over it. Instead of being interpreted as an act of principle, her resolve was interpreted as a 'dummy spit', a babyish tantrum from a young woman unaccustomed to the heat of the political fray. The fact that it ended up being her primary qualification for the leadership, along with her high profile and popularity, shows how skewed that commentary was.

Before the GST legislation had passed, she was isolated by her colleagues for saying the Democrats had 'no room for compromise' on the GST, and was warned not to speak on the subject by leader Meg Lees. Then, in the defining moment of her political career, Meg Lees negotiated a compromise with John Howard which enabled the passage of the GST with caveats: it would not apply to fresh food; income tax cuts for high earners would be cut back; diesel fuel excise cuts would be restricted; and almost $1 billion would be put into environmental protection. Stott Despoja declared that she would exercise her right to a conscience vote under the party rules to oppose the GST. Initially she intended to vote against the clauses dealing with books and newspapers — which she called a 'tax on knowledge' — but later she decided to vote against the entire package.

According to a senior lecturer in politics at Monash University, Nick Economou, each time the party had done deals with the government instead of keeping the 'bastards honest' their vote had plummeted. He believed voters were angry about the GST and did not want to see the Democrats as a mainstream party that did deals with the government of the day. The media monitoring group Rehame found that after the passage of the GST 70 per cent of talkback callers supported Stott Despoja, and less than 3 per cent had anything positive to say about Lees — most were vicious. Rehame's managing director, Peter Maher, said the Lees GST deal was 'as big an issue with the public as we've ever analysed. Most people think the Democrats let them down.' People thought Lees compromised too quickly, and could have won more concessions if she had toughed it out. Stott Despoja, meanwhile, came out 'smelling of roses', Maher said. 'I've never seen a politician do as well, when her party was being vilified, as Natasha this week.'[13]

From this point Stott Despoja became a lightning rod for discontented Democrats. Stott Despoja wrote letters insisting she was not petulant, but principled. Cartoonist Alan Moir depicted her from this point on with a dummy in her mouth, sucking vigorously and looking cross — her eyes wide, eyebrows knitted, folding her arms tightly across her chest. He called her 'Gnashing Despot Spoiler'.[14] When I asked him about this, he pointed out he had drawn other Democrats — Andrew Bartlett and Meg Lees — with dummies in their mouths, and that it was a reflection on the party:

> *AM*: The bigger parties ... crush each other like dinosaurs. The Democrats tend to be so polite about it that in the end when they got angry about something it just sounded like a hissyfit ... She made a big thing of being the baby of the Senate of course when she came in, so it became

an amusing thing, so I put a dummy in her mouth. Just as
with a baby, it became a good tool when she became a bit
angry about things; I'd have her sucking very hard ...

JB: Did you think she was too young for the job?

AM: Yeah. Yes, especially when in leadership you have to do
deals. Meg Lees was a realist. Cheryl Kernot at her best
was good ...

JB: Why did you think she was too young?

AM: Politics is the art of compromise. She's still a little
bit too idealistic, and not sceptical enough of other
politicians.

Journalists soon began to ask if Stott Despoja could withstand
the pressure. She was not sure if she would run for her seat
again, because she was sick of the scrutiny, personal intrusion
and name-calling.[15] An article in the *Sun-Herald*, headed 'Suicide
Blonde: Stott Despoja under pressure over GST — and love life',
reported that Stott Despoja enjoyed the limelight, which she
had cultivated, but when it turned into a spotlight, 'the pleasure
turn[ed] sour.' The journalist's cynicism about Stott Despoja's
motivations was clear: 'While her leader, Meg Lees, and fellow
Democrats were grappling with the massive tax package 10
days ago, Stott Despoja was preoccupied with herself.' The list
went on: her health was suffering, she was too thin-skinned
to be leader, she was hurt by a media backlash, and she was
offended by questions about her private life.[16] The next day, Stott
Despoja fired back, claiming party members were undermining
her because of her position on the GST. In an outburst she later
regretted, she accused party elders of trying to white-ant her with
malicious, vexatious comments. This is what senior journalist
Christine Wallace of the *Australian* says was her great tactical
error — letting people know she was sensitive to this criticism:

> She allowed herself mentally to be vulnerable to that
> campaign against her. If she had continued on her merry
> way generating reams of publicity, getting huge amounts of
> media space and continuing to be a charismatic and popular
> Democrats leader, she'd be there today. But she was a little
> young, not quite seasoned and ... she allowed herself to be
> seen to be publicly sensitive to it and respond to it, and once
> that starts happening things are going to begin to unravel.[17]

Stott Despoja's complaints about media intrusion also galled those who had seen her enjoy, and exploit, the media attention. The *Australian* called her naive and asked her to choose between 'playing at politics and being in a very tough business. It is essentially a choice between thick skinned participation and no petulance — or no participation at all.'[18] Frank Devine told her to get over her 'spotlight withdrawal pains' and start 'filling her pretty head with knowledge and ideas' on youth unemployment and education.[19] The *Australian*'s Peter Nicholson drew a cartoon which showed Stott Despoja lying on her bed writing in a diary how enemies were spreading rumours she was a 'political BULIMIC and lightweight ... I must never trust anyone over 30 — specially now I'm 29¾.' News Limited columnist Piers Akerman, who reserved a particular brand of vitriol for female politicians, said she had enjoyed too many years 'of revelling in her role as Princess Leia, the virgin victim of Australian politics'.[20]

After the passage of the GST legislation, journalists were obsessed with a potential leadership spill, and followed the daily movements of the fractured parliamentary group of Democrats — and an increasingly isolated Stott Despoja — with interest. In late 1999, the *Sydney Morning Herald* sooled triple Walkley Award-winning investigative journalist Gerard Ryle onto her case. The resulting article, 'Behind the Party Girl', which appeared on 8 January 2000, was the first serious, forensic treatment of her public statements and the image she had presented for the media. Ryle found some inconsistencies, and described her as a woman no longer considered the heir apparent to the leadership. He accused her of exaggerating some of the details of her family background to create a story of hardship.[21] He mocked the idea that her 30th birthday celebrations were private, arguing that weeks before, details of her search for the right dress had appeared in gossip columns: 'And in case you missed anything, there were the dress and the woman, three weeks later, spread over two pages of the *Australian Women's Weekly*.'

Stott Despoja told me she thought this was 'the most startling, most appalling piece of journalism about a woman in public life'. She contacted the *Herald* half an hour after her second interview with Ryle. The *Herald*'s editor at the time, Paul McGeough, said, 'There was some communication over this story, but in fairness to her, I don't think she wanted the story pulled so much as she was troubled by how Ryle might use some information that he had ... All I can say about the story that was published was that it went through the normal *Herald* editing process.' Ryle told me that by the end of his research he had come to the view that she had manipulated the media, but that he was conducting a legitimate and fairly standard investigation into a public figure:

> I understand she blames that article for ruining her career. In truth, I was just the first one to question her ... I always liked her and still do, but she was not different to other politicians; she had carefully built this image herself. She was a public figure, she had willingly sought publicity, and had been profiled hundreds of times before ... live by the sword, die by the sword. It wasn't brilliant; it was just basic journalistic research.

Running for leader: January 2001

In February 2001, after the ACT Democrats called for a leadership ballot, Stott Despoja decided to run. The duel was largely between the left-leaning Democrats and those who wanted a more mainstream party which would negotiate over key legislation and extract concessions. But the focus on appearance was paramount throughout: it was portrayed as a contest between a young, good-looking lightweight and a more substantial but dowdy elder. Lees was given a very hard time. Peter Ruehl described her as having 'all the charisma of a laxative'.[22] Mike Seccombe wrote that Lees had 'as one commentator cruelly wrote last weekend, "the demeanour of a deputy headmistress you'd be anxious to avoid in the corridor".'[23] While the *Advertiser* suggested she needed a 'Hillary Clinton style makeover', entire articles were written about whether Stott Despoja was 'more than just a pretty face'. The old *Cleo* and 'tattoo' shots were dragged out of the files yet again.

Both candidates resented the focus on their age. Lees told the Ten Network: 'I find it very difficult when people say ... [you're] past your use-by date because you're into your 50s.' She told the *Australian* that she felt the media were supporting Stott Despoja because she was 'attractive and youthful'. Sandra Kanck, the Democrats' deputy leader in South Australia, inflamed the issue when she told ABC Radio that ageing male Democrats were fuelling sexual fantasies by supporting Stott Despoja: 'She is incredibly attractive, whereas Meg is on the back foot all the time because there's none of the heavy make-up ... Women over 50, we are basically told that we ought to, I guess, don a habit and go hide in our homes. There is a resentment from society that we give way to gravity, that our breasts are no longer pert. Our mouths drop and we get crow's feet around our eyes.' The headline in the *Age* read: 'Claws unsheathed in she-battle'. Lees still believes the competition boiled down to appearance, and Stott Despoja 'was a lot younger and for many people that was always one of the points of judgement, all these sorts of assessments, that she can do a better job because she is more attractive.'

Most of the major newspapers backed Lees in their editorials as the more credible and effective politician, and portrayed Stott Despoja as a populist weak on policy. But the polls showed Stott Despoja had the lead.[24] Seventy per cent of Democrat members voted for Stott Despoja, and she was elected leader on 7 April 2001, with Indigenous senator Aden Ridgeway as her deputy.

The Leader

> You once wrote that manipulation of the media by women
> is [necessary] to get your voices heard. Does that include sex
> appeal, for example?
> — Tony Jones, 'Lateline', ABC-TV, 11 March 2001

As leader, the first question fired at Stott Despoja by a local radio station was, 'So, Nat, has your partner popped the question yet?' She replied, 'Just been elected leader of the Australian Democrats; thought we might talk politics.'

The party's support immediately shot up, at the expense of One Nation, to 7 per cent, according to an ACNielsen Age poll. One in three voters was more likely to support the Democrats.[25] Thousands of people started switching on to the Democrats, and the number of party members increased by 80 per cent. But some of the older male commentators were disdainful of the fact that the new leader did not play the game the way it always had been played. The best example of this was an episode of the ABC's 'Media Watch' in April 2001, in which Stuart Littlemore profiled Stott Despoja in a grossly unfair way. He said she was purely a media creation: 'Here we have a woman of 31 ascended to the leadership of a party wholly and solely on the appeal of her assiduously developed celebrity.' He scoffed at her suggestion that marijuana was a 'health and social issue' and advised her to 'stay off substance' as a 'spokeswoman for the me generation'. He showed clippings of her in *Cleo* and *Who Weekly*, and shots of her appearing on various television shows. 'What is it that a 30-something politician, with a background solely in the Democrats, could possibly have to say?' he asked. 'Her policies include tattoos ...' he answered, as he cut to the photograph of her at the ARIAs, '... but not permanent ones; public relationships ...' cutting to a paparazzi photograph of her having breakfast at a cafe with her boyfriend, and 'being seen in all the right places, including the Packer wedding.' Considering she was snapped firstly while at a party and, secondly, while having a private breakfast, this was quite unfair. The dismissive attitude to magazines like *Cleo* and *Vogue* revealed a condescending attitude to what millions of women read for pleasure.

Stott Despoja's problems as leader stemmed from the fact that she was voted in by a majority of her party members, but was not supported by all of her party colleagues. Meg Lees remained angry about being elbowed aside by an 'autocratic' younger colleague, and refused to recognise her leadership. Deputy leader Aden Ridgeway hinted that he believed the party would be better off under Lees's leadership. Andrew Murray backed Lees, Andrew Bartlett backed Stott Despoja, and the two began to publicly throw punches as the party imploded.

As Stott Despoja struggled to regain control, comments about her age and looks peppered news reports. It became the norm to see snide references to the fact that she was young, blonde and 'only 32'. The implication was that her alleged 'inexperience' (read age) was the root of the Democrats' problems. Yet with census figures showing 35 was the average age of Australians, 32 was not particularly young. At the age of 30, Gary Punch was

minister for arts and territories, and Andrew Peacock was the
minister for the army. Michael Lavarch was attorney-general at
31. Joe Hockey was 33 when he was made minister for financial
services and regulation. Peter Costello was opposition spokesman
on corporate law reform and consumer affairs at 32. Paul Keating
was 31, when he was, briefly, minister for Northern Australia, and
32 when he was opposition spokesman on agriculture, minerals
and energy. Michael Yabsley was NSW minister for corrective
services in 1981, aged 32. John Brogden, the NSW opposition
leader, was just a few months older than Stott Despoja. In 2001,
ACT MP Roslyn Dundas became the youngest woman to enter
any parliament in Australia at the age of 23.

The press gallery, never favourably inclined to the Democrats
(most saw them as a distraction from the two major political
parties), attacked Stott Despoja when her party fractured,
dismissing her as the 'newly engaged', the 'princess of hype',
a 'drama queen', a 'spoiled yuppie' lacking in life experience
but not 'postfeminist coquetry' and ambition — someone
who was 'telegenic but inexperienced' and 'lacking in political

Cartoon published in *The Australian,* March 2001. *Jon Kudelka*

gravitas', with 'more style than substance'. Even praise was often patronising: she was 'an appealing political commodity' who was 'perky, pert and progressive', but 'for all her charm, missed a chance to clearly state the party's goals'.[26]

As the party fought, Stott Despoja went to England to meet her seriously ill future father-in-law. The spat escalated when she was gone, and Lees, who went on a trip to central Australia with her daughter, was still being called to account for her behaviour. In what *Australian* columnist Matt Price believes was the biggest act of political bastardy he had ever witnessed in politics, Lees returned, then resigned from the party before her leader was back in the country. Stott Despoja heard the news while flying over Turkey. Andrew Murray, a Lees supporter, said he was withdrawing to the back bench and becoming a Democrat in exile. Stott Despoja made overtures and issued ultimatums, asking if anyone wanted to challenge her leadership, but it was to no avail. On 21 August 2002, four of the seven senators presented her with a 'ten point plan' they wanted her to agree to, including making concessions to Lees, and greater accountability for her own staff. To have accepted the demands would have meant abdicating any authority as leader.

Stott Despoja resigned on 21 August, saying she had no option: 'I don't have the support of my colleagues in the party room and when it matters.' She offered support to the next leader the party chose and fronted for a party room meeting later that day.

Stott Despoja's colleagues were fools. They disobeyed their party's wishes, ousted her without a back-up plan, then dwindled into insignificance, their profile risible, their impact virtually nil. While they were all slipping around in the mud pit, commentators condemned Stott Despoja at every turn, as they tried to interpret her exercise of power as the lack of it. If she failed to speak, she was weak. If she issued ultimatums, she was accused of an unattractive 'Tarzan approach'. It's true she was unable to pull her colleagues into line, because of a lack of professional authority or personal rapport, but she made no major gaffes, no silly comments, no grandstanding postures. She came back from London to try to take control of the brawling, dysfunctional group of Democrats and found herself constantly undermined. As Louise Dodson wrote in the *Age*, accusations of being autocratic, failing to communicate with colleagues, and having controlling, powerhungry staff were not unique to Stott Despoja.[27] And she had her assets as leader — certainly more so than any of the other Democrat senators, who have occupied the leadership position since she resigned without making an impact.

*

Alan Ramsey was the most vehement of Stott Despoja's detractors. He sat alone in an office around the corner from the chief newspaper bureaus, and had worked in the Canberra press gallery since 1966, before Stott Despoja was born. He was an irascible, widely respected columnist whose office was piled ceiling-high with transcripts, and who was legendary for his elephantine memory and fearlessness. Young journalists revered him. He is, along with Laurie Oakes, Michelle Grattan and Paul Kelly, one of the gallery gods, although he hates the term. He operates alone and doesn't give a stuff what anyone thinks. What struck me when I interviewed him was that he was both deeply angry about the way politics was and passionate about the way it should be. He paced his office, fitfully glowing red as he recounted his fury about various political sins. And Natasha Stott Despoja triggered his alarm bells:

> She was all about herself ... She paraded herself, it wasn't
> about politics, anything she could get herself onto,
> particularly television ... She was the leader, and you

thought, hang on, what about the Democrats, what about the party, what about policy? You are out there promoting yourself. You never thought in those game shows, all those silly things she was on, you thought what does this do for the Democrats? ... She was swept up in the glamour of the whole bloody business, about being somebody. But it was about being herself ... In the same way that Bob Hawke was, for Christ's sake. Bob Hawke was about being Bob Hawke — 'I'm the one! Look at my opinion polls! I am the most popular person!' ... I detested him for it.

At the time of her leadership problems, Ramsey dismissed Stott Despoja as 'a media-created political misfit', a 'flibbertigibbet' with ambitions which 'exceed her competence but not her ego', and a 'young woman far out of her depth who has no business being taken seriously'.[28] He also likened her to the glamorous tennis player who reporters celebrated more for her tanned thighs than her ability, Anna Kournikova. He wrote: 'Each is a beguiling clothes horse with minimum talent in what they do for a living. Kournikova can't play tennis. Stott Despoja is a complete political and parliamentary dunce. That is not to say they're not smart. Of course they are. What each does, and superbly, is captivate the media. The media, in turn, titillate sponsors and/or public opinion ...' Photographs of the two women were puffed on the front page of the *Sydney Morning Herald*. Stott Despoja said later that she was amazed by his comments, because he had never spoken to her in the eight years she had been in politics. 'He's never met me, he's never wanted to interview me, he won't deal with me on any policy issues, he won't respond to my press releases ... as far as I know he's never done a Hansard search on me. He wouldn't have a clue what my work is.'

When I sent Ramsey an email asking him for his response to Stott Despoja's remarks, he fired back this missive:

That sort of crap is why Natasha isn't worth a bumper
as an ordinary MP, let alone a party leader. This isn't
undergraduate playtime. I don't have to ask a politician's
permission to write about him or her, to have an opinion. I
write about George Bush and what an appalling US president
he is, and I don't have [to] interview him to think so. I'm
a political columnist, a political observer. There are many
MPs I don't interview and don't personally know who I write
about far more often than I ever wrote about Natasha. She
was never WORTH interviewing! That's the whole point.
I've been observing Natasha in Parlt [sic] since she got here,
just as I do every MP ... This childish view I must interview
her, that I have to meet her, before I can decide she is just a
piece of selfaggrandising political froth is why she shouldn't
be within a bull's roar of the business. I mean, how long did
she last as leader, ask yourself?

Just over 16 months.

Ramsey's view was significant because so many in the gallery
agreed with him.[29] The consensus appeared to be that she just
did too much of the wrong kind of publicity. The *Australian
Financial Review*'s Tony Walker believes she was 'undercooked'
for the job, and that she did not have 'the maturity to take on
the demanding reins of leadership, irrespective of age'. ALP
pollster Rod Cameron claimed, as few today would, 'You can't
mix celebrity and political leadership ...'[30] Paul McGeough told
me he blamed her demise on the inexperience of the party as
well as her youth: 'I think all of those who really believed in her
potential failed her by not giving her the advice and wise counsel
she needed as such a young political operator.'

Under her leadership, the party did lose some ground electorally.
In a by-election held three months after she became leader, in the
Melbourne seat of Aston, the Democrats increased their vote by a

tiny margin: 300 votes. In the November election later that year, held in the wake of September 11 and the *Tampa*, only four out of five senators were retained, and the lost seat was picked up by the Greens. Their vote in the House of Representatives increased by a fraction, but overall they lost votes to the Greens. The Democrat Senate vote went from 8.5 per cent under Lees in 1998 to 7.25 per cent in 2001. The Greens went from 2.7 to 4.9 per cent. The Democrat vote overall was 5.4 per cent.

The Democrats could have run a better election campaign in 2001, and they struggled to get the media to report on their policies instead of just photographing Stott Despoja in a crop top at the Barrier Reef (which was worn with pants, not a bikini as was widely believed), a Mambo t-shirt, and grimacing as she held a baby. The personality politics had come back to bite. The Greens poached many of their voters; possibly, wrote Mike Seccombe, because Bob Brown was perceived as 'the serious minor player; she was the one in cute clothes on the beach'.[31] But he also pointed out, Stott Despoja did 32 policy launches, 38 speeches, and more than 80 media interviews and conferences. She addressed the Asia–Australia Institute, the Deakin School of Law, the Sydney Institute, and the National Press Club. With September 11 clouding the political climate, the slogan 'Change politics' lost its resonance when voters decided they'd rather not.

Still, the evidence shows that most of the damage to the party's standing, and polling, happened on Lees's watch after she struck the deal on the GST. Democrat defections were not unusual, as three other leaders — John Coulter, Janet Powell and Cheryl Kernot — had left the party for various reasons. Janine Haines also had to deflect abuse from Senators John Siddons and David Vigor when they resigned from the party in the 1980s, under her leadership.[32]

*

After resigning from the leadership, Stott Despoja appeared in the *Australian Women's Weekly* talking about her relationship with her fiancé and the ring he'd bought her from Tiffany's, and was photographed at their home. She also did a fashion shoot for *Harper's Bazaar*, choosing to wear a black suit and white shirt. Even in late 2003, she was in the *Weekly* again, wearing a black dress and talking about her plans to marry over Christmas. It was difficult to work out why. Why give your critics so much ammunition? Why criticise the press for sticking its beaked nose too far into your life, shoo it out, then invite it back in? This was really the only fundamental problem with her media strategy: complaining for something caused, at least in part, by her own actions. But when she did try to keep her wedding private, she was accused of being delusional. Naomi Toy and Fiona Connolly mocked her in the *Daily Telegraph*:

> The Jennifer Lopez of the Australian Democrats, Natasha
> Stott Despoja, is today marrying PR boss Ian Smith in
> Byron Bay. Whoop-de-doo! ... Tash darling, you need not
> have gone to all that trouble of keeping the details of the
> big day such a secret ... Puh-lease ... the silly attempts to
> avoid publicity have raised suspicions that the former media
> darling is either deluding herself about the real level of public
> interest, or is worried that there was none.[33]

Commentators were wrong to assume Stott Despoja was a lightweight because of a deliberate and effective strategy to maximise her exposure and votes in the broader population. She was at her most effective when she undercut the stereotypes, not when she played to them. But the vast majority of her press appearances were necessary for both herself and her party. Without her stellar profile, and obvious ability to communicate through the media, she would never have become leader.

Politics has always made otherwise sensible people do silly things in the pursuit of publicity but the assumption that this means people are stupid or shallow only seems to apply to women. Many male politicians are photographed exercising — swimming, running, doing aerobics, or posing bare-chested with a surfboard, like Tony Abbott — yet seem to escape ridicule. Peter Costello danced the macarena on daytime television with Kerri-Anne Kennerley, and Cheryl Kernot followed suit with the cha-cha. Paul Keating appeared on the front cover of *Rolling Stone* wearing dark sunglasses, and Jeff Kennett also called the 'rock star of Australian politics' — modelled suits for *Australian Style*. He was snapped draped with beautiful young models for the front cover in April 1999, under the headline 'Model Premier'.[34] The then editor of *Australian Style*, Wendy Squires, said 'As a woman, I found it quite offensive, because he made it look like, "Here I am, lord of the domain and here are my pets."'[35]

Can you imagine the storm if Stott Despoja had posed for the front cover of *FHM* in a frock, fondling men who draped her shoulders and knees? Glamour photos and the cult of personality are far more dangerous for women. Does this mean it reflects an unfair, deep-rooted sexism? Absolutely. Should women protest against it? Of course. Should they allow themselves to be made over and pose like models? Only with considerable caution.

Most of the time what Stott Despoja was criticised for was behaviour considered normal in other politicians. She was not the only MP to appear on mainstream, lightweight television shows. ALP president Barry Jones and National Party MP Ian Sinclair appeared on 'Good News Week', for example. Stott Despoja came on 'The Panel' twice, but Peter Costello, Kim Beazley, Bob Brown, Mark Latham and Tim Fischer have also been guests. John Howard and wife Janette have appeared on Channel Ten's 'Healthy, Wealthy and Wise', and Kim Beazley also walked television viewers around his garden on Channel Nine's 'Burke's

Backyard'. Sports minister Jackie Kelly gave the photos of her wedding day to the *Australian Women's Weekly*. Labor leader Mark Latham was on 'Burke's Backyard' and 'Enough Rope'. Cheryl Kernot — who made her derisive views of what she saw as Stott Despoja's 'any publicity is good publicity' approach publicly known — appeared twice on 'Good News Week' and 'Club Buggery', as well as on 'The Panel'. Kernot also took the nation through her garden on 'Burke's Backyard', and featured in the pages of magazines including the *Australian Women's Weekly*, *Ita*, *Elle*, and *New Idea*. She ended one show singing a duet of 'You've Lost That Loving Feeling' with Paul McDermott. 'Anything to gaze into those mischievous baby blues,' she wrote in *Speaking for Myself Again*. The difference was that Stott Despoja was courted more, and was better at it than most. Max Walsh, who joined the gallery the same year as Ramsey, 1966, wrote that Stott Despoja had 'that quality Paul Keating identified as necessary for a leader — the ability to throw the switch to vaudeville'.

The success of Stott Despoja's approach as a vote-puller is undeniable. As many recognised, the success of minor parties had always been dependent on charismatic leadership. In the 1996 election, she gained what the *Sydney Morning Herald* called a 'near record' 14.7 per cent of the vote. In 2001, she polled better than any of her Democrats colleagues, with 12.6 per cent of the primary vote. In 1998, she was named the most popular role model for working women in a survey by the NSW Chamber of Commerce, and the nation's second most influential woman, after Cheryl Kernot.

Christine Wallace dismisses any suggestion she lacked substance as 'bullshit':

Natasha was brilliant. This publicity seeking is used as a slur; in fact, it was one of the things that made her a great politician. That's what politics is, it's about getting space in

the public realm, in the media and fighting your corner ...
And she was a very attractive figure, she won votes for the
Democrats. At the next election the Democrats are going
to disappear, they will be replaced entirely by Greens,
all because she was assassinated by her own, by another
woman ... Getting column inches is one of the things
politicians have to do. Unless you do it you can't influence
people. If you can't influence people you can't get votes, you
can't get your agenda up in policy and in legislation. It's the
currency of politics and Natasha was great at it.

Even Laurie Oakes, political editor at Channel Nine since 1984,
believes she was a 'terrific performer' whose celebrity profile was
useful: 'What happened to Natasha is that she got outnumbered.'

*

I finally interviewed Natasha Stott Despoja at the Commonwealth
parliamentary offices in Elizabeth Street, Sydney, where she sat
with her press adviser and clutched a cup of coffee. She was
reserved, and her thoughts rambled a little. I had been warned
that her charm was disarming. But I was just struck by how
normal she was. When I told her I had spent the week reading
Cheryl Kernot's press clippings, and had found it a depressing
story, she agreed: 'I know! I think mine is depressing, but hers is
much worse.'

After an hour of justifying her media strategy and insisting
she had no regrets, she finally said perhaps her approach had not
been ideal:

If I was doing it all again, would I do it differently? You
bet I would. Because I would want a really nice life where
people said nothing but nice things about me. And then on

the other hand I think people make mistakes ... [and] a lot
of other women won't make those same choices because
of what I have done. Or maybe they'll go further and do
something completely radical, because they figure, what does
it matter ... When I look back I think if I was an adviser
charting the perfect political ascension for a woman in
politics today, it would be head down, talk about nothing
but your policy work, don't let them see a human side, don't
be multi-dimensional, definitely don't be attractive, never
dress up in public, try not to pose with any alcohol in your
hands, certainly don't wear any low-cut dresses, never go to
any public events with your partner, and basically just talk
jargon the whole time and they'll respect you.

I interviewed her again a few months later, in December 2003,
just after her party had announced that Andrew Bartlett was
going to be leading the Democrats to the next election, provided
he stayed sober. He had been forced (briefly) to step aside after
admitting he had been drunk in parliament when he assaulted a
female Liberal senator, and that he had an alcohol problem. All
day she had been swatting away accusations that she was being
disloyal to a friend — Bartlett — because she believed that his
behaviour was inappropriate. She had also just received a phone
call from a journalist asking if she had just become eligible for
her parliamentary superannuation (she had), and if this was
why she had not stood for leader, suggesting that she would not
want to lead her party because she could now take off with the
loot. There had also been some unfounded rumours circulating
that she was not running because she was pregnant. I had just
filed a column for the next day's paper on ten reasons why the
Democrats should ask her to be leader again.

She came out of her office looking pale, exhausted and shaken.
'Why is it, every time I see you,' she said, 'something is happening?'

I had the feeling that there was usually something happening. When we sat down on her couch, I asked if she was okay. Her eyes went red; she blinked quickly and her voice wobbled. The attacks had been vicious that week, she said, and she was thrown by it, and did not understand why she was the focus when she had ruled herself out of running for leadership. She was genuinely perplexed, and sought my thoughts a couple of times during the interview as to why some particular journalists had disliked her, why the press turned in unison sometimes. When I left, we shook hands and she laughed, 'That was just like therapy!' She seems so immersed in public life that she genuinely struggles to understand what continually happens to her, to match her view of herself with the celebrity politician in the news pages.

Stott Despoja's major problem was her colleagues, of course. But the way she was hyped then trivialised by the press did not help. Her experience with the media has been another cautionary tale. It would be worrying if the message young women — or men — gleaned from her story was that a high profile is a dangerous thing. Because, as all politicians know, this is also a key to success. Stott Despoja has always recognised this, although she assesses the power of the press more soberly now: 'The level of influence the media has [is] totally extraordinary, just amazing, and certainly was beyond my wildest dreams. I will never underestimate the role of the media in Australian political life ... I think the media is actually culpable in selecting, electing, producing leaders and determining who stays.' And Stott Despoja was selected by the media, elected by her party then ousted by her colleagues — who were partly fuelled by the negative articles which dismissed her as a glamour girl. But as soon as she resigned as leader, the party disappeared from view.

CHAPTER EIGHT

Cheryl Kernot:
from Wunderfrau to whore

For a time, journalists worshipped Cheryl Kernot. Almost literally, on one occasion. In the mid-1990s, she invited journalists for evening drinks in an alcove in Parliament House. She played the Beach Boys on her ghetto blaster and chatted until somehow the journalists, drunk and silly, found themselves circling her, bowing down in turn, both mocking and playing to the adulation which then came from many quarters of the press. Hearing the story now, it seems an odd, orgiastic ritual late at night in the shadowed corners of the sprawling office block on the hill in Canberra. Kernot remembers the party, not the incident, but according to one reporter who was there, Margo Kingston:

> By the end of the night everyone was very drunk, and
> she stood in the middle and the journos were around her
> and ended up walking around her in a circle and doing a
> ritualistic bowing, like a wave. It was a sendup but also a
> bit weird. The media had loved her — she was open, she
> was available ... [the] impression was given that there were

no barriers, she saw us as her friends, we were all working for the same great goal, and so on. Anyway, she walked out and I followed her. She went into her office and did not turn on any lights. It was dark, and she turned on the television and watched herself on the late night TV and asked me my thoughts on how she went. She was in love with her image, she had merged with it. It's one of the dangers of being open, of transcending the roles assigned ... [Now] she is a pathetic figure. [But] I loved her ideas, I loved the way she expressed them; she was full of really wonderful ideas.[1]

The public shaming and stoning of Cheryl Kernot, at one time the nation's most popular and successful female politician, is an extraordinary, tragic story. Many of us watched the disaster unfolding on television from the cracks between our fingers: her sudden changing of political parties, the red dress, the tendency to blame other people for her mistakes, the way the press simultaneously turned on her like sharks chasing a fish. Her career reads like another cautionary tale: do not cry, do not complain, do not pose in raunchy dresses, do not defer blame for your behaviour to colleagues or hormones, and — *above all* — do not sleep with your political colleagues.

Today she is both pilloried and pitied, but it is important to remember how huge Kernot was, how bright she shone. She was the dream girl of the press gallery for several years. The accolades poured thick and fast, treacle spreading on newsprint. She was the saint; the rational, no-nonsense negotiator; the 'attractive blonde' interviewee. As Democrat leader, she was unaccountable in the way government ministers were, but increasingly wielded some power in the Senate and wreaked some significant changes to key legislation: Mabo, workplace reform, and budgets. She was a serious threat to conservative politics — and hugely successful.

Then, on 15 October 1997, she lobbed a grenade when she announced she was resigning from the Democrats and joining the ALP. Her defection to — or 'seduction by' — the ALP proved to be a monumental mistake. But the imagery pumped out from television screens and on the front pages of newspapers was powerful: she did look very pleased, wistful almost, as she smiled and looked skyward while the men on either side of her — Kim Beazley and Gareth Evans — spoke to the astonished media throng. The Labor Party was ecstatic. She was the first in the country's history to rat *to* Labor; other defectors — Joseph Cook, Billy Hughes, Joe Lyons — had left the ALP and headed to more conservative parties. John Howard immediately said her move was 'all about personal ambition', not principles. It was a risk. As she said in her defection statement, 'Being a creature of one political culture moving into another, there are no guarantees for me. Perhaps this experiment will fail.'

It did. A year later her credibility was tattered, her Labor colleagues wary, her former Democrats colleagues hostile, and her strength in shreds. Once she was heralded as the woman who could win the election for Labor, the media — goaded by her opponents — sank their teeth into her reputation and shook it, which clearly contributed to what was a very public unravelling of a woman once widely respected. At the end of 1999, she was hospitalised with exhaustion. In the process, she blamed everyone but herself: the leader of the Labor party, Kim Beazley; blokey elements of the party; a male-dominated media; unsupportive staff; an affluent and increasingly Liberal electorate; Liberal opponents who did everything in their power to destroy her. Her anger seemed to warp her judgement as she continued to lay herself bare for the journalists she accused of intruding too far into her life. There is no doubt, however, that she was treated differently from the men who lined the benches on either side of the house as the issue became how she performed in the media, not how she performed in the parliament.

*

Throughout the 1990s, Kernot was a star. Former ALP pollster Rod Cameron was still rhapsodic when he talked about her years later: 'The world was hers for the taking. She was absolutely at the pinnacle for quite some time; she was terrific; she was everything you could hope for.' At the time of her defection, he described her as the perfect leader: 'If you had to put together an identikit picture of the ideal political leader in Australia, you would come up with a person who is strong — not in the macho sense but in the sense of having inner strength — [who has] conviction; [is] highly credible and believable; someone who is good-looking but not to the extent of being glamorous; [is] articulate and media-wise and comes across well in the media. You get someone like Cheryl Kernot.'

After entering parliament in 1990, Kernot's political ascension was smooth and uninterrupted. She gained respect after she extracted some key concessions in the superannuation legislation, slowing the introduction of the 'superannuation guarantee levy' and reducing its impact on business. She represented reason and commonsense. The *Sunday Telegraph*, in excitement characteristic of many papers when a political woman was seen to be competent or influential, declared her 'SUPERWOMAN'.

Shortly afterwards she became leader, deposing environmental scientist John Coulter, who lacked her charisma and media rapport, and insisted he wanted to appeal to people's minds with thinking, not the quick grab. Kernot was ambitious, credible and likeable. In her leadership campaign, she had played to her media strengths, saying the Democrats had to think about 'what their public face should be', and that the leader should be a woman. Most reporters urged the party to support her. She was 'mumsy', a 'non-militant feminist', 'a thinking politician', effective but feminine: a woman who was 'as mild as milk, [had]

205

the demeanour of a schoolmistress and a voice not known to rise a decibel above its measured pitch'.

Kernot won 81 per cent of the vote and was welcomed by journalists, many of whom had become personal friends. She was widely praised a few months later for her negotiations over the 1993 Budget, particularly for exacting concessions that were revenue neutral. She recognised that the government had been elected to carry out its agenda, and should be allowed to aim for a deficit, and was respected for it. She won almost $500 million in changes. The *Sydney Morning Herald* declared it 'the Kernot budget'. Richard Farmer from the *Canberra Times* wrote that she 'looked and sounded like sweet reasonableness itself ', and had 'emerged as a person of substance': 'A new force has arrived in Australian politics. She just looks and sounds so refreshing.' The core of her 'absolutely beautiful politics' was that she had accepted 'governments should be allowed to govern while reserving the right to look after all the little people'.[2] By December, Alan Ramsey wrote that while the media was doing handstands around Bronwyn Bishop as a 'political curiosity who seeks to be Australia's first woman prime minister', Bishop was a bizarre caricature compared to Kernot's substance, discipline, 'great commonsense and generosity of spirit'. He concluded: 'Cheryl Kernot has arrived.'[3]

Soon, the headlines read: 'Is this woman Australia's best politician?' There appeared to be a consensus in the reportage — she had made a name for herself, made the Democrats relevant, and made the big players of the chief parties take notice. She was also commended for the role she played in negotiating the native title legislation at the end of 1993. As Diana Bagnall wrote in the *Bulletin*, 'The press gallery, which is notoriously hard to impress, fell about praising her political skill and maturity.' The Democrats, now a significant minor party, were polling better than they had for years.

The media hype was so prolonged that other MPs began to call her 'Saint Cheryl' and laughed at her 'halo'. But Kernot deliberately sought to represent honesty and credibility, positing herself as someone who would clean up the muck of the political fray.[4] For years she pursued the idea of government accountability and a code of conduct for MPs. She was tough on Ros Kelly over the sports rorts affair, and received some of the credit for Kelly's scalp.

With the exception of a few financial commentators, Kernot was not seriously criticised by the press until after the 1996 election, which John Howard won.[5] The Democrats doubled their vote, jumping to 11 per cent, after a 5 per cent swing towards them. Kernot began to talk of the Democrats having their own mandate — which meant undermining the Coalition's claim they had a mandate to implement policies like the sale of Telstra because of a 5.4 per cent swing towards them, the third-largest at a federal election since 1949. Most of the quality press urged her to be responsible, and not compromise the government, which John Howard had promised would deliver policies to the Australian people.[6] She still played an important part in negotiations over the industrial relations legislation, extracting more than 170 concessions.[7] She was widely praised for having 'mainstream political skills'. She became friends with Howard, but particularly with industrial relations minister Peter Reith — they were described as a courting couple searching for a relationship of mutual convenience. Kernot and Reith were photographed shaking hands and beaming at each other after their deal on the legislation, which saw sweeping changes to the industrial relations law, scrapping Labor's unfair dismissal laws and giving greater scope to non-union enterprise agreements. Kernot was often described in old-fashioned romantic terms (until she defected to the ALP, when the terms became more sexual). As early as 1991, Kernot was described as someone the government needed to 'woo', 'court' or 'seduce' in order to ensure the passage of their legislation through the Senate.

When Mal Colston defected from the ALP in late August 1996 and moved to the crossbench as an independent senator, the Democrats lost the balance of power and were instantly diminished. Kernot no longer had enough numbers to ensure the passage of legislation and lost some of her status as a major political player.

*

The defining day of Kernot's political life was 15 October 1997, when she left the Democrats to join the Labor Party (the page one headline of the *Daily Telegraph* the next day was 'Cheryl goes into Labor'). Greg Turnbull, then Kim Beazley's senior media adviser, told me he had never seen political journalists in such a frenzy: 'The barometer of media demand went higher that day — certainly as high as anything I had known in five years with the prime minister [Paul Keating] and five years with the opposition leader. Every magazine in Australia, every television — 'Burke's Backyard' to 'Harry the Vet' everybody wanted Cheryl that day, and every day for the next few weeks ... it was amazing interest. And that did surprise me. She was attracted to the media like a moth and the media were attracted to her like a swarm of bees: it was extraordinary.'

Kernot was crushed at the media's response. The worst was to come, but the reports of 16 October marked an instant shift in her media fortunes as she was accused of selfish ambition, betrayal of her staff, hypocrisy about keeping the bastards honest, and general selfinterest. It was at this point that the linchpin of her public image — her honesty and the purity of her ideals — was pulled.

Hyperbole was rife. Shaun Carney wrote in the *Age* that on that day, 'Australian politics blew apart.' Many key commentators wrote that Kernot's credibility would forever be tainted by the fact that she had abandoned her party to join the bastards (especially as she had been critical of the ALP in the past). The newspapers jumped on her in their editorials. Her ambition was her worst sin, compounded by the fact that she had not informed her colleagues or staffers about her decision. The *Sydney Morning Herald* slammed the move as an act of treachery, saying she had damaged her party, her own credibility, and let down voters for the sake of personal ambition: 'There is no doubt that the halo of "Saint Cheryl" ... has been severely tarnished.' The *Australian*, which immediately backed Natasha Stott Despoja as her successor, along with the *Sydney Morning Herald*, suggested her move had more to do with a grab for power than her antagonism towards the Howard government.[8] The *Daily Telegraph*'s Piers Akerman, who was caustic whenever he wrote about the woman he called 'Senator Moonbeam', wondered what good she would be to the ALP: 'Cheryl Kernot is probably best known for silly dancing on a midday television program, not for her contribution to the political debate.' Labor voters would be asked to ignore her past criticisms of their party and think of her as a 'vote-pulling celebrity: a Barbie doll of the ballot box'.[9]

A few individuals cheered. The *Australian*'s Paul Kelly applauded her 'for having the courage to seek executive power. She has chosen to become a serious politician instead of wasting her career as a senate spoiler. That decision is a bonus overall for Australian politics.' Laurie Oakes praised the way the 'Queen Rat' had handled her news conference with 'extraordinary strength and calm' and credited her with a fundamental switch in Australian politics, and renewal for the ALP. In a sense, he wrote, 'it was her coming out as a serious politician'. She would do what it took to win.

Kernot herself has always claimed her decision was primarily intellectual. She told me:

My biggest shock was the conservative agenda of John
Howard because I had just happily been going along under
a Labor agenda, meeting with the Labor Party to hammer
out improvements to things I thought basically were okay
to start with — Mabo, all of [that] superannuation stuff,
the '93 budget, and I hadn't been in parliament under
a conservative government ... [I thought] I can't just sit
here playing negotiator compromiser on things I do not
fundamentally believe in ... I was uncomfortable in my
own skin ... There was this big discord again between
those who'd heard my words — those who'd wanted a
different agenda from what Labor was offering to the
conservatives at that stage, who thought I might bring
some of my Democrat agenda to Labor — and what the
press were saying. There was a huge disjunct, and so,
while they were all writing their formulaic stuff, I was
getting thousands of faxes and letters from people.

ABC reporter Fran Kelly was one of the few who said she
understood the move — Kernot was a driven ambitious woman
who was being courted. Kelly thought: people change and
develop, why not move from a minor to a major party? It was
a 'logical ambitious career path'. Kernot also maintained her
integrity by relinquishing her senate seat.

Whatever the real reasons for the switch, though, from the
point of her defection Kernot was accused, in crude terms, of
screwing her way to the Labor Party. The sexual innuendo was
rife — and unfortunate in retrospect. The lusty parallels poured
forth: she was Labor's bride they had wooed and seduced, a
sex-goddess, Boadicea in bed with Beazley and Evans. One
caller to a Canberra radio station asked, 'Why has the Mother
Superior of the parliament decided to become a political harlot?'
The *Bulletin* headline read: 'Will the marriage last?' Senior

reporter Peter Bowers, then at the *Australian Financial Review*, wrote that the Coalition's charge that she had gone from '*Wunderfrau* to whore' reflected its panic at her boost to the ALP's electoral appeal. One journalist, Marion Smith, accused her of 'dickstroking', or flirting with men to get to the top, in an extraordinary piece for the *Courier-Mail*. Smith referred to comments Don Chipp had made about Kernot's 'coquettishness', and added: 'In the circles of women with attitude, it's called something rather more crude — "dickstroking". But, by golly, it works for those women prepared to use it as a tool on their way to the top. Anyone who has seen Kernot twinkling beguilingly through interviews with the mostly middle-aged men of the Canberra press gallery would recognise it.'[10]

Looking back, knowing Kernot was having an affair with Labor cabinet minister Gareth Evans before and after her defection makes the sexual innuendo seem even more blatant, and the continual references to a seduction, sickening. In the *Australian*, cartoonist Bill Leak depicted her in bed with Beazley and Evans, asking 'Now ... who is going to be on top?' Evans's name was sprinkled liberally throughout the news reports of her defection, and he was seen to have played a core role in her move: he suggested it, acted as her sounding board, and was effusive when it was successfully executed. Many journalists acknowledged their close friendship. Paul Kelly wrote at the time, 'The personal bond between Gareth Evans and Ms Kernot was fundamental in her decision.' In hindsight, some of the reporting was creepy. Mike Seccombe wrote that Evans had played the main part in her seduction:

We use the word advisedly, for Evans described their
relationship in almost erotic terms on ABC-TV's 'Lateline' ...
He recounted how he slowly wooed her: 'It started out with
a lot of casual, off-the-cuff, almost wistful exchanges,' he

sighed. And it was consummated, he recounted, after he put the rather raffish proposition: 'What about it, kiddo, any chance of coming across?'[11]

While journalists were hesitant, the public response was overwhelmingly favourable. The managing director of the media monitoring group Rehame, Peter Maher, said 'no issue has generated as much concentrated caller comment since the death of Princess Diana'. The Sunday Telegraph Quadrant poll found 60 per cent approved of her decision, 72 per cent said it was good for Labor, 37 per cent were more likely to vote for Labor, and 60 per cent said they would like to see her become the first woman PM. The front-page headline of the *Sunday Telegraph* cried, 'Cheryl for PM!' Similarly, the *Sun-Herald* yelped, 'Voters Back Kernot!', with a Taverner poll which found that, while 44 per cent thought her reputation as a principled politician had been damaged, Kernot was the most popular choice for Labor leader after Beazley, and Australia's most popular female politician. Pollster Ian McNair said he could not recall, in 25 years of polling, such a huge swing to a federal opposition in such a short time. Brian Toohey wrote that she may have to become leader if the party was going to truly capitalise on her. Finally, a Bulletin–Morgan poll found a 10.5 per cent swing towards Labor, which would bring them victory if an election were held then.[12]

The final decision by the ALP to bring Kernot over to the party was made just after the 1997 South Australian elections, when they had polled poorly and the Democrats' primary vote had soared, largely, they believed, due to Kernot's leadership. Their election prospects looked grim. National secretary Gary Gray told me: 'Ultimately my reason for approaching Cheryl was to destroy her as a potential Democrat. To destroy the essential element that was defining the Democrats, that was such a potential danger to the Labor Party.' Gray pointed out, however, that there were others who wanted her to join the party because 'she genuinely represented a major break in the political circuit'.

Kernot was a coup for the Labor Party. She was meant to bring credibility, integrity and a female influence. Many believed she could bring them victory in the 1998 election by attracting women from middle-class backgrounds, whom Beazley described as the 'soccer mums'. Because of this, from this point she became a target for the Coalition. Paul Daley wrote in the *Sunday Age*: 'If she has any skeletons [the Coalition] will exhume them.' They were already rattling the cupboard door. When the first skeleton was dug out and dangled in the press, its bones were picked over for months.

*

On 13 December 1997 — just two months after her defection — the *Sydney Morning Herald* published a profile written by Paul McGeough headed 'The other side of Saint Cheryl'. This other side, apparently, was saucy, sexy and ruthless, with a scandalous past, the side 'where ambition and determination lie'. It would be hard to imagine a profile about a male MP revealing his 'true side' to be ambitious and determined. It's hardly surprising for a politician. But then few men in politics are called saints. The most important revelation was buried halfway down the story: her past relationship with the school captain of St Leo's College, a school the recently seperated Kernot was teaching at in 1975 in leafy Wahroonga, part of the bible belt of Sydney's North Shore.[13] In 1976, she was living in Queensland with the former school captain: they went on to have a five-year relationship. The man's mother insisted the relationship started when he left school, even if reporters continued to imply it had not. It had happened over 20 years before. Significantly, the story was published on the day Kernot was due to be preselected by Queensland Labor for the seat of Dickson.

An avalanche of stories was to come. Some of the commentary was vicious, much of it gleefully claiming this was proof she was no saint. Victorian premier Jeff Kennett said she deserved it because she had 'set herself up as an angel'. Conservative columnist Christopher Pearson, then writing for the *Australian Financial Review*, implied she was a paedophile. 'Just imagine the outcry,' he wrote, 'if the subject had been a male politician rather than the most sanctimonious woman on Capital Hill.' He wanted to know more: how old was the boy 'at the crucial moment'? Was it an isolated incident, he asked, or did she have sex with any other boys? 'Was it a victimless entanglement, a breach of trust or a criminal matter?' Even if these questions were answered in a 'relatively reassuring way', he continued, he doubted 'that middle Australian parents will take an especially mellow view. However broadminded in theory, many of them understand how destabilising and potentially disastrous for adolescent boys and their families such affairs with manipulative older women can be.' Her hopes of becoming leader had been dashed by this scandal, and 'no amount of confected righteous indignation, simpering or wistful head-on-one-side girlishness will altogether make things right, and penitence is not in her repertoire'.[14] But according to polls, people were outraged, not by Kernot's behaviour but the publication of the story.[15] Readers wrote indignant letters to the editor, and rushed indignantly to her defence. Tom Uren, a former minister in the Hawke and Whitlam governments, wrote to the *Sydney Morning Herald* claiming he had 'never read such a bucket job on a politician in all my years in politics', and was sickened by the sexual overtones in the article. Fran Kelly told me she believed the publication of the story was 'outrageous': 'What annoyed these blokes was what they saw as the saintliness, preciousness of this woman; there is something in there but it's hard to tie down. There was no public crime here if she and he are to be believed. The relationship was finished, it was ongoing and happy. The story was trying to say she is not the saint you think she is, but she was at that point a definite political asset for the ALP and a threat to government. I believe this was part of a campaign to diminish her political potency and it worked.' Still, the story rolled on for weeks. Kernot claims Sinclair's youngest child was chased at her pre-school, as was his mother at her home.

There are three important things to note about this story. First, it did not come from the press gallery, but from a Sydney journalist. The convention about private lives had largely been observed until that point by the gallery. Laurie Oakes later said he had 'strong reservations' about the publication of this story: 'I couldn't see how it was relevant to Cheryl's political role. It didn't seem to me to go even to character. Had the relationship been with someone who was *still* a student, I would have seen it differently.'[16] Other reporters were also angered by the decision to run the story. Margo Kingston and McGeough, formerly close friends, fell out over it. McGeough said the story was the 'very enthusiastic' suggestion of his then editor and editor-in-chief, who had wanted a story on the political gossip surrounding 'an incident' when Kernot was at St Leo's. While he remembers debating the issue with Kingston, he says, 'In the same way that I would not let a politician dictate what was going into a piece I was reporting, neither would I allow a colleague to do so.'[17]

Second, the story had been around for months, as many journalists attested. They had been lobbied by senior Liberal figures, including Tony Abbott, to publish it as a way of undermining Labor's prize asset. Independent MP Graeme Campbell had been asked to raise the matter in parliament but had refused.

Third is that this story was published only after she went to the ALP.[18]

The critical question is why Kernot's affair, which was clearly irrelevant to her political career, was revealed when those of her colleagues were not? And why the vehemence of the response?

The *Daily Telegraph*'s political editor, Malcolm Farr, was at pains to point out to me that the story was not broken by a tabloid newspaper:

> It really shits me when people say what a ghastly intrusion on private life, they say those tabloid journalists — and often they say those Murdoch tabloid journalists — when in fact it came out in a Fairfax broadsheet first ... I would have found it difficult as a journalist to justify writing that and claiming that the public had the right to know that it was something that affected the public duties of Cheryl Kernot ... There were all sorts of weird justifications for it; there were all sorts of inferences that she might be a paedophile or something. As far as I know there was lots of gossip and hearsay but no evidence that she was bonking this chap when he was at school. I don't know. Nor do many of the people who wrote columns and great creeds condemning her for whatever happened. Now they lived together afterwards, it's not the first time an older woman has fallen for a younger man. Then they broke up and I just think it's a matter for them ... if we are going to start imposing standards of public morality, I think we'd better find someone else to do that, rather than journalists; that's not our job at all.

The *Sydney Morning Herald*'s political commentator, Alan Ramsey, was long emphatic that publication of the story was wrong:

> I always thought if it was a bloke, it would never have been written. Blokes fuck around, you know, in their young life, whatever. If we had gone after Tony Abbott and his extraordinary life in the same way and given it the same sort of treatment, and the same sort of presentation, but it doesn't

happen … Journalists usually are the last people in the world
who can afford to be holier than thou about their bloody
personal life or their morals, for God's sake. I mean, they really
do, most of them, have none. And yet they are throwing the
stones — but they don't throw them at the men.

Kernot was still struggling to find her footing within the ALP, and
believes the story established a climate of negativity compounded
by judgement from some of her colleagues.

After the publication of this schoolboy story — dissected in
detail for weeks — Kernot appeared to start feeling the strain. It
was a complex entwining of cause and effect: the media dogged
her, provoked her, and then leapt on any sign of discomfort and
annoyance as a signal of her inability to cope with pressure. At
the same time, Labor staffers said, she became obsessed with her
own image. Greg Turnbull says he thought to himself after the
McGeough story broke, '"You are now a shadow minister in a
Labor opposition. You either get on with it or you don't." But I
think part of her subsequent downfall was she kept wanting to
chew on the bone of the issue of her privacy and her relationship
with the media. And that just got everyone swarming all over her
again and again. And she appeared more interested in that than
in her shadow portfolio … We had about three good days and
they were the first three.'

Kernot's first public snap at journalists was during the ALP
annual conference in Hobart in January 1998. On the first night,
she heard her husband had almost been killed by a removal truck
that smashed into her new home. She was at the airport at 6.00
the next morning, and faced a throng of reporters, telling them
wearily, 'It's this kind of thing that makes people really get sick
and tired of your intrusions into our lives.' When a female ABC-
TV reporter called out, 'How come your move was organised
during the Labor Party conference?', she turned and said, 'Are

you serious? That is a disgraceful way ... to treat me in the circumstances.' At Brisbane airport, she wondered aloud if it had been worth it: 'You've got to ask yourself if it's worth the cost. I've got to ask my family if it's worth the cost.' Senior Labor figures were disgruntled. Her words were widely reported, and regarded as evidence she was not tough enough to make it in the big time of politics.

Her response may not have been textbook, but it was understandable. She pointed out that night on 'The 7.30 Report' that it was her first outburst in eight years and she was exhausted. She had also been accused of neglecting her family in order to attend the conference. It was a human response. But journalists wondered if she was cracking.[19]

At this stage, Kernot still largely had public sympathy.[20] But complaints about the media were not taken kindly by journalists who had helped build her million-vote profile. Her next slip-up came at the ALP conference. Many reporters were astonished by a reference to her impact on the party in a draft of her otherwise successful speech. In her draft, she wrote: 'In a way I didn't expect it to, the earth moved on October 15. A fault line opened up at Kirribilli and now it's running all the way to the Prime Minister's office in Canberra.' This was changed to: 'In a way I certainly didn't expect it to, there did seem to be a shift in Australian politics on October the 15th. Now maybe the entire earth didn't move, but certainly a fault line opened up at Kirribilli and now thanks to Kim Beazley's leadership, and his decency and his magnanimous nature, that fault line is running all the way to the Prime Minister's office in Canberra.'[21]

After seeing the draft version, Laurie Oakes had called Beazley's adviser, Greg Turnbull, and said it seemed arrogant. She changed the speech, with the help of Evans and Faulkner, but it was too late, journalists had seen the draft and she was criticised for an apparent ego. Kernot then discussed media management with some of the key party figures and was given Mark Nolan, who had been secretary of West Australian Labor, to work with until the election.

In a matter of months, Kernot's relationship with the media had soured. She stopped talking to journalists. She was under pressure to contain herself emotionally.[22] Any time a crisis arose, her disgruntled former Democrats staffers were available to journalists to explain her behaviour — she was often volatile, they explained; she had a nasty, emotional side, was 'high-maintenance', and was prone to furious outbursts signalled by 'that look'. She also made some fairly public gaffes. When, at the conference, she was given responsibility for a 'project' policy development on middle-aged unemployed, she twice suggested she would be shadow minister for baby boomers, with unwelcome yuppie connotations. She was contradicted by Beazley twice, adding to suspicions she was uncomfortable in the ALP hierarchy. The Kernot story was now almost pure personality.

The next body blow came a few days later, on 13 March. In parliament, West Australian MP Don Randall accused her of having the morals of an alley cat on heat and suggested — correctly, we later learned — that she was having an affair with Gareth Evans. He was forced to apologise, and was locked out of the Liberal Party convention, but the damage was done. This time, public sympathy was on her side. She became a martyr, and again gained the support of the press for what was widely considered a low act.

Randall had said he wanted to dispel some myths about her before she visited his electorate the following week. After a string of allegations, he raved, 'She is about as honest as Christopher Skase and Nick Bolkus. She is about as loyal as Benedict Arnold, and she has the morals of an alley cat on heat. I was a teacher and I can assure you that if I had had an affair with somebody ten years younger than me I would have been in trouble. You might then say, does this affection extend for the Member for Holt [Evans], we often wonder?' Alan Ramsey called it 'the shabbiest, most cowardly personal attack under the protection of parliamentary privilege in recent memory'.[23] Robert Manne, Fairfax columnist and associate professor of politics at La Trobe University, was similarly disgusted. He said he could not recall a 'more vicious parliamentary slander', and Randall should be disendorsed. Manne argued Kernot, as the first woman not only to have a serious chance of becoming PM but who represented 'an idea of a feminised political sphere', had something 'which seems to threaten the identity and cultural self-confidence of a certain kind of traditional male'.[24] But Gareth Evans, as we later discovered, while refuting Randall's allegations had lied to parliament to protect his marriage.[25]

Kernot had now become the scarlet woman. Which is why her decision to allow herself to be photographed in a fancy red and black dress for the *Australian Women's Weekly*, sitting on a red bench with a feather boa draped around her shoulders, was such a disaster. The timing was appalling. The image conjured up a host of seductive female figures, including 'Mae West meets Tilly Devine' and 'vampy showboat queen'. Miranda Devine wrote in the *Daily Telegraph* that it was 'more wild-west madam than putative prime minister'.[26] Kernot completely underestimated the nature and extent of the public and press reactions, in part because their velocity was unprecedented. Had she known what other 'cover girl' MPs had experienced over the previous two decades, however, she may have thought twice.

Kernot blamed the *Weekly* for not warning her which shot they were going to use. She said she was shocked when she saw the photos, but was also defensive: 'Don't you think I dress up? Don't you think I wear evening dresses? Haven't you ever seen John Howard in a tuxedo? He is often photographed in a tux ... I am not going to lose sleep over it.' After her complaints that the media were intrusive, the photos — along with an interview about her 'dark and disturbing times' — were not well received. A perceived hypocrisy was at the core of the criticism.

Still, the reaction did seem excessive. Greg Turnbull said he was amazed by 'some of the utterly humourless and sanctimonious commentary', and wondered if there was a law which said female politicians could not wear evening gowns. Many commentators said she looked silly, like a tart. Peter Cole-Adams, political editor of the *Canberra Times*, argued Kernot wanted it both ways: 'She denounces the media for trivialising her, even as she trivialises herself. She rightly condemns the stereotyping of women politicians while, in this episode, capitalising on the stereotypes.'[27] Brian Toohey asked, 'Are we to believe that Cheryl Kernot does her best policy work dressed in a red duchess satin gown and feather boa?'[28]

Michael Gordon from the *Age* came to her defence again, and declared that Kernot had become a target since her defection: 'Now the stream of critical commentary has become a torrent, suggesting a consensus among elite media opinion that Kernot is not only fair game, but that she is no longer to be taken seriously.' Her real problem was that she was not able to balance such spreads with policy work, and show substance: 'Having snared one of the most remarkable political catches in memory, Labor had no coherent strategy to put her to work. It seemed content to wing it.'[29]

The oracle-polls were again consulted and the general public proved to be far less judgemental then the press gallery. A Bulletin–Morgan poll found 60 per cent believed the 'red dress' photographs made no difference to Kernot's credibility as a politician. Asked if these kinds of photographs were good or bad for female politicians' images, 55 per cent said they made no difference, and 13 per cent were undecided.

By this time, Kernot was clearly depressed and disillusioned. Her profile was flattened, as she campaigned around the country

The Au$tralian **Women's Weekl**

Clever storage ideas

APRIL 1998
$3.80*

KERRYN PHELPS
Why I married a woman

BIG READ
Tragedy of a supermodel

NONI & JOHN
Counselling saved our marriage

CRAFT
A cosy cat bed

Exclusive interview
CHERYL KERNOT'S
Dark and disturbing times

BEAUTY
Gorgeous new colours

FASHION
Great suits for winter

9 313006 000105   04

Commentators howled when they saw the famous photo that led Cheryl Kernot, the ALP's prize recruit, to be labelled a hussy and a shameless publicity seeker.
Australian Women's Weekly, April 1998. *Australian Women's Weekly*

and refused personal interviews. Journalists were describing her as wary, as she cut herself off from many of them for fear of saying the wrong thing — something she later said she regretted.

Kernot attributes her private struggle to her feeling of impotency within the ALP, and the lack of intellectual recognition. 'What had the biggest impact on me psychologically,' she says, 'was the dawning realisation that Labor wasn't going to do anything constructive with me ... I became completely depressed about it ... I thought, "What's the point?" And I was in a marginal seat, which was killing me. It was a 24-hour a day job in a relentlessly scrutinised local electorate where the local Libs were hostile in the [national] press and the local paper all the time. It was like being in hell 24 hours a day.'

The fact that Kernot was struggling was stark on the night of the 1998 election. It was unclear if she had won her seat, and she was tired and angry. Asked in an interview with ABC-TV if she regretted not holding out for a safe seat, Kernot replied bitterly: 'I'll just say this: Mary Delahunty is in parliament. I'll let everybody decode that.' In other words, a safe seat had been found for another high-profile candidate, former ABC-TV reporter Mary Delahunty, in Victoria, while she was struggling in a marginal seat. Again, the Labor Party collectively groaned. Her constituents were angry, too. Earlier in the interview Kernot had also blamed the possible loss of Dickson on 'the demographics of the seat and maybe those who chose it for me not fully appreciating that'. Former party secretary Bob Hogg said she had 'burnt her bridges' with the ALP, although other senior figures denied this. Journalists were quick to point out she'd said she had insisted on a marginal seat so she could prove herself to the ALP.

Three days later, Kernot apologised for her comments, saying she deeply regretted them.[30] Her remarks had been widely condemned as a dummy spit, although there were two men who were also credited with dummy spits on the same night: Gareth

Evans, who said he would be resigning if Labor lost, and Mark Latham, who resigned from the front bench because he said he felt excluded from policy development. They were all criticised. After two weeks of counting, Kernot finally claimed victory in her seat — by only 176 votes. She was appointed spokeswoman on regional development, infrastructure, transport and regional services, but she failed to make an impact as a shadow minister. She survived two more years, losing her seat in the 2001 election with a 7.3 per cent swing against her. Kernot said there were many reasons for her defeat, and 'they're not all called Cheryl Kernot'. She retired, bruised and exhausted, planning to write a book about her experiences.

*

Over time, Kernot lost many supporters, and, because of her erratic behaviour, people now scoff at the suggestion her gender played any part in her bumpy slide to the bottom of the political heap. As Christine Wallace says:

> Cheryl was on a suicide mission the minute she went to the Labor Party. Her completely obsessed behaviour and her need, Germaine Greer-like, to play out her internal psychic drama on a public stage were a tragedy to watch unfold … once she started spinning out, it was impossible to stop. She was the author of her own downfall despite tremendous efforts behind the scenes to help her, prop her up and make every post a winner. So I just don't buy the blokes-did-in-Cheryl argument; I think it's complete bullshit. The fact is, behind the scenes, a lot of the women who were trying to help Cheryl would say candidly to each other 'she's a dud', she used to be great but she's lost it now, it's a matter of damage control and trying to paper things together.

The ALP didn't seem to handle Kernot brilliantly; she needed more staff, minders and sound advice. She also should have had a safe seat, and access to the inner circle. When she defected, someone anonymously sent her a black condom, 'for use when the Labor Party fucks you over'. But many people in the ALP — politicians, staffers and the executive alike — had worked hard to try to give her the support she needed. The Labor Party spent an estimated $650,000 on 'Project Cheryl', largely on salaries, removal costs, a car, and other incidentals in the year after she had resigned from parliament and before the 1998 election. With the enemies she had in the party, however, and her reluctance to network, it was not enough. Former national secretary Gary Gray says, 'I spent an absolute fortune trying to make it a success and I am convinced that if she hadn't been undermined by people in the ALP that she would have been a success and we would have won in 1998.'

Kernot was brilliant when she feminised the public sphere in a positive way, when she was on a high and tried to usher in honesty, accountability, transparency, and accessibility. These are not inherently female traits, but by refusing to play to some of the male conventions of closed doors and media spin, her approach was heralded as a refreshing breakthrough. But when she represented meltdown, failure, and loss of control, her defence on the grounds of gender — a male-dominated media — failed because of her own culpability. Even though she was judged harshly, it is simply wrong to blame men — in politics or the media — for bad decisions, churlish behaviour and poorly handled public appearances.

At the same time, Kernot was under pressure most of us can barely imagine, and was right to argue that sometimes the scrutiny on high-profile MPs is unbearable. Mike Seccombe told me he could not remember 'any politician ever being subject to that sort of thing'. Who would not struggle under that kind of strain? Dennis Shanahan believes 'it was pretty clear she was cracking up in a psychological way, there's no doubt about that'. Nor should anyone underestimate how much some parts of the media hated her. As Robert Macklin wrote in the *Canberra Times* on 24 October 1998, there was 'a substantial segment of the media who cannot speak her name without fashioning a sneer'. She told one reporter, 'I can't guess what motivates some people to froth at the mouth at the thought of my existence.'

It was not that Kernot was grilled, scrutinised and criticised for an ill-considered — but understandable — move to the ALP that was surprising. What was unnerving to observe was the level of hostility towards her. Greg Turnbull attributes it to the 'wounded antelope' syndrome: 'If you are up on the echelon of this political game where you attract attention, you are fair game, and if there's a wounded one who drops around the back, the lions will get you, and they got her.' She was loathed and widely dismissed as a whinger. In the *Herald*'s Sydney office, some people would hiss and boo at the television screens perched high above the news desk when she appeared — particularly when she was perceived to be complaining one time too many. She seemed to inspire a level of hatred or opposition that is rare. Part of the reason was that journalists despise people who depend on good relations with journalists to cultivate a solid and trustworthy profile, then proceed to complain about media attention; or who lay their souls bare, then complain of intrusion. Turnbull, who was on constant damage-control duty for Kernot, said she 'liked nothing more than talking about and analysing the media and its relationship to her. When you go public demanding privacy from the media, it's kind of a contradiction in terms. And also, if you don't want public intrusion into your private life, get out of the game. Get out of the game.'

Eventually Kernot was caught in a cycle she could not control. As the opposition spokeswoman for health, Julia Gillard put it:

I think it was easy for those women to get sucked into the golden girl vortex where the media decide they're the next big thing, [and] the reporting quickly changes from what they do to who they are. The feminist movement, women in the party for a whole lot of absolutely good-hearted reasons are so happy to see a woman achieving that that they are pretty keen to hold the pedestal aloft and make it even higher. So they are actually adding to the golden girl vortex themselves. And it feeds a cycle where the news becomes not what these professional women politicians do — do they ask good questions in Question Time? Do they release a good policy? — but who they are, and then once you are in that cycle, even though the media has been the driver of the start of the cycle, the media then uses that as a justification for getting into a whole lot of personality-based inquiries, and at the end of the day a whole lot of personality-based criticism. So the issue about Cheryl Kernot became not whether or not she was good at what she did, which should be the test for all of us ... the test for Cheryl became whether people liked her or not.

While all of this was going on, Kernot was voted the most influential woman in Australia in a NSW Chamber of Commerce poll. This again confirmed Kernot's belief that there was a strong dissonance between the views of the press gallery and the public. Political analysts believed Kernot added between 5 and 10 per cent to her party's vote in that year's election. Sue Williams, writing in the *Sun-Herald* at the end of November 1998, reported that internal party polling showed Kernot's approval rating was just as high as when she was leader of the

Democrats. But she was avoiding journalists, and speaking to an ever-shrinking group of them. Tony Wright, then at the *Age*, described her as guarded: 'It is no longer possible to imagine her leaping on a table at her birthday party, as she did a few years ago for the television cameras, and belting out a version of "It's My Party (And I'll Cry If I Want To)".'[31] When it was no longer her party, she was certainly not allowed to cry when she wanted to, if at all.

CHAPTER NINE

Sex and the 'Stiff-Dick Syndrome'

It was a regrettable fact that disgraced females found 'their
character is utterly gone, may never be retrieved', whereas
disgraced males 'after many errors, may reform and be
admitted into that same society and meet with a cordial
reception as before' — but there it was, nature's way …
— Siân Rees, *The Floating Brothel: The Extraordinary
Story of the* Lady Julian *and Its Cargo of Female Convicts
Bound for Botany Bay*

Australians go for the underdog and now she's the
underbitch, isn't she?
— John Laws, 4 July 2002

It was 29 June 2002 and Kathy Bail, feminist author and deputy
editor of the *Bulletin*, was driving down the road from Sydney
to Canberra. She was carrying with her an advance copy of
Cheryl Kernot's book *Speaking for Myself Again*, for delivery
to the house of Australia's most influential political reporter,
Laurie Oakes. A large man, with a phlegmatic, authoritative

style, Oakes was Channel Nine's political editor and a columnist for the *Bulletin* and broke some of the biggest stories in our political history. In 1974, one of his stories prompted an election (after he revealed that Gough Whitlam was planning to appoint a Democratic Labor Party senator, Vince Gair, as ambassador to Ireland in order to change the composition of the Senate). In 1980, he had an entire budget leaked to him.

HarperCollins publicist Christine Farmer said Oakes had spent the previous day charming and cajoling her in an attempt to get a copy of the book, which Kernot had insisted all journalists should receive at the same time: on Sunday, the day before the launch. Farmer said he maintained he needed time to read it before writing his column for the *Bulletin* on Monday. She wavered as Kernot insisted he not receive an early copy. 'I just didn't want any journo's spin in the first 48 hours,' Kernot said. But Oakes persisted, Bail agreed to sign a confidentiality agreement, and Farmer caved in.[1]

Bail, who said the first question in their minds was whether Kernot had spilled the details of an extramarital affair in what had been promised to be a 'tell-all book', delivered the book to Oakes on Saturday night. Kernot had not. As Oakes read through the book over a cold Canberra weekend, on his mind was the smoking gun in his possession: leaked emails that proved Cheryl Kernot had had a five-year relationship with senior Labor minister Gareth Evans.

On Monday morning, as Baptist minister Tim Costello launched Kernot's book at the Sofitel in Melbourne, Oakes sat down to write his column at his office in Parliament House. Farmer told me that the launch had a strange vibe in the air; that the publishers felt nervous, and were surprised by some of the hostile questioning from the gathered media throng: 'We didn't get that warm fuzzy feeling about a book launch. It was pointed and political, people sizing each other up in the room. There was an air of aggressiveness about it at the time … The Beazley launch was warm and fuzzy; the Hayden launch was warm and fuzzy, all matey, even though he had a few paybacks in the book.' Following the launch, Kernot spent time with her friends after sending her daughter to the airport. In Canberra, Oakes went for lunch with his longstanding friend, Kim Beazley's former chief of staff, Michael Costello.[2]

On Tuesday, Kernot was back in Sydney doing a round of interviews on radio and television. That night, fax machines in the major newspaper bureaus in Canberra started whirring as a press release from the *Bulletin* came through, along with a copy of the Oakes column. Alan Ramsey wrote, 'Nobody I'm aware of took it up, though they all knew instantly what cat Oakes was belling.'[3] Kernot was in the car with Farmer when a HarperCollins staffer called to tell her about Oakes's column. Kernot said she was genuinely surprised: 'Having told Gareth that I wouldn't be referring to it, and having discussed it with others, I had decided not to refer to the relationship in the book, one of the main reasons being that I would have to have exposed Gareth's lie to parliament to placate his wife. I really didn't count on Laurie's demonic zeal.'

On 3 July, as Kernot rose early in her room at the Sydney InterContinental Hotel for another day of interviews, copies of the *Bulletin* were being delivered to newsstands. Both Kernot and Evans had left politics, and it was more than three years since the affair had ended, but the trigger for the column was the book, which Oakes said should have been called *Making Excuses for Myself Again*. He slammed her for failing to tell Australia about her extramarital affair in the account of her political demise, writing:

> For a long time now, some members of the Fourth Estate
> have been aware of the biggest secret in Kernot's life. If
> made public, it would cause a lot of people to view her

defection from the Australian Democrats to the Labor
Party in a different light. It helps to explain some of her
erratic behaviour. It was a key factor in the erosion of
her emotional and physical health that contributed to her
political disintegration. It even caused a lie to be told to the
parliament — not by Kernot, but by a colleague. But it was
also personal, so as far as the media was concerned it was
treated as out of bounds.

While it is one thing for journalists to stay away from
such a matter, however, it is quite another for Kernot herself
to pretend it does not exist when she pens what purports to
be the true story of her ill-fated change of party allegiance.
An honest book would have included it. If Kernot felt the
subject was too private to be broached, there should have
been no book, because the secret was pivotal to what
happened to her. Had Kim Beazley, John Faulkner and other
ALP leading lights been aware of it when then-deputy leader
Gareth Evans proposed bringing Kernot into the Labor fold,
they would have thought twice about the idea and probably
said 'no'. Without the distraction and distress it caused
Kernot at crucial times, she would certainly have been a less
flaky and more effective shadow minister. To white out such
a major element results in serious distortion.

Oakes wrote that Kernot's expectations of the role she should
have had in the Labor Party were 'ridiculous'. She had proved to
be 'unable to properly handle the responsibilities she was given.
But basically, she couldn't stand the heat so the voters of Dickson
showed her the kitchen door.' This, for a woman who Oakes said
in 1998 had 'the kind of credibility that most politicians can only
dream about'.[4] Oakes didn't say what the 'secret' was — something
he said he later regretted, as withholding the information seemed
too cynical and calculated a move when he revealed it later that

night on Channel Nine. He said he had wanted to goad Kernot into baring her secret instead, but she refused to say what it was, making light of it on the 'Sunrise' program that morning: 'There is no big, deep, dark secret. I don't have any comment on that particular article. [The secret] could be that I've got flabby arms.'

Titillated by the fact that the relationship had been hinted at but not fully disclosed, by 11.00 a.m. former political staffer and business journalist Stephen Mayne, operator of the political and media gossip website Crikey.com.au, had leapt into cyberspace. In an email to his then 3600 subscribers, Mayne wrote: 'Crikey only regarded it as an unsubstantiated rumour but Oakes has come out and effectively said, "Gareth and Cheryl had an affair, which was pivotal to her defection and subsequent political failure."' Mayne was the first to refer to the affair, insisting, 'Oakes should have gone all the way and actually spelled out what it was.'

A few hours later, Oakes led the Nine Network's 6.00 p.m. news with the claim that Evans and Kernot had had a 'grand consuming' affair for five years. He said he had solid evidence of the affair: emails between the two. In one, Evans admitted lying to parliament about having the affair to protect his marriage, saying he could not yet 'live with the consequences of that revelation'. Then, demonstrating the story was, almost immediately, as much about Oakes as about Kernot and Evans, Oakes was interviewed on 'A Current Affair', to discuss the 'steamy affair' which he said he had uncovered 'some years ago'. He told the television cameras he had worried and thought very carefully about it, but could not allow a 'false version' of 'something that was important to political events of this country' to be out there. Oakes denied it had been calculated for maximum publicity for the *Bulletin* or Channel Nine, but conceded his staggered disclosure had not been the most appropriate way to handle it. He said he had wrestled, worried and agonised — and that there was no 'right' decision. Kernot was still being driven around by Farmer when

Farmer's assistant called and said Oakes had spoken in full about the affair on Channel Nine, and that they had asked for a transcript. Kernot said her reaction was 'fatalistically calm': 'So the bastard's still pursuing me ... when I've been out of parliament for eight months.' When opposition leader Simon Crean, then in London, strangely demanded that Evans and Kernot give a full explanation, the story was guaranteed front-page status in every major newspaper.

Throughout Cheryl Kernot's career, a chasm had yawned between the views of the press and the usually more tolerant public. At no time was this greater. On 4 July, according to media monitor Rehame, 85 per cent of radio talkback calls opposed Oakes's actions to break the story.[5] In the words of the *Australian Financial Review*'s chief political correspondent, Laura Tingle, 'Most people were just saying "yuk".' SBS, which refused to touch the story, received numerous calls of congratulation.

Oakes's decision to expose the affair was dissected for weeks. Journalists were divided. In newspaper offices outside Canberra, there seemed to be general approval for what he did. Most of the journalists I knew thought Kernot was fair game simply by virtue of having written a book. In the nation's capital, however, many powerful journalists, especially those who had for decades respected the convention on not writing about politicians' personal lives, raged. Ramsey called it 'the cheapest, grubbiest cheap shot of all'. The *Australian Financial Review*'s political editor, Tony Walker, said the story could not be justified on public interest grounds, and that it was a case of the media manipulating the media: 'Anyone is entitled to seek to correct a record they believe might be blemished; journalists can hardly argue otherwise. But should a reporter in a privileged position set him or herself up as judge, jury and executioner in such matters? I think not.' Oakes, who insisted he was not a 'muckraker', and that these were exceptional circumstances, did have some support from his colleagues, including the *Australian*'s political editor, Dennis Shanahan, and conservative commentators Piers Akerman and Andrew Bolt. The argument centred on whether or not a private matter impacted the performance of public duties.

Australian columnist Glenn Milne said both sides of politics agreed the affair had 'absolutely no effect on contemporary politics'. Laura Tingle wrote, 'Most in the Labor Party do not believe the fact that Kernot and Evans were involved materially changed the party's fortunes.'

But Michelle Grattan believed Kernot's 'private situation affected her political conduct — her decision to switch parties and why it ended in tears — and she omits this from an account that lashes out at many people'. Grattan told me she had thought at the time Kernot changed parties that her decision must have been driven by a relationship with Evans, because it was so strange, to move from a position of power to an unfamiliar, possibly hostile political culture: 'I thought at the time ... that this was the only explanation for one doing this, for this behaviour. I didn't buy her intellectual justification. I thought the influence brought to bear on her had to be other than the Howard government. If she wanted to be a major player she would have been better to stay the balance of power player ... It was also the way that she did it, the way that she eloped politically; it was like she was under the sway of someone.' Who can judge?

*

So what exactly is the convention about politicians and their private lives? It had been described in the same way for decades, but occasionally broken for different, often subjective reasons. Historically, it has meant that journalists pride themselves on not reporting the sexual liaisons or 'indiscretions' of politicians, including affairs, alcoholism, and broken marriages, in the belief that personal affairs should not spill into the public domain unless there is a significant public interest. The convention has long been used to protect men who cheat on their wives, attempt to seduce journalists, sexually assault or harass women, drink heavily, or take drugs. It appears an underlying assumption has been that when men do these things, the way they think or work is not affected — that politics remains untainted by their personal predilections, the distractions of lust and rejection, the heartache of relationship break-ups, the struggle with addictions. Men can, apparently, separate work and play, their loins disconnected from their brains. Nick Greiner, who was NSW premier from 1988 to 1992, wrote in 1993 that 'Australian journalists go out of their way to avoid attacking politicians' personal lives — unlike their counterparts in the US, UK and elsewhere. One can philander, get drunk, gamble to excess and be treated with sensitive ignore.'[6] In 2001, Laurie Oakes said private lives were still off limits 'almost entirely, unless it's something directly relevant to the way politicians do their job'.[7] Which means the onus is on the journalist to prove the revelation or story affected the way that politician *did their job*. When I spoke to him again in 2004, Oakes told me he would add to his proviso: 'or to why political events occur'.

The convention is still largely intact, and has been eroded only gradually and with great reluctance on the part of most journalists, who have decried any moves towards a more tabloid, American style of political reporting. Underpinning their reluctance is a fear that once someone throws stones, rocks will be thrown back, and politics will be nastier for it. A belief that on the one hand people are flawed and human, and may make brilliant politicians but lousy husbands or wives, and on the other expecting all politicians to be personally pious and flawless is unrealistic and unrepresentative.

But it is now clear that the group this convention has mostly protected is men.

In the mid-1970s, at the time the press was daily dogging the heels of the Whitlam government, innuendo that emerged in news reports was not to do with female politicians but with glamorous young female staffers, or 'supergirls', thought to be turning the heads of the men they worked for. Stories were written ridiculing Liberal prime minister John Gorton when he took a 19-year-old female journalist to top-secret briefings at the US embassy in Canberra after the press gallery's annual dinner. There was ongoing speculation about his appointment of a woman in her early 20s, Ainslie Gotto, as his principal private secretary, considered to be attractive to reporters. The press also salivated over the relationship of Whitlam minister Jim Cairns and his principal private secretary, Junie Morosi — but not only was that relationship current at the time, both parties spoke of a 'kind of love' for each other, fanning the rumours. Many words were written about her 'exotic' (read: Asian) looks. After successfully suing newspapers that suggested their relationship was sexual, Cairns admitted many years later in 2002 on ABC Radio that it was true.

The first time the convention was broken for a female politician was in 1976 when Mungo MacCallum alleged in the *Nation Review* that federal social security minister Margaret Guilfoyle was having an affair with colleague Jim Killen. The front cover read 'The Romantic Ministers', and featured a cartoon by Michael Leunig of a man and woman walking hand in hand through the rose garden, as it was alleged Guilfoyle and Killen had done at Parliament House. MacCallum wrote that fears of a divorce had caused Prime Minister Malcolm Fraser to warn them he would not appreciate a public scandal, which in turn provoked a question to be asked in parliament. MacCallum defended his decision to break the story on the grounds of hypocrisy:

No one objects to a little public hypocrisy from politicians, but when you have a Social Security Minister lauding the virtues of the nuclear family for page after page of the women's magazines, and defending a policy which says that men and women — particularly women — should lose their pension rights if they live in the same house, and then strolling around the parliamentary rose garden hand in hand with one of her colleagues — well it gets a bit much.[8]

After MacCallum broke ranks, few followed his lead as they were to do years later for Kernot. There was only one article that reported the story, in the tabloid newspaper the *Sun*, which splashed it on the front page under the headline '"Cabinet Ministers' Romance" Story', and claimed the government was concerned.[9] Guilfoyle refused to comment.

The second was in 1991, when a relationship Democrat leader Janet Powell had with a colleague emerged in the press during a bitter leadership battle. The initial charges against Powell were that she had failed to consult on some policy matters and that she had a low profile. On 20 August, some journalists reported Powell had been ousted in a party room coup amid claims she was a victim of innuendo about her private life.[10] Tasmanian Senator Robert Bell implied that some kind of 'scandal' was involved, and that Victorian Democrats senator Sid Spindler had become the 'defacto deputy leader' of the party. He also referred to a relationship between Powell and Spindler.

Powell then confirmed the relationship. The story was given prominence for several days. Many reporters regretted this, and told readers so. Tony Wright from the *Canberra Times* wrote that several Democrats senators had told reporters in off-the-record chats that Powell's relationship with Spindler had affected her performance. The information was 'so solid and so persistent' that some had considered reporting it when the first tensions emerged. 'But we all decided to abide by the tradition that stories of a politician's personal relationships were not part of the Australian political reporter's repertoire. Once you go down that path, many issues would become very clouded indeed. All of us know sexual adventures involving politicians, but the tradition has — by and large — held.' The *Sydney Morning Herald*'s Mike Seccombe claimed that because Australian politics was unused to muckraking, 'the sympathy went all Powell's way'. But senior political journalist Michelle Grattan believed the same thing would have happened to then prime minister Paul Keating if he'd had an affair with a female member of cabinet: 'I just think that if you have an affair with someone who is in your party, you're asking for trouble.'[11]

Powell defended herself on the grounds that it was not an affair but a long-term relationship that had ended several months previously, and argued that it had not interfered with her leadership. She blamed her colleagues, and pointed out that she had been attacked while Spindler had not.

Press gallery journalists claim Cheryl Kernot was one of the group of women backgrounding them and using the affair to destabilise Powell. Kernot denied it, holding a press conference with Meg Lees to insist they had never publicly discussed Powell's personal life. However, they produced a press release which listed a 'range of concerns' about Powell, including 'impingements of aspects of private life on party professional judgement'. Powell remained bitter about the incident, telling journalists later that she blamed Kernot for the story, and that Kernot could ask for no sympathy if her own private life were pawed over.

Party politics is grubby and ruthless. Many politicans will use whatever dirt they can against their enemies, including sexual preferences, the presence or absence of children, and custody disputes. Women do not shy from this. These rumours — many of which are grossly exaggerated, unfair and wrong — abound in parliaments and press galleries, and always have. It is then just a case of finding a reporter willing to risk the scorn of his or her colleagues for writing it. Many journalists sympathise with those attacked about their private lives. By the mid-2000s, when one of the tempted media pack broke ranks, he or she was often castigated by opinion leaders — but floods of stories still followed.

Most scandals about male politicians have been brought into the public eye by disgruntled ex-wives or family members, not journalists. One exception occurred in 1995, when journalist Margo Kingston reported that an apprehended violence order had been taken out against West Australian Liberal Noel Crichton-Browne by his wife, Esther, in 1989 after an alleged assault at their home. The order alleged he had beaten her so badly that her eyes were black, an eardrum was perforated, and her neck severely bruised. The court restrained Crichton-Browne from causing 'personal injury' to his wife, and behaving 'in an offensive or provocative manner' towards her. The AVO was later withdrawn, but the story emerged several years afterwards during a nasty Senate preselection contest in Western Australia, when documents were sent to preselection delegates as well as some Liberal MPs by Crichton-Browne's enemies.

In the *Sunday Age*, Michael Bachelard claimed the *Perth Daily News* had had a copy of the restraining order at the time it was issued, but decided against reporting it. Not so in 1995. Crichton-Browne was forced to resign his position as representative of then opposition leader John Howard on the West Australian Liberal executive, and then as deputy president of the Senate. He was also banned from Liberal Party meetings in Canberra. He said he was deeply ashamed of the incident, then inflamed the story by threatening a female journalist that he would 'screw [her] tits off'.

There has been one story similar to that of Kernot's past relationship with a student, involving Tony Abbott, who was a senior Liberal and former trainee Catholic priest. The story was that Abbott impregnated his then girlfriend at university and gave the child up for adoption. The man who first carefully aired this story was a friend of Abbott, and the same columnist who attacked Kernot so viciously for her past relationship: Christopher Pearson. He wrote a story for the *Courier-Mail* in April 1997 decrying poisonous stories which he said had spread about Abbott: 'Most concerned a girlfriend with whom he was said to have fathered a child before fleeing the country, denying paternity. In fact ... there was a longstanding girlfriend in his first year at Sydney University and an unplanned pregnancy. [Abbott] says about it: "We thought of getting married but, in the end, we decided we were too young and the baby was adopted out."'[12] Pearson knew Abbott well, and the story was clearly deliberately released to prevent someone else breaking it as a 'scoop', as well as to correct any wilder versions that had been circulating.

Abbott was not criticised for his actions, aside from the odd letter, and there was little follow-up. There were no stories, for example, about journalists trying to hunt down the woman or the child involved, unlike those who tracked down Kernot's former lover, his mother and even his child at school. However, Labor MP Mark Latham attempted to resuscitate the story several times to damage his political foe. In March 2002, he told the parliament, 'There is a convention in this place that members shouldn't drag each other's families into parliamentary debate. I respect and admire parents like [former deputy PM] Frank Crean ... they have always raised their children and protected their genes, rather than giving them away.' Latham brought it up in parliament and at conferences in 2002, but was strongly criticised for the attacks.[13] Abbott retaliated the next year, when Latham's first wife emerged after his leadership win to tell journalists he was a nasty, self-serving narcissist. Abbott called him 'brutal' in the house.

The final stretch of this story was genuinely astonishing. The child was identified as an ABC sound recordist, and Abbott was publicly and privately reconciled with him. The plot then twisted, though, when Abbot's ex-girlfriend's former flatmate saw the story on the TV news and came forward to confess that in fact he believed he was the true father. DNA tests confirmed this.

Other stories have only come to light because spurned lovers, angry wives or hurt children have handed them to journalists.[14] In 1996, for example, former opposition leader Bill Hayden's 'lovechild', Robert Licciardo, outed himself as the secret his father had hidden for almost 40 years. Licciardo, who was given up for adoption at birth, said he'd decided to tell his story when Hayden released an autobiography and did not mention him. The story, which did not spark much interest, was first revealed in the Melbourne *Herald Sun*. Licciardo, a Victorian restaurateur, then gave an exclusive interview to the *Australian Women's Weekly*, which was reported in the *Daily Telegraph*. He said his mother never recovered from giving him up and did not have any more children, even though she later married. Licciardo was a ward of the state who had moved among foster homes, and wanted his famous father to publicly acknowledge him. Hayden refused to comment. The story died quickly.

Senator Bob Woods was similarly embarrassed when a former lover, Roxanne Cameron, took her story to the media.[15] Former Victorian finance minister Ian Smith was forced to resign after his pregnant ex-lover, Cheryl Harris, filed a court action in 1995 alleging he had put pressure on her to abort their child so it would not damage his career, had assaulted her, and had breached her employment contract.[16] He denied these claims, retaliated with a defamation action against her and her solicitors, and received a substantial payment from her solicitors in an out-of-court settlement. All legal disputes with Harris were settled without any admissions.

A story about John Hewson's first marriage was not reported until an interview with his former wife, Margaret, was published in the *Australian Women's Weekly* in 1991.[17] Mrs Hewson told the magazine her former husband moved out four days before Christmas in 1985, saying, 'You can't cope. You won't be able to cope with being a political wife.' She admitted she had struggled: 'I felt very inadequate. I would be seated between two very high-profile men and you could feel that just as soon as they found out you were a housewife looking after three children — dull and boring — you could sense them turning their backs on you.'[18]

Later that month, Mrs Hewson appeared on '60 Minutes', after celebrity agent Max Markson procured payment for her. The show was heavily criticised because reporter Jeff McMullen also interviewed the Hewson children, then aged 18, 15, and eight. Immediately after the show Hewson's popularity surged.[19] A Herald Saulwick poll taken in Sydney and Melbourne showed 71 per cent of voters thought neither better nor worse of Hewson after his ex-wife's revelations. Eighty per cent also thought politicians' private lives should not be a matter for public debate. Pollster Irving Saulwick attributed the surge to 'visibility, handling and sympathy'. It is difficult to work out what kind of impact this tell-all had on Hewson's political career, and if it contributed to his failure to win what had been called the unlosable election in 1993. Hewson told me he has no idea but 'suspect[s] not much'. He said he found it very hard and was called 'a monster' by some, but had refused to comment because Margaret was going through a difficult time. After having suffered this humiliation, it seems peculiar that Hewson would later make comments about the childlessness of then NSW opposition leader Bob Carr, for which he was condemned.[20]

At other times, journalists have refused to report on stories unless they emerge in court, or at trials. When NSW minister Sandra Nori's affair with Labor colleague Paul Gibson was revealed during an Independent Commission against Corruption inquiry, she was devastated. Again, it was not the media who were responsible, but ICAC commissioner Barry O'Keefe, who declared the affair to be of public interest, and ruled that the media could report on it.[21] O'Keefe was not the first to air the affair. Former premier Nick Greiner had alluded to it on 6 March 1992 in parliament. According to the *Sunday Telegraph*, the reference did not escape politicians, reporters or parliamentary staff. It was, however, not reported on until O'Keefe deemed it could be. A senior political journalist recalled that 'Everybody knew about it. They didn't go out of their way to hide it ... [But] none of the journalists ever wrote about it because, frankly, it wasn't an issue.'[22]

*

So what was different about Kernot? Journalists have often hinted at the active sex lives and affairs of MPs, as though referring to a kind of erotic tension swirling in the insular environment of federal politics, fuelled by the sexual allure of power, which is often incomprehensible to people outside looking in. Fia Cumming wrote in the *Sun-Herald* in 1997 that 'sexual dalliances' had been part of federal political life for decades: 'With companionship a rare commodity in the vast Parliament House, lonely and bored male MPs often still seek female company ... For the great majority of MPs who are heterosexual males, there are always plenty of young, intelligent, attractive and ambitious women around Parliament House.' She listed some indiscretions, including a conservative cabinet minister who 'made out' in the toilets or the back of ministerial cars, a married Labor MP who'd had an affair with one of his staff, then her daughter — whom he went on to marry. Another married MP had three mistresses in Canberra.[23] How standards have changed. There were many others. In the *Australian Financial Review,* Lyndall Crisp and Jill Margo wrote that 'the list of dalliances goes forever; it would be easier to name those who didn't stray'.[24] When National Party leader John Anderson said politicians who could not keep their marriage vows should not be in parliament, Mungo MacCallum responded that if these standards were applied vigorously 'he'd be a mighty lonely politician in the cabinet room, the party room and indeed the entire building.' Of the 11 prime ministers since World War II, he wrote, he would 'confidently back just two' to pass the Anderson test.[25] There are many men who could be charged with hypocrisy, because they have mouthed rhetoric about family values while cheating on their wives. As Michael Bachelard wrote in the *Sunday Age*:

> Some political observers refer to a 'stiff-dick syndrome',
> which causes men in politics, infatuated with their own
> professional and personal potency, to become serial
> propositioners and adulterers. But until they cross that line
> and do something either illegal or impossible to ignore, their
> colleagues, political opponents and the media usually pretend
> not to notice. Or show no sign of being concerned.[26]

How many cases of harassment and assult were explained away by the 'stiff-dick syndrome'?

In 1984, then Democrat leader Janine Haines threatened to break some conventions herself by talking about a sexual double standard in politics. Her comments, made to 5DN Adelaide radio announcer Jeremy Cordeaux, about the alleged infidelity of her parliamentary colleagues sparked headlines across the country in what was called the 'bed-hopping row'.[27] The straight-shooting Haines said most of her colleagues had 'a friend on the side', or at least 'casual or regular alternative partners', and blamed it on a double standard which meant 'being away from a spouse for whatever period of time is a jolly good reason for playing around'. She also said she had been propositioned herself. In a statement that was prophetic in light of what later happened to her successors, Janet Powell and Cheryl Kernot, she said this behaviour was considered acceptable in male MPs but 'a woman who plays around gets thoroughly derided — women MPs would be drummed out of the service if they tried it'. Not surprisingly, her remarks were greeted coolly by her colleagues.

When the story about the Evans–Kernot relationship was aired, then, many of their colleagues would have squirmed. The reason the convention is in place is not just about a moral integrity, a desire to keep politics clean, as argued earlier, but because no one wants to be under that kind of personal scrutiny. As Robert Manne argued, 'The instinct to leave the private lives of our politicians alone is, in the end, grounded in something deep, an understanding that a certain kind of social logic governs our collective life. This logic can be summarised swiftly thus: one thing leads to another.'[28] Those who throw stones will be quickly bruised themselves. When Hewson spoke about Carr's childlessness, for example, Ramsey wondered if he wanted journalists to write about the fact that his own wife was having problems conceiving. And, in 2002, it was not long before nasty gossip about Oakes started circulating around newsrooms, which some journalists were eager to confirm and report on. News Limited columnist Glenn Milne wrote that some politicians 'were muttering that Laurie might have a few dark secrets of his own'. Kernot told me people contacted HarperCollins with their own unconfirmed rumours:

> My publishers started getting all these calls from people saying that they knew about Laurie Oakes's own sexual peccadilloes. The first time they laughed. By the tenth time they said, 'Oh we'll tell you this, it's amazing how the

Australian people react when they think someone is being treated unfairly; they come out of the woodwork.'

In 2004, Kernot hinted she was longing to tell stories about Oakes: 'My eyes are twinkling as I say this, but I think I might write an unauthorised biography about him.'[29] Asked for his reaction to this innuendo, Oakes hinted that his critics had motivations of their own and shrugged it off: 'I put my head above the parapet, a lot of people took shots at it. It sort of goes with the territory, doesn't it? ... I haven't set out to be prurient about anyone's private lives, that wasn't my motivation.'

*

Millions lapped up the Kernot and Evans stories thirstily, gripped by the unfolding saga of the reckless, powerful lovers: the woman, alone, unemployed yet unabashed; the man, still married, still employed, but caught out. But there was still a feeling of unease for some about the fact that again this woman, who had held significant power, was being sexually scrutinised. And this was evident in the letters that choked the fax machines and flooded the inboxes of letters editors.

Malcolm Farr says he would not have written the story himself, but once it had been reported it was worthy of dissection and comment:

> With profound moral cowardice, I have a bob each way. If I
> had the emails, it is quite likely I would not have published
> them. It would have been an absolute agony, the sort of agony
> I don't think Laurie went through. I saw no evidence of that;
> it was quite a deliberate, structured thing, the release. But —
> and this is where my moral consistency disappears — having
> become public knowledge, it was a valid thing to be debated,

if you know what I mean; it did have a significance. And part
of that significance was that Kernot had not been honest in
the book.

Alan Ramsey was livid. While their offices were just metres away
from each other in the hindquarters of Parliament House, and
they had been friends for 25 years, he told me he and Oakes have
not spoken since.[30] He still blazes when he talks about it:

> I thought he was so fucking unctuous, this business about,
> oh I *agonised*, I had to tell the truth, poor old Beazley — I
> mean that was just appalling. Just *appalling*. There can be no
> justification for it. I mean why didn't he do it to his mate ...
> [a Labor politician] who was one of the great pokers around
> the place, and was known as such? ... But most people
> thought, it's his private life, for God's sake.[31]

Let's examine the key justifications Oakes used: first, that if
someone writes a biography, or book about a recent experience,
they must 'tell-all'. This demand has been made rarely, and it
seems odd to suggest that when someone writes a book about
their own life they will, or even must, put in all the information
we would like to read, particularly about their sex lives, health
problems, or flirtations with drugs or various addictions. An
autobiography is a voluntary act, from a private citizen. Even
biographers sometimes protect their subjects by omitting details
that might embarrass them, especially if the subject or their
family are still alive. We might want to know more about what
drives and influences our public figures, but who has the right to
reveal — or demand — the information?

Three years before Kernot's book was published, in October
1999, Allen & Unwin published a biography of Gareth Evans,
written by former staffer Keith Scott. If Oakes was right, this

was just as the affair was ending, yet no mention was made of it. The publishers described the book as 'a comprehensive and engaging exploration of the public and private life of one of Australia's most substantial politicians and accomplished foreign ministers'. Scott even wrote about Kernot's defection, arguing: 'Evans played a central role in convincing Kernot to make the switch, and in helping engineer the move once she'd made her decision, over a plunger of coffee, with Evans, Beazley and Labor senator John Faulkner in Faulkner's office.' Oakes said, in a column written a week after the story exploded into print, that he had become convinced the pair were having a relationship in the second half of 1999. When I asked him why he did not write the story then, Oakes said he did not have the emails and did not read the book: 'At that stage I had no particular interest in Gareth's personal life.'

The story could have been run when Evans publicly lied about the affair, on the grounds that he was misleading the parliament. It could have been run when Kernot defected, if there was solid proof that Evans was the major reason for her move. It could have been run when she was struggling to gain a foothold on the edifice of the ALP and make a substantial contribution to her portfolio — again if there was empirical evidence of a causal link. But Oakes decided to run the story after he read Kernot's book — and, critically, once he had the emails that confirmed the affair. He said the book was the prompt because in it she did not reveal everything, and blamed everyone but herself: the ALP, Kim Beazley, the media.

To the second justification. The fact that Oakes was in part writing the story to protect Beazley, who was heavily criticised in Kernot's book, is a troubling one. On 4 July, on the ABC's 'World Today' program, he justified his decision by saying: 'If I'd done nothing, in my view I was allowing a particularly false version of what happened to be accepted and a lot of people getting the blame for things that I don't believe they should have been blamed for. I am thinking particularly of Kim Beazley.' Wouldn't the protection of a politician be the last concern of a journalist?

Third, Oakes claimed the affair was significant in the defection. There are two factors to consider: the mindset of the Labor powerbrokers, and the mindset of Kernot. Oakes believed the ALP would not have recruited the popular Democrats leader if they had known she was in love with one of their senior ministers. In a letter to the ABC's 'Media Watch', Oakes wrote:

> Did I have evidence the affair was a significant factor in
> the defection? What I said was that knowledge of it would
> change many people's view of the defection. That was
> certainly true. I knew that John Faulkner had told colleagues
> that if he had known of the affair at the time of the defection
> he would have vetoed it. I had been told by very good sources
> that Beazley would almost certainly have taken a similar
> view. That, to me, made the affair relevant to the defection.

To the behaviour of some key figures in the ALP, perhaps, but not to Kernot. And it is all very well in hindsight — could others have convinced them otherwise, that it would be for the good of the party that they still brought her over; that the press would continue to observe the convention, if they knew? One of the key players, the national secretary of the ALP, Gary Gray, told me he did not know if knowledge of the affair would have affected his decision.[32] He said the ALP powerbrokers did not work it out until three weeks after Kernot had switched camp. Kim Beazley's chief of staff at the time of the defection, David Epstein, wrote in the *Australian* that he also did not know if they would have spurned Kernot if they had known earlier, but they would have 'paused for thought'.[33]

Kernot said Evans's advice formed 1 per cent of her reason to jump ship. If it were 30 per cent, or 49 per cent, would that justify the story?

The fourth, and related, justification is Oakes's claim that the affair made Kernot a flaky, less effective shadow minister. As mentioned earlier, journalists have long concurred that the only excuse for writing about someone's private life is when it affects their public duties, so this is probably the most critical test. Oakes claimed the affair began when Kernot was Democrats leader and Evans the foreign affairs minister. He said it ended in November 1999, after a 'long period of recrimination'. He then added: 'Within days, Ms Kernot entered hospital suffering from what she describes in the book as immune-system breakdown as a result of emotional and physical exhaustion.' He argued in the *Bulletin* that the affair was instrumental in 'the erosion of her emotional and physical health that contributed to her political disintegration'.[34] He also said that it was relevant because the 'gradual break-up' had an impact on Kernot's behaviour 'and therefore on Labor's election prospects'. David Epstein backed him up, saying, 'The intensity of the relationship befuddled the political judgement of those involved and, in turn, made it virtually impossible for the ALP leadership to engage in rational dialogue with them.'[35] It appeared that he believed Evans's behaviour was affected too.

What this claim lacked was proof of a causal connection between a love affair's bloom and decline, and Kernot's poor performance as a shadow minister or her obvious depression. If Oakes's rationale were applied universally, anyone in a prominent position — say a minister — could have their political judgement or acumen eroded by engaging in an affair. Surely the sex lives of prime ministers should be on the public record if this is the case — we deserve to know which bad policy decision can be attributed to a night on the tiles, or between the sheets. Prime ministers have often admitted retrospective affairs, many of them to sustained and numerous ones. In 1989, after Prime Minister Bob Hawke tearfully admitted he had cheated on his wife, 80 per cent of respondents to a Herald Saulwick poll said it made no difference to the way they thought about him.[36] The last person to see Harold Holt before he was swept out to sea at Portsea in 1967 was his mistress, Marjorie Gillespie. Zara Holt later said he had lovers in Portsea, Melbourne, Canberra, Sydney, and Hong Kong. Ben Chifley's personal secretary was also his mistress, according to his biographer, David Day. This did not become public knowledge until after his death.

This part of Oakes's reasoning is crucial, because if the affair was not the key reason, or even a substantial reason, for Kernot's inability to be an effective shadow minister, then it unnecessarily lends weight to archaic views about the intemperance of women; their instability; being ruled by their hearts; and that their heads are clouded by emotion, especially desire. If there was evidence of this — an email perhaps, of Kernot saying she could not work or think properly, or was making mistakes when the affair soured — it was certainly not made public, so conjecture and assumption took the place of fact. According to Oakes, the emails provided the proof that the affair caused her breakdown but he chose not to reveal them:

> LO: No one could say I raked over her personal life. I
> used hardly anything ... I had a lot of material which
> illustrated what had happened to Cheryl, and the dates
> that it had happened — who had said what to whom and
> so on. There was no way that I would have written what
> I wrote without being sure of those things.
> JB: But she appeared to be unravelling on a number of
> fronts: her bad decision, being in the Labor Party, and I
> guess what it is difficult for an observer, without having

the material you've got, is to ascertain how significant a
contribution it was — if the breakdown of the relationship
was one factor or the defining factor.

LO: Without going into detail — and I haven't gone into
detail over it and I don't want to, I don't think it's fair
to either of them — all I can tell you is that it is an
important factor.[37]

Gerard Henderson asked, 'If Kernot was so knocked off course
by her ongoing romance with a senior ALP politician, why did
she negotiate an important deal with the Coalition on industrial
relations in the lead-up to the 1996 election?'

If it did have a profound impact on her, can anyone seriously
argue no other Australian politician in the past two centuries
has not been affected by an affair, relationship breakdown or
marital problems? Where were the stories about how Evans's
foreign policy announcements were coloured by his nocturnal
activities? Who drew up a timeline with the dates of Bob Hawke's
proclivities next to the major decisions his government made?
And are we to assume that having sex with a third party is more
likely to affect your judgement than having sex with a spouse; or
indeed than not having sex at all? That breaking up with a lover
is more emotionally or professionally damaging than a divorce?
Many politicians have split up with their wives with only a flicker
of media interest, if any. And it is just as easy to argue that an
affair can sustain you, as it is to argue it can distract you.

Kernot, in her attempt, however clumsy, to explain her
behaviour, said there were three major reasons for the debilitating
depression she experienced while a Labor politician. By far the
greatest, she said, was the ALP: enemies who undermined her;
a problematic relationship with the leader, Kim Beazley; and the
fact that she felt sidelined. She told me, 'The biggest stress on me
was the dawning — which came pretty early on — that there was

going to be no role for me. And what had I done, and could I ride it out?' The next was the media — 'oh, she's gaffe prone, she's not performing' — and last was a strong Liberal campaign against her in the parliament and the electorate. I then asked her about the break-up of the relationship: how much that had contributed to her stress.

It was there but I was hoping that by throwing myself into the policy [I would cope] ... I was in therapy, Gavin and I were in counselling, I mean I was dealing with that. My therapist thought the biggest stress on me was the detribalisation I suffered as a result of leaving the Democrats and going to Labor, as a result of what happened. He thought that was a huge, huge stress. I would be silly to say it wasn't there ... But if you are looking for a thesis which supports Laurie Oakes's view, it's wrong. That was part of the depression I was already feeling. But I was feeling that when Gareth was there. He knew that I was just quite desperate ... I knew that what affected my performance as a shadow minister was Labor's unwillingness to include me in anything that mattered ... I considered myself an ideas person, I went into politics for ideas, and as soon as I went to the Labor Party I had no intellectual respect ... and that damaged me a great deal ... I think what happened to me was incredibly complex and it would be too trite to say it was my relationship with Gareth and it was my being a woman who took a risk. It was a much more subtle and complex interrelationship of all these things which I don't think we'll ever know.

Kernot told the ABC's Monica Attard that Oakes never came to her with the story, and had never asked her what impact the affair had had on her, or what was causing her decline. So who do we believe? The woman or the observer? Kernot claims that because Oakes did not check facts with her, he made some errors. When I asked her if she had thought her relationship with Gareth would last forever, for example, she said, 'Not forever but it had potential to continue ... it was very, very special. Even after Gareth left we had made plans to meet up and see each other and see how things worked out away — with one of us away — with him away from parliament. But of course it didn't happen that way.'

Laurie Oakes was initially very reluctant to be interviewed for this book, insisting that if he had any more information he would reveal it himself, and that it was too long ago (18 months) to remember details. When we eventually spoke he was defensive, partly because, as he told me at the end of the interview, he had 'reason to be wary' after the abuse he'd copped at the time of publication. He maintained his decision was correct:

> The key thing that made me decide to write it was what
> Cheryl wrote in the book about why her period in the
> Labor Party was so difficult, how the media drove her to
> a breakdown. And I knew all of that was untrue. I knew
> what had caused the problems and I knew what had caused
> her ... even those emotional problems that she had. I had the
> knowledge. Also in there was the statement by Gareth Evans
> saying Kim Beazley had done the wrong thing by Cheryl,
> and I had the background to that. So I am in the position of
> fact. Which conflicts with important strands in her book.
> That was the kind of thing I was thinking about.

I don't think Laurie Oakes had a particular bias against Kernot. He often praised Kernot in his columns. Many found his rationale compelling. But his action played into a lot of sexist assumptions that observers were unable to properly evaluate without being given the evidence.

*

The significance of this story should not be underestimated. Laurie Oakes is an enormously respected, powerful press gallery leader. This was not an inexperienced reporter trying to be controversial, it was the heaviest of the heavyweights making a calculated and considered decision about a long-held convention. The final irony is that in writing a book that attacked the media as sexist, unethical and untrustworthy, Kernot was placing trust in a group of gallery reporters to protect her, to contain her open secret within the confines of Parliament House. Her mistake was to believe that the media would treat her as they treated the men — while writing a book to prove the opposite. But it would be wrong to blame Kernot simply for writing a book, as many did. It was not a great book; it was hastily written, often jumbled and contradictory, and basically amounted to a long, drawn-out self-justification, blaming instead the Labor Party, the leader, the press, and men everywhere — running newsrooms, taking photos, doing backroom ALP deals. Underpinning it all is a great sense of loss and grief.

Despite this, it's hard not to have a human response to Kernot; to the woman who broke down then was stoned in public. She made a bad decision, she was somehow diminished as the years passed, but she was certainly sorely judged for it. She left politics without a husband (their marriage fell apart after the 2001 election), a lover, the loyalty of either the Democrats or the ALP, the friendship of her former staffers, and with faint prospects of a future career in Australia.

While the media were not to blame for what happened to Kernot, they were critical in her downfall. It was not just the scrutiny, it was the level of scrutiny; it was not just the attack, it was the intensity of the attack. And it was not just the fact that the conventions were broken for her — it was the velocity with which they were followed up, and the scale and vehemence of the coverage. The media did not break Cheryl Kernot, but they exacerbated the pressure a thousand-fold, and effectively destroyed her reputation. And fierce debates about gender, power, privacy, sexual behaviour, and ethics all sprang from public discussion of who she had slept with and when.

What was it about her that sparked such fervent admiration then such unforgiving hostility in the press? Many politicians are hated, but few at that level. HarperCollins publicist Christine Farmer said she went from amazement at the number of attacks to disgust at the salaciousness in the media reports: 'It was like she was Princess Diana and had done something wrong.' Monica Attard, who procured an exclusive radio interview with Kernot in which she spoke of her relationship with Evans, said she was stunned by the emotion Kernot stirred in other journalists. She took more than 70 phone calls the day after she interviewed Kernot — a few days before the program was aired — from reporters wanting to know what she'd said, what she looked like: '"Is she going to break down? Is she going to kill herself?" A lot of the feedback from women were saying good on you, but a lot of the men were very, very hostile towards her, and that translated into media reaction as well ... There is something about Cheryl that seems to rile the media but it was pretty amazing to be there in the eye of the storm when it was happening with her.'

What was most surprising, according to Attard, was 'the ferociousness with which some of my journalist colleagues approached the whole thing'. She found it difficult to distinguish between the professional desire to get information about what Kernot had told her before the program went to air, and just sheer hostility towards Kernot because 'she was such a despised person at the time ... I found it quite shocking and a bit disturbing because we all know that there's no such thing as absolute objectivity but I expected a bit of deference to the idea.

I found none in relation to the Kernot story; there was just anger and pissed-offedness.' When I asked Mike Seccombe about the vitriol, he replied, 'I don't quite understand the psychology but there's a pigeon coop mentality, once someone falls to the bottom of the cage with a spot of blood on them, everyone picks them to death.'

*

It's 1.30 p.m. and I am sitting in my car with Cheryl Kernot, stuck in traffic in Cleveland Street, heading for Sydney airport. She has a flight to Brisbane at 2.00 p.m., and is, understandably, starting to panic. I realise I have miscalculated how long it will take to drive her from Newtown to the airport. A strained note appears in her voice, and she calls her friend — who is waiting at the terminal with her luggage — who advises her to hop across the cement road barrier and catch a cab in the other direction. I fall silent, embarrassed. Then a gap appears in the traffic and I slam my foot down, veering into the right lane. A prolonged horn blast comes from the truck behind us as I sneak a sideways look at her. A second, longer blast follows. 'I bet it's a man,' mutters Kernot. A glance in my rear-vision mirror proves it is. We both laugh, a little anxiously, as I continue to veer in and out of the traffic as quickly as I can.

Eight minutes later we are at the airport. I am still driving way too fast, and almost don't see a man walking across a median strip, daydreaming. I brake, and gesture apologetically. He stops and glares, stepping around the bumper bar and pointing to his eyes. '*LOOK!*' he shouts, angrily. 'Yep, yep, I'm really sorry,' I mouth back. His mouth then curls and he brings his hand up in the air, waving it like a talking puppet, shouting, 'Yap, yap, yap.' We both groan at his assumption: two women in the car; it's not bad driving, it's that we are *talking* too much. 'Now that's rude,'

Kernot says. 'Very male.' She shakes my hand then hurries off in her bright red jacket, disappearing into the crowds at the Qantas terminal.

I drove off wondering if that was the way the world was — or seemed — for Cheryl Kernot: men sounding horns, gesturing rudely, misreading her. Throughout our interview she had often referred to men, a masculine media, blokey parliament, a male way of operating, a rigid wall of testosterone in political parties, a culture that had deified then derided her — saint to scarlet women. As Democrats leader, Kernot was a highly respected politician and effective negotiator. She promised to try to change politics. When she changed parties instead, in order to better access power, she lost the respect of much of the gallery, who claimed her political purity had been key to her success. And that ambition was an ugly trait in a woman. From then it was open slather — her past sex life, a host of transgressions, her current sex life. It went on, month after month.

Kernot was living in London at the time of writing this book, working as a consultant and thriving, she says, on being regarded for her intellect once again. When I first contacted her, she told me to read Siân Rees's book *The Floating Brothel*, about the voyage to Australia of female convicts, many of whom had been convicted of trifling crimes, who eventually served as prostitutes in the new colony. She reminded me of the book several times, and when I finally read the tales of these women, caught between poverty and penury, it became clear why. 'It was a regrettable fact,' Rees wrote, 'that disgraced females found "their character is utterly gone, may never be retrieved", whereas disgraced males "after many errors, may reform and be admitted into that same society and meet with a cordial reception as before" — but there it was, nature's way, God's will, human nature. Female crime was like terminal illness, terribly sad, sometimes brought on by circumstances outside the victims' control, but irreversible.'

Postscript, 2021

It was only in the first few months of 2021, thanks to the courage of Brittany Higgins and others, that people began to speak openly about the sleazier aspects of political culture in Canberra, and how toxic and obnoxious it can be for women. It is patently clear that lack of reporting on, or truthful discussion of, this environment has protected not women but primarily predatory men.

A short time after becoming an MP in 2004 Labor's Kate Ellis was approached in a bar by a Liberal staffer (later a senator) who said to her: 'The only thing anyone really wants to know about you, Kate, is how many blokes you had to fuck to get into parliament.'[38] *As she wrote in her book,* Sex, Lies and Question Time, *that was just the everyday 'run-of-the-mill sleaze and innuendo' in federal politics: rumours about women having sex with drivers, staffers and colleagues. She demonstrates beautifully how sexual gossip is primarily targeted at women, and weaponised against them. Greens senator Sarah Hanson-Young had to deny rumors she had been 'busted having sex in the prayer room' to her then leader, Bob Brown, while Ellis found herself on the phone to a newspaper editor denying she was entangled in a love triangle in her office, vowing: 'I've never even kissed him.' The rumour, she says, came from her own colleagues.*[39] *Ellis even discovered it had been widely rumoured that she had 'vajazzled' — or decorated her pubic area with little fake jewels — in preparation for the Midwinter Ball, where the media mingles with politicians and powerbrokers.*

Far from dying out, slut-shaming is now common practice for some in federal parliament. When women get to their feet to speak, they are sledged by opponents who call out the names of men they are supposed to have had sex with. Amanda Rishworth told Ellis that people have yelled at her across the chamber: 'We all know you effed such and such!' In the case of Greens senator Sarah Hanson-Young, this went on for months, until it made her so anxious she began to avoid going to parliament. Then, when David Leyonhjelm, a senator for the Liberal Democratic Party, shouted out while she was debating the protection of women against sexual assault that she should 'stop shagging men', she accused him of 'slut-shaming', took him to court and successfully sued for defamation. Justice White agreed that Leyonhjelm was aiming to 'shame her publicly' by later saying 'the rumours about her in Parliament House are well-known', that 'Sarah is known for liking men', and Sarah 'is known for having lots of relationships with men' were 'calculated to embarrass, and done with malice'.[40]

Throughout the case, Hanson-Young told the court she had to endure abuse, phone calls and emails from people calling her a 'hypocrite and misandrist', because, they said, she was a 'slut who had sex with men'. Her daughter's classmates asked her daughter repeatedly: 'How many boyfriends has your mum had?' On 3 July 2018, her chief of staff told her: '[Your media advisor] just received a call and the caller said, "If you do not stop saying that all men are rapists, there is a group of us who will rape you. Many men are angry at [you] and ... we will punish [you] by raping [you]."'

It is worth remembering that Brittany Higgins was raped not long afterwards, in Parliament House.

And instead of trying to prevent sexual assault, parties and even pre-selectors continue to sexualise the women in their midst, or on their peripheries. Wanting to avoid an avoidable scandal is one thing, and discriminatory prurience is another. As Ben Smee revealed in the Guardian *in July 2020, nine former Queensland LNP candidates had been asked intimate questions when being vetted by male party officials. One was asked to write down the name of her former sexual partners on a piece of paper, and asked if she also slept with women. Another woman was asked, 'What is your favourite sexual position?'*

This prurience can be hugely damaging — even fatal — to a political career. In July 2018, Labor MP Emma Husar found herself the subject of an internal party review into staff complaints — at least half of which were from a single employee who had been fired — including bullying, inappropriate behaviour and sexual harassment. Then Buzzfeed published an unsubstantiated allegation from the review that Husar, a single mother and survivor of domestic violence, had exposed her nether regions to a colleague, Jason Clare, in her office. Husar says the relevant staffer was not even with her on that day, or in Canberra at all, and Clare had denied the allegation, but Buzzfeed reported the story without calling either Husar or Clare. The headlines accused her of 'doing a Sharon Stone', referencing an iconic scene in Basic Instinct *where a character — a bisexual, murderous novelist — uncrosses and crosses her legs while being interrogated in what appears to be a deliberately provocative move. The policemen stare and sweat. (It is only now that we know that Sharon Stone claims she was manipulated into doing this scene: she says she was asked to remove her white underwear on the grounds that they were reflecting the light. She writes in her book,* The Beauty of Living Twice, *that when she first saw the 'up-the-skirt shot', she was in 'a room full of strangers' and that 'it was humiliating and upsetting'.)*

Husar says that after this, she was effectively forced to quit politics. Even before the ALP review had been completed, she says she was asked by senior party operatives to 'fall on her sword' or face consequences. Husar, who had won her seat in Sydney's west with a swing of 4.1 per cent in 2016, did not stand at the next election.

While the ALP review had found she had behaved unreasonably towards staff, a report by lawyer John Whelan found there had been no basis for her to resign from parliament and that allegations of sexual harassment and lewd conduct were not supported. To date, the Whelan report has not been released, and Husar has not sighted a copy.

Almost three years on, Husar is considering her legal options and seeking advice on suing the ALP on the grounds of unlawful sex discrimination and sexual harassment. In July 2019 she had settled a defamation action against Buzzfeed, forcing them to apologise for not seeking comment from her, and to retract the story.

So how should MPs be treated after the airing of untested allegations?

In comparison to Husar, after the ABC published a story that an unnamed cabinet minister was alleged to have raped a woman in 1988, the attorney-general Christian Porter held a press conference in which he identified himself as the subject of the story. Again, Porter forcefully denied the allegations and pursued the ABC for defamation before dropping the case after mediation. He was moved from his position of attorney-general to minister for industry, innovation and science during the legal process — but has, significantly, remained in cabinet. But the question of what consequences there are for women, and for men, in political life, remains a burning one.

CHAPTER TEN

Saint Carmen: canonisation and crucifixion

Below and beyond all this is the question, banal but insistent — why? How did this happen? What weakness, what action on my part put me here? At one level this invites analysis of the sequence of events, the roads not taken, the choices wrongly made, the careless words, the inattention, rip-tides not discerned ... Yet it also invites the ... question 'Why me?' Even if the worst possible construction is placed on my actions, they amount to so much less than is said and done daily in public life ... It raises the question of what I represent that makes me a target for such action.

> — Carmen Lawrence, personal diaries, 1997[1]

All week, Carmen Lawrence has played the part of cool woman. Reasonable, logical, understanding rather than angry towards the man who is accusing her, censorious of muckraking, and with just a touch of suggesting that she is being put upon because she's female. It's the Lawrence style. She's all about control. Not cracking. Being highly organised.

And, above all, appearing to conduct her politics a good deal more attractively than those macho boys do.

— Michelle Grattan, the *Age*[2]

When Carmen Lawrence moved to federal politics in 1994, four years after becoming Australia's first female premier, the hype was extraordinary. Prime Minister Paul Keating lured her with the promise of a cabinet position, recognising her potential as a symbol of progression and regeneration. She was dubbed 'Saint Carmen' and depicted by cartoonists with halos and wings, as a woman who would sweep into Canberra and clean up the grubbiness, bringing the ethical ambiguities of federal politics into sharp relief. A close-up of her face was put on the front cover of the *Bulletin* on 15 November 1994 with the headline: 'Carmen Lawrence: Is she Labor's Next Prime Minister?' Greg Turnbull, then senior adviser to Prime Minister Paul Keating, said it was like Elvis coming to Canberra.

A decade later, when I went to interview her, she was a backbencher. Since she had gone to Canberra she had been blamed for a woman's suicide, and called a murderer. She had endured a royal commission in 1995, which found that when she was premier of West Australia she had misled the parliament regarding her role in the airing of a family court dispute. This finding was later overturned by a court, but the scrutiny by the press was acute and protracted.

The central question was whether she, as premier, had previous knowledge of a petition tabled in the WA Upper House claiming that the opposition leader had improperly provided information about a public servant's finances to his wife, Penny Easton. A few days later, Easton committed suicide. Liberal MP Wilson Tuckey declared Lawrence 'had blood on her hands'. After the royal commission handed down its findings, she was then charged with perjury. Lawrence was finally exonerated when a District Court jury found she had in fact not lied.

She had survived, but many predicted her career would be irreparably damaged. Throughout the commission and the court case, journalists wondered at her resolve, her toughness, and her ability to somehow distance herself from the viciousness of the attacks. She did not crack, break down or get angry in public. While she was acquitted by the court, her credibility had been severely battered. When she resigned from the front bench in December 2002 out of anger at Labor's refusal to differentiate itself from the Coalition's policy of keeping asylum seekers in detention centres, she was mocked — a liar claiming to be morally superior? At the end of the following year she was voted in as the president of the Labor Party in the first ballot open to grassroots membership. Political enemies had attacked her for ten years, journalists doubted her, but the party faithful still believed in her. It was not just that she acted as a lightning conductor for Labor dissidents. Somehow she represented something they craved.

*

I found myself, at six o'clock on a Thursday night in May 2003, sitting in Lawrence's tidy Canberra office, interviewing her over a glass of white wine. It was the end of an uneventful parliamentary sitting week. We talked about the press, politics, the court case, and the royal commission. I asked her, 'Do you think it all — the Easton affair — had an impact on you that it wouldn't have had on others?' To my surprise, she blinked, and her mouth started to tremble.

She paused, then said quietly, 'I don't know. What it played into for me were a couple of things I suppose, which are me rather than somebody else. One is the fact that I think I am careful of other people's feelings, most of the time.' She apologised as she began to cry.

> Destroying other people's reputations or saying harmful
> things about them, I don't do that. So it played into that view
> of myself ... Some of them were quite keen to point out the
> inconsistency between my expressed values and the claims
> that were being made about my knowledge and the notion
> that I had somehow contrived a set of circumstances which
> produced this outcome [Penny Easton's suicide] knowingly,
> callously — so they pushed that hard. So I am not unique
> in that but that is one of the characteristics that I have that
> I suppose they perceived as a potential weakness. The other
> thing, I suppose, as a psychologist I saw the situation as
> much more complex than other people would, knowing
> about the circumstances in which people commit suicide.
> And you know, feeling that — if there was anything I could
> have done to prevent ... [starts to cry harder] — poor woman
> — obviously I would.

I turned the tape-recorder off but again she kept talking, still composed as the tears dripped down her cheeks. I switched it on again.

> I suppose they are the things that are particular about
> me that might have made it harder ... And why should
> [journalists care], they see death and destruction every day.
> I mean [former foreign correspondent] Paul McGeough sees
> people blown up; why would he care about the sensitive
> feelings of a politician [laughs]? I understood that and
> I didn't ever in a sense blame the media either. I mean I
> don't like the way a lot of the media operate. I think it is
> superficial and tabloid and destructive. But I have seen

other people *really* destroyed, other people really put
through the wringer. I survived.

I then asked if it was actually her sense of self, her identity, that
her enemies had got to: 'Who you said you were and who you
were believed to be?' She answered:

CL: Yes, yes it was. The thing about who I was believed to
be mattered less to me frankly. Because ultimately you
have got to look at yourself in the mirror in the morning,
because no one else is looking for you. And to that extent
it was a very carefully targeted … [*blows nose*] but who
knows how conscious that was on the part of the people
who did it.

JB: To target you?

CL: To target in that way.

JB: Your sense of self?

CL: Yeah. I'm not saying they were sophisticated about it but
they would have seen it as pricking some inflated idea of
my own rectitude. I am not straight laced, I don't think I
am pompous about the values that I hold. But you could
see it and hear it in some of the things they said. Howard
in particular was good on that. He obviously felt that I
had somehow put myself above the political fray, that I
[was saying I] wasn't some kind of dirty operator, and
this was illustration of the fact that I was, really. I was
no different to the rest of them. [There was a] kind of
sneering: 'Who the hell do you think you are? We know
what you're really like, you're a hypocrite.'

JB: The saint stuff doesn't do anyone any favours.

CL: No, it doesn't. And that was the exaggeration I suppose
that put me in a position where that was likely to happen
one way or another.

JB: When you are seen to be acting like just another
politician?

CL: Yes. Just another politician, or just another bloody
politician, and in a sense I had already been blooded in
that I had been the premier of a state at a very difficult
time, and it wasn't as if I claimed purity. I had admitted
making mistakes, very public mistakes ... So it was not
as if I was wandering around the place saying look at
me, I'm wonderful, but that was what they said in a way.
Underneath that, what they got to was the core belief in
my own compassion I suppose [*starts to cry again*].

JB: They say that's what you believe about yourself, but
that's also what the public believed. That was your
greatest asset, and being a woman is —

CL: Is part of it. It is unsexing you in a way [*blowing nose*],
it is. But I am not saying they wouldn't have done it to a
bloke. Different style maybe, different target in terms of
the characteristics they might choose to focus on [*tears*].

JB: So what do you attribute your survival to?

CL: [*Still teary*] Not doing this too often [*laughs*]. Just let me
compose myself.

She disappeared into the bathroom for several minutes. I sat in
her office, staring at her bookshelves, waiting. I was taken aback,
after having read all the press reports praising her composure,
and toughness in the face of fierce attack — and those accusing
her of being cold and aloof as a minister and premier. When
I ended the interview 20 minutes later, we both apologised.
She responded: 'Well you didn't know. I didn't know. A small
Krakatoa happened [*blows nose*]. In a sense it's good for me to
know that I am still not quite there. Maybe I never will be.'

This was in fact the ultimate triumph of those who successfully
— and unfairly — linked Lawrence with Penny Easton's suicide.

They got to her. Inside her. At the time, she was admired for her resolve. Eight years later, her suffering was still apparent, although she was clearly vulnerable for other reasons — her mother was very ill and one of her closest friends had just died. I walked back to the press gallery, remembering that the day before a bureau chief had laughed and told me, 'I never feel sorry for politicians. Never.'

After what happened to Carmen, one senior political columnist told me, women gave up. If she could not make it, who could? Why bother trying to change the system? The disquieting part of her story is that her appeal, her immense popularity, was largely due to the fact that she was a woman. It was not just that she was an articulate, charismatic politician. She was perceived to be different from the men — who then expended considerable amounts of energy and millions of dollars to prove that she was not. She was just like them, they argued — she lied. And worse — she was a murderer.

*

In 1990 Rod Cameron famously predicted that we were about to witness the 'feminisation' of Australian politics. Other things being equal, women were 2 or 3 per cent more likely to vote for a female candidate and men were split close to 50–50. It was an unstoppable trend. This was because, he said:

> The increasing community cynicism, the eventual
> realisation of the gravity of national economic problems,
> and the growth of division over consensus in social issues
> will reinvigorate the search for a new style of political,
> corporate and community leadership, and a new order
> of political values in which Australians will have faith.
> Increasing divisiveness in our society will result in a

different approach to resolving complex debates. The old
macho ways of proving leadership credentials will decline
and the community will respond to a commonsense,
managerial style which is in touch, honest and direct.
This new basis I have called the feminisation of the social
agenda — a move away from the masculine aggression and
confrontation formula of the old order.[3]

Leaders would need to show a human side, and would be valued
more for intelligence, honesty and creativity than for brute
strength. Except that instead of bringing on or elevating women
to feminise politics, the threat of highly electable women led to
the feminisation of the men instead. The consensus style of Steve
Bracks took over from the remote authoritarian approach of Joh
Bjelke-Petersen, for example.

It was not just Cameron. Many reporters hailed the early 1990s
as the time when a small group of women were transforming
politics. Senior political correspondent Geoff Kitney wrote in
1994 that in national politics, 'women are increasingly setting
the pace, setting the agenda and setting the standards', even if
their numbers were small: 'Never in Australia have women had
the influence, or the opportunity, that they now have.' Bishop,
Lawrence and Kernot were 'approaching crucial tests which
will determine which of them plays the most influential role in
Australian political life through the balance of the '90s ... Where
these three women go from here will be one of the great political
stories of our time.'[4]

Yet each of them flamed then faded.

For many, Lawrence provided hope that politics could be done
differently. She had a disarming effect on people. One journalist
described it as a 'magnetic pull', another as a 'crusading aura', and
others as a charisma that made people warm to her immediately.
Jane Cadzow wrote in March 1995 that 'Lawrence can't venture

into a public place without well-wishers urging her to go all the way to The Lodge. Mal Holmes, her Commonwealth car driver in Perth, says he hasn't seen this much excitement about a politician since he chauffeured former prime minister Bob Hawke at the height of his folk-heroism … While other parliamentarians compete with varying success for media attention, Lawrence gives the impression she has only to clear her throat to attract a crush of camera and microphone.'[5]

It was not just voters. Paul McGeough, originally from Perth, described her as 'a truly remarkable politician' who was 'held in awe by many in the national press gallery … [and] treated with a reverence that has blessed few Australian politicians'.[6] Political columnist Matt Price — who was the *Australian*'s bureau chief in Perth between 1997 and 2000, and state political reporter for Channel Nine between 1991 and 1996 — said he observed an 'incredible suspension of normal cynicism and scepticism towards Carmen' in many political journalists. When he came to Canberra covering Richard Court at a premiers' conference in 1995, and told a group of gallery reporters that he thought Lawrence had always known about the Penny Easton petition, they were visibly taken aback: 'She was treated completely differently. I hadn't seen anyone treated like this before. She was held up as a great hope. I didn't get into an argument, but it was pretty uncomfortable. It was a peculiar reaction for journalists; it was like I'd insulted them.'

The uncommon faith Lawrence inspired in many journalists appeared to be particularly evident in some of the women in the press gallery, who were bitterly disappointed when she came under serious attack. Eventually their disappointment turned to her. ABC political reporter Fran Kelly says she was 'heartbroken to see such a high-calibre politician be ruined like this', and sickened by the political pursuit of Lawrence to the point of a royal commission and perjury trial. Margo Kingston says she and

Dr Lawrence can stand the heat . . . inspecting the kitchen of an Aboriginal centre — Picture: ERNIE McLINTOCK

Carmen heads for the top, naturally

When Carmen Lawrence was made Australia's first female premier, *The Australian* pulled out an old photograph of her in a kitchen to splash on the front page.
Ernie McLintock/Newspix

Kelly 'went through agony' trying to understand it, but that she finally confronted Lawrence and told her she had decided she did not believe her: 'It was very powerful. There was a real emotional connection with her. I was just devastated; I was a true believer, I thought she was wonderful, but after [I told her I did not believe her] we didn't talk for six years ... It took me a long time to get over Carmen ...'

Kelly says, 'While everyone else was pursuing her I was holding back — still doing tough interviews, I think, but allowing her answers and her denials to stand. Other politicians have been caught out or not believed and haven't been pursued to royal commissions. It was a political exercise purely and simply. The level of attention it attracted and the vehemence of the comment were much greater because the expectation of her was so high. I was offended by the way it happened.'

Lawrence says she was aware that some reporters were keenly disappointed by the findings of the Marks Royal Commission: 'There was a certain sense of them having been betrayed, as if I had personally gone out of my way to do something to harm them. That was a bit odd.'

Most journalists I spoke to described the pursuit of Lawrence as purely political, and the punishment excessive. When she came to Canberra, held aloft on the shoulders of the prime minister and touted as a possible deputy or even successor, the Liberals sized her up and were waiting. At the same time, almost all journalists thought she'd lied about the Easton affair — although few were prepared to say that on the record. Geoff Kitney attributes her 'immense appeal' to the fact that she was incredibly articulate, and had original ideas. But male or female, he continues, 'I think a fallen politician really cops it. Really really cops it.' What happened to Lawrence has also happened to some men: gruelling public trials; sustained, vitriolic attack; undermining from their own party as well as their opponents. Many leave politics feeling bitter, unappreciated and keenly aware that they have suffered in a way their colleagues have not. Many feel that were it not for timing, cruel fate, a certain story, a particular colleague, they would have been leaders. But Lawrence was the only woman who could have led the country if things had been different.

*

This is what we know about the Easton affair. On 8 April 1995 Paul McGeough broke a story in the *Sydney Morning Herald* — bizarrely tucked away on page eight — in which Keith Wilson, formerly the health minister in the Lawrence government, said

Lawrence had lied about the tabling of a petition in parliament before the suicide of Penny Easton in 1992. McGeough told me he had always suspected that she lied, 'for the simple reason that the issue at the time was too big to have been left in the hands of backbenchers or party aides'. Lawrence had said she knew of the petition, and the 'general thrust' of it, when it was tabled, but claimed she had been briefed 'only just before it was tabled and then only in the broadest of terms'. But, almost three years later, Wilson challenged her recall and suggested she was not telling the truth. He claimed the petition had been discussed at cabinet, and that some ministers had warned against its tabling, but she had gone ahead because she wanted to damage the opposition leader, Richard Court. He also said she had promised to come back to cabinet before anything further happened. Lawrence, then health minister in the Keating government, denied his claims.

The Easton petition was the latest manoeuvre in a messy personal dispute over a divorce settlement between Brian and Penny Easton. It should never have ended up in parliament. Political point-scoring with a family break-up isn't particularly decent, let alone feminist, behaviour. It was grubby, although not particularly unusual, politics, and both sides of the house were guilty of allowing themselves to be used as pawns in an acrimonious private battle.[7]

In 1992, Brian Easton used the support of ALP backbencher John Halden to present a petition in parliament accusing his former wife, Penny Easton, of perjury. The petition also claimed opposition leader Richard Court had supplied Penny Easton — who was falsely rumoured to be his lover — with sensitive and confidential material. The petition was immediately declared to be unfair and incorrect, as the perjury charge had been thrown out of the Family Court. Still, the media eagerly pursued the story and front-page headlines blared daily. The day after the petition was tabled, Channel Seven reporter Geoff Parry chased Penny Easton into her garage, and shot footage of her standing, silent, in her nightgown, with her back to the camera, trying to shield her face with her hand. According to a letter sent by Channel Seven to the ABC's 'Media Watch', the crew 'taped Mrs Easton in her garage at the rear of her home unit from a right-of-way and as she was driven away in a car'.

Four days later Penny Easton was found in her car in the hills that surround the coastal city of Perth. She had committed suicide. She left a note which began: 'No one committed perjury in my family ... I have been set up so well that I have no way out but this. I cannot live with the hurt that is being done to my family. I know it's all political.' Angry and grieving, Easton's family demanded to know if Lawrence knew about the petition. Many believe that what went on to be a destructive, protracted saga could have been stopped at this point if Lawrence had taken responsibility for the petition but not the suicide, apologised to the family and called an inquiry. But she insisted she was telling the truth. She did not say she never knew about the petition, but that a staffer, Ed Russell, only told her about it the night before it was tabled, and Halden spoke to her about it on that morning. It became a question of how many days in advance she was told.

Months after the story broke in 1995, Lawrence's star was still bright. There was speculation that she would become deputy to Keating when Brian Howe retired. Then, as the federal Labor Party was preparing for an election, Richard Court, then the Liberal premier of Western Australia, called for a royal commission. Headed by Kenneth Marks, the commission's task was to examine 'the circumstances and events preceding and following the presentation of a petition' to the upper house of the West Australian parliament on 5 November 1992. The key question was whether the tabling of the petition was a premeditated move which Lawrence had been planning for some weeks in order to distract from other problems the government was facing, or something she had only been told about briefly the day before it was taken to parliament.

Eight cabinet ministers testified that Lawrence had brought it up at a cabinet meeting on Monday, 2 November 1992. There were six ministers, including Lawrence, who either did not recall or said no such discussion had occurred. Paul Keating lent his full weight to support Lawrence, attacking the veracity and process of the commission, insisting it was a politically motivated 'very nasty extension' of executive power.[8] Penny Easton's parents attended the entire trial.

The commission concluded Lawrence had lied about what she had known, and had 'supported the use of Easton's grievances and allegations for her own political interests — and at the expense of the parties to the Easton matrimonial dispute and their families'. Commissioner Marks also found that 'there was no need for her, as Premier, to intervene in the Easton matter, which was an essentially private grievance.' The next day, the front page of the *West Australian* shouted: 'SHE LIED'.

Not everyone was crowing. On 16 November, Milton Cockburn in the *Sydney Morning Herald* argued that it was an extraordinary and dangerous precedent: 'A politician, who has not acted illegally, has been found to have acted improperly because she sought to gain a political advantage over her parliamentary opponent. Only a very naive person could come to such a conclusion.' What riled her supporters most of all was that the subtext of much of the comment, and dirt throwing, was that she was guilty of murder; that there was a simple causal connection between the petition and Penny Easton's suicide, and there were no other factors — like nasty family disputes, a vindictive former husband, media harassment, and depression, for example.[9] Many saw it simply as a witch-hunt. It was known Lawrence had some enemies in the

West Australian ALP. Much of the hostility followed her decision to establish a royal commission into WA Inc., which resulted in the jailing of Brian Burke — the former premier — and David Parker, former deputy premier. Her refusal to give character evidence at Burke's fraud trial caused further resentment.

Paul Keating dismissed the findings of the Marks royal commission as blatantly political, and Lawrence remained health minister until the government lost the election in 1996. She was still a shadow minister when she was charged on 21 April 1997 by the West Australian police with having given false evidence to the commission. She faced a maximum penalty of five years imprisonment. She was charged on three counts, and she pleaded not guilty to all of them. After a three-week trial she was acquitted by a District Court jury. The *West Australian*'s headline proclaimed: 'SHE'S BACK'. In the 1998 federal election, she substantially increased her majority in her Fremantle seat.

In an article written for the *Eye* in December 1999, senior gallery journalist Christine Wallace argued the media had repeatedly and effectively drawn a connection between the suicide and the petition: 'In almost every one of the hundreds of news stories for four years about Carmen Lawrence and the Easton petition, is a sentence like, "Four days after presentation of the petition, Penny Easton committed suicide." It created a Pavlovian connection in people's minds between the two events. Alternative possibilities like "… after realising what an unremitting bastard her husband was", "… after being hounded by the press", or "… being cumulatively depressed to the point of hopelessness" never appeared.'[10]

The pursuit of Lawrence was clearly politically motivated. Was it worse because she was a woman? Of course. Who else, apart from Cheryl Kernot, has been so powerfully and lethally dubbed a saint? It is only natural that over-hyped expectations lead to disappointment. It is rare for politicians to see journalists personally wounded by their demise. But was she targeted because she was a woman? No. Her uniqueness and perceived virtuosity added to her profile and popularity, but she was also targeted because she was potentially capable of leading her party and helping Keating win government again. And while she was acquitted of any charges of perjury, the stain remained.

Lawrence says it was her political opponents, in both the Labor and Liberal parties, who did the most damage. She believes the media generally have taken her seriously: 'Whatever other things have happened I don't feel that my views have been discounted or set aside because I am a woman of a particular kind. Quite the reverse if anything.' Meanwhile, journalists justified their scrutiny of her by saying she had claimed to be different but was found not to be, and must be held to account. Michelle Grattan wrote in 1995 that 'Lawrence is a classy politician. There is no reason to believe she is any worse than her peers when it comes to standards and ethics. But when she talks about wanting "to conduct politics in a different way", without the male characteristics of aggression and strutting, as she did in a *Canberra Times* interview recently, she invites us to scrutinise her approach carefully. The main thing that seems to be different about Lawrence is the method she brings to doing things, and her public presentation, rather than the substance of what she does.'[11]

The ghost of the Penny Easton case trailed Lawrence for the rest of her political career. After the court case was over, she returned to the front bench. In 2002 she resigned from the shadow ministry over the party's position on the war in Iraq and support for mandatory detention of asylum seekers. She was condemned by commentators who saw her drift to the Left as piety, and disloyalty to the party that had stuck by her during the Easton years. But her resignation served as a beacon for Labor voters who were dissatisfied with the leadership's failure to counter the Howard government's hard-line views on asylum seekers. This, along with her own strength and ability, is why Carmen Lawrence survived. Her election as Labor Party president — another first for women — proved her grassroots support remained. Matt Price believes voters forgive her because they like her, and believe her when she speaks:

> Carmen has made a lot of mistakes over a long career but people just like her, and it really frustrates some of her more strident critics. She has some enormous critics in the West Australian Labor Party, but she pops up and says what she thinks and people like her ... She is an impressive woman with a hide of a rhino ... But it's not all image. The reality is, when she talks about issues, she talks pretty good common sense about it. She's an extraordinary politician, and like other extraordinary politicians, there is substance behind it. There's still a feeling out there that it's a shame what happened to Carmen Lawrence.

*

Were the 1990s a mere blip on the landscape, when an unfortunate group of women just made too many mistakes or didn't have enough talent to make it? Rod Cameron thinks so. When I interviewed him, he said his thesis still held up: 'The general point is that sheilas are going to be generally better viewed, and a good female candidate will these days, generally speaking, beat a good male candidate.'

Cameron argues that the feminisation thesis means male leaders are becoming more accessible and human, while women are having more success at a community level. And while, he said, Labor was still placing factional hurdles in front of many women, the Liberals were putting more women in marginal seats: 'The Libs realised it's not the high-fliers we are searching for, with some exceptions, but a community-minded, strong but ordinary woman in marginal seats, like Dana Vale and Jackie Kelly — they are not much as ministers, but are wonderful local members ... What lies at the heart of their electability is that the community-type people, strong and dynamic but ordinary — I don't mean to be offensive, but natural for their community — usually go very well.'

The grassroots is well and good, but what is stopping women from becoming leaders?

The female meteor syndrome — where women flame then fade to black — has demonstrated a clear gap between the expectations and judgements of the press and the public. It has long been established that there are many advantages to being a woman in politics. An ANOP poll commissioned by Susan Ryan as far back as 1982 found good female candidates appealed more to swinging voters than men did because they appeared more human, more honest than the men.

The canonisation of female MPs has been fuelled by a public distrust of politicians in general, and a desire for difference, integrity and honesty. As James Oram put it in the *Sun-Herald*, 'The public would rather trust a junkyard dog with rabies than a politician howling at election time.'[12] Former NSW community services minister Carmel Tebbutt believes there is a lot of pressure on women to be 'the humanising force in politics ... Women do tend to be more consensual, focus more on outcomes, and are put off by the rough and tumble of politics ... but I am not convinced that's not the product of the way women are brought up ... and over time that will change.'

With the notable exception of Carmen Lawrence, who initially held sway over the press gallery, voters are frequently more receptive to women in politics than journalists are.

Reporters are astonished when they travel with politicians who are swarmed and embraced by people on the street, possibly reflecting a conflation of politics and celebrity. Even Margaret Guilfoyle, who was not a celebrity, was likened to the Queen. Reporters stood by as Pauline Hanson was mobbed in shopping malls, people asked Natasha Stott Despoja for her autograph at airports, and cricket fans shouted out to Bronwyn Bishop. Polls regularly defied pundits: Bishop was shown to have popular support (at least ahead of Hewson), Hanson had surprising success, and Stott Despoja at one point polled as Australia's most popular politician, even though political journalists thought each of them lacked depth and substance. The reason for the popularity of so many of these women is precisely that they were seen to be different from conventional politicians. They spoke openly, wore different — and often feminine — clothes, did not snub mainstream television shows or women's magazines, and they cried and got angry with the media. Each in turn seemed vulnerable. But while their humanity endeared them to voters, in many guises it turned journalists against them — they should be stronger and not look good, or enjoy looking good; they should turn photographers away and insist journalists only ever write about policy. If they'll listen.

Stott Despoja was keenly conscious that the views of journalists did not reflect those of the community:

> For a while there we just read the letters [page] because we
> thought, we just want to know what you guys are thinking.
> We don't want to know what the opinion makers are
> thinking. And obviously focus groups and things like that
> are fascinating too ... And for a while there I was thinking,
> what am I going to do? Everyone thinks I am stupid. And
> you go out into the community and people say, 'Oh I can't
> believe it, oh you are so articulate, thanks for standing

up for ...' and you just think 'You do? What are you
reading?' ... As I've always said it's about the community,
it could never afford to be about the press gallery because if
it was [I would be in trouble].

What was most lethal for many female politicians in the 2000s
was not the disdain of the press but the excitement about possible
female leaders, and women who have the potential to penetrate
or change in some way the blokey political culture so many
voters are tired of witnessing. There was, however, still a bias
underlying much coverage, demonstrated in sideswipes at good-
looking women, a distaste for celebrity, almost a hatred of those
seen to complain about their treatment at the hands of the media.
The standards of behaviour are higher, and therefore the attacks
more vicious for those who transgress them. At the same time,
in the 2000s, many women MPs struggled to get any coverage
at all.

Julia Gillard believes there was an intensity about the
experience of Carmen Lawrence as 'the woman most likely' that
was unprecedented in Australian politics:

And I think whilst Carmen endured and survived it, the black
motive that drove the Libs on that occasion, you'd have to say
they actually got a bit of what they wanted. They did have a
fair bit of success with taking her out of what she could have
been doing and shoving her talents into an ongoing defensive
struggle over many years ... I think probably the lesson for
everybody and probably the lesson a bit more acutely for
women, because women are still a bit unusual in politics,
is you don't want to underestimate the ferocity of what the
political system is about.

Lawrence says her advice to the next generation of young women, would be 'not so much to try and hide but to repudiate exaggerated perceptions. What I should have done more often than not was say "don't be ridiculous", and I didn't do that often enough I suspect.'

*

I do not know if Carmen Lawrence lied, but I do know that Australians have witnessed numerous political fictions in recent times. It is as though we expect politicians to fib. Spin, fudge, duck, weave, cover-up. Children overboard, *Tampa*, intelligence about weapons of mass destruction, threats of terror within our region. We were told that a group of asylum seekers arriving by boat threw their children overboard, which was false.[13] We were told Iraq possessed weapons of mass destruction, which was false.[14] We were told Australians knew nothing of the abuse at the Abu Ghraib prison in Iraq, which was false. But while these were exposed as lies, they had negligible impact on the politicians responsible for them. As for driving people to kill themselves, there have been at least a dozen suicide attempts in our detention centres by desperate asylum seekers, and we have sat by and watched. Who is responsible for those? Will we hold a royal commission into conditions in detention, and the psychological deterioration of children we left behind razor fences in the desert for years?

Two days after I interviewed Lawrence, former governor-general Sir William Deane, in a speech given at the University of Queensland, criticised the Howard government's lack of truth in incidents such as the children overboard inquiry, and the lack of justice in mandatory detention, and said the greatest challenge for future leaders was to be just and truthful.[15] In November 2003, Richard Woolcott, a former secretary of the Department of Foreign Affairs, concluded in an opinion piece in the *Age* that 'many Australians no longer believe their government'. In the public imagination, political rhetoric is conflated with fudging, with half-truths and quarter-truths, with blatant lies. The most recent have been protested, ironically, by Lawrence herself. Her survival is due to the fact that to many she still represents integrity, a new kind of politics.

When I dropped into her office, a couple of weeks after she had burst into tears while talking about Penny Easton, I asked how she was feeling. 'Oh,' she laughed, 'I recovered pretty quickly.'

CHAPTER ELEVEN

How to Succeed in Politics Without a Penis

I am not going to change my hairstyle, I'm not going to clip my eyebrows, I'm not going to change the clothes that I feel comfortable in and I'm certainly not going to start working out whether I'm going to offend somebody if I say something.[1]

— Janine Haines

You need to have a cardinal rule, and I think the one is, always opt for never playing the victim. If it happens, just wear it. Because ... when you use the victim card, no matter how many times you use it, that will be the end. Some misdemeanour, bad deed, misjudgement or whatever, that's unfairly used against you, you will survive that. Each one of those individual ones you will survive. But if you get typecast as a victim, you won't. So it doesn't matter how bad it is, just remember this too will pass, but labelling the victim won't.[2]

— Amanda Vanstone

In 1994, the former premier of Victoria, Joan Kirner, donned leather pants and gelled her hair for an appearance on 'The Late

Show' singing Joan Jett's raunchy rock classic, 'I Love Rock and Roll'. It was a visual treat: she howled, rocked and strutted her way through the performance, camping it up in a way that endeared her to thousands. It was not just the abandon and apparent lack of self-consciousness that was so appealing, but the fact that it is so unusual to see politicians goofing around happily in public. Years later, she told me it was her most successful media appearance: people still wanted to come up and shake the hand of the feisty politician who for a moment looked like any of us up onstage at a corny karaoke night, with a few lagers under our straining belts. Many female politicians have gained the media's respect through competence and talent. Others have done it simply by appearing human.

By 2004, there were 60 women in federal parliament. It was no longer a novelty to see women lining the green and red benches. Older female MPs told me this next generation was quieter, more determined to play by the rules, to trade and fight in factions, to sing the party anthems. Some, like the opposition spokeswoman for immigration, Nicola Roxon, said they were treated well by the press, and were more frustrated that 'issues that are seen to have an impact on women get sidelined in the reporting or in the political hierarchy'. Still, they closely watched the female political celebrities of the 1990s and the acne of sexism that continued to break out across the media.

So what are the lessons?

One feature many successful female politicians share is a forthright, straight-shooting approach. Janine Haines was a fine example. Her most refreshing characteristic was her candour, the fact that she was unapologetically herself. She refused to pander to critics of her image, on the grounds that a politician's personal or physical characteristics were irrelevant. 'What you see is what you get,' she said, 'and that basically is what the Democrats are all about. We're not operating a puppet show behind a thin veneer of political ideology.'[3] When she sacked a press secretary three weeks after he told her to change her hairstyle, clothes and glasses, journalists applauded. 'If he'd succeeded,' wrote one, 'he may have undone the very factor which sets Janine Haines apart from her rivals, Andrew Peacock and Bob Hawke ... the fact that she is not the plastic creation of media advisers and image makers.'[4] Haines said vanity and image-making was a travesty of what politics was about, and journalists approved: 'With Janine Haines, what you see is what you get; the image is reality.'[5] The polls showed the 'natural untutored approach to politics' was working, and Haines had plucked the Democrats out of obscurity and put them onto the front page.

Former immigration minister Amanda Vanstone, also from South Australia, is similar in some ways. Her attitude to the press was 'ignore them' and 'wear them down'. Her candour was unusual. She told me, 'People are sick of plastic politicians. Why have this veneer? Why not be yourself? It's just a lot easier. People will respond to that a lot better in the end.' Her caveat is that her personal life should remain private: 'It doesn't mean you have to open up a cupboard and say here is my mind and my heart and you can have a look at every little piece of it.'

Vanstone shrugged off the relentless comments on her weight, her loud clothing and — the press gallery favourite — the 'exploding pineapple' shirt:

> I don't care. They can say what they like. See basically, before I got into politics I would have worn mostly black and navy ... And then I had a coloured shirt for some reason, I can't remember why, and they made such a thing of it at the time, and I've just done it and done it and done it. And I've worn them out now. Surely you'll agree — if a journalist went to an editor and said, 'I've got a great story about Vanstone's new shirt that she's got,' the editor would say

'Really? Well, aren't you a genius, we've been there and done that.' I've just worn them out.

She also gives as good as she gets, and is admired for it. When Labor senator John Faulkner kept commenting on her weight from the other side of the chamber, she finally called him the 'King of Comb-over' to silence him. She's still proud of the comment: 'The comb-over was a ripper. That fixed him up. He used to get stuck into me all the time. The King of Comb-over used to sit there going snip snip. Just for a couple of weeks — then no more trouble ... It was not [intended as] public humiliation for him; it was to teach him a lesson, that if you want to play like that, well, girls can play like that too.'

Few people know that Vanstone is also an amateur cartoonist, who applied to *Herald* cartoonist Alan Moir's school of cartooning when she was minister for justice. At the end of 2003, she called Moir asking for his permission to reprint a drawing of Bronwyn Bishop's head. He told me she wanted to copy it onto glass plates, glaze them, and give them to her colleagues for Christmas. Moir is an admirer of Vanstone. He describes her as 'a good, strong, effective [politician], but she's jolly, she's very down-to-earth, that's the way I depict her ... she's full on, she's straight on. And she makes mistakes, but she's not embarrassed about it. She's a person who will apologise. She's quite refreshing.'

Vanstone was clearly able to laugh at herself. On her website — which includes pictures of her dogs and her staff's pets — she has written her own captions under some photographs: one talks about 'bad hair days'; another says 'OK OK, 19 years in the Senate has taken its toll.' Alan Ramsey wrote Vanstone was marked not just by her durability, strong personality, refusal to suffer fools, or ability, but 'above all, her great commonsense and her get-out-of-my-face attitude to the remorseless business of politics, a business of men run by men under men's rules.'[6]

Vanstone was, for some time, the most senior female minister in the government. In 2002, she regained cabinet rank after losing it in 1997, and in 2003 she was promoted to minister for immigration and multicultural and indigenous affairs. Many journalists say they admired her blunt and aggressive approach, but disliked her politics, considering her to be a moderate who sold out in her tough attacks on welfare fraud, in cutting funds in the university sector, and maintaining government policy on keeping asylum seekers in mandatory detention. She was also regarded coolly by women's groups, who saw her as an unenthusiastic advocate of their interests when she was minister for the status of women. She had often raised eyebrows over her apparent eagerness to attack other women, particularly fellow South Australian Senator Stott Despoja, but also women like Carmen Lawrence and Cheryl Kernot. When Stott Despoja's profile loomed as an issue for the then Democrats leader Kernot, Vanstone famously quipped that there was only room for one blonde in the Democrats. The remark appalled Stott Despoja, who argued that Vanstone, as one of the few women in politics, should be the last to ridicule other women on the basis of their appearance. Recalls Vanstone: 'I went back into the Senate and said to Natasha, "Look, I've been attacked by the appearance police for years and you know there is nothing wrong with being blonde — otherwise you wouldn't have dyed your hair that colour."'

Another federal Liberal MP, Jackie Kelly, had great success endearing herself to her electorate as a down-to-earth young mother. She did not want to be seen as a well-heeled Liberal, so played down her law degree and other achievements. But when she struggled to be taken seriously as a minister (which few young mothers ever have been) she tried to try to shape her image as more serious, and policy-oriented:

In my electorate they love the fact that I am approachable, warm and fuzzy, and that I am a real person, whatever that means. And I think you are complicit with the media in that. You always have a choice about whether to do a piece of media or not and it certainly suited me I think for my first two terms in parliament to have that image. Now I am on 5 per cent [margin] I am actually trying to adjust that image, which is why you go to ground a bit, then you come back and start building an intellectual base to it. You go too far with it and you start becoming an airhead and fluffy and PM's pet, and you become this thing that's highly electable but doesn't have the intellectual rigour to have some clout in media policy debates ... Now every time I go to the media I am trying to make it meaty. And it's very hard.

Like Vanstone, Kelly believes you should never 'whinge' about media treatment: 'They're a pack of bastards [*laughs*]; don't expect any favours.'

Part of the problem with this analysis, though, is that when women pointed to obstacles, or bias, they were more likely to be labelled whingers, while blokes were seen as forthright and direct. In powerful men, anger is seen as natural, almost to be expected, whereas with women, it is seen as a sign of instability, of being unhinged.

Postscript, 2021

In 2004, having read and analysed several decades worth of press reportage of women in politics, I was determined to find some easy solutions to game the system, so women could bypass the nonsense of celebrity profiles, the distraction of reporter's interest in their personal and domestic lives, and make their way into cabinet. This is the part that I have reflected on most since finishing the book, and rued because I now think women should just be themselves, and blow up a system that would shame or tame them.

It's not easy, I know, so let me explain how I came to this thinking, which I then summarised in several tips. My first — which I cringe at today because while it was a reflection of the times, where women were so constantly derided and many gun-shy as a consequence, it still seems patronising — was to 'Establish a serious profile, as someone who is policy-oriented and has the respect of your colleagues.' Sigh. Respect should be theirs automatically. And, to explain, I wrote:

NSW Liberal Virginia Chadwick, who was considered a possible premier, and generally well liked by the press, said she was always cautious about doing any media not directly to do with her portfolio. She believes many women have suffered from the 'Icarus principle': when they fly too high, journalists will melt their wings. The other kind of publicity did not appeal to her personally, but was also politically a 'dangerous way to travel'.

The former Liberal minister for family and community services Jocelyn Newman, while insisting that she was 'mystified' that she did not attract more attention, said she had deliberately kept a low profile: 'Most of the senior women in politics have been raised by the media and dashed by the media ... it's made me very wary.'[7]

My second hot tip was to 'Avoid the celebrity shots, posing in ballgowns or bikinis.' Now I think: 'Do what you want'. Surely we can move past the idea that women are stupid because they look nice in a dress. Of course, bikini shots probably don't serve any politician well, because editors still love to ridicule powerful women by highlighting the fact they also have bodies — unlike men who can parade about in little costumes just as former PM

Tony Abbott did often in his budgie smugglers (mostly when swimming). But the point of this section was to show that this was the lesson younger generations of women MPs had learnt: to police themselves, tone themselves down, be careful not to display any overt signs of femininity or being female. One was a future PM. I wrote:

Victorian MP Julia Gillard is frequently referred to as a 'rising star'. She is an impressive politician — smart, analytical, and clearly a tough operator — with a distinctively gravelly voice. When she was made opposition spokeswoman for population and immigration in November 2001, her photograph was placed on the front cover of the *Age*. A former staffer called her and said, 'I'm just unpacking the suitcase we've been keeping Cheryl's feather boa in.' Gillard told me, 'It was a joke, but what he also meant — and I took it to be good advice — was watch yourself. It's all very nice when it's all very nice, but if you let it get out of control, it can get all very nasty too.' She would definitely not agree to dress up for women's magazines:

> I'm a professional politician. I went into politics to be
> involved in implementing positive changes for this country ...
> the Cheryl stuff getting dressed up I wouldn't do. Because
> it's got no connection [to my work] ... And I think one of the
> great advantages we've got, and we have to acknowledge it
> time after time, is that we're able to make those judgement
> calls having seen what's happened to women who went
> before us. So I'm not critical of Cheryl or anybody who made
> different decisions because they were the first and I've had
> the ability to watch that and learn from it.

Many of today's female politicians say they too have learnt from Kernot's red frock experience. Jackie Kelly says while she believes 'if you've got it flaunt it', it would not be right either for her electorate or her image: 'I would have done it I suppose when I first entered parliament and had something worth flaunting. But these days, two kids later, I just don't think it's me. I think I'd be caught out same as Cheryl, it's just not you, come on. That stuff just isn't relevant to my electorate.' It's hard for busy women to concentrate on their clothes, she says: 'I've actually got bagged for my dress sense. I've had lots of barbs for being quite dowdy. It's hard because you've got a lot of things on your mind ... If I was Elle Macpherson and making a living out of it, sure, spend some time on it but ...'[8]

I wonder, though, if part of the Cheryl Kernot lesson was about not just gender, but height, power and success. As time has gone on, women in the lower ranks of political life have found themselves treated more even-handedly, but the higher they climb, the more the old stereotyping emerges, and in even more acute forms. Julia Gillard is the greatest example of this.

But I will get to that. My third piece of advice was 'Steer attention away from your personal life.' In 2021, this seems to be is as obvious as it is patronising. My fourth was similar: 'Avoid a personality cult.' This was all about the fervour Natasha Stott Despoja inspired. I wrote:

Many younger MPs now talk about 'the Natasha lesson'. Don't do the wrong sort of publicity, or you'll be seen as a bimbo. Federal Labor MP Tanya Plibersek, who is a couple of months younger than Stott Despoja, has consciously taken a different approach. She is cautious about discussing her private life, and has said 'no' to fashion shoots with women's magazines: 'First, because they can go disastrously off the rails. Second, it's very hard for your colleagues to take you seriously after that. Also, if you look at the people living in your electorate, how many can you assume buy

Woman's Day in one week ... for how many is it a vote changer? So there are very obvious costs and not very obvious benefits.'

Asked about Stott Despoja, Plibersek says:

> I would not take her as a model for how to manage a media campaign strategy because I think she did too much frivolous stuff ... What is the reason we are there? If you actually want to get legislative change through, you need to be able to convince your colleagues that the program you want implemented is well thought out and will change people's lives, and if they are used to thinking of you as a flake they won't take it seriously, and if the only media you get is flaky, they will write you off. So you could be a household name but unable to do anything in parliament ... I don't know where she should have drawn the line, but she should have said 'no' more often. It's the difference between being popular and being respected.[9]

West Australian Liberal Julie Bishop said her approach with the press was to 'be accessible, up-front and tell it like it is'. While she agreed to walk down a catwalk in a fashion parade in 2003 with Kim Beazley, she said it was only because it was for a charity fundraiser: 'Would I have done it because a fashion house asked me to do it? No, because I am the member for Curtin. Hopefully I don't portray myself as someone who gets dressed up and poses for fashion magazines. I have been elected to do a job, not get into a personality cult ... It's not about me, it's about the government and the people.' If you want to be photographed in your swimmers to make a point, that's fine, she says, but you need to be conscious how that will be used in a different context: 'I think there are better ways of drawing attention to good policy than posing in extreme ways.' (Years later, as foreign minister and deputy prime minister, Bishop was photographed often in glamorous couture; behind her back, some colleagues sniped, but her public popularity was remarkable).

The fifth suggestion was: 'Cop criticism.' This was inspired by the string of complaints Cheryl Kernot made before and after her political exit, which may have been called-for, but were poorly timed. Still, why should women have to silently 'cop' a criticism that is different, more vicious and more damning than their male colleagues? Why accept the bogus and distracting stereotyping and othering? Janine Haines was right when she told the Australian Left Review, *in answer to more questions about having been portrayed in a 'kaleidoscope' of images ranging from 'prissy' to 'bimbo', that she did not want to be pigeonholed: 'I'm not abandoning the complexity of my personality to fit some black and white image. Complexity, that's what life's all about.'*[10]

Sixth, 'Understand that journalists are not your enemies. Nor are they your friends.' Again, pretty obvious. But to be fair, the sense of false intimacy was long a particular pitfall of working in close proximity with the press gallery, and still stands, especially for women who want to avoid the sleaze, innuendo and compromise apparent in much of Canberra's political culture. This is what I wrote:

Julia Gillard puts this perfectly. The job of journalists, she says, is:

> ... to develop a relationship with people that is sufficiently
> disarming so that they get information that they otherwise
> wouldn't. Their job is one of engagement ... trying to get
> to know people, disarming people a little bit, and our
> job is to understand that and not fall victim to it. At the
> end of the day it's not that they're nasty people or people
> without ethics, they are doing a job and their job is not to

act as our advocates or press secretaries or ciphers … They rightly should be critical, probing, questioning, and I think you've got to be ready for that no matter how disarming the personal engagement with them might be.

Some MPs are even more cautious. Nicola Roxon did not socialise with journalists because she wanted to avoid being trivialised: 'I am sure it would be enjoyable and I am sure I would make some better friendships and contacts, but I just think it's also got a lot of risks that I didn't want to take … I am a young woman, I am single, I want to do the x, y and z things, how am I going to get into a position where people treat me seriously … People do underestimate that as a young woman, [they think] you are not going to be as capable as a 65-year-old man, so you've got to build that, give people less reasons to underestimate you.'

Seventh, 'Try, in the midst of it all, to be yourself.' This I still agree with. Especially when 'it all' involves spin, obfuscation, policy paralysis and outright lies.

Eighth, I somehow felt compelled to tell women not to 'assume that female journalists will be more sympathetic because you're a woman'. This largely came from the myth that arose in the 1990s, during scandals centreing on Ros Kelly and Carmen Lawrence, that young female journalists 'carved them up' with greater vigour than the men. The examples I gave were as follows:

When I asked the former *Australian Financial Review* political editor, Tony Walker, if he would advise an up-and-coming woman MP differently to a man, he answered: 'Yes. Bear in mind whatever misty-eyed notions you might have about the sisterhood, female reporters won't necessarily cut you slack when the chips are down simply because you are a woman. In fact, possibly less so than males because of the disappointment

factor ... that somehow you'll be seen to have let down the side.'
But press gallery veteran Michelle Grattan dismissed the assertion
that women go harder on fallen women as 'a bit of a cliché' and
an instance of stereotyping of female journalists.[11]

*Today, any suggestion female journalists would 'go softer' on
any woman in the public eye has long gone. But what is obvious
is that when it comes to sexual assault, bullying, harassment
and the intimidation of women in political cultures in Australia,
it is women who have broken the stories, and pursued them
most vigorously: Samantha Maiden, Lisa Wilkinson, Katharine
Murphy, Amy Remeikis, Louise Milligan, Laura Tingle, Leigh
Sales, Karen Middleton and more. Their forensic work was cast
as 'angry coverage that often strayed into unapologetic activism
... from a new, female media leadership' in the* Australian
Financial Review, *the AFR's senior correspondent typically
reverting to the idea that women's work comes from emotion —
even hysteria — and not diligence and competence.*

As Katharine Murphy retorted in the Guardian: *'Investigating
allegations of rape and sexual harassment in a sustained way,
requiring people to be accountable for how they manage their
own workplaces, isn't activism. It's public interest journalism by
any working definition.' Nor is it a female concern, but a human
one. As to the suggestion this is a new clutch of women raging
up to the ramparts, Murphy wrote: 'I have worked on this beat
since 1996. I've covered eight prime ministers. I arrive early and
I leave late.'*

*Lisa Wilkinson was blunt on Twitter: 'Welcome to the new
world order, boys.'*

*Ninth — and here is a fraught one — 'Beware the gender
card.' The gender card is a term used to dismiss women who
speak up about sexist treatment. It is also used to silence those
who witness, and document, sexist treatment, by implying that*

*by recognising bias, observers will be immediately blinded to
any other context, contributors or reasons a woman might be
under attack. In the 1990s and 2000s, it was a potent way to
ensure political women stayed quiet about discrimination, for
fear of recrimination. In 2004, I wrote:*

Former Labor MP Ros Kelly is one who fell foul of the gender
card debate. As a federal minister in the 1990s, Kelly, who was a
close ally of Labor prime ministers Bob Hawke and Paul Keating,
constantly faced allegations of tokenism and political window-
dressing. She was also derided for her ambition. In 1992,
evidence emerged to confirm the suspicions of cynical onlookers.
The 'sports rorts affair' emerged after she was exposed as having
engaged in $30 million of pork barrelling with sports grants
when she was minister for the environment, sport and territories.
In 1992, an officer at the Australian National Audit Office
was told by the Finance Department that there was something
wrong with the way the sports grants were being administered.
In 1993, the auditor-general, John Taylor, sought details of
the grants appraisal processes, but was told by Kelly that there
was little or no documentation. She told him it was up to her
'as minister to make the final decision on which projects are
funded'. The ANAO report found the money allocated in those
grants was obviously skewed: the average grant to a Labor seat
was $257,000, compared to $141,000 to a Coalition seat. The
auditor-general refused to rule out political bias in the way the
grants had been allocated. He told the House of Representatives
committee investigating the scheme that fraud 'was more likely to
have occurred than not'.

Kelly was pilloried by the opposition. Any suggestion by her
Labor colleagues that the ferocity of the criticism was to do with
her gender was scoffed at. Mike Seccombe called it a kind of
'victim feminism' which implied journalists should go easier

on women. Joan Kirner was one of those who defended Kelly, arguing there was a tougher standard for women, and that Kelly had been pursued more viciously by opponents and the media because she was 'an attractive blonde woman'. Journalist Geoff Kitney slammed this argument as 'both wrong and dangerous ... What it implicitly argues for is a lesser standard for women because they are women.' Kelly had failed to meet a minimum standard of ministerial accountability, and was being punished for political ineptitude, not her gender.[12]

But can gender play a part in the way attacks are carried out, and in the weight given to mistakes made? Christine Wallace was one of the few who came to Kelly's defence, writing in the *Australian Financial Review* that Kelly's limitations were 'all out of proportion to the background sniping, bitching and badmouthing she has attracted during her 14 years as a federal MP'.

Senior gallery journalist Michelle Grattan told Susan Mitchell:

> Most women journalists are feminist and so are most
> thinking women, so women like Kelly and Bishop are up
> against it if they're not prepared to take that on. My view is
> that Kelly is no better and no worse than a lot of politicians.
> She was over-promoted, there's no doubt about that. [But] I
> have to admit that I was genuinely surprised that the sports
> rort affair ran as hard as it did.[13]

Margo Kingston, who covered the sports rorts issues intently when she was at the *Canberra Times*, under the editorship of Michelle Grattan, said the idea that Kelly was hounded because she was a woman was 'crap':

> She made a decision not on need but [on] re-electing Labor
> in marginal seats, with public money meant for real people
> in real need. But the real need in many cases is in safe Labor

seats where people are shit poor and have no supporting facilities. They are spitting on their own people ... I thought she behaved abominably and I was incensed that she was refusing to be accountable and was just sweeping the questions under the carpet ... I went down and introduced myself when she became minister. She patted me on the knee, offered me coffee but I couldn't make any sense of her in terms of policy. I just walked out and said I don't want to talk to her again, she's not interesting, there's nothing there. But I certainly didn't look at her and think she is blonde therefore she is dumb.

Not all would agree. Ramsey, for one, saw her as ruthless, ambitious, and with 'a lot of political ability'. He added, though: 'She's got this lovely coquettish style, particularly when dealing with men in politics.'[14]

Kelly felt more vulnerable because, she believed, people thought she was stupid. She still claims her looks detracted from her credibility: 'being good-looking and dressing the way that I like to dress — a bit outlandish and stylish ... That's just the way I am and then that was a problem in being taken seriously.'[15]

Kelly told me feminists were generally hostile to her, but said she was still surprised by the vitriol she saw in stories by female journalists. She and Kingston never liked each other and never connected, she said, probably because Kingston was a lesbian and she was 'normal, an ordinary mum with two kids'.

*

It is difficult to talk about gender when your behaviour is under scrutiny because ensuing media debate usually reduces it to simplistic terms which make feminists seem one-eyed and perennially naive. If women are in any way analytical about what is happening to them in public commentary or in the parliament, it often is interpreted as an attempt to avoid blame. It is reasonable to walk into a debate where there are a number of factors at play and wonder how men would be treated for the same behaviour. Playing the victim is one thing; being treated differently is another.

There were, then, different approaches to talking about discrimination. The first was Vanstone's, which advocates roughing it out. The second was Joan Kirner's. In her time as premier, Joan Kirner was treated poorly by the media: her weight was exaggerated and mocked, she was caricatured as a flustered housewife wearing a large spotted dress, and she battled to gain credibility as the leader of a state in serious financial trouble. She identified that the way she was being portrayed was a political, not a personal problem and fought back in a very public way, articulating what she was doing very clearly and garnering support for it. ABC journalist Fran Kelly said she was a 'huge fan' of Kirner as a politician: 'There was nothing cloying, selfrighteous about her, she was tough and fought the boys at their own game. She never asked for anything special because she was a woman but pointed out what was problematic in terms of gender within the political system.'

While she was in a somewhat privileged position as premier, Kirner's success demonstrated a way ahead. That after decades of discrimination against women in powerful positions, the protests of the women themselves — and many journalists — had led to a recognition that sexism frequently colours reporting on powerful women, and leads to a flawed interpretation of events.

There had been many changes in the press since women like 'Housewife MP' Joan Child first posed next to her Hills hoist, and the 'kissable' Kathy Sullivan, stubbed out her cigars and walked into Canberra's Parliament House. Female journalists entered their profession at a far more rapid rate than the female politicians they reported on. Women formed about 12 per cent of the journalistic workforce in 1960 (compared to 25 per cent of the total workforce), when it stabilised for years.[16] There was a substantial influx of women in the 1970s and 1980s, but this was usually into junior positions. A study carried out in 1984 found that the *Courier-Mail*, the *Sunday Mail*, the *Telegraph*, and the *Sun* all employed roughly four times more men than women, and there was a total absence of women in the highest positions.[17] Photojournalism also remained stubbornly male dominated for decades. A survey of regional metropolitan daily newspaper photographers in 1992 found 91.5 per cent of respondents were male, and 8.5 per cent female.[18] (More recently, a 2014 Women in Media Whitepaper found that while the media reporting workforce was roughly evenly split between women and men, in print and broadcast, women journalists were only named or acknowledged as journalists of 30.8 per cent of media coverage. Three out of every four political reporters were male.)

It was not until 1993 that a woman edited a major daily metropolitan newspaper in Australia — Michelle Grattan, for the *Canberra Times* — although she was only in that position for two years. The lack of women editors has undoubtedly influenced the reporting of news stories in Australia. Others have followed her lead, but in many places the higher echelons of media groups remain stubbornly male. It was only in 2020, for example that the *Australian* appointed its first female editor in its then 65-year history — Michelle Gunn.

Over the last three decades, there has also been a transformation in the nature of political reporting, and a growth in the size of the press gallery. In the early 1930s, there were six or seven in the permanent press gallery corps in Canberra, and by 1951 it was approximately 30. The number crept to 50 in the late 1960s. By September 2003, the prime minister's press gallery list had 270 people on it, including mainstream reporters in print, radio and TV, Rehame and Capital Monitor, as well as reception and administrative staff. (According to the Parliamentary Education Office, there are still about 250 people in the press gallery in 2021.) Over this period, journalists became more competitive, and more independent of the government.

As the ranks of the press gallery journalists grew, the circulation of newspapers dropped substantially, relative to the post-war growth in the urban population. The proportion of people reading a newspaper dropped from 84 per cent to 73 per cent between 1966 and 1978. In 1987, the combined circulation of all major daily metropolitan and national newspapers was over 3.5 million, and 71 per cent of the population read a newspaper regularly. By 1990, it was three million and by 1994 it had dropped to 2.4 million. The number of newspapers shrank following changes to the cross-media ownership laws in 1987, with 14 major newspapers closing between 1987 and 1992. (In 1987 News Limited, owned by Rupert Murdoch, took over the Herald and Weekly Times newspapers. This meant there were then two major groups who owned most of the newspapers in Australia: John Fairfax Limited and News Limited.) While in 1988 there were 16 national and capital dailies, there were 11 in 1995. The concentration of media gave more power to those who remained.

*

Sometimes, through the refracted lens of the press, we are schizophrenic about our politicians — do we want them to be human, or superhuman? In an increasingly sophisticated political environment, there are plenty of contradictions about acceptable ways to behave. Some women break through conventions of behaviour and are affectionately regarded for doing so, while others are castigated for being flippant or shallow, for not conforming to the way men do politics. There is no simple formula.

And context is crucial. If Stott Despoja squeezed into tight leather pants and sang 'I Love Rock and Roll' for a television show, she would have been roundly condemned for trivialising herself with such a stunt. The older, earthier Kirner made a triumph out of something that would make other politicians appear media hungry or just silly. Perhaps it's also a question of the balance of coverage. Or even what your politics are. Pauline Hanson was certainly herself when she entered politics, unfettered by inhibitions of political behaviour or rhetoric, and untutored in how to handle the media. But hostility to her intolerant right-wing views coloured the response to her: instead of being praised for her lack of pretence and unaffected speech, she was lampooned and pilloried, and probably satirised more than any other politician that decade. She was made grotesque, subhuman, demonic. Just as she broke through a few rigid patterns of political behaviour, while reporting on her, the press broke a few of their own.

Pauline Hanson: 'a man's woman'

Don't overlook or deny the most obvious thing about Pauline
Hanson. In the eyes of many, she is an attractive, sexually
alluring woman. This is not an explanation of her popularity
— but it is the doorway of instinctive appeal through which
her message enters ... About Hanson there hangs the potent
scent of late-blooming sensuality.[1]
— journalist Nicolas Rothwell

When feminists advocate the election of more women to
parliament, we can be sure they don't have women like
Pauline Hanson in mind ... it is men who comprise the
majority of her candidates — and it is men who fall at
her feet and sweep her up into their virile arms. Make no
mistake, Pauline Hanson is a man's woman.[2]
— historian Marilyn Lake

On 6 November 2003, Pauline Hanson walked out of Brisbane
Women's Prison to face a panting media throng. She was thin,
vulnerable and clearly shaken by the 11 weeks she'd spent in a

high-security wing of the prison. Into her words, usually spiked with censorious and intolerant tones, came a note of compassion. After saying she wanted to hug her children and father, she said:

> PH: The message that I'd like to say is — I got caught up in the system that I saw fail me and I just, I am so concerned now for the other women behind the bars here — and men — that have also seen the system fail them and that's my biggest concern. And I — my love and wishes to the girls that I've shared the last 11 weeks with and I'd like to say a big thank you to the prison staff who've done an excellent job and I would like to send an extra special thank you to Alan Jones and to Bronwyn Bishop for their support and not giving up on me, especially the people of Australia.
>
> Journalist: Did you get a hard time in jail?
>
> PH: The system let me down like it's let a lot of people down. And there are other girls in there that the system has let down. And it's only because of money, power and position that stops them from getting their freedom.

At this moment, the martyrdom of the incendiary redhead who'd dragged the entire country to the right — particularly on border security and immigration — was complete. The public flocked to support the woman who had taken on the major political parties, sparked a phenomenally successful movement, been emulated by conservatives and vilified by progressives, until she was convicted of electoral fraud and landed in jail. She had waited for almost three months before the Court of Appeal overturned her conviction. As Cosima Marriner wrote in the *Sydney Morning Herald* that weekend, she had been elevated 'from a politically controversial figure to a modern-day martyr — Australia's Joan of Arc, complete with red tresses'. In a significant shift, she was no longer viewed as the victim of the media and 'elites', but of the 'system', political and legal, which had conspired to put her into a jail cell. The fact that she had registered the party with a list of 500 supporters, while there were only three official members — some called it a clumsy attempt to maintain control of Pauline Hanson's One Nation political party, others called it a $500,000 fraud — was largely glossed over. (The Court of Appeal held that the supporters believed they had become members, and therefore the application was valid.)

She was out. The pundits licked their lips, the political analysts scratched their heads, the fingers of the pollsters clicked against the abacus of public opinion. Hanson's appeal had always been her status as a 'non-politician'. She did not talk like them, look like them, or act like them. She flouted codes of behaviour, conventions of dress, and stumbled over big words. The major parties, long afflicted with the curse of narcissus in selecting candidates that looked like themselves, repeating generations of pale men equipped with the rhetoric of political compromise, were stumped. And feminists — who historically have found it far easier, or been far readier, to defend women on the Left — were uncomfortable as the import of her right-wing and racist policies was swamped by the apotheosis of the Woman Who Defied the System. As one reader, Harry Heidelberg, wrote to Margo Kingston's web diary on smh.com.au: 'I am spellbound. She's a gutsy woman and I'm sorry — I can't help but like her. Also, she's HONEST ... In a time when we have never been more oppressed by the system, doesn't she still have some resonance? She once said she was the mother of the nation. Mothers teach. Maybe she can educate us given the extraordinary trip she's been on. I want to hear more. It's not about 'we are in danger of being swamped by Asians' or 'please explain' or 'Easytax' or all the rest of it. She's a mirror and it's a journey.'

In the mid to late 1990s, Hanson's fame sprang from xenophobic ideas about immigration, race, welfare and globalisation that male politicians like Graeme Campbell had been hawking for years.[3] She was noticed because she was a woman, because she was so utterly unlike anyone else in federal politics. Her timing was right, and her gender was right. She was thought to be honest at a time when a growing acreage of the community distrusted and disliked politicians, believing them to be dishonest and corrupt.

*

By the 2000s, more column inches had probably been devoted to Pauline Hanson than to any other Australian female politician. She claims her major battle had been against the elite in the media who recoiled at her policies, and that this defined her identity. Her hostility today is palpable. She refused to talk to me for this book, and her best friend told me that after she left jail she decided she was tired of the media and would refuse any of their requests. She had always been naive when it came to the press, inexperienced and uncomfortable under scrutiny. Margo Kingston, who followed her on the campaign trail for the 1998 election, wrote a book about her experiences, which is a superb study of the heat, chaos and confusion that marked the campaign — as well as the complex interplay of personalities, conflicting emotions and the personal involvement of some journalists, particularly Kingston.[4] She revealed that many journalists and media outlets made political decisions about the coverage of Hanson. They did not want to help make her more popular because many were alarmed by her views, but they were fascinated by the spectacle of an untutored political novice making policy on the run.[5]

The role the press played in the spread and conflagration of 'Hansonism' was endlessly debated as commentators watched the flames in the late 1990s. Some incorrectly claimed her success was simply due to the media, and that she did not represent a 'spontaneous grassroots movement'. As academics Iva

Deutchman and Anne Ellison have noted, women MPs often win the attention of the press if they contradict female stereotypes.[6] Some journalists have also blamed the media for elevating her far more than was commensurate with her ability or political influence, and others have wrestled with their own culpability.[7]

During the 1998 election campaign Hanson once held an off-the-record meeting with journalists (to tick them off about their reporting), where she declared defiantly: 'If I lose my seat, it will be on the basis that people don't want my policies, that they don't want me or what I stand for. But there's no way in the bloody wide world that I am going to allow the media to make me lose it.'[8] Her political biography suggested that a lack of clear policy and structural cohesion in the party, and the distribution of preferences, probably had more to do with her demise than the prolonged, intense scrutiny by the press. She was disendorsed by the Liberal Party for the seat of Oxley in 1995 following some inflammatory comments she made about support for Indigenous people. She stood as an independent in 1996 and won the seat with a swing of more than 23 per cent. The next year she formed Pauline Hanson's One Nation Party, and in 1998 the party won 11 seats in the Queensland election. She quickly became a celebrity and the most famous Australian woman in the world. But in October that year, after a series of preference deals that worked against her, she failed to win a seat in parliament. The party won only three seats in the 2001 Queensland election, and Hanson quit as president in 2002. In 2003 she failed in her attempt to get elected to the NSW upper house, and several months later was sent to jail for fraudulently registering One Nation in Queensland.

The truth is, the significance of the election of the woman from Ipswich initially eluded most commentators. Her experience was similar to that of other women who found that their popularity in the polls or the grassroots of their parties cattle-prodded the media into recognition of their influence. Coming at the end of the progressive Keating era, Hanson articulated the whispered, muttered resentments of a part of the Australian community who had felt sidelined and silenced for years, unsettled by the impact of globalisation on their livelihoods and uneasy with the values of 'new class elites'.[9] The response to her on talkback radio and television fuelled some of the attention, but it was only once her party demonstrated serious electoral pulling power that the press was transfixed, and serious. According to Kingston it was not until Hanson's party won 11 seats at the Queensland election in 1998 that the *Herald* stopped seeing Hansonism as a 'sick joke' and 'waiting for the laughter to die down'.[10] Hanson defies the experience of many 'media tarts'. She was a subject of fascination, but was not pursued by the press because they liked her but, for many, because they despised her. There was not a point at which they turned on her, or brutalised her. There was rather a point at which they softened, and took her more seriously than they had initially. Hanson drove political reporting widdershins, making a mockery of conventional journalistic propriety or caution, as well as objectivity. Two things journalists frequently fretted over were their role in her rise and whether they had the power to subvert her success.

Was Hanson framed by the press? None of the traditional sexist categories applied to her, few of the clichéd slurs stuck, but the sexism was obvious and her critics were unabashed in their attacks — it was open slather on her appearance, sexuality, dress, voice and working-class background. The usual restraint was abandoned for the 'Oxleymoron', the 'Evita of Ipswich'. It is an interesting exercise, placing Hanson within the stereotypes, or frames, that have historically applied to political women in Australia, and seeing how they fit.

1. The steel sheila

Hanson's ambition was not questioned, although the apparent contradiction of her power and her appearance was constantly mulled over. The long-running jibes that female politicians were really men in drag, hiding male genitals under their skirts, were taken one step further in Hanson's case, when satirist Simon Hunt created the drag character Pauline Pantsdown, parodying her views and juxtaposing recordings of her voice in songs like 'I'm a Backdoor Man' to ridicule her. Hanson — or the photographers who shot her — did play with the imagery of the female warrior, or martyr, at times; she was pictured saluting, standing in a tank and wearing a helmet, for example. But she was not the Steel Sheila journalists had been hunting for decades. She came from outside the main political parties, had no chance of leading the country, and her potency as a leader was seen as inexplicable and weird, instead of a logical or hoped-for career progression. She lacked the 'respectability' necessary to be seen as a Thatcher clone.

2. The housewife

Hanson was a working woman who ran a fish and chip shop in Ipswich, not a demure domestic creature happy to do the housework. At least one photographer tried to get a photo of her pegging out her washing, but she was more likely to draw the tag 'fishwife superstar'.[11] She did not have a romantic view of marriage and told journalists she liked casual sex. She was widely reported to have advised one of her shop employees to use men for their bodies — 'get what you can out of them, then give them the flick' and told journalist David Leser that the best moment of her life was getting divorced. When he asked whether this was from her first or second husband, she laughed: 'That's two good things.'[12]

3. The mother

While in her personal life she had fractured relations with her sons to whom she did not speak for years at a stretch — Hanson fancied herself as a mother to the nation. In 1998, she declared: 'I care so passionately about this country, it's like I'm a mother. Australia is my home and the Australian people are my children.' This sparked a fascinating debate on maternity and politics. Prime Minister John Howard said he was the 'servant' of the nation; Treasurer Peter Costello said, 'She's not my mother'; and Labor leader Kim Beazley said his mother's philosophy was inclusive: 'The view of Australian mums, as I have found, is that while you love everybody, there's always the vulnerable in your family that you take care of most. That is motherhood Oz style. It is not motherhood Pauline Hanson style.' But, musing on the one-time popularity of Bronwyn Bishop, and the desire of the electorate for a strong female leader, then press gallery president Malcolm Farr summed it up as: 'We want mummy. And I think Hanson instinctively realised that when she called herself the mother of Australia and wrapped the flag around her. She knows men, and men like being mothered. They like a striking authoritative female figure to do things for them.'[13]

4. The feminist

Hanson claimed to despise feminists, and said she was not one because when she was married she always had a hot dinner on the table for her husband when he got home.[14] She lumped feminism in with a host of other social ills, criticising what she saw as 'a new religion of internationalism, of anti-white racialism, multiculturalism, feminism and Asianisation'. Equally, when sexist comments were made about her dress, body, brain, or right to be in parliament, feminists were quiet, many offended by her racism and her belief that the 'most downtrodden person in modern Australia' was the white Anglo-Saxon male. Her former adviser, John Pasquarelli, said: 'I laugh when I think of those ball-breaking, hairy-legged feminists who find themselves on the horns of a dilemma. On the one hand they would dearly love to embrace Pauline Hanson the Amazon, who wears a belt strung with dripping male scalps, but they also find themselves totally repulsed by their perception of her policies.'[15]

There was a substantial gender gap in the support for Hanson: in the late 1990s, 60 per cent of Pauline Hanson's One Nation Party's support was from men and 40 per cent from women. The gap existed in every age group.[16] Historian Marilyn Lake's theory was that disaffected rural white men were looking to Hanson to 'restore their stolen masculinity'. According to Pasquarelli, her 'sex appeal became very evident in the weeks after her maiden speech. Those men seeking dates with Pauline sent her gifts of chocolate and flowers, together with letters couched in polite but amorous language ... A few dispensed with the preliminaries altogether and made proposals of marriage! These Sir Galahads saw Pauline as a classical damsel in distress — feisty and tough, yet vulnerable and almost girlish as she stood alone against her assorted foes.'[17] Lake argues her sex appeal was crucial: unlike other female MPs, who tried to downplay their sexuality,

> Hanson flaunts her sexual difference and in the process of
> fashioning her as a celebrity, journalists have come to the
> party, their gaze gravitating to the signs of sex on her body:
> the red hair, the green eyes, the painted mouth, her sexual
> persona signified by her class, as well as her gender.[18]

One female media commentator told me she thought Hanson was portrayed as the 'town bike', with the connotation not just of sexiness but sexual availability and accessibility, a woman who enjoyed sleeping with men. Another female journalist wrote that Hanson had a certain sexual confidence: 'Thirty years ago, she'd be the girl who laughed with the blokes, unafraid of the rough joke, unafraid of being called 'common'.[19] The interest in the sex appeal of Hanson quickly translated into speculation about her sex life, particularly a rumoured affair with the Machivellian David Oldfield, and his influence over her.[20]

5. The cover girl

This was the stereotype Hanson exploited relentlessly. At first the media wrote disbelievingly about her sex appeal, then, as she morphed into a model, they played up to it, splashing her on front pages in her halter dress, bright yellow jackets, and knee-length skirts. At the same time, mostly female commentators mocked her leopard-print cowl necks, Hawaiian-style muu-muus, and love of loud colours. Much of this coverage was overtly snobbish. Then, of course, there was the extraordinary front-page headline 'Forget policy — I've got great legs'. According to Kingston, Hanson was surprised by the media interest in this black 'regulation height' skirt. She describes a scene where journalists were relaxing in a bar with One Nation members and police, and a News Limited journalist was receiving phone calls from *Daily Telegraph* editors asking for more miniskirt quotes: 'Oldfield suggested Hanson say she had better legs than Beazley or Howard. She didn't want to say anything, but when pressed hard came up with the line that if she had good legs at 44 then that was good going.' That was the last time she wore a short skirt during the campaign.[21]

Hanson was voted one of Australia's sexiest women in an *FHM* poll in 1998 — scraping in at 100. She 'polled particularly well', wrote the editors, on which basis, they mocked, they suspected 'many FHM readers to be of dubious mental health, or at least decidedly bent sexually'. The attraction was undeniable, but it was considered perverse. Bob Ellis described her on the Queensland election night standing 'in a pale gold spotlight with a jostling swarm of paparazzi, like Kim Novak at a Hollywood premiere, to gloat and preen and prattle and raise her strange yellow devil-cat eyes while everyone looked at her with a kind of erotic, stirred revulsion: how could this dread improbability be happening?'[22] Hanson was often caricatured as grotesque, monstrous and inhuman.

At the same time, Hanson was portrayed as a woman who was both a political fool and a canny flirt who knowingly manipulated men to get votes. Mike Seccombe wrote: 'Pauline Hanson might not know what xenophobia means, or who the police commissioner is, but she sure knows the political value of a revealing dress ...'[23]

Sonja Koremans wrote in the *Courier-Mail* in 2001:

Who on earth was Pauline Hanson trying to be yesterday? Was it one of Charlie's Angels or Princess Diana? Sharon Stone perhaps? It's anyone's guess, but one thing seems certain, she was more intent on flaunting flesh than projecting political acumen. Dressed in an ode-to-the-'80s halter-neck dress — canary yellow and worn with that signature scarlet lippie — Hanson projected an image of a woman more intent on taking a romp in the top paddock than dealing with deregulation of the dairy industry. But, with 60 per cent of One Nation's support coming from men, why wouldn't Hanson want to egg on her biggest fans with sexy frou frou frocks?[24]

There was no shame. It should be noted that while Hanson might have liked dressing up, she said she refused to pose in overtly sexual, or artificial, ways. In 2001, when she was polling highly in another *FHM* poll, the then editor, John Bastick, said he wanted her to pose for the magazine — doubtless in typically revealing outfits. She told a journalist, 'No thanks. But if a woman who has

'Forget policy, I've got great legs'. Headline in the *Daily Telegraph's* election coverage, September 1998. *Michael Klein/Newspix*

had four kids can be asked to do something like that, it's a great compliment. I'll leave it at that and just stick to politics.'[25] She indicated to News Limited journalist Emma Kate Symons that she had limits, and there was 'no way in the world' she would pose with a feather boa like Kernot: 'I am not a fashion model and I am in politics.'[26]

*

Less than three weeks after she was released from prison, Pauline Hanson appeared in the *Australian Women's Weekly* in a series of photographs: in an aqua blue cardigan, a black strapless cocktail dress with a beaded choker, a sparkly black shirt and pants, and chic white shirt and black skirt ensemble. The words — billed as her secret prison diaries — contrasted sharply with the glamour shots, as she detailed strip searches and the indignities of prison life. It had been an alarming place for her to find herself, and the stories that emerged about senior Liberal minister Tony Abbott and his establishment of a trust fund called 'Australians for Honest Politics' to help fund court cases against Hanson doubtless confirmed her suspicions that 'the system' was out to get her. As she told the reporter who wrote up her 'diaries': 'I remember Dad telling me not to go into politics because it was a dirty game. I didn't know what he meant then. Now I was experiencing it first hand.' The article ended with the declaration that if she were to stand for parliament it would not be as a member of the party she founded, One Nation, but as an independent: 'I have been through the court system, the litigation, the party politics, the in-fighting and that took me away from what I set out to do in the first place — to give people a voice.'[27]

Hanson both defied and embodied the bias against women in politics. She made her maiden speech exactly 20 years after Margaret Thatcher packed her bags for her visit to Australia in 1976, and the two women differed sharply: the cool, articulate, brilliant, blonde British woman and the inarticulate, unpolished, angry, redheaded Australian. Thatcher was the *über*-politician who was feared by her colleagues, and Hanson the anti-politician who was loathed by hers. Thatcher eventually became Britannia, while Hanson draped herself in the flag and declared she was the mother of all Australians. Thatcher controlled the media, cynically manipulating stereotypes when she was establishing a profile as leader of the Tories, then ignoring them as she cultivated the steely persona instead. Hanson defied the media, and subverted the conventions by playing to them. This may have been because her supporters were immune to attacks on her in the press — which they took as further evidence that she was fighting the elites.

Just as Natasha Stott Despoja was jeered at for wearing an evening dress, and Cheryl Kernot for a red feather boa, Hanson sashayed into polling booths and election parties in flesh-flashing numbers, delighting admirers with sundresses, high heels, and a collection of fetching frocks. When she did what other women were not supposed to do, it often worked in her favour. Hanson was then, perhaps, our first post-modern media tart who unwittingly and clumsily played the media at their own game and, briefly but spectacularly, won.

Conclusion

> It's not just what we inherit from our mothers and fathers
> that haunts us. It's all kinds of defunct theories, all sorts of
> old defunct beliefs, and things like that. It's not that they
> actually live on in us; they are simply lodged there, and we
> cannot get rid of them. I've only to pick up a newspaper and
> I seem to see the ghosts gliding between the lines.
>
> — Henrik Ibsen, *Ghosts*, 1881

All politicians are media tarts. Former Queensland premier
Peter Beattie admitted as much, saying that pursuing publicity
was part of a politician's job. It was a bit rich, he said, that his
colleagues in opposition should make a song and dance about
it: 'It's like two prostitutes standing on the corner talking about
virginity.' This is increasingly the case in an age of electronic
media grabs, and image-driven makeovers. But when women are
the ones with bulging newspaper clippings files, overworked press
secretaries, and stellar profiles, they are frequently dismissed
as vain, superficial and narcissistic; as being ego-driven, and
therefore lacking intellectual or diplomatic ability — even though
politicians who lack egos are pretty rare. Right now, those who
have fought to keep women out of powerful positions have had

some success. Younger women have learnt to keep their heads down. They dress soberly and shy from self-promotion. They play the game better, but they play it more like men. Overt claims that women improve politics have largely disappeared — anyone who is seen to imply they are more moral because they are female will be either thought naive or proved wrong. But accepting that politics is dirty, nasty, and dishonest is not the way forward. Men and women need to tackle and confront the political culture together. In politics, women remain a symbol of what the problems are, as would any marginalised, disenfranchised group. Some women will fail. Some will be mediocre performers, average policy promoters, uninspiring legislators. Just like a lot of the men. But the exclusion of women and people of colour still represents lack of justice, and they remain, despite all their protestations, hoped-for change agents.

Many criticisms have been levelled at the gallery over the past 20 years: they move in a pack, are insulated from 'real people's lives', are too close to their subjects, and are prone to create and fuel controversy and conflict in the search for a good story. Despite its faults, the gallery has often acted as a buffer against the worst excesses of political behaviour — the rumour, innuendo, and use of personal information to destroy opponents. There are unspoken codes and conventions of behaviour that are unknown to most people. But they also condemn politicians for behaviour many of them are guilty of.

The *Australian*'s Dennis Shanahan, who has worked in the gallery for almost two decades, is both a fierce defender and a harsh critic:

> We are unelected, unaccountable, sanctimonious,
> parsimonious in our attitude to politicians and generous
> in our attitude to ourselves, hypocritical, two-faced,
> contradictory ... yeah, we're all of those things. And this is

the defining difference. We don't put our hand up to take
taxpayers' money to represent the public and to make an
oath of office. I always maintain that personal stuff can
remain in the background unreported as long as it doesn't
interfere with office or hide rank hypocrisy. While journalists
[are allowed to] be blatant hypocrites, politicians aren't,
so that's the tough rules. I think it's very, very difficult on
politicians, and overall to the detriment of public service in
the wider sense, because of the difficulty of actually finding
people who will put themselves forward.[1]

A close look at polling and focus studies over the 1990s reveals
a sharp dissonance between female politicians favoured by the
electorate and those journalists respected. Bronwyn Bishop
was very popular in 1993, but caricatured by the gallery as a
manicured dragon lady. While journalists threw up their hands
in horror when Kernot defected to the ALP, the electorate said
they understood her motives. When she wore a raunchy red dress
for the *Australian Women's Weekly*, the press errupted, but then
conducted polls that found people did not mind. When Laurie
Oakes wrote about Kernot's affair with Gareth Evans, the public
strongly objected. Stott Despoja was dismissed as a lightweight
by gallery veterans, but adored by her party. These differences —
which are also seen in Pauline Hanson's experience and, in the
noughties, that of Carmen Lawrence — are vital to understand:
basically, Australians want a female politician who is honest,
down-to-earth, and does not play the boys' games. But this is
exactly the kind of woman who, once she reaches the higher
echelons, is destroyed. Their enemies achieve this by tackling
their most powerful asset — their image, linked to their standing
with the community — by urging the press to publish dirt.

Several journalists told me they had often worried, or wondered,
if Cheryl Kernot would commit suicide after some stories were

published. The scrutiny was fierce and intrusion intense: she was even interviewed in her hospital room. She was clearly cracking psychologically under the strain, and journalists were there to hold the bucket as she threw up bile then splash it on the front page. To ask questions about this is not to excuse anyone of bad behaviour, to plead for their special treatment, or ask if they can be excused from the scrutiny that comes with being a public figure. It is simply to question how far we need to push, or punish, our elected representatives when they fail us. And whether simply what was seen as whinging or wilting demands punishment or intense scrutiny.

Monica Attard is a highly respected journalist who has been awarded an Order of Australia for services to Australian journalism and has won four Walkley Awards. She told me her interview with Kernot about the affair with Evans (which won her another award) changed her perspective on the media:

> I suddenly got a taste of how intense the media scrutiny was of her and how difficult it was, not being able to walk around your suburb, in which you lived, not being able to leave your apartment or answer your phone. I could see it in her face ... What did we want? Did we want Cheryl to top herself? ... It's the ugly side of the Australian media, when we pick, pick, pick, hound, hound, hound, and what do we want from that person? ... In Cheryl's case, it was not enough for her to be out of the public eye; they wanted blood ... It was not my business, but half the time I just felt like saying, just bugger off, leave her alone, she has gone through an awful time, just back off. Unless we want her to put her head in the oven ... It makes you wonder about our humanity, how cruel we can be. She was obviously suffering, she was really falling apart, and for people to be so cruel and stick the boot in was awful.

Sometimes it seems women are praised then punished for overt signs of femininity. Or at least any obvious reminder that they are unlike the men who have run Australian politics for the past hundred years. It is wrong to assume they are morally superior to men, or even loath to play the same games, but it is disappointing to think that the growing presence of a previously excluded group does not matter, and will not have any impact on the whole, even if just by breaking certain codes or demanding accountability.

*

Some say the 1990s was just a freak set of circumstances for women, an unfortunate chain of events that led to them being pushed from leadership positions into the mud — if they had not leapt themselves. Michelle Grattan argues the 'meteors' of the 1990s 'were very peculiar stories; they were extraordinary stories: Bronwyn who wanted to take the leadership by siege, Cheryl who did something very unusual, Carmen who was destined for high things and had been exposed as not telling the truth and pursued hard by the opposition.[2]

The reason these events of the 1990s are difficult to quantify is that underpinning each of the cautionary tales — Bronwyn (the woman who sought too much power without permission) Bishop, Carmen (the woman who claimed to be better than the men) Lawrence, Cheryl (the woman who complained too much) Kernot, and Natasha (the woman who got too much publicity) Stott Despoja — are flaws and mistakes. But over and over, these mistakes are considered to be so much worse in women than in men, and attract a greater volume and length of attack: ambition, chasing publicity, claiming to dislike aggressive politics, or complaining. Worst of all is to claim you have been unfairly treated by the media — if you have ever had any positive publicity, you will never be able to make this claim without journalists turning on you. One by one, these women became caricatures — hyped, sanctimonious saints, heroines, ambitious bitches, shallow party girls — and eventually their policy work was obscured by a cult of personality over which they had very little control. As Shaun Carney wrote in the *Age*, 'The Australian political scene seems capable of dealing with only one prominent woman at a time ... many male political players are locked into seeing prominent women as bit players or novelty personalities.'[3] They were pursued by their opponents not because they were women, but because they were potentially serious vote-pullers, electoral drawcards with the kind of popularity party strategists fantasise about.

What drove a lot of the press coverage of female MPs then was a questioning of their humanity. Those with right-wing views, who are not seen as particularly compassionate, were portrayed as almost subhuman monsters, with grotesque features ripe for satire or caricature — Bronwyn Bishop and Pauline Hanson. Those seen as honest, decent and warm-hearted were canonised and showered with praise for being human, relatable and real — Carmen Lawrence, Cheryl Kernot and even Natasha Stott Despoja. They were cheered for representing the politics of change. But then, when they showed emotion, made mistakes, or behaved like the men in playing political hardball, they were fiercely castigated.

So where do we go from here? First, media outlets that are intent on luring more women readers should resist patronising women when the temptation arises, and salivating over those considered photogenic, or leadership material. The Australian Journalists Association's Code of Ethics provides that we should not 'place unnecessary emphasis on personal characteristics, including race, ethnicity, nationality, gender, age, sexual orientation, family relationships, religious belief, or physical or intellectual disability'. Second, it's important for women, and men, to continue to question the dominant political culture, and hopefully undermine it with their presence. If the next generation's Stott Despoja completely shunned the spotlight, aped the behaviour of the political head-kickers, cut off her hair, dressed in nothing but suits, and refused to be seen at parties, would that be a victory for women? Perhaps, if she became prime minister. But people are sick of the pretension, lies, aggro and name-calling of traditional politics. Australians are cynical and increasingly distrust their politicians. For a democracy that prides itself on social values and the importance of public participation, this is hardly an inspiring scenario.

The challenge for women is to be wary of the problems the media poses, while remaining accessible and open. As history has shown, they have not stood idly by as the press has built — or trashed their reputations in the press. They have refused requests, manipulated attention, exploited stereotypes, called out sexism and continually attempted to shape the way they have been portrayed. They have proved the public craves a different style of politics, and pricked the interest of journalists who are curious about whether women can usher in this change.

There are many talented young women in parliaments across the country, one of whom, it can only be hoped, will become the Steel Sheila journalists have dreamt of for so long. Sugar and steel, and a capacity to feel — that's what we want media tarts to be made of.

Epilogue

capital

in grade five

they bus our children
to the capital

to the long white building,
high-majestic, on the hill

where the boys mostly learn:
you study hard,
and you might well
work here one day, mate

and the girls hang back,
and button their collars:

cause this place
is where women
get raped

Maxine Beneba Clarke[1]

The Valkyries

On 10 April 2021, the day after Prince Philip died at the age of 99, I was sitting on an ABC News desk co-presenting a weekend special on the royals, when Malcolm Turnbull walked on set, beaming and chatty. 'What about Laura Tingle?' he said to us while we were off-air. 'She's been absolutely on fire!'

We all nodded in agreement about the stellar work of the chief political correspondent for the ABC's '7.30' program, especially her recent coverage of the rape allegations, the misogyny in Canberra culture, the video that emerged of staffers masturbating over a female MP's desk.

Tingle had steel in her voice when she'd challenged Prime Minister Scott Morrison on how he had palmed off matters regarding accusations against Christian Porter (that he strongly denies) to police, who were unable to investigate the relevant rape claims anyway (as the accuser had taken her own life); night after night, she had stared down the barrel of the camera, addressing Morrison directly and with force.

Turnbull kept talking about her, searching for words: 'It's not just about her words, it's her –' he gestured to his head, his jaw '– face! She's like a Valkyrie!'

I thrilled to this description, sitting up straight before the red camera lights switched back on and I began asking him questions about his recollections of the man who was married to Queen Elizabeth II for 73 years.

In Norse mythology, the women called Valkyries oversee battles and pick who may live and who may die. They represent honour and uncompromising justice. The literal meaning is 'chooser of the slain'.

We are so used to women being slain, being prey. We are not used to women being the hunters, the protectors.

Imagine if this new era could be one of the Valkyries, doling out justice.

This is a movie we have not seen before, a narrative we don't know.

*

It's an era of restrained, steady anger. Women have long been punished for anger, for railing against the way things are. They are accused of hysteria, emotion, loss of control while blokes storm and rage as though it is expected of them.

Even in 2021, when women, and men, began to ask that allegations of rape be properly examined, scrutinised and taken seriously, the female journalists were accused of being angry activists, motivated by emotion.

So much has changed since I wrote the first edition of this book. Even the debate over the word 'feminist' has somehow been quashed or quietened. In 2014 Beyonce, the world's most lauded popstar, performed her single 'Flawless' at the MTV Music Video Awards in front of a screen festooned with the word FEMINIST in capital letters; her silhouette was one of strength. The song samples a TED talk by Nigerian writer Chimamanda Ngozi Adichie calling for gender equality, in which she says:

> We teach girls to shrink themselves. To make themselves
> smaller, we say to girls, 'You can have ambition, but not
> too much, you should aim to be successful, but not too
> successful, otherwise you will threaten the man' ... We teach
> girls that they cannot be sexual beings in the way that boys
> are. Feminist: the person who believes in the social political,
> and economic equality of the sexes.[2]

We have long taught women those things, too. Even politicians.

Today, media reportage remains a real problem for prominent women, mostly because of the hatefulness that can accompany it:

the inferno of criticism on social media. The confidential report prepared for the Liberal Party Executive in 2015 found that 'the media's scrutiny of parliamentarians has been one of the biggest deterrents for women seeking a career in politics', especially the potential implication on their children and families.

The report also found a perception 'that female politicians are discriminated against by the media', that 'the media focus more on the appearance of women than in the message' and that potential female candidates are deterred from politics by watching what happened to other women shot by cannon into the political circus: 'Women can cope with playing the ball in politics, but not playing the man or woman.'[3] After all, two of our female politicians have had to stomach protracted discussions about whether they were 'sluts'. Sarah Hanson Young sued, won and is still a senator. Emma Husar sued, settled and is no longer in politics.

It's clearly not just gender diversity that is a problem in our parliaments, but all kinds of diversity; ability, ethnicity, culture, sexuality, race, class, age. If all of this effort — a drive to a more inclusive, transparent polis — just amounts to more white women being elected, we will have failed.

But women MPs are no longer staying quiet, bending like pretzels to fit into politics as they once did. And women like Kate Ellis, Tanya Plibersek and Julie Bishop are eager that young women know how incredibly worthwhile they have found their political work to be, despite all the rubbish. It's crucial that talented women run for parliament, and that the blokey culture that would block or mock them is made accountable and more transparent.

When I wrote this book, women were carefully, cannily, learning to play the system. It was an era of sober reckoning with what had happened to the women in this book, and a reflection of the constraints of the time. In many cases this has worked —

female premiers, a governor-general and one prime minister. And some highly talented frontbenchers. But this requires patience — and patience is wearing out. The closer women have inched to power, the more visible an undercurrent of sludge has become, exposing an ongoing sexualisation, stereotyping and sidelining, a refusal to accept a woman wielding authority. Social media — especially the anonymous and gutless users on there — has pushed this to a more extreme and relentless form. Much has changed in terms of sheer numbers but the treatment of Julia Gillard shocked many; it was so ugly, visceral, unrestrained, damaging and unfair.

It's not rooted in social media. It's rooted in history. It has just found expression in another form. Which is why if we do not recognise and understand this history, it will continue to morph and repeat.

We need, now, our Valkyries — in politics, the media, the courts, in every place that has systems that diminish and exclude the voices of women — to call people to account. We need, now, for all this research and reporting, all of the forensic work and first-hand accounts of women calling for a fairer, more equitable culture, to be heard. That's the challenge here; parliamentary chambers were designed for male voices. Even lapel microphones are designed for male clothes. Politics was designed for white men. But it's not working any more.

The lava, quietly, is flowing.

Julia Baird, 2021

Acknowledgements

A book like this, with its roots in years of research for my PhD, has many debts. First the research was made possible by the expertise of numerous librarians across the country. The staff at the NSW Parliamentary Library, including Rob Brian, David Clune, Stewart Little, Greg Tillotson and Richard Baker, have been particularly helpful. I am also grateful for the assistance of the staff at the Federal Parliamentary Library, especially Roslyn Membrey and Bernice Donellan.

I interviewed many people for this book who are too numerous to mention but were generous with their time. I would, however, like to thank those female MPS I spoke to, including Franca Arena, Louise Asher, Gracia Baylor, Flo Bjelke-Petersen, Bronwyn Bishop, Julie Bishop, Anna Burke, Jan Burnswoods, Valerie Callister, Virginia Chadwick, Joan Chambers, Kerry Chikarovski, Joan Child, Joan Coxsedge, June Craig, Mary Crawford, Janice Crosio, Lyla Elliott, Wendy Fatin, Rosemary Foot, Pat Giles, Julia Gillard, Marlene Goldsmith, Julie Greig, Deidre Grusovin, Margaret Guilfoyle, Janine Haines, Kay Hallahan, Yvonne Henderson, Maggie Hickey, Jane Hill,

Caroline Hogg, Beryl Jones, Jackie Kelly, Ros Kelly, Cheryl Kernot, Lis Kirkby, Joan Kirner, Sue Knowles, Di Laidlaw, Carmen Lawrence, Meg Lees, Susan Lenehan, Wendy Machin, Margaret McAleer, Jeanette McHugh, Jean Melzer, Sandra Nori, Pamela O'Neil, Jeanette Patrick, Tanya Plibersek, Margaret Ray, Margaret Reid, Nicola Roxon, Susan Ryan, Kay Setches, Prue Sibree, Heather Southcott, Natasha Stott Despoja, Kathy Sullivan, Ann Symonds, Carmel Tebbutt, Jo Vallentine, Amanda Vanstone, Judyth Watson, and Barbara Wiese.

Dozens of my *Sydney Morning Herald* colleagues have given me support or assistance over the years, from talking through ideas to tolerating long writing stretches, and helping with dozens of dilemmas over the years, including Richard Coleman, Linda Doherty, Gabe Hooton, Michael Howard, Peter Fitzsimons, Margo Kingston, Heather McKinnon, Alan Moir, Ron Nicolle, Belinda Pratten, Judy Prisk, Max Prisk, Alan Ramsey, Mike Seccombe, Flicc Walsh, and Cathy Wilcox. Paul McGeough, Mark Scott, and Robert Whitehead all allowed me to take time off to work on the thesis and then the book. Simon Holder provided research assistance in Canberra at a critical time. Other journalists have also helped with interviews and various queries, particularly Monica Attard, Malcolm Farr, Michelle Grattan, Fran Kelly, Laurie Oakes, Matt Price, Peter Rae, Dennis Shanahan, Tony Walker, and Christine Wallace.

Thanks must go also to those people who read and commented on chapters of the book, including Geoff Kitney, Gerard Henderson, Anne Summers, and Rob Manne. And finally, a big shout out to those of my friends who have talked over ideas and read drafts, especially Michelle Arrow, Katherine Biber, Jo Chichester, Jo Fox, Josie Gresch, Sarah MacDonald, Dan McMurray, and Andrew Rayment.

I raise my glass to my yum cha partners in crime — Tim Dick, Joel Gibson, Cath Keenan, and Sacha Molitorisz (and Jo).

Particular thanks also goes to Judith Whelan and James Woodford. There is a trio of tarts who have helped me in every way — Kimberley Lipschus, Jacqui Jones, and Martha Sear, who read every word and inspired me to keep going. My parents, Bruce and Judith, have been fantastic, along with the rest of my family. Without them, and the unstinting support of Morgan Mellish, this book would not have been written.

Julia Woodlands Baird
July 2004

Notes

Introduction to 2021 edition

1   Kate Ellis, *Sex, Lies and Question Time: Why the successes and struggles of women in Australia's parliament matter to us all*, Hardie Grant, Sydney, 2021, p. 125.

2   Blair Williams, 'A gendered media analysis of the prime ministerial ascension of Gillard and Turnbull: he's "taken back the reins" and she's "a backstabbing" murderer', *Australian Journal of Political Science*, 52:4, 2017, pp. 550–564.

3   Ibid, pp. 555–559.

4   Jessica Sier & Vanessa Desloires, 'The Abbott government breaks more promises than it keeps', *Australian Financial Review*, 5 September 2014.

5   Kate Ellis, op cit. p. 7.

6   Ibid. p. 124.

7   Ibid. pp. 124–125.

8   Abigail Lewis, 'The Way In: Representation in the Australian Parliament, Per Capita', 2019.

9   Eryk Bagshaw, 'Parliament is no more diverse now than it was in 1988 as political staffer ranks explode', *Sydney Morning Herald*, 19 Jan. 2019.

10 Women's Working Group chaired by Rosemary Craddock, *Room for Movement: Women and Leadership in the Liberal Party*, A Liberal Party Federal Executive Initiative, 2015.

Introduction to 2004 edition

1   Journalist Anne Deveson, as chair of the National Working Party on the Portrayal of Women in the Media, 1992, quoted by Geoff Turner,

'Towards equity: women's emerging role in Australian journalism', *Australian Studies in Journalism*, vol. 2, 1993, p. 161.

Prelude

1 Patricia Morgan, 'Mrs Thatcher will warn Australians: Russian threat not just a European problem', *Advertiser*, 3 Sept. 1976, p. 5.
2 T. S. Monks, 'The Iron Lady is set fair for Downing Street', *SMH*, 28 Aug. 1976, p. 14.
3 Ros Dunn, 'Not just a pretty face', *Australian*, 11 Dec. 1974.
4 Letters to the editor, *SMH*, 21 Feb. 1975, p. 6.
5 Patricia Morgan, op. cit.
6 Thatcher's memories of the trip to Broken Hill were dominated by the strength of the unionism in the mining town. The union leaders, she later wrote, 'informed me proudly that no one could live or work in the town without belonging to the union. A bar in the town which had recently challenged the rule had simply been boycotted and forced to close down. My guides were completely unabashed, indeed perversely pleased, about this blatant infraction of liberty. I could not help wondering whether I had had an insight into Britain's future.' Margaret Thatcher, *The Path to Power*, HarperCollins, London, 1995, p. 387. The only other comments Thatcher made about her trip to Australia involved her admiration for former Liberal prime minister Robert Menzies.
7 Editorial, untitled, *Sun-Herald*, 19 Sept. 1976.
8 Martin Beesley, 'Twelve thousand mile run to Downing St', *Australian*, 21 Sept. 1976, p. 15.
9 Margaret Thatcher, op. cit.
10 Editorial, 'Lady in waiting', *SMH*, 13 Feb. 1975, p. 6; Editorial, 'Petticoat government', *Daily Telegraph*, 14 Sept. 1976.
11 It also should be noted that during this time, media mogul Rupert Murdoch, who owned newspapers the *Australian,* the *Daily Telegraph* and the *Daily Mirror* in Sydney, the *News* in Adelaide, and the *Daily Sun* in Brisbane, supported Thatcher in the 1979 election. His support continued in the early 1980s in both Britain and Australia.
12 Beatrix Campbell, *The Iron Ladies: Why Do Women Vote Tory?*, Virago Press, London, 1987, p. 233.
13 Kathy Sullivan speaking on ABC Radio, 11 Jan. 1991, Federal Parliamentary Library transcript, p. 9.
14 Quoted by Wendy Webster, *Not a Man to Match Her*, Women's Press, London, 1990, p. 71.

Chapter One: Steel Sheilas: female MPs, ambition and power

1   In hindsight, there are many similarities to the Hanson phenomenon
    which occurred three years later: she had immense grassroots support,
    though most of her colleagues despised her; the media paid her much
    attention but little respect; she was a populist who engaged in repetitive
    and simple rhetoric; and politicians were forced to take her seriously by a
    series of polls that proved she had electoral pulling power.

2   Glennys Bell, 'Rise of the prettier polly', *Bulletin*, 21 April, 1981, p. 7.

3   Untitled, *Time*, 24 Feb. 1975, p. 10.

4   Donald Horne, *A Time of Hope: Australia 1966–72*, Angus &
    Robertson, Sydney, 1980, pp. 2–3.

5   'McMahon: women too soft to be PM', *Age*, 21 June 1978.

6   'A mother with political ambitions', *SMH*, 10 April 1975, p. 14.

7   Ralph Sharman, 'Minister promises end to dole cheats', *Daily Telegraph*,
    Dec. 1975.

8   Chris Anderson, 'Woman Senator to Lead Liberals?', *Sun-Herald*,
    9 March 1975, p. 3.

9   She told the National Press Club in November 1977 she had not seen
    a possible candidate for the first female prime minister, and she was
    certainly not one, despite being one of the Fraser government's most
    effective ministers.

10 Claudia Cragg, 'Rosemary Foot: the Iron Lady of Down Under', *South
    China Morning Post*, 27 May 1984.

11 Nikki Barrowclough, 'Rosie', *Sydney*, Feb. 1982, p. 42.

12 Catherine Menagh, 'Dedication to a career', *West Australian*, 8 June
    1981, p. 46.

13 Matthew Moore, 'Chadwick in need of correction', *SMH*, 7 April 1990.

14 Many journalists admired her success in resisting cuts, as she repeatedly
    battled attempts by treasurers (first Phillip Lynch, then John Howard)
    to restrict eligibility for family allowances and over-70s pensions. The
    fact that a woman could continually stand up to, and get the better of,
    a group of men, and prevent them from cutting her department's budget
    was a subject of perpetual fascination for members of the press gallery.
    However, this in itself could distract from the real story. In October
    1979, the chief political correspondent at the *Age*, Michelle Grattan,
    questioned the 'ballooning cost' of welfare recipients. She pointed out
    federal budget expenditure on social security and welfare had increased
    from 17.3 per cent of the 1969–70 budget to estimates of 28.2 per cent
    for 1979–80. (Michelle Grattan, 'The giant jelly, welfare', *Age*, 24 Oct.
    1979.) The *Australian Financial Review* editorialised that Guilfoyle's

ability to resist the pruning of her department's budget was not evidence of her invincibility, but a worrying sign of a government being held hostage by a Senate which refused to cut public spending on welfare. The annoyance at the attention paid to Guilfoyle instead of the state of the budget was reflected in the headline 'How a lady senator distracts the eye' (*AFR*, 4 June 1979).

15 Terry Slavin, 'Yes Virginia, the Minister is a woman', *Sun-Herald*, 3 April 1988; Nick Yardley, 'Meet Greiner's Iron Maiden', *Sunday Telegraph*, 22 May 1988. Note that a series of budget cuts led to closure of one-quarter of district offices, amalgamation of more, and widespread job losses. Demonstrations and public protests followed. At one point, nearly 150 welfare agencies took out a $4000 full-page ad in the *SMH*, calling on the premier to stop the cuts. At the same time, there was a series of problems in juvenile detention centres, including escapes and suicides, which coincided with a more punitive approach to juvenile detention taken by Chadwick. She was going, the *Sunday Telegraph* opined, 'from crisis to crisis'.

16 Reflecting what was a growing consciousness of sexism in reportage, the reporter agreed: 'Right down to the irrelevant description of trim, petite, blonde, blue-eyed mother of three'. ('A woman with $9000 million a year to spend', *Courier-Mail*, 1 Sept. 1979.) When asked by one journalist about labels like tough, aloof, cold, steel butterfly and ice maiden, Guilfoyle said cautiously, 'I suppose I am a lot of things to a lot of people … It's not easy to be close to people and … I am not necessarily what people always say I am.' She insisted competent was a more accurate description of her than tough. (Gail Franzmann, 'No soft job for the Senator', *Herald* (Melbourne), 10 Dec. 1979.)

17 Anne Summers, '"I think you grow every day in a job like this" — an interview with Margaret Guilfoyle', *National Times*, 6–11 Sept. 1976, pp. 52–54.

18 Guilfoyle, uncharacteristically, attributed the tag to a double standard or discomfort with powerful women: 'I feel that image is one which women in top positions attract by making decisions that, while necessary, are unpopular. A man making the same decision would be seen as strong and competent but a woman attracts descriptions such as uncaring, unfeeling.' (Alex Kennedy, 'Calm during the storms', *Advertiser*, 4 April 1979, p. 4.) Asked what she considered the most unfair publicity she and the department received, Guilfoyle cited television programs or articles that portrayed the department as 'needlessly cruel, heartless and not doing its job properly'.

19 Michael Harvey, 'The Dame bows out with her customary grace ...',
    Herald (Melbourne), 2 June 1987. Harvey also recorded that she rejected
    the idea of having harboured leadership ambitions, and referred to her
    lack of complaint abut gender bias: 'If being the lone woman on both the
    pilot razor gang and the renowned Fraser Cabinet was a constant battle
    against male prejudices, Senator Guilfoyle was not about to let on.'

20 Reporter Belinda Luscombe wrote that while Greiner believed Metherell
    would be remembered as the punitive father of the NSW modern
    education system, Chadwick 'may well be remembered as its mother':
    'Like the archetypal father of Victorian romantic novels, Metherell took
    an out-of-control child and beat him into shape. He cut out his pocket
    money, threatened to disinherit him, banned him from going out and
    even (in reintroducing the cane) spanked him. Exit Metherell, leaving
    child resentful, hurt, confused and angry. Enter Chadwick, soothing,
    gentle and kind — she tends to her charge's wounds, gives him a hug and
    puts him gently to bed.' Luscombe, however, warned against thinking
    of the 'marble minister' as a soft touch, writing that on the issue of the
    Teachers Federation and the Parents and Citizens Association she was
    'as firm as sugar-coated granite'. (Belinda Luscombe,'Mother Superior',
    Daily Telegraph, 22 Sept. 1990.)

21 Jeremy Moon and Imogen Fountain argue this is more reflective of
    'women's areas of community and parliamentary specialisation'. (Jeremy
    Moon and Imogen Fountain, 'Keeping the gates: women as ministers in
    Australia, 1970– 96', *Australian Journal of Political Science*, p. 465.)

22 'Action woman', *New Idea*, 16 Dec. 1989, p. 10.

23 Jodie Brough, 'An entirely different lady', *Canberra Times*, 31 Oct. 1992,
    pp. C1– C2.

24 He said when Bishop lost preselection in 1974, she was consumed with
    the fact that this had happened because she was a woman: 'I have vivid
    memories of her ... telling me privately at that preselection that she was
    so incensed about the way the world treated women that she'd taught her
    daughters to urinate standing up. She used another word, and it really
    stuck in my mind.' (David Leser, *Bronwyn Bishop: A Woman in Pursuit
    of Power*, Text, Melbourne, 1987, p. 39.)

25 *Australian Women's Weekly*, June 1993.

26 Mike Gibson, *Daily Telegraph Mirror*, 4 Oct. 1993, p. 10.

27 Alan Ramsey, 'Bishop fights her way to public notice', *SMH*, 22 April
    1989, p. 31.

28 Frank Devine, 'Bronwyn's push may soon turn to shove', *Australian*,
    12 Aug. 1993.

29 Jodie Brough, op. cit.

30 Gerard Henderson was sceptical: 'In a recent editorial in the *Australian Business Monthly*, Bruce Stannard referred to (unnamed) individuals who had described Bishop as "Menzies in a frock". I wonder.' (*SMH,* 1 Feb. 1994, p. 13.)

31 Sue Williams, 'Now trendy Wendy must wear the flak', *Telegraph Mirror,* 18 Feb. 1991.

32 She also cultivated connections with Rodney Adler, then FAI chief executive; celebrity agent Harry M. Miller; and Mary Fairfax. Alan Jones was also a key backer, and defended her in *Sunday Telegraph* columns as the victim of jealousy.

33 In February, according to another Newspoll, given the choice between Hewson and Bishop, 48 per cent chose Bishop and 34 per cent Hewson. If Bishop were leader, 56 per cent said they would vote for the Liberal Party at an election, and 47 per cent of those polled said the same of Hewson. Fifty per cent of voters thought she would make a better PM than Keating. According to another poll in February, she was perceived to be stronger, more competent, and more intelligent than Hewson.

34 Quoted by Michael Millett, 'Voters: Women want Bishop', *SMH,* 4 Feb. 1994, p. 1.

35 This is not actually correct. Bishop was preselected on 11 December. Carlton left on 14 January. Reporters wrote at the time that a by-election was not expected until February or March. It occurred on 26 March 1994. At the time of this interview in 1992, according to the Commonwealth Parliamentary Handbook, there had been six occasions on which the gap between the vacation of the seat and the by-election date had been longer than Bishop's.

36 Ellis agreed the swing against Bishop was exaggerated in the press, but claims he had a 'considerable impact' on her campaign: 'With a high-profile candidate you'd expect a swing to her of 3 to 4 per cent. On first-party preferred there was a swing against her of 5 per cent, overall there was 1.5 per cent against her, which was fuck all and had me quite depressed on election night. It was exaggerated in the press; they were sick of her and needed a moment like that. But ... it could have been better.'

37 Staley now says that while he was not certain she would have become leader, he recalls sympathising with Bishop and saying, 'If she'd had a huge win and pulled the votes, you never know.' He told me he was supporting John Howard but said to her something like, 'Bad luck. If you'd pulled a bigger vote you never know.'

38 Kate Legge, 'The making and remaking of Bronwyn Bishop', *Australian Magazine*, 2–3 Oct. 1993, p. 14.

Chapter Two: Housewife Superstars

1   Henrietta Dugdale, *A Few Hours in a Far Off Age*, Melbourne, 1883, p. 67.
2   Doris Blackburn, MHR from 1946 to 1949, had left the ALP over her involvement in the International Peace Campaign, and stood for federal parliament as an Independent Labor candidate.
3   'Labor's woman MP flies banner for PM', *SMH*, 20 May 1974, p. 2.
4   Marilyn Lake, 'Feminist history as national history: writing the political history of women', *Australian Historical Studies*, vol. 17, no. 106, 1996, pp. 154–69.
5   Pat Mainardi, 'The politics of housework', in Ellen Malos (ed.), *The Politics of Housework*, Allison & Busby, London, 1980, pp. 99–104.
6   Betty Friedan, *The Feminine Mystique*, Penguin, Ringwood, 1963, pp. 13–29.
7   See Catherine Hall, 'The history of the housewife', in Ellen Malos, op. cit., pp. 44–72.
8   Commonwealth Bureau of Census and Statistics, *The Labour Force*, ABS, February 1975, p. 16.
9   K. Richmond, 'The workforce participation of married women in Australia', in D. Edgar (ed.) *Social Change in Australia: Readings in Sociology*, Cheshire, Melbourne, 1974, p. 269. In 1947, 8.6 per cent of married women worked outside the home, while 18.7 per cent did in 1961. By 1971 it was 32.7 per cent. Note these statistics are based on women who were employed full-time or part-time, or looking for employment.
10 'Winds of change in the suburbs', *SMH*, 1971, Federal Parliamentary Library press clippings files. See also Rosemary Mayne-Wilson, 'Lonely, out in suburbia', *West Australian*, 25 Aug. 1973.
11 Stanley Hurst, 'The lone woman helping to change South Africa', *West Australian*, c. 28 Aug. 1973, Federal Parliamentary Library clippings files.
12 Peter Blazey, 'Battler Joan Child still takes it all in her stride', *Australian*, 20 July 1983, p. 9.
13 'Angry alderman hits back at home role for women: mother attacks bachelor's view', *Daily Telegraph*, 23 June 1975. Note: Taylor later received the 1975 'thumbs down award' in the 'LOOK!' awards, *SMH*, 1 Jan. 1976, for these comments.

14 *Pix*, 2 Oct. 1943, p. 5. Note: Cathy Jenkins, in a study of the press treatment of Dame Enid Lyons and Dorothy Tangney in 1943, argued that while their private lives were not emphasised, newspapers contained references to their roles as wife, mother and — in Tangney's case — aunt. (Cathy Jenkins, 'Press coverage of the first women in Australia's federal parliament', *Australian Studies in Journalism*, no. 5, 1996, pp. 82–100.)

15 Quoted by Marian Sawer & Marian Simms, *A Woman's Place: Women and Politics in Australia*, Allen & Unwin, Sydney, 1993, p. 83.

16 'Woman for polls', *Mirror*, 21 Oct. 1961.

17 'Candidate is a housewife, but not a superstar', *SMH*, 28 May 1979, p. 2.

18 Sue Johnson, 'Women go for a share of politics', *Sun-Herald*, 21 Sept. 1980, p. 11.

19 Interview with the author, 21 Feb. 1997.

20 Transcript, Pru Goward interview with Janine Haines, ABC Radio, 5 Nov. 1990, Federal Parliamentary Library clippings files.

21 Interview with the author, 19 Nov. 1996.

22 Malcolm Mackerras, 'Do women candidates lose votes?', *Australian Quarterly*, Sept. 1977, p. 7. After further research from subsequent elections, Mackerras argued in 1980 that 'it makes little difference whether the candidate is a woman or a man ... women will be elected when parties select them for safe or winnable seats.' (Malcolm Mackerras, 'Do women candidates lose votes? — further evidence', *Australian Quarterly*, summer 1980, pp. 450–54.)

23 See table in Marian Sawer, 'Two steps forward, one step back: women and the Australian party system', in Joni Lovenduski and Pippa Norris (eds), *Gender and Party Politics*, Sage, London, 1993, p. 23.

24 David Hickie, 'Women: the housewife is still the dominant image in Australia', *National Times*, 3–8 Oct. 1977, p. 10. Hickie concluded that this poll, conducted among 1000 city dwellers over 18, both male and female, showed Australians had 'significantly more male chauvinism in their attitudes than their British counterparts'. The major areas of difference were beliefs about non-discrimination against women, and whether children suffer if they have working mothers.

25 Interview with the author, 20 Nov. 1996.

26 Interview with the author, 17 Feb. 1997.

27 *Lillydale and Yarra Valley Express*, 16 May 1979, p. 12; interview with Gracia Baylor, 20 Feb. 1997. Baylor was still accused of neglecting her children because her youngest child was 18 months old when she was elected in 1979.

28 'Women go for a share of politics', *Sun-Herald*, 21 Sept. 1980. There

were some men who gave out recipes when asked; for example, Andrew Peacock's recipe for Nut Crust Apple Pie. (*Woman's Day*, 14 Jan. 1985, p. 27.)

29 Interview with the author, 27 Aug. 1997.

30 The caption informed us that during her campaign 'her sons helped with the housework, including cooking'. Selena Summers, 'The lady of the house', *Australian Women's Weekly*, 5 June 1974, p. 2. Interview with Joan Child, 27 Feb. 1997.

31 Lorraine Palmer, 'The new blonde Senator with "plenty of fight": "Women *need* women in parliament"', *Woman's Day*, 15 July 1974, p. 16.

32 Interview with the author, 27 Oct. 1997.

33 Interview with the author, 2 Dec. 1997. Elliott was a member of the WA upper house for the ALP from 1971 to 1986, and was deputy ALP whip from 1976 to 1978.

34 The *Australian Women's Weekly* was the oldest — first published on 10 June 1933 — and most widely read women's magazine in Australia. McNair Print Readership Survey, *National Magazine Readership Survey, Sydney, Melbourne, Brisbane, Adelaide, Perth*, 1972. Briefing papers in the Women in Politics Conference files claim there was a significant growth in the readership of women's magazines in the early 1970s, from 2 per cent in 1962–67 to 33 per cent of women in 1968–73. The source cited was J. S. Western, *Australian Mass Media Controllers, Consumers, Producers*, AIPS Monograph No. 9, Women and Politics Conference, Canberra 1975 papers, NLA.

35 According to the *Age*, in 1971, women spent approximately $325,000 each week on the three major women's magazines. By 1975, Australians spent $43 million per year on 13 million locally produced women's magazines. (Dennis Minogue, 'A war for women', *Age*, 31 May 1975, quoted by Anne Summers, *Damned Whores and God's Police: The Colonisation of Women in Australia*, Penguin, Ringwood, 1994, p. 482.) At the time of the first publication of *Media Tarts* in 2004, *New Idea* averaged more than 400,000 copies per issue, *Woman's Day* was purchased by more than half a million people, and the *Australian Women's Weekly* was still Australia's bestselling magazine, with an average 688,000 buyers a month. (David Dale, 'We love our celebs, but not naked or gardening', *SMH*, 16 Feb. 2004, p. 3.)

36 Interview with John Hill, then a reporter at the *Sun*, 20 Apr. 2001.

37 Gay Alcorn, 'Women make their mark: trio enjoys battle in the House', Living and Leisure section, *Courier-Mail*, 14 May 1986, p. 13.

38 Letters to the editor, 'Happy in the kitchen?', *Courier-Mail*, 6 Sept. 1988, p. 8.

39 *Australian*, 8 Feb. 1990.

Chapter Three: Florence Bjelke-Petersen: pumpkin politics

1 'Senator Flo is feeling scone-hot for Canberra', *Daily Telegraph*, 14 March 1981.

2 Jane Cadzow , 'The ebb of Flo', *Age*, 14 Sept. 1991, p. 12.

3 Clive Hale, 'Nationwide', 7 Oct. 1980, transcript, Federal Parliamentary Library Current Information Service.

4 Bob Hawke was prime minister of Australia from March 1983 to December 1991.

5 It should be noted that Flo Bjelke-Petersen continued a long tradition in Australian and international history of women who were elected to parliament by virtue of being related to politically prominent men, although most had gained a reputation for talent and oratory in their own right (see Melville Currell, *Political Woman*, Croom Helm, London, 1974, pp. 167–72). Of the nine women elected to state parliaments in Australia prior to World War II, four were political widows or daughters. The first woman to be a member of the House of Representatives, in 1943, Dame Enid Lyons, was married to the former prime minister of Australia, Joe Lyons, who had died in 1939. Lyons had established a reputation as a popular speaker before entering parliament, and had travelled widely campaigning with her husband, despite the pressures of illness and the responsibility of raising 11 children. This syndrome, which implied women's work as politicians was legitimised by their relation to — or representation of — their husbands or fathers, has become known as 'male equivalence'. The first three women to sit in the House of Commons and the first woman to be a member of the New Zealand parliament were political widows. Of the first four women in the world to lead their countries, two were widows of former leaders (Sirimavo Bandaranaike, who became prime minister of Ceylon in 1960, and Isabel Peron, who was president of Argentina in 1974) and one, Indira Gandhi in India, was the daughter of a former prime minister. (Marian Sawer & Marian Simms, *A Woman's Place: Women and Politics in Australia*, Allen & Unwin, Sydney, 1993, p. 75.)

6 Margo Kingston, 'The Boswell files', *SMH*, 3 March 2001.

7 See discussion in Donald Horne, *A Time of Hope: Australia 1966–72*, Angus & Robertson, Sydney, 1980, pp. 2–3.

8 Editorial, 'It's the go of Flo', *Herald* (Melbourne), 13 March 1981;

Jacqueline Rees, 'Joh's Flo — firing with both barrels', *Bulletin*, 1 Oct. 1977.

9 In a study of the *Australian Women's Weekly*, Shirley Sampson found women existed only as wives and mothers in the pages of the popular magazine: 'They are not portrayed as active and independent units in an economic system, and so provide no choice of role models for young girls. The image of the role of women is of home duties as central.' (Shirley Sampson,'The *Australian Women's Weekly* today', *Refractory Girl*, no. 3, winter 1973, p. 17.)

10 Hugh Lunn, 'Flo solves Joh's ticket problem', *Australian*, 29 Sept. 1979, p. 1.

11 Columnist Tess Lawrence argued Bjelke-Petersen's political future was assured 'for little reason other than she beds the Premier of that State'. (Tess Lawrence, 'Must Women Come Third?', *Sunday Press*, 21 Oct. 1979.)

12 Editorial, 'It's the go of Flo', *Herald* (Melbourne), 13 March 1981.

13 Hugh Lunn, 'Flo's political recipe', *Australian*, 2 Oct. 1979, p. 9. This copy was also used in the *Sunday Mail*, headed 'Flo ready to tackle the Iron Lady', 7 Oct. 1979.

14 Peter Trundle,'The female of the species:Yvonne: I believe in consensus, Flo: I try to be nice', *Courier-Mail*, 2 Aug. 1980.

15 Janet Hawley, 'A day in the life of Florence', *Courier-Mail*, 24 Sept. 1980.

16 Jane Sullivan, 'Mrs Bjelke may get $150,000 Senate windfall', *Age*, 2 March 1981.

17 Editorial, 'The fortunes of politics', *Australian*, 17 March 1981.

18 Florence Bjelke-Petersen, 'Mr dear Mr Mitchell', *Australian*, 12 March 1981.

19 Don Dunlop, *Herald* (Melbourne), 2 June 1981. Note the *Courier-Mail* published a highly positive review by a staff reporter, 'Having a go at Flo', 13 June 1981.

20 Hugh Lunn, 'Pikelets and politics! Senator elect Flo will still feed the chooks', *Sunday Mail*, 10 Aug. 1980.

21 Tess Livingstone, 'Flo gets her unit in Canberra', *Sunday Mail*, 15 March 1981.

22 While reporting her complaint, Sally Loane pointed to the fact that the press also reported on her becoming an honorary Avon lady in February 1985. This, she wrote, was an unprecedented award given because 'although she has never sold an eyeshadow or demonstrated a lipstick, she has true Avon characteristics: a high achiever, who had successfully

combined being a wife and mother with a career.' (Sally Loane, "Honorary Avon lady' too busy to sell lipstick', *CourierMail*, 7 Feb. 1985.)

23 Being married to her husband had given her 30 years of political experience, she said, denying that she was politically naive. (Laura Veltman, 'Flo's rising faster than pumpkin scones', *Daily Telegraph*, 28 March 1981.)

24 'Senator Flo is feeling scone-hot for Canberra', *Daily Telegraph*, 14 March 1981.

25 Philip Castle, 'Senator Flo: half of a formidable combination', *Canberra Times*, 19 April 1981, p. 7.

26 Quoted in John Lahr, *Dame Edna Everage and the Rise of Western Civilisation: Backstage with Barry Humphries*, Bloomsbury, London, 1991, pp. 21, 66, 82. Edna Everage was often photographed reading the *Australian Women's Weekly*.

27 ibid. Note Humphries, on p. 184, argued that Thatcher had come to resemble Edna: 'First she was a housewife, then the politician, then finally she became the star. And now she likes to show that she's still a bit of a housewife.'

28 Christabel Hirst, 'I don't mind the pumpkin scone image: Flo', *Advertiser*, 20 Sept. 1982.

29 Laura Veltman, op. cit.

30 He also said she reminded him 'in a rather chilling way' of Margaret Thatcher. Barry Everingham, 'Flo flies in with a cause', *Sunday Mail*, 29 March 1981.

31 Alan Reid, 'The Flo dough show', *Bulletin*, 31 March 1981.

32 Neil O'Reilly, 'Flo loses a mentor', *Sun-Herald*, 5 May 1985; Sally Loane, 'The Queensland puppets and their puppeteer', *Times on Sunday*, 12 April 1987.

33 David Broadbent & Michelle Grattan, 'Bjelke is gloating over talks with PM', *Age*, 15 May 1981; Michelle Grattan, 'Premier's wife makes her presence felt', *Age*, 16 May 1981; Wallace Brown, 'Flo the peacemaker ends bad blood of states funds wrangling', *Courier-Mail*, 16 May 1981.

34 Anne Summers, 'Senator Flo confounds her critics', *National Times*, 21 June 1981.

35 Wallace Brown, 'Flo supports Democrats in tax vote', *Courier-Mail*, 17 Sept. 1981; Warwick Costin, 'Flo becomes the battlers' friend', *News* (Northern Territory), 24 Sept. 1981.

36 Michelle Grattan, 'The Canberra–Bjelke power game', *Age*, 16 Nov. 1981.

37 Jane Cadzow, op. cit., p. 15.

38 Michael Gawenda, 'A home-made homily: ding dong, Flo calling', *Age*, 19 Feb. 1985.

39 The legislation was the *Sex Discrimination Act 1984* (Cth) and the *Affirmative Action (Equal Employment Opportunity for Women) Act 1986* (Cth). Significantly, the *SMH*, in an editorial that supported the legislation, reminded Bjelke-Petersen she was there not because of who she was, but because of who she'd married. That she had proved to be a shrewd, populist politician only provided proof of the discrimination women faced: '... without her husband's name and influence, she would never have had the chance to show her qualities. Yet as her vigorous opposition to the sex discrimination legislation indicates, she has political talents that would have blushed unseen.' ('Women in the House or home', *SMH*, 17 Sept. 1983, p. 12.)

40 Most commentators believed it was Joh's idea, and Hugh Lunn, in his book *Joh, The Life and Political Adventures of Johannes Bjelke-Petersen* (University of Queensland Press, St Lucia, 1978), argues it was Joh's press adviser Allan Callaghan. However, one journalist argued Lunn was culpable for breaking the story that Flo was going to run, which, Flo said, put the idea into their heads (Philip Castle, 'Senator Flo: half of a formidable combination', *Canberra Times*, 19 April 1981, p. 7).

41 Sylvia Costa-Roque, 'Gough leads cheers for Flo', *Sunday Mail*, 20 Dec. 1981.

42 Joh Bjelke-Petersen narrowly escaped a jail sentence after a jury was unable to reach a verdict at his trial in 1991 for perjury and allegedly accepting $100,000 from an Asian developer.There was some controversy over the fact that one of the jury members was a Young National and member of the Friends of Joh support group.

Chapter Four: Political Superwomen and MP Mums

1 Letters to the editor, *SMH*, 14 May 2004, p. 12.

2 Bettina Arndt, 'Combining motherhood and politics harder than a triple twist with a flip', *SMH*, 10 Sept. 2002, p. 11.

3 Reported by Kate McClymont, 'Sauce', *SMH*, 23 Aug. 2003, p. 24.

4 Melbourne *Punch*, 14 April 1887.

5 In Australia, there has been a higher proportion of women in ALP ministries (13.3 per cent) than in other ministries (7.3 per cent) since 1970. However, there was some discrepancy between individual governments. The 1972–75 Whitlam government had no women ministers, although the preceding and succeeding Liberal–National

governments did. (Jeremy Moon and Imogen Fountain, 'Keeping the gates? Women as Ministers in Australia, 1970–96', *Australian Journal of Political Science*, vol. 32, no. 3, p. 460.)

6 Andrew West, 'Gabrielle, MP: politics is not a place for a mother', *Sun-Herald*, 25 Nov. 2001, p. 30.

7 Elizabeth Gosch & Adam Cooper, 'MP kept baby news a secret to save her job', *Daily Telegraph*, 11 Dec. 2001, p. 9.

8 Elizabeth Johnston, 'The grind of electioneering pregnant with possibilities', *Australian*, 17 Oct. 1983, p. 11.

9 Kate Legge, 'Mother knows best — Goodluck, MP, knows better', *Age*, 19 Aug. 1983.

10 Jerry Fetherston, 'Ros Kelly's politics are home-based: ambition's on the backburner as tipped Cabinet minister sorts out her priorities', *Woman's Day*, 28 July 1986, pp. 8–9.

11 Her ability to manage a hectic schedule was, according to the subheading of another article by a woman journalist, 'proving again that a woman's place is in the House as well as in the home'. Liz Porter, 'A mother's place in politics', *Mirror*, 29 Sept. 1983.

12 Rosemary Munday, 'Ros Kelly: finding the time for politics ... and a new baby', *Australian Women's Weekly*, 1 Jan. 1985, pp. 10–11.

13 Interview with the author, 2 Feb. 1997.

14 Leslie Anderson, '"I'm not going to resign yet," says Mrs Craig', *Sunday Times*, 9 Aug. 1981.

15 From an interview with the author. Bronwyn Bishop also claims her divorced status was used against her by Bob Ellis in the 1994 Mackellar by-election: 'It was pretty ugly ... I think one of the ugliest ads he ran was: "Here is a picture of me with my family. I am a married man and she is divorced."' Ellis describes the ad as a photograph of himself with his family standing on the ashes of the house he had lived in for 17 years, which had burnt down. 'I said I invite Senator Bishop to provide a similar photo. She ran one in response with a photo of her and her daughter saying, "Families come in all sizes."'

16 Commonwealth of Australia Parliamentary Debates, 23 April 1902, vol. ix, p. 11937. The 'honorable gentleman' he is referring to is Sir William Lyne.

17 'Busy life for Senator mum and wife', *News* (Northern Territory), 20 Aug. 1981; Kate Legge, 'Wanted, dead or alive', *Age*, 13 Oct. 1984; 'The most powerful woman in Canberra', *Bulletin*, 6 Nov. 1984.

18 John Hamilton, 'Democrats' voice that won't be silenced', *Herald* (Melbourne), 26 Aug. 1985.

19 Karen Harbutt, 'Wounded Janine Haines parries Siddons' sword', *Canberra Times*, 18 Jan. 1987.

20 Amanda Buckley, 'Janine Haines: balancing on a two-edged sword', *SMH*, 30 Nov. 1985, p. 44.

21 Lyndall Crisp, 'High moral ground in a snappy sweater', *Times on Sunday*, 5 July 1987.

22 Greg Mayfield, 'Mr Haines to become a Mr Mom', *News*, 18 Dec. 1986; also printed in the *Herald* (Melbourne), 'Mum's the word for Senator's husband', 18 Dec. 1986.

23 Transcript, Pru Goward interview with Janine Haines and Janet Powell, 5 Nov. 1990, Federal Parliamentary Library clippings files.

24 Madonna King, 'Canberra wives unite', *Mercury* (Hobart), 27 July 1989; Laurie Oakes, 'The miseries of an MP's wife', *Bulletin*, 20 June 1989, p. 28; 'Roslyn Kelly', *Bulletin*, 3 July 1984.

25 Peter Coster, 'The man who waits at home for Haines', *Herald* (Melbourne), 16 June 1987.

26 Chris Purcell, *Sun-Herald*, 20 July 1986. See also Rosanne Robertson, 'Behind these successful women, there's Hu, Harold and Ivo', Good Weekend, *SMH*, 9 Feb. 1985, p. 30.

27 Gerard Ryle, 'Meg Lees — the unauthorised story', *SMH*, 19 June 1999.

28 Sawer and Simms, *A Woman's Place: Women and Politics in Australia*, Allen & Unwin, Sydney, 1993, p. 141.

29 Peter Coster, op. cit. Note this was also printed in the *Sunday Mail* (Brisbane) under the same headline on 28 June 1987.

30 Farah Farouque, 'House and home', *Age*, 12 Oct. 2003, p. 1.

31 Ian Henderson, 'A job only a politico could love', *Australian*, 6 Nov. 2001, p. 9.

Chapter Five: Feminist Politicians: 'waving the flag of feminine feminism'

1 Prime Minister Gough Whitlam was dismissed by the Governor General, Sir John Kerr, on 11 November 1975, following the decision by the Liberal Party to block the supply of money bill in the Senate. This was ostensibly done on the grounds that the ALP government had mismanaged the economy through excessive expenditure, pushing up unemployment and inflation as well as interest rates. In April the government had been subject to criticism following revelations that the Minister for Minerals and Energy, Rex O'Connor, had attempted to borrow up to $4000 million from overseas sources in a bid to buy back Australian resources from overseas investors. He resigned in October. On 16 October, the Senate voted to block supply until Whitlam agreed to call

an election. The ALP lost the following election, held in December. For a discussion of Rupert Murdoch's apparent campaign against Whitlam, see George Munster, *A Paper Prince*, Viking, Ringwood, 1985.

2   'Talk but no action', *Daily Telegraph*, 1 Sept. 1975.

3   Quoted by Virginia Haussegger, 'Has feminism let us down?', *Age*, 23 April 2003, p. 15.

4   Elisabeth Kirkby, 'When the Air Force holds cake stalls', in Jocelyn Scutt, *Different Lives: Reflections on the Women's Movement and Visions of its Future*, Penguin, Ringwood, 1987, p. 87.

5   Pat Nigra, 'Women in politics', *Daily Telegraph*, 3 May 1972, p. 43.

6   She told one journalist the single exception was when she was trying to be elected mayor of Fairfield. (Toni McRae, 'Wran to get a fighting lady', *Australian*, 9 Sept. 1981.) Crosio told another reporter: 'I have never experienced being disadvantaged because I am a woman. Female politicians are concerned more with the quality than the quantity of life. Women are more questioning and perceptive.' (Jill Gainsford, 'A woman's place is in Labor', *Sunday Telegraph*, 21 June 1981.)

7   Jill George, 'Politics is Jan's real bread and butter', *Sunday Telegraph*, 27 Sept. 1981.

8   Chris Blanche, 'Janice wins her way up', *Daily Telegraph*, 24 Sept. 1981.

9   When she was federal minister for aged care, Bronwyn Bishop told me in an interview on 25 July 1994 that 'the word feminist has a pejorative meaning in that I am just an individual and I live in a country which gives me opportunities to use the talents that I have and you have and everybody else has ... To me, feminism focuses on, instead of the positives, the negatives.'

10 Ann Curthoys writes the women's liberation movement sprang from the New Left and was 'concerned with imperialism, socialism, and the oppression of Third World and minority groups, with the ideologies sustaining an evil capitalist system, with revolutionary strategy and tactics'. (Ann Curthoys, 'The women's movement and social justice', in Dorothy Broom (ed.) *Unfinished Business: Social Justice for Women in Australia*, Allen & Unwin, Sydney, 1984, p. 162.)

11 Noel Francis from the *Canberra Times* said 'feminists, or members of women's lib ... will feel some exultation that the voice of woman is being heard more widely throughout the land.' (Noel Francis, 'Seat in the House for mother of five', *Canberra Times*, 25 June 1974.) Child was not entirely hostile towards the women's movement. She told journalists she was not a 'staunch Women's Lib supporter' but that the movement had 'opened closed doors and stuffy rooms and brought a much needed

change to attitudes in Victoria'. (Don Baker, 'Joan may be in select few',
Sun-Pictorial (Melbourne), 1974, Joan Child Federal Parliamentary
Library clippings files.)

12 Interview with the author, 27 Feb. 1997.

13 Stephanie Bunbury, 'The Liberal who is at home in the House and the
kitchen', *Age*, 22 Feb. 1985.

14 When Liz Reid was appointed women's adviser to the Labor government
in 1972, a journalist wrote: 'Would the sisterhood please stand still for a
moment and stop wobbling under their t-shirts? I have just been talking
to ... Miz Liz — in flared jeans, tank top and no bra.' (John Hamilton,
'"But what do I tell my Girl?" asks the PM's Miz', *Herald* (Melbourne),
21 August 1973.)

15 The term 'bra-burning' evolved from a demonstration against the Miss
America pageant in 1968, where women threw bras and other items of
feminine dress and make-up into a garbage bin. They were not actually
burned; a journalist wrongly reported that they were. But press reports
emblazoned 'bra-burning' into public consciousness, and it became an
enduring symbol of women's rejection of patriarchy, and a reminder both
of feminist debates about women's bodies and a cultural fascination with
breasts. Susan Faludi points out there was scant evidence of underwear
torchings at women's rights demonstrations in the 1970s, and only two
displays that came close were fabricated, and organised by men. (Susan
Faludi, *Backlash: The Undeclared War against Women*, Chatto &
Windus, London, 1991, p. 99.)

16 'ALP picks woman for state post', *Australian*, 12 July 1971, p. 2. Even
Enid Lyons, the first woman MHR, who had been retired for 25 years,
told a journalist she did approve of women's lib, and that one of her
many greatgrandsons had brought her a box of matches, telling her she
could burn her bra with them. (Anne Dupree, 'Dame Enid looks at life ...
the family role', *Sun*, 23 Sept. 1976.)

17 The term originated in France in the 1880s, surfaced in England in
the 1890s, and several years later appeared in the United States (and
Australia). (Leonie Huddy, 'Feminists and feminism in the news', in Pippa
Norris (ed.), *Women, Media and Politics*, Oxford University Press, New
York, 1997, p. 185.) Activist Ann Curthoys argues the term rested on
different political perspectives in what she calls a 'very chequered history
of naming'. Before 1970, she argues, there was a large gap between those
who called themselves feminists and those who fought for what they
called 'women's equality'. Women active in the Left (including those who
came from the anti–Vietnam War movement, the Labor Party or the

Communist Party) saw the former as decrying class analysis. According to Curthoys, the term 'women's liberation' emerged in the early 1970s and comprised a rejection of both positions: '"Feminism" was seen as describing an older women's non-libertarian anti-sex position, while "women's equality" could never do (equality with what? men? them? no thanks!).' (Ann Curthoys, 'Where is feminism now?', in Jenna Mead (ed.), *Bodyjamming*, Vintage, Sydney, 1997, p. 189.)

18 Anne Summers, *Damned Whores and God's Police*, Penguin, Ringwood, 1994 (1975), p. 509.

19 Ann Curthoys, *For and against Feminism*, Allen & Unwin, Sydney, 1988, p. 64.

20 Juliet Mitchell, 'Women: the longest revolution', *New Left Review*, no. 44, 1966; Pat Mainardi, 'The politics of housework', in Ellen Malos (ed.), *The Politics of Housework*, Allison & Busby, 1980, pp. 99–104; Kate Millett, *Sexual Politics*, Rupert Hart-Davis, London, 1969; Shulamith Firestone, *The Dialectic of Sex: The Case for Feminist Revolution*, Paladin, St Albans, 1972 (1971).

21 For a discussion of the split between reformists and revolutionaries, see Patricia Grimshaw, ibid., pp. 66–86.

22 Some women journalists were founding members of WEL, and Kate White argues they tailored the organisation to meet with media acceptance. (Kate White, 'Women and party politics in Australia', *Australian Quarterly*, vol. 53, autumn 1981, p. 32.)

23 Quoted in Joyce Nicholson, The Women's Electoral Lobby and women's employment: strategies and outcome, MA minor thesis, Women's Studies, University of Melbourne, 1991, p. 27.

24 The National Women's Consultative Council, quoted by Marian Sawer, *Sisters in Suits: Women and Public Policy in Australia*, Allen & Unwin, Sydney, 1990, p. 3. The newspapers surveyed were the *Nation Review*, the *Age*, the *Australian*, the *Bulletin*, the *National Times*, the *Australian Financial Review*, *Woman's Day* and the *Sunday Telegraph*.

25 A survey conducted in 1983 found 28 per cent of women from different political parties, who were state and federal MPs, had been or were still WEL members, including Susan Ryan, Ruth Coleman, Kathy Martin, June Craig, Anne Levy, Grace Vaughan, Robyn Walmsley, Margaret Reynolds, Pat Giles, Kay Hallahan, Carmen Lawrence, Yvonne Henderson, Barbara Wiese and Virginia Chadwick. (Kate White, 'Is the women's movement turning inward?', *National Times*, 20–26 May 1983; Karen Kissane, 'Can the family cope, Senator?', *Age*, 14 April 1982.) Note that in the 1970s and 1980s, what Marilyn Lake calls

'state feminism' emerged in state and federal governments, including the introduction of legislation and bureaucratic programs to promote the status of women, equal opportunity, affirmative action, and to prevent sexual discrimination. (Marilyn Lake, *Getting Equal: The History of Australian Feminism*, Allen & Unwin, Sydney, 1999, p. 253.)

26 Lyndsay Connors, 'Women are here to stay, particularly at the polls', *National Times*, 4–9 Dec. 1972, p. 14.

27 Wendy McCarthy, *Don't Fence Me In*, Random House, Sydney, 2000.

28 Alex Kennedy, 'Senator beats the odds', *Advertiser*, 17 April 1979.

29 See discussion in chapter six.

30 Alex Kennedy, 'The Senator is a "together lady"', *Advertiser*, 15 Sept. 1981.

31 *Sun-Herald*, 10 Feb. 1980; Alex Kennedy, ibid. For a discussion of the search for the 'first woman Premier' or prime minister, see chapter one.

32 Lenore Nicklin, 'Labor's optimist in the Senate', *SMH*, 11 Nov. 1978.

33 The paper was by economist Anne de Salis, analysing male and female voting patterns since World War II. (Susan Ryan, *Catching the Waves: Life in and out of Politics*, HarperCollins, Sydney, 1999, p. 177.) Empirical analyses of the gender gap in federal elections have revealed that women have generally favoured conservative parties since gaining suffrage at the turn of the century. Don Aitkin found that approximately 10 per cent more women than men voted for the Liberal and Country parties than the Labor Party in the 1960s, but by the late 1970s the gap had almost halved. However, after this point, momentum slowed. (Don Aitkin, *Stability and Change in Australian Politics*, Australian National University Press, Canberra, 1982; Carmen Lawrence, 'The gender gap in political behaviour', in Kate Deverall et. al. (eds), *Party Girls: Labor Women Now*, Pluto Press, Sydney, 2000.)

34 According to the *Australian*, 'Her detractors reckon she's a tough, unbending feminist. Radical feminists toughly and unbendingly accuse her of dumping their issues. You get the feeling that ACT Senator Susan Ryan is beginning to get tired of being typecast as the Labor Party's answer to Everywoman. "I get annoyed when I'm characterised as only interested in women's issues," she says ... "A difficulty I've had is explaining that I have broader interests than just women. And women have sometimes interpreted that as dropping their cause."' (Susie Foster, 'The passionate senator seeks broader scope', *Australian*, 7 Oct. 1980.)

35 Jenni Hewett, 'The Senate's changing feminist', *SMH*, 29 July 1981, p. 7.

36 Mary-Louise O'Callaghan, 'Oh! Susan! — But it wasn't always so', *SMH*, 26 Feb. 1987, p. 9.

37 Andrew Symon, 'In the political trenches', *Advertiser*, 12 March 1984, p. 2.

38 Chipp had been a Liberal MHR since 1960, and resigned from the Liberal Party to form the Democrats. The first Democrat MP was elected in South Australia in September 1977, while two senators, including Chipp, were elected in December 1977.

39 Marian Sawer, 'Topsy-turvy land — where women, children and the environment come first', op. cit., pp. 238–39.

40 Tracey Aubin, 'Sexy? Ruthless? Funny? Will the real Janine Haines please stand up?', *Australian Magazine*, 17–18 June 1989. Note that Haines told me in an interview in 2000 that she did not call herself a feminist because she hated labels.

41 See, for example, the articles that followed her remarks about the political ignorance of the ordinary Australian. (Don Aitkin, 'Democracy, more an ideal than a reality', *Age*, 3 July 1987; Suzanne Pekol, 'A smooth campaign for Haines' Democrats', *Courier-Mail*, 3 July 1987.)

42 Angela Long, 'Men, take a look at yourselves', *Herald* (Melbourne), 13 March 1978.

43 Another example of Haines being ridiculed for drawing attention to sexism was in September 1986, when she inflamed some commentators with a speech she gave at a housing and planning conference in Adelaide. She argued male planners and developers were partly to blame for stress-related illnesses suffered by housewives because they were ignorant of the stresses of looking after children, being isolated in the suburbs, and catching public transport. ('Haines blames male planners', *Advertiser*, 30 Sept. 1986; 'If suburbia seems a nightmare, blame him', *Age*, 30 Sept. 1986; Max Fatchen, 'The best made plans', *Advertiser*, 2 Oct. 1986.) Comments like this were immediately linked to others she had made about sex and sexism. The Melbourne *Herald* of 30 September 1986 asked, 'Is this the Senator for sexism?' and attacked her in an editorial for being simplistic and sexist, with 'a touch of the high school debating society' in her 'fuzzy thinking'.

44 In 1983 she issued a *Position Paper on Women* and put out press releases urging women not to be hoodwinked by 'promise her anything' political platforms from male-dominated parties. The position paper, which promised more concessions than Ryan could as part of the ALP, covered discrimination against women, rights in marriage, legal status, employment, childcare, education of medical and legal professions, reform of rape laws, and sexual stereotyping in advertising.

45 Sue Bailey, 'Someone has to lead, says Janine Haines', *Mercury*, 19 Oct. 1984.

46 Lee Tulloch, 'The new political power brokers', *Vogue Australia*, April 1981, p. 149.

47 'Democrat resigns over "feminists"', *Advertiser*, 9 Oct. 1984. Cliff Boyd announced he was going to run as an independent because the Democrats were 'putting feminism before the family'. He said that the importance of the role of the woman who chose to stay at home was being eroded by 'a frenetic push to get them to do everything from walk in space to driving front end loaders'. Janet Powell attributed the breakaways to baggage from 'old boys' networks' which some men had brought with them from other political parties to the Democrats. (Janet Powell, 'Representation of women in Australian parliaments — why is it so?' *National Women's Conference 1990: Proceedings*, 1990, Write People, Canberra, p. 53.)

48 Andrew Fraser, 'Haines and Siddons: the differing plans', *Canberra Times*, 2 July 1986.

49 Christine Rau, 'Democrats exult in poll gains', *National Times*, 7 Sept. 1986.

50 Barbara Hutton, 'The party that put a woman first', *Age*, 20 Aug. 1986.

51 Janine Haines, 'Readers' Forum', *News*, 16 Feb. 1981.

52 'Haines may bid for Lower House at next election', *Advertiser*, 13 July 1987. By January 1988, Haines was the most popular of the four major party leaders, according to a Morgan poll conducted in her home town of Adelaide. She had a 64 per cent approval rating from women, compared to 53 per cent for Labor prime minister Bob Hawke, 44 per cent for Liberal Party leader John Howard, and 29 per cent for National Party leader Ian Sinclair. ('Haines pips Hawke in leadership stakes', *Australian*, 23 Jan. 1988; Rex Jory, 'Democrats stronger now, says Haines', *Advertiser*, 23 Jan. 1988.)

53 John Sampson,'Haines & Co: why this time they matter', *Sunday Age*, 11 March 1990; Phil Jarratt, 'What makes a great politician', *Bulletin*, 11 April 1989; Richard Farmer,'Why Janine Haines will win', *Australian*, 23 Feb. 1989; 'Where the cup is Kingston', *Age*, 18 Oct. 1989; Jacqueline Lee Lewes, 'Canberra on the line', *SMH*, 15 May 1989; Jane Cadzow, 'Women about the House', Good Weekend, *Age*, 26 Nov. 1988, p. 21.

54 Paul Willoughby, 'Haines sacrifices all for Hindmarsh', *Advertiser*, 1 Dec. 1988.

55 Glenda Korporaal, 'Forward and left with the Democrats', *Bulletin*, 20 Feb. 1990; Richard Farmer, 'Janine Haines, the Democrats and the high cost of giving', *Australian*, 21 Jan. 1990.

56 Rod Cameron claimed in 1990 that 'a woman with experience in bringing up a family is now worth an extra advantage point on polling day … In the past it was the man who would have had such an advantage.' (Rod Cameron, 'Feminisation: the major emerging trend underlying future mass audience response', unpublished address, 11th National Convention of the Public Relations Institute of Australia, 19 October 1990. See also Paul Kelly, 'Real muscle, vain hopes', *Australian*, 3 March 1990.) A survey conducted in Brisbane in 1983 found 65 per cent of respondents believed men entered politics because of ambition or a desire for power, while only 11 per cent of women had similar motives. (Wendy Richards, quoted by Marian Sawer, 'From motherhood to sisterhood: attitudes of Australian women MPs to their roles', *Women's Studies International Forum*, vol. 9, 1986, p. 539.) This idea is similar to the theme in press coverage that Pippa Norris identifies as women leaders being portrayed as 'agents of change' who will clean up corruption in politics. She acknowledges that 'in part this frame reflects campaign themes by some of the women.' (Pippa Norris, 'Women leaders worldwide', in Norris, op. cit., p. 163.)

57 In the mid-1990s, Carmen Lawrence was referred to as 'Saint Lawrence' when she moved to federal parliament, and Democrats leader Cheryl Kernot was also referred to as 'Saint Cheryl' before she switched to the ALP.

58 David O'Reilly, 'Haines: honest, trustworthy', *Bulletin*, 5 Sept. 1989.

59 Peter Smark, 'The descent of Saint Janine not to be taken as gospel', *Age*, 24 Feb. 1990.

60 To have won the seat, she would have needed to finish second to draw the preferences of the major parties. Figures are as reported by Mark Bruer, 'Powell volunteers as Democrats begin search for new leader', *Age*, 26 Mar. 1990. Slightly different figures were reported by Roy Eccleston, 'Leader's loss sours victory for Democrats', *Australian*, 26 Mar. 1990.

Chapter Six: The Cover Girls: 'Forget policy, I've got great legs!'

1 Marion Frith, 'For Ros, a picture for everyday use, and another to put over the Cabinet', *Canberra Times*, 19 July 1990, p. 1.

2 Mike Seccombe, 'Between the sheets, but no smut, *SMH*, 19 July 1990, p. 1. Several years later, Smith said the shots of Kelly had hardly ruined her career, but she was critical of Cheryl Kernot for posing on the front page of the *Australian Women's Weekly*: 'I think anyone who looks as if they are dressed to kill or looks as if they are trying too hard has a problem … In that shot of Ros Kelly there was no jewellery, no feather boas.' (Pilita Clark & Margo Kingston, 'Dress sense', *SMH*, 25 March 1998, p. 13.)

3   Front cover, *Australian Magazine*, 17 June 1989.

4   Angela Donaldson, 'Yes Minister!', *Woman's Day*, 8 March 1993, p. 28.

5   'Kissable Senator', *Australian*, 23 May 1974.

6   Digby McLean, 'Meeting the kissable senator', *Canberra News*, 6 June 1974.

7   ABC Radio, 11 Jan. 1991, Federal Parliamentary Library transcript, pp. 8–9.

8   A year later an article appeared about how Sullivan's husband coped with earning less than her, doing chores and 'people referring to him as Mrs Martin'. ('Her job has to come first', *Australian*, 20 Nov. 1976.) Note also that all newspapers reported, despite the headline in the *Courier-Mail*, that she would continue to use her maiden name in politics.

9   'Senator "evicts" estranged husband', *Advertiser*, 14 Feb. 1978; 'Kathy … it's over', *Sun-Pictorial*, 14 Feb. 1978; '"My wife evicted me" — Senator's husband', *Courier-Mail*, 14 Feb. 1978.

10 Sullivan sued the Melbourne *Truth* over an article it ran on the break-up of her second marriage. (Lyndall Crisp, 'The MP who shot herself in the foot', *Bulletin*, 18 July 1989.) She told me that, becauses no one from the *Truth* arrived for the hearing, the judgement went against them, with damages and costs negotiated.

11 Hugh Lunn, '"I take the rap for being a woman," says Senator Kathy Martin', *Australian*, 15 Feb. 1978.

12 Editorial, 'Politician knocking', *Australian*, 16 Feb. 1978; Hugh Lunn, 'Queensland Liberals live in fear of the pumpkin-scone vote', *Australian*, 9 Feb. 1983.

13 Wallace Brown, 'Canberra's Blonde Bombshell', *Courier-Mail*, 24 Feb. 1977. See also articles in the *Australian* and the *Age*, but note the headline was used only in the *Courier-Mail*.

14 Lyndall Crisp, 'The MP who shot herself in the foot', *Bulletin*, 18 July 1989.

15 The only period during which Sullivan was not on the back bench was a few months in 1983, when Andrew Peacock promoted her to the shadow ministry as opposition spokesperson for home affairs and administrative services, before he was deposed as leader after losing the election.

16 Tony Baker, 'The day the ALP went chic!', *News*, 17 June 1980.

17 He was indignant in 1983 when Wiese was not given a ministry because, he argued, she had been 'good enough to be a showpiece party president'. (Tony Baker, 'Women take a wallop', *News*, 27 April 1983.)

18 Randall Ashbourne, 'Barbara's beauty is a barrier', *Sunday Mail*, 18 April 1982.

19 Samela Harris, 'Wiese: work is a lifestyle for her', *Advertiser*, 16 July 1985.

20 Louise Boylen, 'A flourish of flowers for Barbara', *Australian*, 19 July 1985, p. 6.

21 'Promises, promises', *News*, 25 July 1985. When she was elected to the South Australian House of Assembly in 1977, Jennifer Cashmore was called Jennifer Adamson, but she reverted to her maiden name in 1986.

22 Geoff de Luca, 'Bannon "amazed" by tour jibe', *News*, 25 Feb. 1987.

23 Interview with the author, 3 Dec. 1997. Towards the end of Wiese's career, there was an inquiry into accusations she had used her position to help her partner, who had been working with the hotels and clubs associations (to develop a strategy to get poker machines introduced into South Australia) and had been involved as a consultant in a Kangaroo Island tourist development. She believes the media followed it more intently because of a long-standing, media-created perception 'about the attractive minister who had a man and there was the added spice that we weren't actually married and this view ... that women more than men are incapable of separating their personal lives from their business lives'. Wiese called for an inquiry, and was cleared of charges of impropriety, but was found to have breached cabinet conflict of interest rules. (Katherine Towers & Ewin Hannan, 'Retiring MP tells of beating the old guard', *Australian*, 28 Aug. 1995, p. 2.) Journalist Chris Kenny, in an exposé of the manipulation of the media by the South Australian government, believed she should have resigned. (Chris Kenny, *State of Denial*, Wakefield Press, Kent Town, South Australia, 1993, pp. 33–34, 40–41.)

24 Interview with the author, 3 Dec. 1997.

25 Warren Owens, 'Woman to replace Punch', *Sunday Telegraph*, 4 Aug. 1985.

26 Wayne Sanderson, 'Nationals' lady looks a winner', *Daily Telegraph*, 12 Oct. 1985.

27 Liz Van Den Nieuwenhof, 'Wendy's used to breaking tradition', *Daily Telegraph*, 6 Feb. 1989.

28 Dorian Wild, 'Dabs of colour set hearts a flutter', *Daily Telegraph*, 31 Oct. 1985; 'P.S.', *Daily Telegraph*, 1 Nov. 1985; 'Dabs of colour ... '; 'Wendy still the best', *Sun-Herald*, 13 Nov. 1988.

29 Interview with the author, 5 Nov. 1997.

30 Interview with the author, 29 March 2001.

31 Malcolm Farr, 'MP's good looks spark row', *Daily Mirror*, 22 Feb. 1989, pp. 1– 2.

32 Adam Connolly, 'Machin looking good — tipped for a post in next ministry', *Daily Mirror*, 25 July 1990. Note this photograph was printed again, months later, with an article on how she was considered ministerial material.

33 Peter Grimshaw, '"Pretty" Wendy puts politics first in Parliament's bear pit', *Daily Telegraph*, 23 Feb. 1989. Another debate erupted in the press after opposition leader Bob Carr refused to apologise for calling Machin a 'silly bitch' at a press conference in May 1992. He argued it was not public comment and he had been speaking 'off the record'. Alicia Larriera, 'Carr isn't sorry about "silly bitch" criticism', *SMH*, 2 May 1992; 'Carr told to apologise for sexist jibe', *Telegraph Mirror*, 2 May 1992. He had been referring to Machin, who as deputy speaker had prevented him from completing his prepared speech on the Australian flag, saying, 'The silly bitch stopped me getting out half my speech.' Although print journalists did not report it until it was brought up in parliament by the speaker, Kevin Rozzoli, radio journalists had broadcast it. Carr's comments revived the debate about 'sexism and confidences in the NSW parliament', according to *Australian*. Kylie Davis, 'Carr calls Machin a silly bitch, off record', *Australian*, 2 May 1992. It was not a comment quickly forgotten. Mark Coultan, 'Touchy issue with women, so Fahey had no choice but to wield the axe', *SMH*, 28 Oct. 1994.

34 Phillip Clark (ed.), 'Polly wants to be a cracker', Stay in Touch, *SMH*, 11 Feb. 1991. On the first day, photographs of Machin in a leopard print bra top and matching shorts appeared, alongside a photograph of her reclining by the sea in a sundress. The next day, two more photographs of Machin, in a suit and a party dress, were published, and the day after that readers were provided with their own 'Wendy dolls' to dress in 'Dancing Wendy' or 'Working Wendy' cutouts. When she announced her engagement a couple of months later, they provided a wedding dress to add to the Wendy doll collection. (Stay in Touch, 'Remember to chuck the bouquet, Wendy', *SMH*, 6 May 1991.)

35 Tony McGowan, 'Dressing down for a model MP', *Telegraph Mirror*, 14 Feb. 1991.

36 *Telegraph Mirror*, 14 Feb. 1991. The role of the broadsheet political trivia — or satirical — column and of the tabloid newspaper are interesting in this incident: the former 'broke' the story and mocked Machin for baring any flesh for the cameras, while the latter gave the story great prominence, centred it on conflict, and defended her in an editorial for 'correctly' displaying an attractive physique. The satirical nature of Stay in Touch gave it licence to be critical of Machin, and highlight her

appearance in a slightly superior and more mocking way than the tabloid newspapers. The 'humanity' she was cheered for bringing to politics appeared to be in fact a femininity predicated on sexual desirability.

37 Sue Williams, 'Now trendy Wendy must wear the flak', *Telegraph Mirror*, 18 Feb. 1991.

38 Bryce Corbett, 'Regret of her own Machin', *Daily Telegraph*, 6 July 1996, p. 13.

39 'Wal misses out', *Sunday Telegraph*, 22 March 1992; 'Baby boomer', *Sun-Herald*, 22 March 1992.

40 Sandra Olsen, 'New mum first pick for cabinet', *Telegraph Mirror*, 21 May 1993.

41 Janise Beaumont, 'Why Wendy keeps it in the family', *Sunday Telegraph*, 24 Oct. 1993.

42 The odd gratuitous headline continued: 'Blondes have more funds', *Telegraph Mirror*, 20 July 1993. The article was about Chadwick, Machin and Chikarovski talking to female members of the Liberal Party's 500 Club: 'NSW parliament's political bombshells joined forces last night to entertain and inform several hundred of the Liberal Party's female faithful.'

43 Jody Scott, 'Mothers deny the dangers of day care', *Australian*, 30 March 1994; Gabrielle Chan, 'Candidate ignores flak over remarks on widow', *Australian*, 19 May 1994; Paola Totaro, 'Libs fail to find a shining star for by-election fight', *SMH*, 19 May 1994.

44 'Nappy power makes mark in NSW politics', *Sunday Telegraph*, 29 March 1992.

45 Interview with the author, 5 Nov. 1997.

46 Paul Simpson, 'She's up to her neck in it: Janice turns back the tide', *Daily Telegraph*, 21 Dec. 1984.

47 Editorial, 'Don't be wet, Mrs Crosio!', *Daily Mirror*, 21 Dec. 1984.

48 Marian Theobold, 'Minister delays drain relocation', *Eastern Herald*, 21 Aug. 1986.

49 Malcolm Farr, op. cit., p. 2. Janice Crosio was elected to the House of Representatives in 1990 as the member for Prospect, NSW.

50 Interview with the author, 27 Feb. 1997.

51 Quoted in Susan Mitchell, *The Scent of Power: On the Trail of Women and Power in Australian Politics*, Angus & Robertson, Sydney, 1996, p. 91.

52 John Hurst, 'Kirner and the media', *Australian Journalism Review*, vol. 15, no. 1, Jan–June 1993, p. 127.

53 Miranda Devine, 'Success creates big problems', *Daily Telegraph*, 8 April 1997, p. 10.

54 Interview with the author, 6 May 1998.

55 Miranda Devine, op. cit.

56 Janine Cohen, 'The politics of fashion: women MPs get a dressing down', *Herald* (Melbourne), 17 Dec. 1984.

57 Nathan Vass, 'Kelly was a victim of sexist hate mail', *Sunday Telegraph*, 8 July 2001, p. 3.

58 Janine Cohen, op. cit.

59 Michelle Grattan, 'Grass-roots Democrats out to sprout a taller poppy', *Age*, 3 Aug. 1991; Clare Curran, 'Profile: Janet Powell', *Australian Left Review*, no. 122, Oct. 1990, p. 8.

60 Pilita Clark, 'Democrats' tussle has inimitable style', *SMH*, 2 Aug. 1991.

61 Mike Seccombe, 'Janet wants a new image', *SMH*, 3 Aug. 1991.

62 Kay O'Sullivan, 'A change of image: Powell needs updating, experts agree', *Herald-Sun*, 10 Aug. 1991, p. 5.

63 Powell stood on a ticket with the Rainbow Alliance, a Victorian political group with a platform based around the environment, peace and social justice. By this time — October 1992 — photographs revealed she had in fact changed her hairstyle to a softer, lighter, blow-waved look, and wore make-up. However, part of her problem, according to Innes Willox, was that she had 'never fitted the mould'. She was matronly, nice and pleasant: not what you would expect of a leader of the Democrats, he wrote. Innes Willox, 'A long search for political alternatives', *The Age*, 3 July 1993.

64 Luke McIlveen, 'One's a toiler with funny hair, the other is Dilbert', *Daily Telegraph*, 16 April 2004, p. 2.

65 Julia Baird, 'Kemp a victim of the razor gang', *SMH*, 16 Jan. 1999, p. 4.

66 Larry Schwartz, 'Asher takes life in a "man's world" in her stride', *Sunday Age*, 23 July 2000, p. 3.

Chapter Seven: Natasha Stott Despoja: the 'impossible princess'

1 The story has been told many times: On the day of her swearing-in ceremony in 1995, Stott Despoja brought two pairs of shoes to Parliament House: a pair of Doc Martens and some conservative heels. She consulted her leader, Cheryl Kernot, who left the choice to her but later said she had warned against cultivating a personality profile. Stott Despoja's version of the story is different. She says she arrived at work in the Docs she had often worn in Parliament House when she worked there as an adviser: 'I turned up with things to move into an office, I had my high heels ... just a daggy pair of courts that I had, and I brought them up to the Senate chamber and I said to Cheryl, "Are you okay, I brought

these just in case," and she said "Nup, there's no time, come on." And it was just like, "okay".'

2 She also wrote a piece for the *Age* about her first two months in parliament, which asserted, 'As Australia's youngest female federal politician, I am used to people focusing on my age or my appearance', and went on to explain again why she wore the Docs. She said she hoped that her presence would bring young people to the polls, ending with, 'By exercising this democratic right, young people will also have the opportunity to give undeserving representatives the boot, whether they are wearing Doc Martens or not.' (Natasha Stott Despoja, 'There's a new "kid" in town', *Age*, 9 Feb. 1996, p. 20.) In a diary she kept for the *Sun-Herald* about her first days in parliament, she said she had no time to reflect on the 'strange preoccupation of the media' with her shoes. ('Natasha Stott Despoja talks about ... her first day in parliament', *Sun-Herald*, 19 May 1996, p. 3.)

3 In 2001, when weighing her up against Lees in the leadership contest, the *Age* assessed that Lees was famous for determination, while Stott Despoja was famous for Doc Martens in parliament. Annabel Crabb, 'Defiant Lees ready for leadership face-off ', *Age*, 28 Feb. 2001, p. 4.

4 In 1996, she made a strong contribution to debates about tertiary education, and was often quoted on the subject. Matthew Franklin, writing about the changes in university funding for the *Courier Mail*, credited the Democrats for consistency in their opposition to university fees, and argued that the staunch defence of their position by Stott Despoja had launched her political career and marked her as a 'mover and shaker', as she had 'become the rallying point for people opposing the Vanstone changes. Even Vanstone, at the height of the debate on Wednesday, was heard to utter that Stott Despoja at least knew what she was talking about.' ('Education inc.', 7 Dec. 1996, p. 26.) Georgina Windsor also reported this in the *Australian*, writing that Stott Despoja's 'knowledge and straight shooting style on higher education issues has made many in parliament sit up and take notice, and sparked whispers about her look of leadership'. ('Vote battle a tale of two women', 5 Dec. 1996, p. 2.) In 1997, the subjects she was quoted on included bank fees, funding for science and technology research, labelling of genetically modified food, the application of the *Privacy Act*, job training programs, proposed voucher schemes, taxation of postgraduate scholarships, information technology, student protests, cuts to the Aboriginal student supplement, legislation restricting access of the Commonwealth Ombudsman and Human Rights Commissioner

from visiting immigration detainees, interest rate cuts, an online Wik petition, a decline in university enrolment applications, and the failed fraud case against John Elliott by the National Crime Authority. Other topics included the work for the dole plan, internet censorship, the need for data on marine pests, guidelines for social security benefits for immigrants, youth unemployment, compulsory voting, university staff cuts, literacy rates, the information economy, product safety standards, the constitutional convention, and sending plutonium into space. She also regularly attacked One Nation and its policies for young people. She was responsible for the release of the Democrats' youth poll. She submitted a dissenting report in June 1997 to the Senate Select Committee on Community Standards. The majority report argued for an extension of banned material, and greater penalties for the transfer of adult material — porn — over the net. Stott Despoja argued this was too restrictive, and supported an independent complaint handling body, codes of practice for the industry, age verification for net users, and a scheme to label online content.

5 Gerard Ryle, 'Behind the party girl', Spectrum, *SMH*, 8 Jan. 2000, p. 1.

6 Virginia Trioli, 'The new colt', *Age* (Extra), 1 November 1997, p. 5.

7 Over 1998 and 1999, Stott Despoja was quoted in articles about higher education, work for the dole, West Australian abortion laws, the republic, regulation of collection of human genetic information, privacy laws, the GST, voluntary unionism, the scrapping of Abstudy, job allowance, job network, unemployment figures, HECS, gun laws, drug policy, and CD legislation. When she opposed legislation to remove controls on CD imports, many commentators were sceptical of this move, which was at odds with the Australian Consumer Association and Allan Fels, head of the Australian Competition and Consumer Commission. Peter Switzer wrote in the *Australian* that initially her decision had 'added to my suspicion that this was a dizzy Democrat', although he agreed with her after recognising the arguments of an academic who believed CDs would not be cheaper as a result: 'Ring of truth in music reform row', 4 April 1998, p. 54. The Bill was still passed, by a narrow margin. She also spoke about mutual obligation and the dole, the proposed preamble to the Constitution, the constitutional referendum, a GST on books, cyber porn, labelling of genetically modified foods, voluntary student unionism, internet censorship, globalisation, youth wages, school fees, and religious discrimination.

8 Virginia Trioli, 'Rising star', *Age* (Extra), 11 Nov. 1997, p. 5.

9 Shelley Gare, 'Political covergirls find the dress fits', *Australian*, 25

March 1998, p. 2. Gare quoted Hugh Mackay, who said it was not such a risk for Stott Despoja because she was trying to establish herself as a young voice in an old forum, 'but Kernot's baseline is that she has spent a lot of time establishing she's a fairly serious political figure, not to be dismissed as fluff.'

10 Greg Callaghan, 'Internet conduit for senator's dream', *Weekend Australian*, 5 Oct. 1996, p. 5.

11 Natasha Stott Despoja, 'Stott in the name of Love', *SMH*, 22 Jan 1999, p 6.

12 Malcolm Farr, 'Shot down over Kosovo', *Daily Telegraph*, 1 May 1999, p. 11. According to the story, she upset her colleagues by heading off to Albania, thereby missing the tax debate in the Senate, on what was not considered official parliamentary business. Farr claimed she extended her stay in a stopover in Rome because she was tired, and was having problems getting a flight. She then asked for another two days off — thereby planning to spend as much time in Rome as she had with the refugees. It was not what she did that annoyed people, he wrote, it was the way she did it. The next day Stott Despoja issued a press release claiming the story was untrue, and based on malicious gossip. She was only in Rome for a matter of hours between connecting flights, had not asked for an extension of time, and would be seeking legal advice that week.

13 Mike Seccombe, 'Democrat's dilemma', *SMH*, 5 June 1999, p. 36.

14 *SMH*, 12 June 1999.

15 'I'm conscious, too, that I've benefited from the media in as much as you have to deal with flak,' *Sunday Telegraph*, 30 May 1999.

16 Fia Cumming, 'Stott Despoja under pressure over GST — and love life', *SunHerald*, 6 June 1999, p. 51.

17 Interview with the author, 10 April 2003.

18 Editorial, 'Senator faces a fundamental choice', *Australian*, 8 June 1999, p. 14.

19 He gave her credit for hard work, and her contribution to debates about censorship, euthanasia and HECs, as well as her vitality and pose, but claimed she had 'let celebrity get in the way of professionalism' in his column published on 10 June 1999.

20 Piers Akerman, 'Princess Leia's public wars', *Daily Telegraph*, 8 June 1999, p. 11.

21 For example, he wrote she had incorrectly claimed to be the first member of her family to get a university degree (her father, whom she said was not part of her family, had one, and her mother had 'eight-ninths' of one) and

revealed her lack of contact with her half-brother, who lived in Canberra. Note: Lees wrote a letter defending Stott Despoja on various points, saying she had a democratic right to vote on the GST according to her conscience and insisting she was not isolated.

22 Peter Ruehl, 'Are these ying-yangs just playing polly?', *AFR*, 1 March 2001, p. 48.

23 Mike Seccombe, 'The politics of protest', *SMH*, 28 Feb. 2001.

24 In a poll by the Adelaide newspaper the *Sunday Mail*, Stott Despoja was found to be the preferred choice for PM by 23 per cent of voters, with Howard at 25 per cent, and Hanson 11 per cent. A Morgan poll found Stott Despoja was more popular than either major party leader, with a 64 per cent positive rating — Howard had 47 per cent and Beazley 47 per cent.

25 Michelle Grattan and Mark Robinson, 'New team buoys Democrats and jolts Labor', *SMH*, 10 April 2001.

26 Ross Peake, 'A star burns out', *Canberra Times*, 22 August 2002; Dennis Atkins, 'If ratings were votes', *Courier-Mail*, 26 July 2002; Mark Day, 'Balancing act on a precipice', *Daily Telegraph*, 31 July 2002; Mike Seccombe, 'The curse of a political princess', *SMH*, 22 August 2002; Editorial, 'Democrats face sternest test', *AFR*, 22 August 2002; Peter Charlton, 'Dems the breaks', *Courier-Mail*, 27 July 2002; Rex Jory, 'Democrats undone, but who cares?', *Advertiser*, 7 August 2002; Dennis Atkins, 'Historic end for shooting star', *Courier-Mail*, 22 August 2002; graphic with story by Matt Price, 'Gang of Four now holds the reins', *Australian*, 22 August 2002; Malcolm Farr, 'Party's over for adored Natasha', *Daily Telegraph*, 24 August 2002; Editorial, 'Democrats' fate hangs on party reform', *Australian*, 22 August 2002.

27 Louse Dodson, 'Wither the divided democrats?', *Age*, 23 August 2002.

28 Alan Ramsey, 'Lees's stance just a block off the old Chipp', *SMH*, 31 July 2002, p. 13; Alan Ramsey, 'Fools and their flibbertigibbet', *SMH*, 27 July 2002.

29 He did not always dismiss her so easily. During the GST debate, he expressed some respect for the 'ambitious young deputy' who was 'no shrinking violet about self-promotion' but managed to adroitly handle media questions about the GST. He concluded that it would be interesting to see how far she went. (Alan Ramsey, 'Stott Despoja stakes out a bottom line', *SMH*, 29 May 1999, p. 43.)

30 Jason Koutsoukis, 'Party will bounce back, say pollsters', *AFR*, 23 August 2002.

31 Mike Seccombe, op. cit.

32 Gerard Henderson, 'The blonde and the bombshell', *SMH*, 30 July 2002.

33 Naomi Toy & Fiona Connolly, 'A big Natasha secret no one cares about', *Daily Telegraph*, 5 September 2003, p. 14.

34 *Australian Style,* issue 31, April 1999.

35 Note that when, in 1993, the Good Weekend magazine ran a digitally altered photo of a naked Kennett on the cover, he threatened to take legal action, saying it was in bad taste and, while he was happy to be criticised as a politician, he was 'not prepared to be held up to ridicule in that way'.

Chapter Eight: Cheryl Kernot: from Wunderfrau to whore

1 Interview with the author, 12 May 2003. Kernot believes Kingston was exaggerating: 'It was actually a small dancing space. I recall Margo having had a few and trying to get Michelle Grattan to dance.'

2 Richard Farmer, 'Tweak table to become fixture in mass mind', *Canberra Times*, 27 August 1993.

3 Alan Ramsey, 'Big pictures have sharp corners', *SMH*, 4 December 1993, p. 29.

4 When a poll was published which found only 24 per cent of people believed that politicians told the truth, she invited voters to call her office with suggested improvements for federal politics.

5 Max Walsh wrote in 1996: 'You could say that Senator Kernot luxuriates in the situation of enjoying power without responsibility. A British prime minister, Stanley Baldwin, once described this situation (in reference to the media) as the prerogative of the harlot. It says a great deal about Senator Kernot's skills that she not only avoids such a description, but is portrayed as the Mother Teresa of Australian politics.' (Max Walsh, 'Saint Cheryl lets her halo slip', *SMH*, 2 Feb. 1996, p. 25.) But he said her halo had slipped when she said she would not support the privatisation of Telstra, despite the Coalition's promise that they would pour $1 billion into the environment if the legislation went through.

6 The *Australian* said there could be no integrity in making sure the government broke the promises they made to Australian people. The *Australian Financial Review* agreed — keeping a government honest meant they should be free to implement the policy they promised, though the Democrats could delay, debate and negotiate. Don Chipp also pointed out that the Coalition had won 48 per cent of the vote, and the Democrats had no mandate: they should refine, not block, government policies. However, an AGB McNair poll taken on 13 August 1996 found 60 per cent of respondents said they would condone attempts by the

Democrats to block parts of the budget if they were unfair or involved broken promises. On 9 August 1996, the *Australian Financial Review* gave her another serve for her 'disdain for the reasonable functioning of Australian democracy'. The Senate should be a house of review, not obstruction, it argued, and the Democrats did not have the right to reject the government's program of fiscal reform. Max Walsh, then at the *Sydney Morning Herald*, agreed. The *Australian* told Kernot to 'show some responsibility and pull back'.

7   This included allowing vetting by the Australian Industrial Relations Commission of non-union employment agreements, and benchmarking of non-union agreements against awards.

8   The *West Australian* also editorialised that her move was more to do with ambition than with principle, and said she had been tarnished by the process. The *Courier-Mail* wrote that members of the Australian Democrats had every right to feel betrayed, and her personal ambitions may have led her into a political wilderness. An exception was the *Age*, which argued her decision would be good for Australian politics: 'It may, if her hopes are fulfilled, determine the shape of government and people's faith in our political institutions as Australia enters the new millennium.' Praising her integrity and sincerity, common sense and fairness, the *Age* argued her critique of the Howard government would resonate with many voters, and in seeking a role as an initiator rather than a spoiler, 'she presents as the most likely candidate in the country to become Australia's first female prime minister.' (Editorial, *Age*, 16 October 1997, p. 18.)

9   Piers Akerman, 'Cheryl's no saviour', *Sunday Telegraph*, 19 October 1997, p. 63.

10   Marion Smith, 'Kernot's dark side', *Courier-Mail*, 1 Nov. 1997, p. 29.

11   Mike Seccombe, 'Kookaburra', *SMH*, 18 Oct. 1997, p. 34.

12   A Herald ACNielsen-McNair poll found a third of Democrat supporters were now more likely to vote for the ALP, and Kernot was rated highly or very highly as a potential prime minister by 35 per cent of voters.

13   Piers Akerman had hinted at something fishy, but Peter Charlton of The *Courier-Mail* rejected the rumours of Kernot 'running off with a male student' as unsubstantiated, resembling a lurid soap plot. Charlton described the attempt to dig for dirt on her past — by two Sydney journos — as representing a sea change on Australian politics — the press gallery had been 'singularly reluctant to report the known peccadilloes of the serving politicians'. Former student and Australian sports journalist Bret Harris confessed to a schoolboy crush on his attractive blonde teacher: spending time with her was 'teenage heaven'.

14 Christopher Pearson, 'Kernot can't close the door on skeletons', *AFR*, 15 Dec. 1997, p. 19.

15 Only 9 per cent of voters said she had been harmed 'a lot', and 17 per cent said she had been damaged a little (Taverner Research Company for the *Sunday Age*).

16 Email correspondence with the author, 25 May 2004.

17 Email correspondence with the author, 26 Jan. 2004.

18 Previously, the only serious incursion on her privacy was in 1996 when the press reported that her brother was facing charges of attempted murder and attempted sexual assault. He was later convicted.The same thing had happened to Carmen Lawrence when she moved to Canberra — suddenly stories about her de facto relationship and the child she bore while unmarried sprang into print. They died down, however, after her former de facto came out to speak of his love and admiration for her. And perhaps because it was hardly a scandal — it was legal to not be married after all.

19 Journalist Virginia Trioli argued that if Kernot's claims that she had been hounded by the media came as an accumulated response to the shameful reportage of her sexual history story, that was understandable, 'But as a response to the orthodox treatment of a minor story it was excessive and, paradoxically, attention seeking.' The question was stupid but she should have said 'good morning' and moved on. Some came to her defence, most notably journalists from the *Age*. Michael Gordon said it was a minor eruption which 'would not register when compared with the temper tantrums of that other high-profile parliamentary recruit, Bob Hawke, before he was elected in 1980'. Columnist Pamela Bone argued: 'You call that an outburst? She didn't swear, she didn't raise her voice, she didn't cry, or at least not in front of the cameras. Maybe, when she got on the plane, she went to the toilet and shed some tears of anger and frustration. I would have.' (Pamela Bone, 'Should Kernot's life be this hard?', *Age*, 22 Jan. 1998, p. 11.)

20 Her strength was her honesty, and, as Michelle Grattan pointed out, like Bob Hawke she had her own 'special relationship' with the Australian people. This meant her mistakes would emphasise her humanness and enhance, not detract from her appeal — the public would forgive her lapses. (Michelle Grattan, 'Punters recognise Bob's heir', *AFR*, 24 Jan. 1998, p. 24.)

21 Another critical amendment altered this passage in the draft: 'If you look closely in my eyes you will see that I'm a fighter. I'm here to contribute to delivering Australia from one of the worst governments it's ever had. And it will take more than a truck to flatten me.' The final version read:

'I couldn't be prouder than to be a member of Kim Beazley's team, and I'm here as a part of that team, to help deliver Australia from one of the worst governments it's ever had the misfortune to elect. And comrades, it takes more than a truck to flatten me.'

22 Shortly afterwards, on 26 February 1998, when giving a speech at the Quill media awards in Melbourne, she reminded her media audience of Christabel Pankhurst's warning to fellow suffragette campaigners: 'Never lose your temper with the press.'

23 Alan Ramsey, 'Foolish behaviour all round', *SMH*, 14 March 1998, p. 43. A week later Ramsey embarrassed her by accusing her of lifting large slabs of a speech she gave from one given by Evans a few days earlier, and accused her of being obsessed with her own political significance.

24 Robert Manne, 'Attack on Kernot reveals Canberra's double standards', *SMH*, 16 March 1998, p. 15.

25 Evans stood up in parliament and declared that Randall's comments were 'totally baseless, beneath contempt and a disgusting abuse of parliamentary privilege'. 'It takes more than an apology,' he said, 'to heal the hurt, particularly to our families, that this sort of performance causes.' This lie was something which, as he later confessed in an email to Kernot, weighed heavily on his conscience, particularly as the affair continued for a couple of years after this.

26 Miranda Devine, 'Red dress but redder faces', *Daily Telegraph*, 24 March 1998, p. 10.

27 Peter Cole-Adams, 'Beazley gallant while Kernot's critics see red', *Canberra Times*, 25 March 1998, p. 2.

28 Brian Toohey, 'Kernot soap won't wash', *AFR*, 24 March 1998, p. 19.

29 Note Gordon's own newspaper criticised the red dress in an editorial: 'Can a feminist wear lipstick? Of course she can. Can a woman of fairly mature years pose in a scarlet satin sheath and feather boa, eyes heavily made up and toenails painted silver, and still expect to be taken seriously? The proposition is more doubtful. And even more so when the MP in question had in the past complained about the media trivialising her by describing her as 'Labor's new bride'. (*Age*, 28 March 1998, p. 11.)

30 In *Speaking for Myself Again* she wrote: 'The constant barrage of criticism and the pressure on myself and my family was increasingly hard to deal with. At times I was not my best and I readily acknowledge the provocative nature of my election night comments ...' At the end of the night, she wrote, she sat outside on a bus stop seat and wept.

31 Tony Wright, 'Cheryl Kernot — facing my future', *Age*, 16 June 1999, p. 13.

Chapter Nine: Sex and the 'Stiff-Dick Syndrome'

1 Oakes has no recollection of these negotiations.

2 Reported by Alan Ramsey, 'A sly route to the truth', *SMH*, 6 July 2002, p. 37.

3 The AAP wire service ran a story that night about Oakes's column, and the next morning about Kernot's insistence there was no secret. They did not report on the affair until after Oakes revealed details on Channel Nine.

4 Laurie Oakes, *Bulletin*, 3 February 1998.

5 In a letter to 'Media Watch', sent on 6 July, Oakes queried the accuracy of the Rehame figure: 'A 3AW poll conducted by Neil Mitchell was rather different. I am told there was at least one other radio poll that did not back up the Rehame figure. I am also told that Steve Price on 2UE said his calls were not running at anything like 85 per cent against publication. But I am not surprised that many people were offended by my decision to run this story.'

6 Nick Greiner, 'The smart-alec culture: a critique of Australian journalism', *Australian Studies in Journalism*, vol. 2, 1993, p. 4.

7 Quoted by Ruth Wilson, 'Political interviewers: what makes them tick', *Australian*, 13 July 2001.

8 Mungo MacCallum, 'The Killen–Guilfoyle connection', *Nation Review*, 22–28 Oct. 1976, p. 4.

9 Bill D'Arcy & Hugh Crawford, '"Cabinet Ministers' Romance" Story', *Sun*, 22 Oct. 1976.

10 Roy Eccleston, 'Ousted Powell vows to fight on', *Australian*, 20 Aug. 1991. Note the *Australian Financial Review*'s Robert Garran did not mention it: 'Democrats oust Powell for deputy', 20 Aug. 1991.

11 Mike Seccombe, 'Don's Party's over', *SMH*, 31 Aug. 1991; Susan Mitchell, *The Scent of Power: On the Trail of Women and Power in Australian Politics*, Angus & Robertson, Sydney, 1996, p. 30.

12 Christopher Pearson, 'Friends and politics', *Courier-Mail*, 5 April 1997, p. 24.

13 In May 2002, he told a Young Labor conference in Sydney that Abbott was hypocritical to have encouraged journalists to publish stories on Kernot's private life. Latham claimed Abbott told a conference that 'the best support structure in our society is an intact family' and 'we want to discourage children out of wedlock'. Latham then asked, 'Why doesn't he practise what he preaches?' In June 2002, he shouted across the chamber — as Abbott criticised Labor — 'You've had too many unions, Tony, you grub.' In July, in a speech given in Perth about modernising

the ALP, responding to a comment of Abbott's that the ALP was full of 'hereditary peers', Latham attacked him again: 'Tony Abbott is always walking away. As a young man he became a "hereditary disappear".' On 11 August, Susanne Lobez, who had adopted a daughter, wrote an indignant column in the *Sunday Herald Sun*: 'Where do you get off using adoption as some example of moral dubiousness which disqualifies a person from discussing families, responsibilities and commitment?' Miranda Devine agreed: 'Much good came from what must have been a painful process for Abbott and his girlfriend — a boy was alive and parents had been given the gift of a child.' (Miranda Devine, 'Adoption — how did it become a dirty word?', *Sun-Herald*, 11 August 2002, p. 15.)

14 One exception was in 1999, when NSW Liberal MP Michael Photios left his pregnant wife and toddler daughter for his long-standing mistress, fashion designer Mela Purdie. The *Sun-Herald* dubbed him 'The Love Rat', the press trailed him for days, and he lost his seat in the next election. The rationale used for revealing that story was the fact that he had used photographs of his family in the election campaign, while he was having an affair.

15 He was forced to resign after she claimed he had rorted his travel allowance. She appeared on '60 Minutes', and, as Rachel Browne wrote in the *Sun-Herald*, 'with a trembling lip but a steely tone, the 30-year-old blonde dumped on her ex.' She declared he had rorted his travel expenses by taking her on a trip to Europe during their two-year affair. She also took out an AVO against him when the relationship ended. When News Limited newspapers published photographs of Woods and his wife, Jane, at their Sydney home — taken by a photographer standing on the roof of his car, peering over the back fence — in February 1997, politicians condemned them for it.

16 The *Age* reported that Harris was paid out by the state government, but this was not confirmed.

17 A freelance journalist, Phillip Somerset, had squeezed the story out of Mrs Hewson and tried to sell it to various newspapers. It was rejected by *Woman's Day* editor Nene King because Mrs Hewson insisted her remarks had been off the record. King said, 'I felt she was vulnerable and John Hewson is a very prominent man ... Perhaps I may have been alienating the next Prime Minister.' In August the *Weekly*, which had initially been cautious, decided to publish it.

18 Adele Horin was certainly sympathetic, wondering if Hewson would wish that his daughter do as her mother had: sacrifice herself for her

husband's career, then be abandoned for a career woman? ('Strong mother is best gift for a daughter', *SMH*, 3 Sept. 1991, p. 13.)

19 Michelle Grattan was not impressed: the program had left a 'nasty taste'. 'Do we really want to start down the American road,' she argued, 'where every detail of private life is likely to find its way into the public arena, salacious seasoning for the political debate? We've usually operated on different informal rules in this country ... we should be careful of throwing that restraint away in the excitement of one somewhat tawdry tale.' She insisted what made a good politician 'is not necessarily what makes a good family person, or vice versa. Elections are judgements about the former.' If these stories were encouraged, she said, good candidates would be loath to enter politics, and the political process would be debased. ('Ticking off for "60 Minutes"', 1 Oct. 1991, p. 13.) Mary Hennessy, head of Channel Nine publicity, said the station had received more than 100 phone calls after the program was aired, and the 'vast majority' were in support of Hewson.

20 In an address to a NSW Liberal Party convention in October 1992, he said, 'You've got to be suspicious of a guy that doesn't drive, doesn't like kids and things like that. When he's up against a full-blooded Australian like John Fahey, he has not got a hope.' Prime Minister Paul Keating said he was 'flabbergasted' at the move to bring in 'the worst of American politics', and pointed out that not one Labor politician had ever sought to exploit Hewson's own family dramas. Hewson called Carr to apologise. (Oddly, several years later, Liberal MP Peter Collins, when opposition leader, also pointed to Premier Carr's lack of children — which again backfired on him.) Mike Seccombe wrote that Hewson's comments were extraordinary because in federal parliament there were up to a dozen homosexual MPs, and 'plenty of members and senators who have had or are having affairs, have broken marriages, drink to excess, and even some who smoke a little dope. Yet as long as it does not interfere with the performance of their duties, their parliamentary opponents and the press gallery usually ignore all this.' (Mike Seccombe, 'Shock! Horror! The muck stops here', *SMH*, 2 April 1994, p. 5.)

21 The investigation was into whether notorious underworld figure Louis Bayeh had provided 'benefits or rewards' to state MPs from mid-1990. Gibson had befriended Bayeh in the 1990s after Bayeh claimed he had been framed by the police over heroin-related charges, and Gibson was seeking information on corrupt police. Nori was Gibson's lover at the time, and allegedly was the beneficiary of some of Bayeh's largesse, including a holiday to Fiji and gold jewellery. At the time Nori was married to

federal Labor MP John Faulkner, but said she believed her relationship with Gibson, which had begun circa 1988 and ended in about 1993, was 'substantial and serious' with long-term prospects. The story of the affair was good copy, and Nori was pursued over the relationship in a way Gibson was not. The *Sunday Telegraph* managed to get a photo of her at her front door, crying. The reporter described her as anguished, distraught as she admitted she was hurting: 'Take a look at me, will you?' The reporter continued: 'Stripped of make-up and smoking a cigarette, Ms Nori appeared to have had little sleep. Unable to control her emotions, she burst into tears. Ms Nori has had to carry her burden for some time, and what was once a private pain is now clear for all to see.' Indeed. ('The tears of Sandra Nori', *Sunday Telegraph*, 19 April 1998, p. 7.)

22 Gibson had sung out 'Love is in the air' after Terry Metherell had asked a Dorothy Dixer of Greiner. The chamber burst out laughing, but Greiner tartly responded: 'It is rather strange that the honourable member for Londonderry should say "Love is in the air". Of all the people opposite, who but my friend and squash partner, the honourable member for Londonderry, do you think would be stupid enough to say, "Love is in the air"?' After an application from Gibson, the Supreme Court ordered that O'Keefe step down from the investigation because of 'ostensible bias' on moral grounds. Assistant commissioner and retired judge Jeremy Badgery-Parker eventually cleared Gibson of any corrupt conduct but criticised him for a lack of truthfulness and reliability in his evidence. As Kerry-Anne Walsh wrote in the *Sunday-Telegraph*, Nori 'had her past love affair with Gibson plastered over the papers as a result of the inquiry and the end result was: nothing'. ('Does this watchdog have any teeth?', *Sunday Telegraph*, 8 August 1999, p. 141.)

23 Fia Cumming, 'Affairs of State', *Sun-Herald*, 16 Feb. 1997, p. 39.

24 Lyndall Crisp & Jill Margo, 'Sex and power: the liaisons that make history', Perspective, *AFR*, 6 July 2002, p. 24.

25 Mungo MacCallum, 'Sex, power and politics', Insight, *Age*, 6 July 2002, p. 1.

26 Michael Bachelard, 'Men in arms', *Sunday Age*, 21 Dec. 1997, p. 4.

27 The topic of the interview was the ruling of the Remuneration Tribunal that the special minister of state be empowered to decide if de facto spouses should be entitled to overseas travel like legal spouses.

28 Robert Manne, 'Attack on Kernot reveals "Canberra" double standards', *SMH*, 16 March 1998, p. 15.

29 Marion Frith, 'Where Cheryl Kernot is happy to be a nobody', *Sun-Herald*, 28 March 2004, p. 28.

30 The night before Ramsey's Saturday column was due to come out, he was seated next to Oakes at a dinner for a retiring colleague. Ramsey told me, 'It was a jolly evening, but as soon as I sat down I told him I'd taken to him with the cudgels in the paper next morning, that I disagreed strongly with what he'd done, and he responded relatively amiably, saying yes he understood I'd been writing about it, and we proceeded to have a great night with Peter. At the end of the night, Oakes and I shook hands, would you believe, because I said we may never do so again. There was some good-natured argy-bargy between us, with me saying I hoped he'd get over it before my birthday in the first weekend of January — Oakes and Kath had been guests at my birthday lunch the previous two years, a wonderfully riotous affair down at our South Coast house at Tuross, where I cook fish and chips for about a dozen of us (I catch the fish with a friend) — and him saying he hoped so too, because we'd been friends for 25 years. And that was the last time we spoke. He has ignored me ever since. We pass in the corridor in the press gallery without a word. Sad, isn't it?' When I mentioned Ramsey to Oakes, he said, 'If you are going to use Ramsey as a source we can end the conversation now. Ramsey knows nothing and is wrong on many things, quite often, so let's not quote Ramsey as a source.' When I reminded him they had been friends before they fell out over this story he countered, 'Well, it depends what you mean by friends. We've known each other a long while, that's all.'

31 Interview with the author, 9 April 2003.

32 Laurie Oakes claimed Gray told him differently, and also pointed to Ramsey's column, where it was revealed that in 1997 Gray had asked Kernot directly if there was anything they should know that would come back to embarrass the Labor Party, Kernot herself, or the defection deal. (Alan Ramsey, 'Political voyeurism that hides the real sting in the tale', SMH, 6 July 2002, p. 37.)

33 David Epstein, 'Love and other bruises', Australian, 6 July 2002, p. 1.

34 In an editorial, the Australian Financial Review similarly argued the affair 'may help explain many odd things about Ms Kernot's defection to Labor and her decline from a cool, professional Democrats leader to an erratic shadow minister'.

35 David Epstein, op cit.

36 During an interview with Clive Robertson on Channel Seven's 'Newsworld' program, he said his wife 'understood that it was part of a pretty volatile, exuberant character and she knew my love for her had never changed'.

37 While he had heard rumours of the affair for some time — he had even received a phone call from a Qantas steward after a flight they had been on — he said the emails provided 'irrefutable proof'.
38 Kate Ellis, op. cit. p. 27.
39 Kate Ellis, op. cit. p. 55.
40 Hanson-Young v Leyonhjelm (No 4) [2019] FCA 1981, www.jade.io/article/675945.

Chapter Ten: Saint Carmen: canonisation and crucifixion

1 Quoted by Christine Wallace in 'The nobbling of Carmen Lawrence', *Eye*, 16–29 December 1999, p. 50.
2 Michelle Grattan, 'Carmen — a case to answer', *Age*, 15 April 1995.
3 Rod Cameron, 'Feminisation: the major emerging trend underlying future mass audience response', unpublished address, 11th National Convention of the Public Relations Institute of Australia, 19 Oct. 1990.
4 Geoff Kitney, 'Female trio to shape politics', *SMH*, p. 9.
5 Jane Cadzow, 'Carmen Lawrence's year of living dangerously', *SMH*, Good Weekend, 11 March 1995.
6 Paul McGeough, 'Did she know? The teflon-coated woman faces her toughest test yet', *SMH*, Spectrum, 15 April 1995, p. 3.
7 The first political interference came in 1987, after Penny Easton obtained documents from Richard Court, then opposition leader, which included meeting minutes of a company Brian Easton was involved with. She gave information to a Liberal MP, Ross Lightfoot, which he used in an attempt to embarrass the Labor government. He claimed Brian Easton was concealing a $200,000 ex-gratia payment from the Public Service Board in the divorce settlement.
8 The government funded a legal attempt by Lawrence to ask the West Australian Supreme and High Courts to determine the extent of parliamentary privilege.
9 This was made worse because Penny Easton's mother, Barbara Campbell, consistently made the connection and faxed the report of the coroner, who said that the publicity generated by the petition had exacerbated her distress, to journalists. The coroner, David McCann, had concluded that the petition was a contributing factor to her death, writing that: 'As a result of a petition presented to the State Parliament further publicity was generated concerning the deceased and her family ... it is clear that the deceased had been concerned and distressed by past events and that her distress was exacerbated by the more recent events.'

10 Christine Wallace, op. cit.

11 Michelle Grattan, op. cit.

12 James Oram, 'Far from home', *Sun-Herald*, 18 Feb. 1996, p. 12.

13 After the 2001 election the public discovered that the story about asylum seekers throwing children overboard was not true, that the photographs released by the government showed something entirely different, and that the defence minister, Peter Reith, was advised by bureaucrats that they did not depict children thrown in the water. We also learned that although two days before the election the acting chief of the defence force spoke to Reith about the photos, and Reith spoke to John Howard later that night, Howard spent the following day repeating that 'the best advice' available to the government was that children had been thrown overboard.

14 We discovered part of our rationale for sending soldiers to Iraq was false when John Howard admitted intelligence that claimed Iraq had bought yellowcake uranium from Africa was wrong. He said, 'Anything that I have said that might be seen as misleading was not a deliberate misleading.' This information was one of the reasons we went to war, even though spy agencies had warned against its use. The Office of National Assessments (which provides advice to Howard on intelligence) and the Department of Foreign Affairs said they had received a report days before Howard gave a statement in parliament which said the claims were 'uncorroborated and not necessarily believed'.

15 Without directly addressing the government, he said, 'There is one challenge for the future leaders of our nation which I would particularly emphasise ... the challenge of justice and truth, the challenge never to be indifferent in the face of injustice or falsehood. It encompasses the challenge to advance truth and human dignity rather than to seek advantage by inflaming ugly prejudice and intolerance. Who of us will easily forget the untruths about children overboard? Or the abuse of the basic rights of innocent children by incarceration behind Woomera's razor wire? ... Some may think that these and other similar unpleasant things should be left unmentioned. But if our coming generation of leaders refuses to honestly confront the denial of truth or responsibility which they reflect, our nation will surely be in peril of losing its way in the years ahead.'

Chapter Eleven: How to Succeed in Politics Without a Penis

1 Bruce Jones, 'Janine's greatest gamble', *Sun-Herald*, 19 Feb. 1989.

2 Interview with the author, 10 July 2003.

3   Paul Austin, 'Janine Haines — no Chipp off an old Democrat's block', *Australian*, 17 June 1987.

4   Sue Dunlevy, 'Haines — deft use of reality as image', *Herald* (Melbourne), 1 March 1990. It was paralleled to a commitment to feminism by Jane Cafarella in 'The first slice, not just the crumbs', *Age*, 21 March 1990.

5   Sue Dunlevy, ibid.

6   Alan Ramsey, 'If only the seats of power carried more backsides like this', *SMH*, 13 Nov. 2002, p. 15.

7   Jane Cadzow, 'Tasmanian Tiger', Good Weekend, 18 March 2000, p. 16.

8   See also a piece Liberal senator Helen Coonan wrote in the *Sydney Morning Herald* where she argued: 'The cult of celebrity that has been created around certain women politicians distorts the purpose for which we are elected. Women politicians have an unprecedented opportunity to respond to the public disenchantment with political style.' (Helen Coonan, 'Time for a good look in the mirror', *SMH*, 25 Nov. 1998, p. 19.)

9   Interview with the author, 5 May 2003.

10 *Australian Left Review*, vol. 3, July/Aug. 1989, p. 9.

11 Interview with the author, Dec. 2003.

12 Geoff Kitney, 'Female trio to shape politics', *SMH*, 1 April 1994, p. 9.

13 Susan Mitchell, op. cit., p. 29. Not all members of the press gallery would agree. Journalist Peter Cole-Adams, for example, attributed Kelly's problems to a damning report from the auditor-general, criticism from a parliamentary committee, Kelly's refusal to answer questions, and her own lack of competence. However, historian Clem Lloyd saw it as a 'feeding frenzy' of the press. (Australian Press Council Conference Papers, *Public Figures and the Press*, University of Southern Qld, Toowoomba, 24 March 1994, pp. 9, 22.)

14 Jane Cadzow, 'Women about the House', *Good Weekend*, 26 Nov. 1988, p. 21.

15 Interview with the author, 27 Aug. 1997.

16 Geoff Turner, 'Towards equity: women's emerging role in Australian journalism', *Australian Studies in Journalism*, vol. 2, 1993, p. 132.

17 Rosemary Harris, 'Women, workers, ladies or chicks? How the *Courier-Mail* sees woman', *Hecate*, vol. 10, no. 1, 1984, pp. 28–48.

18 Grahame Griffin, 'A profile of Australian newspaper photographers', *Australian Studies in Journalism*, no. 3, 1994, p. 151.

Postlude

1   Nicolas Rothwell, 'Thirteen ways not to think about Pauline Hanson', in Tony Abbott et. al., *Two Nations*, Bookman Press, Melbourne, 1998, p. 162.

2   Marilyn Lake, 'Pauline Hanson: Virago in parliament, Viagra in the bush', in Tony Abbott et. al., op. cit., p. 114.

3   Before the 1996 federal election, Graeme Campbell was kicked out of the ALP because of his anti-immigration, anti–economic rationalist views, and strong criticism of the Aboriginal affairs bureaucracy. He then successfully stood as an independent member for the seat of Kalgoorlie, and formed the antiimmigration Australia First Party. He believes One Nation stole many of his policies.

4   Margo Kingston, *Off the Rails: The Pauline Hanson Trip*, Allen & Unwin, Sydney, 1999.

5   After some weeks, the press themselves became the story, as they were heckled and harassed at meetings, refusing to leave one when police were called, defiantly demanding they be handed budget costings, and that the One Nation Party be as accountable as others. One Nation members became so angry with the media that they began to rely on the internet to disseminate information, setting up websites outlining policy and critiquing the mainstream press.

6   Iva Ellen Deutchman & Anne Ellison, 'A star is born: the roller coaster ride of Pauline Hanson in the news', *Media, Culture and Society*, 1999, vol. 21, pp. 33–50.

7   More research is needed here on the question of whether it was the volume of publicity, the criticism of Hanson, or the support given by shock jocks like Alan Jones which artificially pumped the public figure of Pauline Hanson to loom so large on our political landscape in the 1990s. See Murray Goot, 'Pauline Hanson and the power of the media', in Ghassan Hage & Rowanne Couch (eds), *The Future of Australian Multiculturalism*, Research Institute of Humanities and Social Sciences, University of Sydney, 1999, pp. 205–302, and Murray Goot, 'The perils of polling and the popularity of Pauline', *Current Affairs Bulletin*, vol. 73, no. 4, 1996–97, pp. 8–14.

8   Margo Kingston, op. cit., p. 29.

9   Murray Goot & Ian Watson, 'One Nation's electoral support: where does it come from, what makes it different and how does it fit?', *Australian Journal of Politics and History*, vol. 47, no. 2, 2001, pp. 159–91.

10 Margo Kingston, op. cit., p. xv.

11 Margo Kingston recorded that a photographer asked Hanson, who was having a 'media-free' day, if he could take a photo of her hanging out her washing, but she replied, 'I'm at the office tomorrow, working, and I don't take my washing to work. Have a day off; you need it, you're looking tired.' (Margo Kingston, op. cit., p. 41.)

12 David Leser, 'Pauline Hanson's bitter harvest', *Good Weekend*, 30 Nov. 1996.

13 *New Idea* ran a damaging story during the 1998 election campaign which implied Hanson was a poor mother who had neglected her sick son. The headline on the cover cried: 'Pauline Hanson's dying son, "I can't even speak to her."' Tabloids and broadsheets alike followed it up, despite Hanson's refusal to comment. See Margo Kingston, op. cit., chapter 12.

14 Margo Kingston, op. cit., p. 42.

15 John Pasquarelli, *The Pauline Hanson Story — By the Man Who Knows*, New Holland Publishers, Sydney, 1998, p. 285.

16 Murray Goot,'Hanson's heartland — who's for One Nation and why', in Tony Abbott et al, op cit, p. 72.

17 John Pasquarelli, op. cit., p. 281.

18 Marilyn Lake, op. cit., p. 116.

19 Helen Elliott, 'Hanson's sexual power', *Herald Sun*, 10 June 1998, p. 19

20 The *Daily Telegraph* ran a front-page story headed 'Very close: Hanson and her svengali', with a photo of Hanson resting her head on his shoulder, hinting at a sexual relationship between the two. There was protracted interest in the men running One Nation, especially Oldfield and, to a lesser extent, David Ettridge, and the often condescending tenor of the articles was that they were controlling her like puppet masters. This leads to a critical, but little discussed, factor in the media's treatment of women MPs, which is the key role press secretaries can play in the mishaps and misunderstandings of media relations. As Kingston details, Hanson's adviser, David Oldfield, was widely loathed by journalists, considered narcissistic and patronising towards the woman he called 'the Project'. Other women have suffered from similar problems; it is an area ripe for research.

21 The subeditor at the Melbourne *Herald Sun* rejigged the story so Hanson was quoted saying she had the best 'pins' in the country. Kingston, op. cit., p. 102.

22 Bob Ellis, 'The vote for One Nation was less a vote for racism than a revolt against Economic Correctness', *Sydney Morning Herald*, 22 June 1998, p. 17.

23 Mike Seccombe, 'How Hanson got her men', *Sydney Morning Herald*, 15 March 2003, p. 34. He added: 'And when she was photographed wearing a Bang label evening dress, with what was described at the time as "a revealing lace panel", she got a big, positive response from her constituency.'

24 Sonja Koremans, 'All dressed up and going nowhere', *Courier-Mail*, 14 Feb. 2001, p. 19.

25 'Pauline keeps to dress code', *Herald Sun*, 2 May 2001, p. 16.

26 Emma Kate Symons, 'The evolution of Hanson', *Daily Telegraph*, 17 July 1998, p. 11.

27 'Pauline's secret prison diaries', as told to Michael Sheather, *Australian Women's Weekly*, December 2003, p. 34. The *Daily Telegraph* picked up the story — not to talk about her prison revelations, but about how glamorous she looked in her photographs. It reprinted the photo of Hanson in the strapless dress and likened it to a photograph of Princess Diana on the front cover of *Vanity Fair*, claiming 'The black and white photos of Ms Hanson attempt to capture the same serene mood as the famous pictures taken of Di by the celebrity photographer Mario Testio for *Vanity Fair* magazine in 1997.' (Dora Tsavdaridis, 'From prisoner to princess: Pauline even has a "secret diary" to tell of torment', *Daily Telegraph*, 25 Nov. 2003, p. 3.)

Conclusion

1 Interview with the author, 29 May 2003.

2 Interview with the author, Dec. 2003.

3 Shaun Carney, 'Down to earth for the heavenly body politic', *Age*, 22 Nov. 1997, p. 10.

Epilogue

1 Maxine Beneba Clarke, 'capital', *How Decent Folk Behave*, Hachette, Sydney, 2021.

2 Chimamanda Ngozi Adichie, TED talk, Dec. 2021, www.ted.com/talks/chimamanda_ngozi_adichie_we_should_all_be_feminists.

3 Women's Working Group chaired by Rosemary Craddock, *Room for Movement: Women and Leadership in the Liberal Party*, A Liberal Party Federal Executive Initiative, 2015.

Bibliography

A more extensive bibliography, including the international literature on the subject of female politicians and the press, can be found in my doctorate: Baird, Julia, 'Housewife superstars: female politicians and the Australian print media 1970– 1990', PhD, University of Sydney, 2001. This thesis also includes a substantive discussion of the historiography and political science which provides the theoretical framework for this research, particularly the concept of framing.

Primary sources

Oral history recordings

Dowse, Sara, interview with Susan Ryan, July 1991, TRC 2744, Oral History Collection, National Library of Australia.

Jamieson, Ronda, interview with June Craig, Sept.–Nov. 1987, J. S. Battye Library of West Australian History, Perth.

Pratt, Mel, interview with Dame Enid Lyons, 13–22 March 1972, TRC 121/30, Oral History Collection, National Library of Australia.

Sawer, Marian, 'Women and Politics', address to ANU Convocation Luncheon, 22 July 1982, TRC 1153, National Library of Australia.

Manuscript and archival material

Most of the newspaper articles referred to in this book have come from clippings files held in parliamentary libraries in Australian capital cities, particularly the federal Parliamentary Library in Parliament House, Canberra. I also drew material from archives in the NSW, Queensland, South Australian, Victorian, and West Australian parliamentary libraries.

I have drawn from the following papers at the National Library of Australia Collection:

Lyons, Enid, Dame, Papers of Dame Enid Lyons 1931–1974, manuscript, NLA, MS 4852.

Office of Women's Affairs, *Proceedings of the Women in Politics Conference, Canberra, 1975*, Office of Women's Affairs, Department of the Prime Minister and Cabinet, 1976, NLA.

Summers, Anne, Papers of Anne Summers 1967–2000, manuscript, NLA, MS 7073.

Women in Politics Conference, Canberra, 1975, papers, NLA.

Unpublished theses

Allan, Pam, 'A preliminary sketch of the role of women in the NSW branch of the ALP', BA Hons, University of Sydney, 1974.

Baird, Julia, 'Housewife superstars: female politicians and the Australian print media 1970–1990', PhD, University of Sydney, 2001.

Nicholson, Joyce, 'The Women's Electoral Lobby and women's employment: strategies and outcome', MA minor thesis, University of Melbourne, 1991.

Conference papers, speeches and reports

Australian Press Council, *Public Figures and the Press*, conference papers, University of Southern Qld, Toowoomba, 24 March 1994, p. 9 ff.

Cameron, Rod, 'Feminisation: the major emerging trend underlying future mass audience response', unpublished address, 11th National Convention of the Public Relations Institute of Australia, 19 Oct. 1990.

Cox, Eva, 'Women and the State', Australasian Political Studies

Association 23rd Annual Conference, 28–30 Aug. 1981, Canberra.

Fairfax, John B., 'The press and politics', *Thinking about Australia: the Sir Earle Page Memorial Orations, 1984–1990*, Sir Earle Page Memorial Trust,Woolloomooloo, 1990.

Lewis, Abigail, 'The Way In: Representation in the Australian Parliament, Per Capita', 2019.

Mayer, Henry, 'Dilemma in mass media policies', Academy of the Social Sciences in Australia, annual lecture 1979, Australian National University, 6 Nov. 1979.

Peake, Lucy, 'Press coverage of women candidates for the UK parliament', unpublished paper prepared for presentation at the ECPR 25th Joint Sessions of Workshops, University Bern, Switzerland, 27 Feb. to 4 March 1997.

Ross, Karen, 'Skirting the issue: women, politics and broadcast media in Britain', paper given at Console-ing Passions 98, University of Western Sydney, Nepean, Australia, 1998.

Simms, Marian, 'Women and political power in Australia: a feminist analysis', papers of the second Women and Labour Conference, 1980, pp. 247–67.

Women's Working Group chaired by Rosemary Craddock, *Room for Movement: Women and Leadership in the Liberal Party*, A Liberal Party Federal Executive Initiative, 2015.

Secondary sources

(Note: Where several chapters of an edited collection have been used, only the book is cited.)

Articles

Appleton, Gil, 'Spot the invisible woman', *New Journalist*, vol. 24, 1976, p. 5.

Ashley, Laura & Beth Olson, 'Constructing reality: print media's framing of the women's movement', *Journalism and Mass Communication Quarterly*, Washington, vol. 75, no. 2, summer 1998, pp. 263 ff.

Baer, Denise L. & John S. Jackson, 'Are women really more "amateur" in politics than men?', *Women & Politics*, vol. 5, no. 2/3, summer/fall 1985, pp. 79–92.

Baird, Katrina, 'Attitudes of Australian women sports journalists', *Australian Studies in Journalism*, no. 3, 1994, p. 231–53.

Bellamy, Sue, 'The heroine as myth, or male cultural baggage we've been forced to carry', *Refractory Girl*, summer 1972/3, pp. 30–31.

Bowman, Ann, 'Physical attractiveness and electability: looks and votes', *Women & Politics*, vol. 4, no. 4, winter 1984, pp. 55–65.

Bulbeck, Chilla, 'The stone laurel: of race, gender and class in Australian memorials', *Cultural Policy Studies*, occasional paper no. 5, Institute for Cultural Policy Studies, Griffith University, 1988.

Carlton, Jim, 'Women in parliament', *Canberra Bulletin of Public Administration*, no. 76, April 1994, pp. 13–16.

Clarke, Jocelyn, 'Leaving the numbers game: women, tokenism and power', in Marian Simms (ed.), *Australian Women and the Political System*, Longman Cheshire, Melbourne, 1984.

Conlon, Anne, 'Women and politics — a personal viewpoint', *Australian Quarterly*, September 1977, vol. 49, no. 3, pp. 11–19.

Couldry, Nick,'Disrupting the media frame at Greenham Common: a new chapter in the history of mediations?', *Media, Culture & Society*, vol. 21, no. 3, pp. 337– 58.

Cox, Eva, 'Politics aren't nice — or is the women's movement attitude to politics feminist or sexist?', *Refractory Girl*, summer 1974–75, pp. 29–30.

Craig, Geoffrey, 'Press photographs and news values', *Australian Studies in Journalism*, no. 3, 1994, pp. 182–200.

Creedon, Pamela J., 'Framing feminism — a feminist primer for the mass media', *Media Studies Journal*, winter/spring 1993, pp. 69–80.

Cryle, Denis, 'Towards a history of Australian journalism: research in progress', *Australian Studies in Journalism*, vol. 2, 1983, pp. 38–45.

Curran, Clare, 'Profile: Janet Powell', *Australian Left Review*, no. 122, Oct. 1990, p. 8.

Curry, Rae, 'Women in journalism: why don't they make the grade?', *Australian Studies in Journalism*, vol. 2, 1993, pp. 170–231.

Curthoys, Ann, 'Feminism, citizenship and national identity', *Feminist Review*, no. 44, summer 1993, pp. 33–34.

——, 'Histories of Journalism', in Ann Curthoys & Julianne Schultz (eds), *Journalism: Print, Politics and Popular Culture*, University of Queensland Press, St Lucia, 1999, pp. 1–9.

——, '"Shut up, you bourgeois bitch": sexual identity and political action in the anti–Vietnam War Movement', in Joy Damousi & Marilyn Lake (eds), *Gender and War: Australians at War in the Twentieth Century*, Cambridge University Press, Melbourne, 1995, pp. 311–41.

——,'Towards a feminist labour history', in A. Curthoys, S. Eade & P. Spearitt (eds), *Women at Work*, Australian Society for the Study of Labour History, Canberra, 1975, pp. 88–95.

——, 'Visions, nightmares, dreams: women's history, 1975', *Australian Historical Studies*, vol. 106, 1996, pp. 1–13.

——, 'Where is Feminism Now?', in Jenna Mead (ed.), *Bodyjamming*, Random House, Sydney, 1997.

——, 'The women's movement and social justice', in Dorothy Broom (ed.), *Unfinished Business: Social Justice for Women in Australia*, Allen & Unwin, Sydney, 1984.

——, 'Women's liberation and historiography', *Arena*, no. 22, 1970, pp. 35–40. Curthoys, Ann, Julianne Schultz & Paula Hamilton, 'A history of Australian journalism, 1890 to the present: report on a research project', *Australian Studies in Journalism*, vol. 2, 1993, pp. 45–52.

Daniel, Ann, 'It depends on whose housewife she is: sex work and occupational prestige', *Australian & New Zealand Journal of Sociology*, vol. 15, 1979, pp. 77–81. Deutchman, Iva Ellen & Anne Ellison, 'A star is born: the roller coaster ride of Pauline Hanson in the news', *Media Culture & Society*, vol. 21, 1999, pp. 33–50.

Dixson, Miriam, 'Gender, class and the women's movements in Australia 1890, 1980', in Norma Grieve & Ailsa Burns (eds), *Australian Women: New Feminist Perspectives*, Oxford University Press, Melbourne, 1986.

Eisenstein, Hester, 'Speaking for women? Voices from the Australian femocrat experiment', *Australian Feminist Studies*, vol. 14, summer 1991, pp. 29–46.

Entman, Robert M., 'Framing: toward clarification of a fractured paradigm', *Journal of Communication*, vol. 43, no. 4, autumn 1993, pp. 51–58.

Evans, Ray & Kay Saunders, 'No place like home: the evolution of the Australian housewife', in Ray Evans & Kay Saunders, *Gender Relations in Australia: Domination and Negotiation*, Harcourt Brace Jovanovich Group (Australia) Pty Ltd, Sydney, 1992.

Eveline, Joan & Michael Booth, 'Who are you, really? Feminism and the female politician', *Australian Feminist Studies*, vol. 12, no. 25, 1997, pp. 105–18.

Eyland, Ann, Helen Lapsley & Catherine Mason, 'The attitude of husbands to working wives', *Australian Journal of Social Issues*, vol. 18, no. 4, Nov. 1983, pp. 282–88.

Game, Ann, 'Sexuality and the suburban dream', *Australian & New Zealand Journal of Sociology*, vol. 15, no. 2, July 1979, pp. 4–15.

Glazer, Nona, 'Overworking the working woman: the double day in a mass magazine', *Women's Studies International Quarterly*, vol. 3, 1980, pp. 79–93.

Goot, Murray & Elizabeth Reid, 'Women and Voting Studies: Mindless Matrons or Sexist Scientism?', *Contemporary Political Sociology Series*, Sage, London 1975.

Greiner, Nick, 'The smart-alec culture: a critique of Australian journalism', *Australian Studies in Journalism*, vol. 2, 1993, pp. 3–10.

Griffin, Grahame, 'A profile of Australian newspaper photographers', *Australian Studies in Journalism*, no. 3, 1994, pp. 147–81.

Grimshaw, Patricia, 'Only the chains have changed', in Verity Burgmann & Jenny Lee, *Staining the Wattle*, McPhee Gribble Penguin, Melbourne, 1988, pp. 66–86.

Hamilton, Paula, 'Journalists, gender and workplace culture 1900–1940', in Ann Curthoys & Julianne Schultz (eds), *Journalism: Print, Politics and Popular Culture*, University of Queensland Press, St Lucia, 1999, pp. 97–116.

Harris, Rosemary, 'Women, workers, ladies or chicks? How the *Courier-Mail* sees women', *Hecate*, vol. 10, no. 1, 1984, pp. 28–48.

Herzog, Hanna, 'More than a looking glass: women in Israeli local politics and the media', *Harvard International Journal of Press/Politics*, vol. 3, no. 1, winter 1998, pp. 26–47.

Hickie, David, 'Woman: the housewife is still the dominant image in Australia', *National Times*, 3–8 Oct. 1977, p. 10.

Holmes, Anne & Meredith Edwards, 'Women at senior levels of the Australian Public Service', *Canberra Bulletin of Public Administration*, no. 76, April 1994, pp. 29–34.

Holmes, Jean, 'From husband fodder to supergirl: a cartoon history of Australian women and politics', *Social Biology Resources Centre Bulletin*, vol. 2, no. 5, Aug. 1979, pp. 4–6.

Huddy, Leonie & Nayda Terkildsen, 'Gender stereotypes and the perception of male and female candidates', *American Journal of Political Science*, vol. 37, no. 1, Feb. 1993, pp. 119–47.

——, 'The consequences of gender stereotypes for women candidates at different levels and types of office', *Political Research Quarterly*, vol. 46, no. 3, Sept. 1993, pp. 503–25.

Huddy, Leonie, Francis K. Neely & Marilyn R. Lafay, 'The polls-trends: support for the women's movement', *Public Opinion Quarterly*, vol. 64, fall 2000, pp. 309– 50.

Hurst, John, 'Kirner and the media', *Australian Journalism Review*, vol. 15, no. 1, Jan– June 1993, pp. 126–33.

Irving, Baiba, 'Women in Australian politics: a look at the past', *Refractory Girl*, Summer 1974–75, pp. 27–28.

Jenkins, Cathy, 'Kerry Chikarovski and the press', *Hecate*, vol. 26, 2000, pp. 82–90.

——, 'Press coverage of the first women in Australia's federal parliament', *Australian Studies in Journalism*, no. 5, 1996, pp. 82–100.

——, 'Women in the news: still not quite visible', *Australian Studies in Journalism*, vol. 2, 1993, pp. 233–43.

Jones, Helen, 'South Australian women and politics', in Dean Jaensch (ed.), *The Flinders History of South Australia*, Wakefield Press, Netley, 1986.

Kahn, Kim Fridkin, 'The distorted mirror: press coverage of women candidates for statewide office', *Journal of Politics*, vol. 56, no. 1, Feb. 1994, pp. 154–73.

Kahn, Kim Fridkin & Edie N. Goldenberg, 'Women candidates in the news: an examination of gender differences in US Senate campaign coverage', *Public Opinion Quarterly*, vol. 55, no. 2, 1991, pp. 180–99.

Kelley, Jonathan & Ian McAllister, 'The electoral consequences of gender in Australia', *British Journal of Political Science*, vol. 13, pt. 3, July 1983.

Kerr, M., 'If I were the Whitlam Supergirl', *Pol*, vol. 5, no. 9, pp. 12–13, 16–17.

Kirkby, Elisabeth, 'When the Air Force holds cake stalls', in Jocelyn Scutt, *Different Lives: Reflections on the Women's Movement and Visions of its Future*, Penguin, Ringwood, 1987.

Krinks, Clare, 'Domesticity: patterns of dissatisfaction', *Refractory Girl*, summer 1974–75, pp. 38–42.

Lacey, Geoff, 'Females, Aborigines and Asians in newspaper photographs, 1950– 1990', *Australian Studies in Journalism*, vol. 2, 1993, pp. 244–69.

Lake, Marilyn, 'Feminist history as national history: writing the political history of women', *Australian Historical Studies*, vol. 27, no. 106, April 1996, pp. 154–69.

——, 'A history of feminism in Australia', in Barbara Caine (ed.), *Australian Feminism: A Companion*, Oxford University Press, Melbourne, 1998.

——, 'Women and nation in Australia: the politics of representation', *Australian Journal of Politics and History*, vol. 43, no. 1, 1997, pp. 41–52.

Lawrence, Carmen, 'The gender gap in political behaviour', in Kate Deverall et. al. (eds), *Party Girls: Labor Women Now*, Pluto Press, Sydney, 2000.

——, 'Media representation of politics and women politicians', *Australian Rationalist*, no. 49, 1999, pp. 27–32.

——, 'Women and political life', Women, Parliament and Public Service series, *Canberra Bulletin of Public Administration*, no. 76, April 1994, pp. 1–6.

——, 'Women in government: overview', in Mark Neylan & Rae Wear (eds), *Women in Government: Proceedings of the Royal Institute of Public Administration (Queensland division) Annual Conference 5–6 Oct. 1993*, RIPAA, Brisbane, 1994, pp. 12–24.

Leithner, Christian, 'A gender gap in Australia? Commonwealth elections 1910– 96', *Australian Journal of Political Science*, vol. 32, no. 1, March 1997, pp. 29–47.

Lombard, John, 'Federal parliament/press gallery relations', in David Turbayne (ed.), *The Media and Politics in Australia*, public policy monograph, Department of Political Science, University of Tasmania, Dec. 1980, pp. 110–12.

McCulloch, John, *Women Members of the Queensland Parliament 1929–1994*, background information brief, no. 27, 1994, Publications and Resources Section, Queensland Parliamentary Library, Brisbane.

Macdonald, Ranald, 'Parliament and political journalism', *Media Information Australia*, no. 9, Aug. 1978, pp. 1–3.

McElvoy, Anne, 'Media Woman', *New Statesman*, 19 July 1999, pp. 18–19. McGregor, Judy, 'Gender politics and the news: the search for a Beehive Bimbo-Boadicea', in Judy McGregor (ed.), *Dangerous Democracy? News Media Politics in New Zealand*, Dunmore Press, Palmerston North, New Zealand, 1996.

Mackerras, Malcolm, 'Do women candidates lose votes?', *Australian Quarterly*, Sept. 1977, pp. 6–10.

——, 'Do women candidates lose votes? — further evidence', *Australian Quarterly*, summer 1980, pp. 450–54.

Maguire, Daniel, 'Four newspapers' coverage of the 1993 federal election', *Australian Studies in Journalism*, vol. 2, 1993, pp. 11–19.

Mainardi, Pat, 'The politics of housework', in Ellen Malos (ed.), *The Politics of Housework*, Allison & Busby, London, 1980, pp. 99–104.

Mayer, Henry, 'Images of politics in the press', in John Henningham (ed.), *Issues in Australian Journalism*, Longman Cheshire, Melbourne, 1990, pp. 36–45.

——, 'Voters' media preferences', *Medical Information Australia*, vol. 8, May 1978, pp.16–27.

Miller, Susan H., 'The content of news photos: women's and men's roles', *Journalism Quarterly*, vol. 52, 1975, pp. 70–75.

Milligan, Louise, 'Sex appeal and spotty frocks: representations of women politicians in the news media', *metroeducation*, no. 19, 1999, pp. 13–15.

Moon, Jeremy & Imogen Fountain, 'Keeping the gates? Women as ministers in Australia, 1970–96', *Australian Journal of Political Science*, vol. 32, no. 3, pp. 455–66.

Motion, Judy, 'Women politicians: media objects or political subjects?', *Media International Australia*, vol. 80, May 1996, pp. 110–17.

Mugford, Stephen & D. B. Darroch, 'Marital status and female achievement in Australia: a research note', *Journal of Marriage and the Family*, vol. 42, Aug. 1980, pp. 653–56.

Muir, Kathie, 'Tough choices: news media accounts of women union leaders', *Hecate*, vol. 26, no. 2, 2000, pp. 10–30.

Mulraney, Jenni, 'When lovely woman stoops to lobby', *Australian Feminist Studies*, nos 7 & 8, summer 1988, pp. 95–114.

Nile, Richard, 'The Pauline Hanson One Person Party', *Journal of Australian Studies*, no. 52, 1997, pp. 1–9.

Norris, Pippa, 'The gender gap in Britain and America', *Parliamentary Affairs*, vol.38, no. 2, spring 1985, pp. 192–201.

——, 'Women leaders worldwide: a splash of color in the photo op', in Pippa Norris (ed.), *Women, Media and Politics*, Oxford University Press, New York, 1997, pp. 149–79.

Norris, Pippa & Ronald Inglehart, 'Cultural barriers to women's leadership: a worldwide comparison', paper presented at the International Political Science Association World Congress, 3 Aug. 2000.

Perkins, Jerry & Diane L. Fowlkes, 'Opinion representation versus social representation: or, why women can't run as women and win', *American Political Science Review*, vol. 74, no. 1, March 1980, pp. 92–103.

Petersen, Alan, 'Governing images: media constructions of the "normal", "healthy" subject', *Media Information Australia*, no. 72, May 1994, pp. 32–40.

Powell, Janet, 'Representation of women in Australian parliaments — why is it so?', *National Women's Conference 1990: Proceedings*, Write People, Canberra, 1990.

Puwar, N., 'Reflections on interviewing women MPs', *Sociological Research Online*, vol. 2, no. 1, 1997, http://www.socresonline.org.uk/socresonline/2/1/4.html.

Reynolds, Margaret, 'Women, preselection and merit: who decides?', *Reinventing Political Institutions*, Senate Papers on Parliament, no. 27, March 1996.

Richmond, K., 'The workforce participation of married women in Australia', in D. Edgar (ed.), *Social Change in Australia: Readings in Sociology*, Cheshire, Melbourne, 1974.

Robinson, Gertrude J. & Armande Saint-Jean, 'Women politicians and their media coverage', in Kathy Megyery (ed.), *Women in Canadian Politics: Towards Equity in Representation*, vol. 6, Research Studies Royal Commission on Electoral Reform and Party Financing and Canada Communication Group, Canada, Dundurn Press, Toronto, 1991, pp. 127–69.

Ross, Karen, 'Gender and party: how the press reported the Labour leadership campaign, 1994', *Media, Culture and Society*, vol. 17, no. 3, 1995, pp. 499–509.

——, 'Women and the news agenda: media-ted reality and Jane Public', *Leicester University Discussion Papers in Mass Communications*, June 1995.

Ross, Karen & Annabelle Srebeny-Mohammadi, 'Playing house — gender, politics and the news media in Britain', *Media, Culture and Society*, vol. 19, no. 1, Jan. 1997, pp. 101–09.

Ross, Karen and Annabelle Sreberny, 'Women in the House: media representation of British politicians', in Annabelle Sreberny & Liesbet van Zoonen (ed.), *Gender, Politics and Communication*, Hampton Press, Cresskill, New Jersey, 2000, pp. 79–100.

Ryan, Susan, 'Equality: rhetoric or reality?', in J. Reeves & Kelvin Thomson (eds), *Labor Essays 1983: Policies and Programs for the Labor Government*, Drummond, Richmond, 1983, pp. 95–112.

——, 'Women in government and cabinet: "two steps forward, one step back"', *Women, Power and Politics: An International Conference to Advance the Rights of Women and their Role in Politics, Conference Proceedings, 8–11 Oct. 1994*, Women's Suffrage Centenary Steering Committee, Adelaide, 1995, pp. 31–38.

Sapiro, Virginia, 'If US Senator Baker were a woman: an experimental study of candidate images', *Political Psychology*, vol. 2, spring/summer 1981–82, pp. 61–83.

——, 'Research frontier essay: when are interests interesting? The problem of political representation of women', *American Political Science Review*, vol. 75, Sept. 1981, pp. 701–21.

Sawer, Marian, 'From motherhood to sisterhood: attitudes of
    Australian women MPs to their roles', *Women's Studies
    International Forum*, vol. 9, 1986, pp. 531–41.
——, 'Housekeeping the state: women and parliamentary politics
    in Australia', *Trust the Women*, Senate Papers on Parliament,
    September 1992, pp. 7–25.
——, 'The new era: women in Australian parliaments', *Current
    Affairs Bulletin*, vol.59, no. 1, 1 June 1982, pp. 4–15.
——, 'Political institutions', in Barbara Caine (ed.), *Australian
    Feminism: A Companion*, Oxford University Press, Melbourne,
    1998, pp. 239–47.
——, 'Topsy-turvy land — where women, children and the
    environment come first', in John Warhurst (ed.), *Keeping the
    Bastards Honest: The Australian Democrats' First Twenty Years*,
    Allen & Unwin, Sydney, 1997, pp. 237–50.
Schroedel, Jean R. & Bruce Snyder, 'Patti Murray: the mom in tennis
    shoes goes to the Senate', in Elizabeth Adell Cook, Sue Thomas
    & Clyde Wilcox, *The Year of the Woman: Myths and Realities*,
    Westview Press, Boulder, 1994.
Simms, Marian, 'Affirmative action and the Australian party system
    in the early 1990s: will 1993 be seen as the year of the Australian
    political woman?', *Canberra Bulletin of Public Administration*,
    vol. 76, Apr. 1994, pp. 23–28.
——, 'Two steps forward, one step back: women and the Australian
    party system', in Joni Lovenduski & Pippa Norris, *Gender and
    Party Politics*, Sage Publications, London, 1993, pp. 16–34.
Smith, K. B., 'When all's fair: signs of parity in media coverage of
    female candidates', *Political Communication*, vol. 14, no. 1, pp.
    71–82.
Smith, Tony, 'Death of the "maiden" in Macquarie Street?',
    *Proceedings of the Conference of the Australasian Political Studies
    Association (APSA)*, vol. 3, pp. 751–60.
Sreberny-Mohammadi, Annabelle & Karen Ross, 'Women MPs and
    the media: representing the body politic', *Parliamentary Affairs*,
    vol. 49, no. 1, Jan. 1996, pp. 103–15.
Stoper, Emily, 'Wife and politician: role strain among women in public
    office', in Marianne Githens & Jewel L. Prestage (eds), *A Portrait*

of Marginality:The Political Behaviour of the American Woman, David McKay Co., New York, 1977.

Stott Despoja, Natasha, 'Fem X: a fast track to the Senate', in Kathy Bail (ed.), *DIY Feminism*, Allen & Unwin, Sydney, 1996, pp. 103–08.

——, 'Feminism and public life', in Jenna Mead (ed.), *Bodyjamming: Sexual Harassment, Feminism and Public Life*, Random House, Sydney, 1997, pp. 267–77.

——, 'Gorgeous girls, great women', in Jocelynne Scutt (ed.), *Living Generously: Women Mentoring Women*, Artemis, Melbourne, 1996, pp. 199–207.

Sullivan, Kathy, 'Women in parliament — Yes! But what's it really like?', *Canberra Bulletin of Public Administration*, no. 76, April 1994, p. 7 ff.

Summers, Anne, 'Mandarins or missionaries: women in the federal bureaucracy', in Norma Grieve & Ailsa Burns (eds), *Australian Women: New Feminist Perspectives*, Oxford University Press, Melbourne, 1986.

——, 'Women', in Allan Patience & Brian Head (eds), *From Whitlam to Fraser: Reform and Reaction to Australian Politics*, Oxford University Press, Melbourne, 1979.

Swain, Marie, 'Women in parliament', *Briefing Paper*, no. 19, NSW Parliamentary Library Research Service, 1995.

Turner, Geoff, 'Towards equity: women's emerging role in Australian journalism', *Australian Studies in Journalism*, vol. 2, 1993, pp. 124–69.

Vallance, Elizabeth, 'Women candidates in the 1983 general election', *Parliamentary Affairs*, vol. 37, no. 3, summer 1984.

Van Acker, Elizabeth, 'The portrayal of feminist issues in the print media', *Australian Studies in Journalism*, vol. 4, 1995, pp. 174–99.

Van Tassell, G. Lane, 'Recruitment of women in Australian national politics: a research note', *Australian Quarterly*, spring 1981, pp. 334–45.

Van Zoonen, Liesbet, '"Finally, I have my mother back": politicians and their families in popular culture', *Harvard International Journal of Press/Politics*, vol. 3, no. 1, winter 1998, pp. 48–64.

——, 'One of the girls?: the changing gender of journalism', in
Cynthia Carter, Gill Branston & Stuart Allen, *News, Gender and Power*, Routledge, London, 1998, pp. 33–46.

Whip, Rosemary, 'Representing women: Australian female parliamentarians on the horns of a dilemma', *Women & Politics*, vol. 11, no. 3, 1991, pp. 1–22.

White, Kate, 'Women and party politics in Australia', *Australian Quarterly*, vol. 53, autumn 1981, pp. 29–39.

Williams, Blair, 'A gendered media analysis of the prime ministerial ascension of Gillard and Turnbull: he's "taken back the reins" and she's "a backstabbing" murderer', *Australian Journal of Political Science*, 52:4, 2017.

Williams, J., 'Women in party politics', *Australian Quarterly*, vol. 49, no. 3, Sept. 1977.

Williams, Janice, 'Women in Queensland state politics', *Refractory Girl*, no. 4, spring 1973, pp. 13–17.

Woodruff, Judy, 'Covering politics — is there a female difference?', *Media Studies Journal*, vol. 2, no. 2, spring 1997, pp. 155–58.

Zetlin, Di, 'We're here because we're here: women and the ALP quota', in Barbara Sullivan & Gillian Whitehouse (eds), *Gender, Politics and Citizenship in the 1990s*, University of New South Wales Press, Sydney, 1996, pp. 120–29.

Books

Bettison, Margaret & Anne Summers (eds), *Her Story: Australian Women in Print 1788–1975*, Hale & Iremonger, Sydney, 1980.

Black, David, *Women Parliamentarians in Australia 1921–1996: A Register of Women Members of Commonwealth, State and Territory Parliaments in Australia*, West Australian Parliamentary History Project, Perth, 1996.

Black, David (ed.), *The House on the Hill: A History of the Parliament of Western Australia 1832–1990*, West Australian Parliamentary History Project, Parliament of WA, Perth, 1991.

Braden, Maria, *Women Politicians and the Media*, University Press of Kentucky, Lexington, 1996.

Browne, Geoff, *Biographical Register of the Victorian Parliament 1900–84*, Victorian Government Printing Office, Melbourne, 1985.

Caffery, Cecilia (ed.), *At Home in the House: The Voices of Victorian ALP Women in Parliament*, Australian Labor Party, Carlton North,Victoria, 1993.

Campbell, Beatrix, *The Iron Ladies: Why Do Women vote Tory?*, Virago, London, 1987.

Castles, Ian, *Women in Australia*, Australian Bureau of Statistics, Canberra, 1993. Clarke, Jocelyn & Kate White, *Women in Australian Politics*, Fontana/Collins, Sydney, 1983.

Colquhoun, Maureen, *A Woman in the House*, Scan Books, Sussex, 1980.

Coote, Anna & Polly Pattullo, *Power and Prejudice:Women and Politics*, Weidenfeld & Nicholson, London, 1990.

Cosgrave, Patrick, *Margaret Thatcher: A Tory and her Party*, Hutchinson, London, 1978.

Cunningham, Stuart & Graeme Turner (ed.), *The Media in Australia*, Allen & Unwin, Sydney, 1997.

Curthoys, Ann, *For and Against Feminism*, Allen & Unwin, Sydney, 1988.

Curthoys, Ann & Julianne Schultz (eds), *Journalism: Print, Politics and Popular Culture*, University of Queensland Press, St Lucia, 1999.

Damousi, Joy & Marilyn Lake (eds), *Gender and War: Australians at War in the Twentieth Century*, Cambridge University Press, Melbourne, 1995.

Davies, Kath, Julienne Dickey & Theresa Stratford (eds), *Out of Focus: Writing on Women and the Media*, Women's Press, London, 1987.

Department of Employment and Youth Affairs, Women's Bureau, *Facts on Women at Work in Australia, 1979*, Australian Government Printing Service (AGPS), Canberra, 1980.

Deverall, Kate et. al. (eds), *Party Girls: Labor Women Now*, Pluto Press, Sydney, 2000.

Dixson, Miriam, *The Real Matilda: Women and Identity in Australia 1788 to 1975*, Penguin, Ringwood, 1994 (1976).

Dodd, Helen J., *Pauline: the Hanson Phenomenon*, Boolarong Press, Brisbane, 1990.

Edgar, Patricia, *The Politics of the Press*, Sun Books, Melbourne, 1979.

Edgar, Patricia (ed.), *The News in Focus*, MacMillan, Melbourne, 1980.

Ellis, Kate, *Sex, Lies and Question Time: Why the successes and struggles of women in Australia's parliament matter to us all*, Hardie Grant, Sydney, 2021.

Encel, Sol, Norman MacKenzie & Margaret Tebbutt, *Women and Society: An Australian Study*, Cheshire, Melbourne, 1974.

Evans, Ray & Kay Saunders, *Gender Relations in Australia: Domination and Negotiation*, Harcourt Brace Jovanovich Group (Australia), Sydney, 1992.

Faludi, Susan, *Backlash: The Undeclared War against Women*, Chatto & Windus, London, 1991.

Firestone, Shulamith, *The Dialectic of Sex: The Case for Feminist Revolution*, Paladin, St Albans, 1972.

Friedan, Betty, *The Feminine Mystique*, Penguin, Ringwood, 1963.

——, *The Second Stage*, Abacus, London, 1981.

Fraser, Antonia, *Boadicea's Chariot: The Warrior Queens*, Weidenfeld & Nicholson, London, 1988.

Gardiner, Jane (ed.), *Here We Come, Ready or Not!: A Collection of Papers Analysing the Legal and Political Status of Australian Women, and Exploring New Avenues for Action by Women to Attain Constitutional and Legal Change*, Women into Politics, Sydney, 1998.

Gitlin, Todd, *The Whole World is Watching: Mass Media in the Making and Unmaking of the New Left*, University of California Press, Berkeley and Los Angeles, 1980.

Goffman, Erving, *Frame Analysis: An Essay on the Organisation of Experience*, Harper & Row, New York, 1974.

Greer, Germaine, *The Female Eunuch*, MacGibbon & Kee, London, 1970.

Grieve, Norma & Ailsa Burns (eds), *Australian Women, New Feminist Perspectives*, Oxford University Press, Melbourne, 1989.

Grieve, Norma & Patricia Grimshaw (eds), *Australian Women, Feminist Perspectives*, Oxford University Press, Melbourne, 1981.

Grimshaw, Patricia et. al., *Creating a Nation: 1788–1990*, McPhee Gribble, Ringwood, 1994.

Haines, Janine, *Suffrage to Sufferance: 100 Years of Women in Politics*, Allen & Unwin, Sydney, 1992.

Henderson, Anne, *Getting Even: Women MPs on Life, Power and Politics*, Harper Collins, Sydney, 1999.

Henderson, Gerard, *Menzies' Child: The Liberal Party of Australia*, Allen & Unwin, Sydney, 1994.

Horne, Donald, *Death of the Lucky Country*, Penguin, Ringwood, 1976.

Horne, Donald, *A Time of Hope — Australia 1966–72*, Angus & Robertson, Sydney, 1980.

Howe, Renate, *Women and the State: Australian Perspectives*, La Trobe University Press, Bundoora, Victoria, 1993.

Jones, Margaret, *Thatcher's Kingdom: A View of Britain in the Eighties*, Collins, Sydney, 1984.

Kahn, Kim Fridkin, *The Political Consequences of Being a Woman: How Stereotypes Influence the Conduct and Consequences of Political Campaigns*, Columbia University Press, New York, 1996.

Kaplan, Gisela, *The Meagre Harvest: The Australian Women's Movement 1950s–1990s*, Allen & Unwin, Sydney, 1996.

Kenny, Chris, *State of Denial*, Wakefield Press, Kent Town, SA, 1993.

Kernot, Cheryl, *Speaking for Myself Again: Four Years with Labor and Beyond*, Harper Collins, Sydney, 2002.

Kingston, Beverley, *My Wife, My Daughter and Poor Mary Ann: Women and Work in Australia*, Thomas Nelson, Melbourne, 1975.

Kingston, Margo, *Off the Rails: The Pauline Hanson Trip*, Allen & Unwin, Sydney, 1999.

Kirner, Joan & Moira Rayner (eds), *The Women's Power Handbook*, Viking, Ringwood, 1999.

Lake, Marilyn, *Getting Equal: The History of Australian Feminism*, Allen & Unwin, Sydney, 1999.

Lewis, Russell, *Margaret Thatcher: A Personal and Political Biography*, Routledge & Kegan Paul, London, 1975.

Lloyd, Clem, *Parliament and the Press*, Melbourne University Press, Carlton, 1988.

Lunn, Hugh, *Joh: The Life and Political Adventures of Johannes Bjelke-Petersen*, University of Queensland Press, St Lucia, 1978.

McAllister, Ian, Malcolm Mackerras & Carolyn Brown Boldiston (eds), *Australian Political Facts*, Longman Cheshire, Melbourne, 1997 (1990).

Mayer, Henry, *The Press in Australia*, Lansdowne Press, Melbourne, 1964.

Mayer, Henry & Helen Nelson (eds), *Australian Politics: A Fifth Reader*, Longman Cheshire, Melbourne, 1980.

Mayer, Henry & Rodney Tiffen (eds), *Mayer of the Media: Issues and Arguments*, Allen & Unwin, Sydney, 1994.

Media Studies Journal, 'The Media and Women without Apology', Freedom Forum Media Studies Centre, New York, winter/spring 1993.

Mercer, Jan (ed.), *The Other Half:Women in Australian Society*, Penguin, Ringwood, 1975.

Millar, Ann, *Trust the Women: Women in the Federal Parliament*, Department of the Senate, Canberra, 1993.

Mitchell, Susan, *The Scent of Power: On the Trail of Women and Power in Australian Politics*, Angus & Robertson, Sydney, 1996.

——, *Tall Poppies*, Penguin, Ringwood, 1984.

Moir, Alan & Mac Vines, *Flo Goes to Canberra:The Intimate Diary of a Kingaroy housewife*, Angus & Robertson, Sydney, 1981.

Money, Ernle, *Margaret Thatcher: First Lady of the House*, Leslie Frewin, London, 1975.

Morosi, Junie, *Sex, Prejudice and Politics*, Midescope, Camberwell, 1975.

Murray, Tricia, *Margaret Thatcher*, W. H. Allen & Co. Ltd, London, 1978.

New South Wales Women's Advisory Council, *Occupation: Housewife*, NSW Women's Advisory Council, Sydney, 1980.

Neylan, Mark & Rae Wear (eds), *Women in Government*, based on the proceedings of the Royal Institute of Public Administration (Queensland division) Annual Conference, 5–6 Oct. 1993, RIPAA (Qld division), Brisbane, 1994.

Norris, Pippa (ed.), *Women, Media and Politics*, Oxford University Press, New York, 1997.

Oldfield, Audrey, *Women Suffrage in Australia: A Gift or a Struggle?*, Cambridge University Press, Melbourne, 1992.

O'Reilly, David, *The Woman Most Likely: Cheryl Kernot*, Random House, Sydney, 1998.

Parker, Derek, *The Courtesans: The Press Gallery in the Hawke Era*, Allen & Unwin, Sydney, 1991.

Pasquarelli, John, *The Pauline Hanson Story By the Man Who Knows*, New Holland, Sydney, 1998.

Radi, Heather (ed.), *200 Australian Women: A Redress Anthology*, Women's Redress Press, Sydney 1988.

Randall,Vicky, *Women and Politics:An International Perspective*, Macmillan Education, London, 1987.

Reynolds, Margaret, *The Last Bastion*, Business & Professional Publishing, Sydney, 1995.

Reynolds, M. & J. Willoughby, *HERSTORY — Australian Labor Women in Federal, State and Territory Parliaments*, Senate Printing Unit, Senator Margaret Reynolds, 1994.

Ryan, Susan, *Catching the Waves: Life In and Out of Politics*, Harper Collins, Sydney, 1999.

Sawer, Marian, *Sisters in Suits:Women and Public Policy in Australia*, Allen & Unwin, Sydney, 1990.

Sawer, Marian & Marian Simms, *A Woman's Place: Women and Politics in Australia*, Allen & Unwin, Sydney, 1993 (1984).

Simms, Marian, *A Liberal Nation: The Liberal Party and Australian Politics*, Hale & Iremonger, Sydney, 1982.

Simms, Marian (ed.), *Australian Women and the Political System*, Longman Cheshire, Melbourne, 1984.

Simons, Margaret, *Fit to Print: Inside the Canberra Press Gallery*, University of NSW Press, Sydney, 1999.

Smith, A. Viola, *Women in Australian Parliaments and Local Governments: Past and Present*, Australian Local Government Women's Association, Sydney, 1975.

Souter, Gavin, *Company of Heralds: A Century and a Half of Australian Publishing by John Fairfax Limited and its Predecessors 1831–1981*, Melbourne University Press, 1981.

——, *Heralds and Angels: The House of Fairfax 1841–1990*, Melbourne University Press, 1991.

Sreberny, Annabelle & Liesbet van Zoonen, *Gender, Politics and Communication*, Hampton Press, Cresskill, New Jersey, 2000.

Summers, Anne, *Damned Whores and God's Police: The Colonisation of Women in Australia*, Penguin, Ringwood, 1994 (1975).

Sydenham, Diane, *Women of Influence: The First Fifty Years of Women in the Liberal Party*, Women's Section, Liberal Party of Australia, Victorian Division, Cheltenham, 1996.

Thatcher, Margaret, *The Downing Street Years*, Harper Collins, New York, 1993.

——, *The Path to Power*, Harper Collins, London, 1995.

Tuchman, Gaye, *Making News:A Study in the Construction of Reality*, Free Press, New York, 1978.

Tuchman, Gaye, Arlene Kaplan Daniels & James Benet (eds), *Hearth and Home: Images of Women in the Mass Media*, Oxford University Press, New York, 1978.

Van Acker, Elizabeth, *Different Voices: Gender and Politics in Australia*, Macmillan Education Australia, Melbourne, 1999.

Ward, Russell, *The Australian Legend*, Oxford University Press, Melbourne, 1958.

Warhurst, John (ed.), *Keeping the Bastards Honest: The Australian Democrats' First Twenty Years*, Allen & Unwin, Sydney, 1997.

Warner, Marina, *Monuments and Maidens: The Allegory of the Female Form*, Picador, London, 1985.

Watson, Judyth (ed.), *We Hold up Half the Sky*, Australian Labor Party (WA Branch), Perth, 1994.

Webster, Wendy, *Not a Man to Match Her*, Women's Press, London, 1990.

Witt, Linda, Karen M. Paget, & Glenna Matthews, *Running as a Woman: Gender and Power in American Politics*, Free Press, New York, 1994.

Young, Hugo, *One of Us: A Biography of Margaret Thatcher*, Macmillan, London, 1989.